Radio Benjamin

Radio Benjamin

Edited by Lecia Rosenthal

Translated by Jonathan Lutes
with
Lisa Harries Schumann and Diana K. Reese

VERSO
London • New York

This paperback edition first published by Verso 2021
First published by Verso 2014
Translation © Jonathan Lutes, Lisa Harries Schumann and Diana K. Reese 2014, 2021
Introduction © Lecia Rosenthal 2014, 2021
Translated works originally appeared in *Gesammelte Schriften*, 7 vols.
© Suhrkamp 1972–1989

1 3 5 7 9 10 8 6 4 2

Verso
UK: 6 Meard Street, London W1F 0EG
US: 20 Jay Street, Suite 1010, Brooklyn, NY 11201
www.versobooks.com

Verso is the imprint of New Left Books

ISBN-13: 978-1-83976-416-5
eISBN-13: 978-1-78168-576-1 (US)
eISBN-13: 978-1-78168-701-7 (UK)

British Library Cataloguing in Publication Data
A catalogue record for this book is available from the British Library

The Library of Congress Has Cataloged the Hardback Edition as Follows:

Benjamin, Walter, 1892–1940.
[Broadcasts. Selections. English]
Radio Benjamin / edited by Lecia Rosenthal ; tanslated by Jonathan Lutes, Lisa Harries
Schumann and Diana Reese.
pages cm
Includes bibliographical references and index.
ISBN 978-1-78168-575-4 (hardback)
1. Benjamin, Walter, 1892–1940—Translations into English. I. Rosenthal, Lecia, editor.
II. Title.
PT2603.E455A26 2014
838ʹ.91209—dc23
2014025632

Typeset in Adobe Caslon Pro by Hewer Text UK Ltd, Edinburgh, Scotland
Printed and bound by CPI Group (UK) Ltd, Croydon CR0 4YY

Contents

Abbreviations and a Note on the Texts

GS *Gesammelte Schriften*, 7 vols., with supplements, eds. Rolf Tiedemann, Hermann Schweppenhäuser et al. (Frankfurt: Suhrkamp, 1972–1989).

SW *Selected Writings*, 4 vols., ed. Michael W. Jennings et al. (Cambridge, MA: Harvard University Press, 1996–2003).

Translations in this volume are based on Benjamin's radio typescripts as published and edited in the *Gesammelte Schriften*. Information about individual broadcasts, including dates and location, are provided in a section following each translation, just above the notes. Unless otherwise indicated, all translations, including translations of texts cited by Benjamin, are by the translators. The editor of this volume is indebted to the editors of the *Gesammelte Schriften*; the notes to the translations in this volume borrow from and expand upon their work.

The editor would like to thank a number of friends and colleagues who supported this project along the way: Joseph Massad, Martin Harries, Virginia Jackson, Jonathan Zittrain, Andrew Rubin, Jacqueline Loss, Andrew Coletta, Chris Coletta, Gayatri Chakravorty Spivak, Andrew Magliozzi, Berit Schlumbohm, Till Jesinghaus, and Ryan Shiraki. Ursula Marx at the Benjamin Archive in Berlin was especially helpful, as was Thomas Küpper, who, as co-editor along with Anja Nowak of the volume devoted to Benjamin's radio works in the forthcoming German new critical edition, *Werke und Nachlaß*, shared invaluable information as well as his excitement about the project. I would also like to thank the translators, Jonathan Lutes, Lisa Harries Schumann, and Diana Reese, for their hard work. I am grateful to them for allowing me to work closely with them on the translations, for being so open to my queries, and for their thoughtful contributions to conversations about the volume as a whole. To Jonathan Lutes, who was a collaborator from the start, I owe particular thanks. It was because of his encouragement and enthusiasm that the idea for the volume took off. Lisa Harries Schumann generously agreed to join the project midway, and without her contributions it would not have been completed. At Verso, Mark Martin and Lorna Scott Fox expertly guided the book's final stages. I am indebted to them and to Sebastian Budgen, who supported the project from the beginning.

Walter Benjamin on the Radio: An Introduction

Lecia Rosenthal

Theodor Adorno has used the term "radioactive" to describe the explosive appeal of Walter Benjamin's writings.[1] Unpredictable and wide-ranging, the power of Benjamin's work has registered in its generative, cross-disciplinary effects. Widely associated with his writings on photography, as well as his contributions to fields including film, architecture, Jewish theology, Marxism, translation studies, and studies of violence and sovereignty, Benjamin is far less well-known for his contributions to the early history of radio. From 1927 to early 1933, Benjamin wrote and delivered some eighty to ninety broadcasts over the new medium of German radio, working between Radio Berlin and Radio Frankfurt.[2] These

---

1 Theodor W. Adorno, *Prisms*, trans. Samuel and Shierry Weber (Cambridge, MA: MIT Press, 1983), 229. The full sentence reads, "Everything which fell under the scrutiny of his words was transformed, as though it had become radioactive," and in the German, "Unter dem Blick seiner Worte verwandelte sich, worauf immer er fiel, als wäre es radioaktiv geworden" ("Charakteristik Walter Benjamins," in *Prismen, Kulturkritik und Gesellschaft,* [Frankfurt Suhrkamp, 1955], 232). Although Adorno's metaphor uses a different register of boundary crossing, the German *radioaktiv*, like the English radioactive, shares with *Rundfunk,* or radio, a connotation of atmospheric spreading, dispersal, and uncontrolled movement across and within borders and lines of containment; the airwaves, like the air or the atmosphere, represent a quasi-invisible scene or medium of transmission. While the German does not directly imply the coincidence of these two (roughly contemporary) modes of radiality, the notion of Benjamin's gaze, and from there his work, effecting a radioactive transformation suggests the potentially dangerous, if also exciting and new, power of radio and its power to broadcast. On the early debate in Germany over the use of the Germanized *Rundfunk* rather than "Radio," see Peter Jelavich, *Berlin Alexanderplatz: Radio, Film and the Death of Weimar Culture* (Berkeley: University of California Press, 2006), 42.

2 For reasons discussed below, the exact number of broadcasts has been difficult to determine. To date, the most detailed account of the archival traces left by the radio works—including extant typescripts and announcements of dates of broadcast in the program guides of the Berlin and Frankfurt radio stations—can be found in Sabine

broadcasts, many of them produced under the auspices of programming for children, cover a fascinating array of topics: typologies
and archaeologies of a rapidly changing Berlin; scenes from the
shifting terrain of childhood and its construction; exemplary cases
of trickery, swindle, and fraud that play on the uncertain lines
between truth and falsehood; catastrophic events such as the eruption of Vesuvius and the flooding of the Mississippi River, and
much more. In addition to the radio talks and plays specifically
produced for children, Benjamin delivered a variety of pieces on
subjects from practical advice on how to manipulate the boss, and
the rhetoric of self-help and self-promotion ("A Pay Raise?!
Whatever Gave You That Idea!"), to Enlightenment debates on
literary taste and the popularization of reading practices (*What the
Germans Were Reading While Their Classical Authors Were Writing*).
In the radio play *Lichtenberg*, Benjamin places various apparatuses
of surveillance in the hands of "moon beings," externalized, other-
worldly figures who stand in judgment, not unlike omniscient
narrators (and, Benjamin suggests, followers of psychoanalysis),
over the human capacity for unhappiness. And these are only
some of the texts that we find among Benjamin's total output
for radio.

Most of Benjamin's works for radio have never before been translated into English. *Radio Benjamin* presents, for the first time, a
collection in English devoted specifically and entirely to Benjamin's
work in this medium. Section I presents the surviving texts of
Benjamin's "radio stories for children," the talks he wrote and delivered for the Youth Hour on Radio Berlin and Radio Frankfurt.
Section II includes the two radio plays Benjamin wrote for children,

Schiller-Lerg's *Walter Benjamin und der Rundfunk* (Munich: K. G. Saur, 1984). In the
Appendix to this volume, I have followed and added to Schiller-Lerg's chronology of the
broadcasts, where she lists a total of eighty-six known and dated broadcasts by Benjamin.
Some typescripts of broadcasts Benjamin is known to have given are, however, missing, lost,
or undatable. Given the possibility that Benjamin gave additional broadcasts, and that for
some of the known broadcast dates the titles remain uncertain, it is not possible to provide
a complete account of the history and dissemination of Benjamin's radio archive. According
to Schiller-Lerg, "Around ninety scripts have been found or reconstructed" ("Walter
Benjamin, Radio Journalist: Theory and Practice of Weimar Radio," trans. Susan Nieschlag,
Journal of Communication Inquiry 13.1 [1989], 45). One should note, however, that this
number refers to the total number of *broadcasts*, in other words the readings and
performances of Benjamin's radio scripts (in most but not all cases, Benjamin read the
works himself or participated in their production). In some cases, Benjamin delivered the
same or similar material on Radio Berlin and Radio Frankfurt (and in one case Radio
Cologne). For further information about Benjamin's broadcast output and the known dates
of his radio performances, see the Appendix.

Much Ado About Kasper and *The Cold Heart* (the latter co-written with Ernst Schoen). Section III comprises selections from Benjamin's "literary radio talks," his lectures and readings as well as the surviving texts of radio dialogues and *Hörmodelle*, or listening models, along with two radio plays not written specifically for children's programming. Finally, Section IV presents selections from Benjamin's writings on radio that were not written for broadcast or delivered on air.

Interrupted Reception

Despite their thematic and formal richness, and notwithstanding the seemingly inexhaustible interest in all things Benjamin, the radio works have received surprisingly little critical attention. Even as Benjamin continues to be known and anthologized for his pioneering study of the effects of technologies of reproduction on the experience, consumption, and understanding of the work of art, his contributions to the early history of radio broadcasting and his thinking on the subject remain relatively ignored or underrepresented in discussions of his legacy, as well as in debates surrounding the last century's proliferation of new media, and of sound media in particular. Faced with this material, we might well ask how such works could have remained so obscured, or, to use a more media-specific metaphor, so comparatively unheard. I shall address this question through two speculative explanations, one related to the history of the medium and to the archival conditions of Benjamin's radio work, the other biographical. In the process, we will follow the publication history of the radio materials, picking up on the interferences that have contributed to their interrupted reception along the way.

The dissemination of Benjamin's radio broadcasts has been subject to the forms of dispersal and loss often associated with the auditory object more generally. As one critic has argued, "As historical object, sound cannot furnish a good story or consistent cast of characters nor can it validate any ersatz notions of progress or generational maturity. The history is scattered, fleeting, and highly mediated—it is as poor an object in any respect as sound itself."[3] In other words,

---

3 Douglas Kahn, "Introduction: Histories of Sound Once Removed," in *Wireless Imagination: Sound, Radio, and the Avant-Garde*, eds. Douglas Kahn and Gregory Whitehead (Cambridge, MA: MIT Press, 1992), 2. Denis Hollier casts the argument for radio's medial specificity even more pointedly, putting it in terms of what he calls the "nonarchivable

it is not only because Benjamin, working for radio in its infancy, delivered live unrecorded broadcasts unavailable for future audio playback, or even because he failed to keep a complete written archive of the typescripts, that we are left with an imperfect account of the radio works as a whole, that is, as scripts, performances, and works of art. Rather, while such contingencies and others, including the difficult, complex history of the extant manuscripts, are certainly part of the history of Benjamin's radio works, and though the story of what has been lost must, paradoxically, be somehow included or acknowledged, the impossibility of giving a complete account remains an essential component of the medium of sound broadcast and audio performance itself.

In Benjamin's radio play for children, *The Cold Heart*, cowritten with Ernst Schoen, the character of the Radio Announcer attempts to entice the other characters (lifted from Wilhelm Hauff's eponymous tale on which the script is based) to join him in "Voice Land," a spatializing trope for the delocalized zone of broadcast, a frame for the uncertain space and invisible borders of radio transmission. He says to them: "You can come into Voice Land and speak to thousands of children, but I patrol the borders of this country and there's a condition you must first fulfill" (224). This "condition," as explained by the Announcer, turns out to be an allegory for one of the material and medial conditions of radio, and of other media of audiophonic broadcast more generally: radio, he insists, will require letting go of the material trappings of the body. The characters must agree to "surrender all finery and relinquish all external beauty," an act of disrobing and disembodiment that places an oddly sartorial

afterlife" of broadcast, or broadcast defined as live, ephemeral, and non-cooptable event. "Unless it leaves a deposit on an archivable support, sound remains merely an event and disappears without a trace, without being able to be repeated, cited, convoked ... The characteristic specific to radio is that it is live. The living word flows from it and expends itself unreservedly. The fact that it leaves no trace cannot be blamed on a temporary defect, linked to the medium's immaturity: that is its very definition. This definition is threatened by the progress of recording technology and by the social success of radio." Hollier describes this specificity as a radical "calling of live broadcasting," or "radiophonic utopia," an impossible, apocalyptic finality built upon the possibility that radio speech, not unlike sacred speech, might remain unrepeatable and therefore beyond contamination. In this sense radio might legitimately, if also forgettably, declare the end of the book ("only radio can proclaim the death of paper"): whereas literary or graphic declarations of the end (of literature, books, writing, archivization, the world) confront the double-bind of their own ongoing iterability, a radio event might plausibly announce itself as the last to speak, the definitive break, the ultimate sign-off. Hollier, "The Death of Paper: A Radio Play," *October* 78 (Fall 1996), 18–19. Benjamin's broadcasts, even those that take catastrophe and disaster as their subject, do not share this taste for positing radio as essentially one-way or anarchival.

emphasis on the otherwise generic problem of radio's need to transform the visual into the strictly auditory. In Voice Land, then,
"nothing is left but [the] voice." A subtraction with a gain: this
"voice will then be heard by thousands of children simultaneously"
(225).

Radio criticism has come to refer to this condition—the strange
and powerful effect whereby a voice, boosted by a medium (sometimes thought of as a "new" one), emanates extra-broadly, becoming
disconnected from body and point of origin—as the acousmatic
voice. The acousmatic voice is a "voice whose source one cannot see,
a voice whose origin cannot be identified, a voice one cannot place.
It is a voice in search of an origin, in search of a body."[4] As the
"condition" stipulated by the Announcer suggests, one of the effects
of the acousmatic voice is that it radiates so broadly, both exceeding
and redefining the limits of the human voice in its ability to make
itself heard.

If the radio voice is always disseminated from afar, from an invisible off-site, the questions introduced by this acousmatic radiophony
(how does the amplification and diffusion of the radio voice produce
new experiences of both intimacy and distance? how does radio's
technologically enabled disintegration of voice and body itself
become invisible, or, as it were, inaudible?) are, in Benjamin's case
multiplied by the strange status of radio works without sound: while
Benjamin is known to have delivered most of his radio talks himself,
and to have "directed, acted in, and narrated" his radio plays and
listening models, there are, unfortunately, no extant audio recordings of his voice.[5] A fragment of one of the broadcasts of *Much Ado
About Kasper* has survived, but Benjamin's voice is not part of the

4   Mladen Dolar, *A Voice and Nothing More* (Cambridge, MA: MIT Press, 2006), 60. In his
book *Radio* (1936), Rudolf Arnheim puts the condition succinctly, stating of the radio
announcer: "His is one of the purest of radio features achievable in words. He is nothing but a
voice, his corporeal existence is not included in the broadcast. He exists, like music, not beyond
but in the loudspeaker." Arnheim, *Radio*, trans. Margaret Ludwig and Herbert Read (London:
Faber and Faber, 1936), 197. For a critical discussion of the acousmatics of sound reproducibility,
see Jonathan Sterne, *The Audible Past* (Durham: Duke University Press, 2003), 20–6.

5   Schiller-Lerg, "Walter Benjamin, Radio Journalist," 45. For the eighty-six broadcast-
events she lists in her book, Schiller-Lerg suggests that Benjamin probably did not participate
in the actual on-air broadcasts of eight of them (*Walter Benjamin und der Rundfunk,* 530–41).
For additional comments on Benjamin's radio performances and his process of improvisation,
see the editors' notes to Benjamin, *Gesammelte Schriften* vol. 7.2, eds. Rolf Tiedemann,
Hermann Schweppenhäuser, et al. (Frankfurt: Suhrkamp, 1989), 584. See also Klaus Doderer,
"Walter Benjamin and Children's Literature," in *"With the Sharpened Axe of Reason":
Approaches to Walter Benjamin*, ed. Gerhard Fischer (Oxford: Berg, 1996), 171–2.

audio-archival residuum.[6] For such works, where the textual trace represents a kind of pre- or post-figuration of an audio event and broadcast performance, we must read and imagine what we cannot hear.[7]

Benjamin's radio texts, produced during what, in retrospect, appears as a medium's period of incunabula—those early works that are "notoriously fragile and difficult to hear"[8]—bear witness to the difficulties of categorizing the written, threshold material prepared in advance of an audio text. Particularly in the absence of any extant recording of the broadcast, how do we understand the archival, object, and textual status of the remaining typescripts, prepared by Benjamin, often through dictation and with the help of a typist?[9] How do we define the shifting boundaries of the radio work—as historical event and surviving text, singular performance and reproducible artifact, live broadcast and published material? In this regard, perhaps most challenging are those broadcasts Benjamin is known to have given but for which there is no reliable surviving typescript.[10]

---

6   On this recorded fragment of the Cologne broadcast of *Much Ado About Kasper*, see Schiller-Lerg, *Walter Benjamin und der Rundfunk*, 252–69; Klaus Doderer, "Walter Benjamins dreifaches Interesse an der Kinderliteratur: Sammler, Theoretiker und Autor," in *Walter Benjamin und die Kinderliteratur*, ed. Doderer (Weinheim: Juventa, 1988), 30, n. 5; and Philippe Baudouin, *Au microphone: Dr. Walter Benjamin: Walter Benjamin et la création radiophonique, 1929–1933* (Paris: Éditions de la Maison des sciences de l'homme, 2009), where what remains of the recorded broadcast is included as part of a CD that accompanies the book. As of this writing, the audio-recording is also available online at youtube.com, under the title "Walter Benjamin: Radau um Kasperl (1932)."

7   Arnheim captures the difficult, and one might say phonocentric, relationship between script and broadcast performance when he claims that the latter necessarily exceeds and cannot be properly captured by the former. On the one hand, Arnheim prescribes a meticulous approach to preparing the broadcast script, such that "when one is drafting out a wireless talk, one must consciously include in the script the personal tone of voice and way of speaking, quite indifferent as to whether the resultant 'score' of the talk makes at the same time a good piece of printed literature or not" (*Radio*, 218). And yet, even the most elaborate script is bound to remain inferior and inadequate to the improvised performance, such that "To print broadcast talks quite literally is in most cases a complete mistake" (218–19).

8   On early radio and its rarefied incunabula, see Sterne, *The Audible Past*, 288.

9   Benjamin comments on his process of dictation, along with its "liberating" effects, in the correspondence. See letter to Scholem of January 25, 1930, in Benjamin, *The Correspondence of Walter Benjamin, 1910–1940*, eds. Gershom Scholem and Theodor W. Adorno, trans. Manfred R. Jacobson and Evelyn Jacobson (Chicago: University of Chicago Press, 1994), 361; letters to Scholem of February 5, 1931 and February 28 1932, in *The Story of a Friendship*, trans. Harry Zohn (New York: New York Review Books, 2003), 209–10, 227–8. For more on the effects of Benjamin's having dictated the radio materials, see the editors' remarks in the *Gesammelte Schriften*, 7.2, 528–9.

10   These are "known" broadcasts in the sense that other archival traces, including announcements in radio journals such as the Berlin station's *Funkstunde* and the Frankfurt station's *Südwestdeutsche Rundfunk-Zeitung*, testify to their having taken place. The lost or

Of the relationship between musical score and performance, Adorno has written: "Every score is, in a way, only a system of prescriptions for possible reproduction, and nothing 'in itself.'" This formulation takes stock of the retrospective investment in the event and experience of live performance as exuding an "aura or authenticity," an auratic surplus perceived as lacking not only from the musical script but also from the recorded performance or radio broadcast.[11] If, unlike musical scores, Benjamin's typescripts represent the traces of materials prepared for one or two broadcasts, rather than initiating templates intended for ongoing or infinitely reproducible future performances, they are nonetheless all that remains of the textual, on-air performances he gave. In at least one instance they have been subsequently taken up for audio dissemination, having been regrouped, reread, and recorded.[12]

The dispersal of Benjamin's radio works—as sound objects, performances, written documents, broadcast material—has been reflected in and compounded by the complex publishing and archival history of the works. The *Gesammelte Schriften* does not gather the radio works together in one place or introduce them as a discrete set of texts.[13] Rather, they remain scattered under various headings and in

missing broadcasts can be divided into two categories: broadcasts for which no typescript remains whatsoever, and broadcasts for which some related material still exists, such as a print version published by Benjamin in a newspaper or journal. For further information on the lost or missing broadcasts, see the Appendix.

11 Adorno, *Current of Music: Elements of a Radio Theory*, ed. Robert Hullot-Kentor (Cambridge, UK: Polity, 2009), 89. Here Adorno attempts to adapt Benjamin's famous discussion of aura beyond the visual to the question of sound reproducibility. After initially concluding that for music, the "idea of reproducibility" is fundamental rather than subsequent or external to the existence of the musical work, Adorno concedes that "in music something very closely akin to Benjamin's observation can be found. *The authenticity which Benjamin attributes in the visual arts to the original must be attributed to live reproduction in music*" (89, italics in original). In other words, the live performance becomes the locus of aura precisely insofar as recorded or broadcast material threatens to compete with or destroy it (89–90). Regarding radio, Adorno is critical not only of the "pre-technical" notion of the live, non-recorded performance as more authentic than the broadcast material, but also of any notion of radio as carrying over the live event's putative uniqueness or the perceived immediacy of its "here and now"-ness. Radio, Adorno argues, may produce an effect of a "here and now" event, but this effect is "illusionary," as it denies radio's essential and ineluctable tendency to standardize, or to make broadcast an experience of the "ubiquitous" (93).

12 Some of the radio stories for children, recorded in 2002 by Harald Wieser and broadcast by Radio Bremen, were made available on audio CD under the title "Aufklärung für Kinder: von Kaspar Hauser, einem alten Gefängnis, Pompeji und Hunden—nicht nur für Kinder" [Enlightenment for Children: On Kaspar Hauser, an Old Prison, Pompeii and Dogs—Not Just for Children] (Hamburg: Hoffmann und Campe, 2003).

13 Walter Benjamin, *Gesammelte Schriften*, 7 vols., with supplements, eds Rolf Tiedemann, Hermann Schweppenhäuser, et al. (Frankfurt: Suhrkamp, 1972–89). Hereafter cited as GS.

different volumes throughout the multi-volume work. The reasons for this are, in part, historical, and the itinerary of some of the radio type-scripts is worth noting; their story, an account of multiple seizures and relocations, not only contributed to the relative inaccessibility and obscurity of the radio works during the years of the production of the *Gesammelte Schriften*, but also bears witness to a Cold War archival history that remains, in large part, still to be written. As an archival history, it is necessarily an account of destruction and preservation, loss and containment; such an account is both part of the archive and its limit. Certainly one hopes that as the Benjaminian legacy contin-ues, and as the works for radio receive more attention, more details will emerge concerning this layered history.

When Benjamin fled Paris in 1940, he left behind a part of his archive in his apartment, including the remaining typescripts of some of his radio texts. (According to the editors of the *Gesammelte Schriften*, these were materials Benjamin felt were "unimportant,"[14] a bias that has been exacerbated in his posthumous legacy.) Confiscated by the Gestapo, they escaped destruction only through a series of chance events: mistakenly packed into the archive of the *Pariser Tageszeitung* [Paris Daily News], they were saved in 1945 through an act of sabotage. Later taken to the Soviet Union, they were transferred around 1960 to the GDR. Initially held in the Central Archive in Potsdam, they were then moved in 1972 to the literary archives of the Academy of Arts in East Berlin. The editors of the *Gesammelte Schriften* were denied access to these materials until 1983.[15]

The collection of typescripts for the radio stories for children was first published in 1985, when they appeared under the title *Aufklärung für Kinder* [Enlightenment for Children] (ed. Rolf Tiedemann, Frankfurt: Suhrkamp, 1985). They were later included in the *Gesammelte Schriften*, where they appear in the final volume as "Rundfunkgeschichten für Kinder" [Radio Stories for Children] (GS, 7.1, 68–249). Other radio-related materials remain scattered throughout the *Gesammelte Schriften*: Benjamin's "literary radio talks" are not presented together, and remain even less visible as a

---

14 GS, 1.2, 759.

15 This account is derived from two slightly different narratives provided in the GS: see GS, 1.2, 761 and GS, 7.2, 525. For an additional account by the GS editors of the archival history of the radio works, including their comments on the problem of access, see also GS, 2.3, 1440–3. For a brief account in English of this part of Benjamin's archive, see Esther Leslie, *Walter Benjamin* (London: Reaktion Books, 2007), 11.

group.[16] The radio plays, as well as the surviving example of Benjamin's listening models and the one remaining radio dialogue, are similarly dispersed. The forthcoming new critical edition of Benjamin's complete works will correct this problem and, for the first time in German, gather these materials in one place.[17]

The difficulty of identifying the radio works within the *Gesammelte Schriften* is compounded by the multiplicity of programming categories into which they fall. Schiller-Lerg has identified at least eight separate programming categories for Benjamin's radio production: Tales, Lectures, Book Hour, Conversations, Radio Plays, Listening Models, Youth Radio, School Radio.[18] While these categories need not govern our reading of the radio texts, the *Gesammelte Schriften* makes some confusing choices, collapsing, for instance, the important categories of the *Hörspiel* [radio play] and the *Hörmodell* [listening model].[19]

Along with the complex archival and publication history of the works for radio, we can cite Benjamin's own "negative attitude toward much of the work he did for money" as one of the factors that has, perhaps, contributed to their continued perception as relatively "unimportant."[20] In his affirmative reassessment of their value,

16   On the scattered status of the literary radio talks, see the editors' note in GS, 7.2, 608–9. In some instances, the scattering of these materials in the GS can be attributed to the fact that while Benjamin's published versions of the essays survive, there is no known typescript of the original radio-broadcast form. This is the case for broadcasts of material such as the famous "Unpacking My Library," which began as a broadcast on Radio Frankfurt on April 27, 1931.

17   The forthcoming volume dedicated to Benjamin's radio work, edited by Thomas Küpper and Anja Nowak, is scheduled to appear in Fall 2014. Entitled *Rundfunkarbeiten*, it is to be Volume 9 of the collective edition, *Walter Benjamin: Werke und Nachlaß*, to be published by Suhrkamp.

18   Schiller-Lerg, *Walter Benjamin und der Rundfunk*, 540–1. On the overlapping, ninth category of *Funkspiele* [radio plays], which she uses in addition to the *Hörspiele* [radio or listening plays] and the *Hörmodelle* [listening models, Benjamin's original term], see ibid., 218.

19   The GS includes the radio plays *What the Germans Were Reading While Their Classical Authors Were Writing*, *Much Ado About Kasper*, and *Lichtenberg* under the category of "listening models" (GS, 4.2, 642–720). These three texts were initially published together as *Drei Hörmodelle* (Frankfurt: Suhrkamp, 1971). Given the specificity of Benjamin's use of the term *Hörmodell*, or listening model, this categorization does not make sense for these radio plays. The miscategorization has contributed to some confusion in the scholarship, for instance in John Mowitt's discussion of Benjamin's *Lichtenberg*, in *Radio: Essays in Bad Reception* (Berkeley: University of California Press, 2011), 63–76.

20   The first quotation is from Scholem's notes to the correspondence, where he comments on Benjamin's "denigratory assessment" of his radio work and other journalistic writings undertaken explicitly for remuneration. Scholem, notes to letter of February 28, 1933, in *The Correspondence of Walter Benjamin*, 404, n. 12.

suggesting that Benjamin's radio pieces "also contain sediments of his decidedly original way of seeing," Scholem has pointed us in the right direction.[21] In an attempt to account for the relatively discounted status of the radio pieces within the Benjaminian *œuvre*, we turn to some of Benjamin's comments on his remunerated work, including the work for broadcast.

Regional radio broadcasting was introduced in Germany in October 1923.[22] By early 1925, Benjamin had begun to think of the radio, or rather of writing for print periodicals supported by the new medium of radio, as a possible source of income. In a letter to Scholem dated February 19, 1925, Benjamin writes from Frankfurt: "I am keeping an eye open for any opportunities that may arise locally and finally have applied for the editorship of a radio magazine or, to be more precise, a supplement. This would be a part-time job, but it probably will not be so easy for me to get because we are having trouble agreeing on the honorarium. The situation is that Ernst Schoen has had an important position here for months now. He is the manager of the Frankfurt 'broadcasting' station and put in a good word for me."[23]

This comment introduces three threads that will persist throughout Benjamin's work for radio. First, it suggests the intertwining and interdependence of print and broadcast media in Benjamin's career. Second, it points to the financial insecurities that will continue to preoccupy him and which will nearly always be in the foreground when he mentions his contributions to radio. And third, it highlights the way in which Ernst Schoen, a school friend of Benjamin's who worked for the Frankfurt radio station *Südwestdeutsche Rundfunk* and who would become, in 1929, its artistic director, will consistently be credited with having helped Benjamin to launch and sustain his radio career, at least until political pressures made it impossible for either of them to go on working in German broadcasting.[24] As Adorno puts it,

---

21 Scholem, *The Correspondence of Walter Benjamin*, 404, n. 12.

22 For a history of Weimar broadcasting, see Karl Christian Führer, "A Medium of Modernity?: Broadcasting in Weimar Germany, 1923–1932," *Journal of Modern History* 69 (December 1997), 722–53.

23 Benjamin, *The Correspondence of Walter Benjamin*, 262. Momme Brodersen gives more details on Benjamin's 1925 application for a position at the radio magazine *Radio–Umschau* [Radio Review], in Brodersen, *Walter Benjamin: A Biography*, trans. Malcolm R. Green and Ingrida Ligers, ed. Martina Dervis (London: Verso, 1996), 191–2.

24 With Benjamin, the issue of help from his friends was always fraught; like any helpful intervention, it signaled the very need for help, or the kind of vulnerability and dependency that for Benjamin began as financial and professional exposure (in part due to his lack of university affiliation and the impossibility of an academic career, Benjamin having been

"The few years during which Benjamin was later able to live relatively free of worry, following the failure of his academic plans and prior to the outbreak of fascism, he owed in no small measure to the solidarity of Schoen, who as program director of Radio Frankfurt provided him with an opportunity for regular and frequent work."[25]

While Benjamin did not secure the position in Frankfurt in 1925, he would continue to consider the radio a source of much-needed income. He gave his first broadcast, a lecture entitled "Young Russian Poets," from Radio Frankfurt on March 23, 1927.[26] In 1929, Benjamin's engagement with radio became more frequent and intensive. That year, he gave at least thirteen broadcasts: a total of eight readings or talks from Frankfurt, and five talks on children's radio from Berlin. In 1930, he gave at least thirty-seven broadcasts, making it his most productive year on the air. In 1931, his work would be heard on the radio approximately twenty-one times; from January through September of 1932, thirteen times; and finally, twice in January 1933.[27]

Yet even as Benjamin's work for radio became more frequent, or perhaps precisely as he became more dependent on it, his epistolary comments on the material remained, for the most part, disparaging. In his correspondence, he almost always mentions radio in the context of pressing financial concerns, anxiety over which only increased in the years leading up to his departure from Germany in March 1933. His work for radio is among "the work I do simply to earn a living," and in response to what appears to be a request from Scholem for an archive of Benjamin's "works for the radio," Benjamin

thwarted in his efforts to successfully submit the *Origin of German Tragic Drama* as his *Habilitation* in July 1925), and that would, through and beyond the period of the radio years, grow into the political and existential duress that famously contributed to his suicide at the border in Spain in September 1940. For Benjamin's comments on the "helpful intervention of [Adorno's] friends," and on the precariousness of dependence and the limits of gratitude, see his letter to Adorno of March 18, 1934, in Benjamin and Adorno, *The Complete Correspondence 1928–1940*, ed. Henri Lonitz, trans. Nicholas Walker (Cambridge, MA: Harvard University Press, 1999), 34. All of this is to say that Schoen's assistance, so crucial to the story and fact of Benjamin's work for Radio Frankfurt, was both invaluable and symptomatic of the precariousness of Benjamin's intellectual life and the professional circumstances that sometimes supported it and sometimes failed to do so.

25 Adorno, "Benjamin the Letter Writer," in *Notes to Literature Vol. II*, trans. Shierry Weber Nicholsen (New York: Columbia University Press, 1992), 237.

26 "Junge russische Dichter" is one of the broadcasts for which there is no precise or reliable surviving manuscript. (See the Appendix.) The GS editors, along with Schiller-Lerg (*Walter Benjamin und der Rundfunk*, 345), agree that this broadcast probably corresponds to Benjamin's article "Neue Dichter in Russland," which was published in the international review *i 10* (Amsterdam, 1927) and can be found in GS, 2.2, 755–62.

27 For more information on the dates of broadcasts, see the Appendix.

writes even more pointedly, in a letter of February 28, 1933, that he hasn't "been successful in collecting them all. I am speaking of the radio plays, not the series of countless talks, which [will] now come to an end, unfortunately, and are of no interest except in economic terms, but that is now a thing of the past."[28] Here we note that amid Benjamin's ongoing disdain for the majority of his work for radio, presumably including the stories for children and the literary radio talks, he spares the radio plays and singles out *Much Ado About Kasper* in particular as "notable from a technical point of view."[29]

By the summer of 1932, Benjamin was to experience the effects of an increasingly constricted set of options for his contributions to radio. In July, he wrote to Scholem that the "reactionary movement . . . has affected my work for radio," pointing to the Papen government's takeover of the airwaves.[30] By the fall of 1932, Benjamin, writing to Scholem from Provermo, where he was staying with Wilhelm Speyer (coauthor of "Prescriptions for Comedy Writers"), would again comment on the increasingly limited radio situation, noting that he was left "completely deprived by the events at the Berlin radio station of the income that I used to be able to count on, and with the gloomiest thoughts."[31]

Benjamin's last transmission from the Berlin station was the children's radio broadcast "The Mississippi Flood of 1927," on March 23, 1932. His last broadcast from Frankfurt was "Aus einer unveröffentlichten Skizzensammlung Berliner Kindheit um 1900" [From an unpublished collection of sketches, Berlin Childhood Around 1900], on January 29, 1933. This was a selection from what would become Benjamin's famous text, *Berlin Childhood Around 1900*.[32] The next day, January 30, 1933, Hitler was appointed chan-

---

28 Benjamin to Scholem, January 25, 1930, in *The Correspondence of Walter Benjamin*, 361, 403–4. See also Benjamin's letter to Scholem on February 5, 1931, where he refers to his radio work in Frankfurt as merely "some piddling radio matters" (Scholem, *Story of a Friendship*, 211). For further mention of the increasingly constricted conditions that leave him with fewer opportunities to work on radio, see *The Correspondence of Walter Benjamin*, 395–6, 399, and *Story of a Friendship*, 239.

29 *The Correspondence of Walter Benjamin*, 404. As his comments suggest, *Much Ado About Kasper* is, with its provisions for various interventions of sound, noise, and audio-signaling, perhaps Benjamin's most radiophonically charged and formally challenging piece.

30 Letter to Scholem of July 26, 1932, in *The Correspondence of Walter Benjamin*, 395. For the effects on radio of the Papen government's coup, including the firing of Hans Flesch as director of the Berlin Radio Hour, see Jelavich, *Berlin Alexanderplatz*, 241.

31 Benjamin, postcard quoted by Scholem in *Story of a Friendship*, 239.

32 Benjamin broadcast the radio version of "Berliner Kindheit um 1900" on January 29, 1933, from 6:55 to 7:20 pm. On this broadcast, see Schiller-Lerg, *Walter Benjamin und der Rundfunk*, 302–3 and 104–7. In their discussion of the complex composition and publication

cellor, and the Nazi torchlight parade was sent out over the airwaves as the very first nationwide live broadcast.

In Benjamin's surviving listening model, "A Pay Raise?! Whatever Gave You That Idea!" (cowritten with Wolf Zucker), Benjamin considers how to argue one's case, highlighting one's own value as an employee. A playfully didactic take on the rhetoric of self-promotion, Benjamin and Zucker argue for learning how to successfully present oneself and ask for a salary increase, at the same time making the case for tuning in, since one might well profit from listening to the radio. Read alongside Benjamin's own disparaging, often discouraged remarks about his own radio career, "A Pay Raise?!" resonates as an ironic commentary on Benjamin's own sense of indebtedness and failure, as well as on the limitations of what the text repeatedly calls "success." If "A Pay Raise?!" puts forward a model of self-interest and self-help in which the individual need only learn to be confident and persuasive enough to transcend any and all resistance to his cause, promoting a self-help ideal in which it is enough to say that success means "contend[ing] with life's difficulties in a relaxed and pleasant manner" (302), Benjamin's ambivalence about his own career suggests that the simplicity of the model is also its flaw. What would it mean to approach life's "struggles [as] a kind of sport . . . as [one] would a game" (302), given an economic and political context in which the stakes of the game make "success" a far less obvious, less clearly achievable ideal as well as a matter of survival?

Was Benjamin's career on radio a "successful" one? Benjamin could hardly have argued his way out of the end of his work for radio. Perhaps, individually and together, the radio texts offer a different measure through which to evaluate his career and to read the value of his on-air achievements. Though they were ultimately unable to lift him above what he called the "ruin" and "catastrophe"

---

history of *Berlin Childhood Around 1900*, the editors of the GS do not mention the piece's radio past (GS, 4.2, 964–70; and GS, 6, 797–9, and GS, 7.2, 691–4). Unfortunately, no typescript of the broadcast survives, and it is not possible to know what selections Benjamin read. He had composed "A Berlin Chronicle" during the first half of 1932, and, during the second half of that year, had started to work on *Berlin Childhood*. The first selections from *Berlin Childhood* appeared in print, under pseudonym, in the *Frankfurter Zeitung* in February and March 1933 (see editors' notes in GS, 4.2, 966, and "Chronology," in Walter Benjamin, *Selected Writings*, vol. 2, 1927–1934, trans. Rodney Livingstone et al., eds. Michael W. Jennings, Howard Eiland, and Gary Smith [Cambridge, MA: Harvard University Press, 1999], 848, hereafter cited as SW; see also *The Correspondence of Walter Benjamin*, 399–404). Thus, the radio reading would have been Benjamin's earliest "publication" of the work.

that threatened his life and work, the radio broadcasts were central to his writings; some of the written works most important to Benjamin were presented, at one time and in one form or another, on the radio.[33] The broadcast pieces further our understanding of a wide variety of Benjaminian themes.

Reading the Radio Works: What Is Radio for Benjamin?

Readers of Benjamin's work will be familiar with some of the thematic concerns of the radio pieces. Just as Benjamin focuses in the "Work of Art" essay on the problematic appearance of the "vanishing point" of aura under the changing conditions of the present,[34] in the radio pieces, Benjamin's gaze often falls upon traces of disappearance and the vestiges of obsolete social forms. Thus, in the radio stories for children that focus on Berlin, Benjamin is interested in presenting a Berlin that is in the process of becoming fossilized. In "Street Trade and Markets in Old and New Berlin," for instance, Benjamin presents the erstwhile market hall as an exemplary scene of outmoded nineteenth-century social relations. After evoking, through the literature of Adolf Glassbrenner, the "market women" and "hawkers" that peopled the markets of "old Berlin," he concludes, "Most of this sort of business has utterly vanished from the streets of Berlin" (14). And, he continues, just as the classic hawkers have disappeared, so too have sand-delivery men and colporteurs.

---

33   In a letter to Scholem of July 26, 1932, Benjamin writes of the "four books that mark off the real site of ruin or catastrophe, whose furthest boundary I am still unable to survey when I let my eyes wander over the next years of my life. They include the *Pariser Passagen*, the *Gesammelte Essays zur Literatur*, the *Briefe*, and a truly exceptional book about hashish" (*The Correspondence of Walter Benjamin*, 396). Versions of segments of at least three of these projects were presented on the radio: from the material that became *The Arcades Project*, we can trace a link to "The Railway Disaster at the Firth of Tay" (see this volume, 171 n.1). The *Briefe* mentioned by Benjamin refers to the collection of German letters, with brief introductions and commentary, that ultimately became *Deutsche Menschen*, in GS, 4.1, 149–233 ("German Men and Women," SW, 3, 167–235). Initially published under the pseudonym Detlef Holz from April 1931 to May 1932 in the *Frankfurter Zeitung*, the text was published in book form in 1936. The related radio piece is "Auf der Spur alter Briefe," in GS, 4.2, 942–4 ("On the Trail of Old Letters," SW, 2, 555–8). For the book on hashish, which was never published as such during Benjamin's lifetime, the related radio broadcast is "Myslowitz–Braunschweig–Marseille: Die Geschichte eines Haschisch-Rausches," in GS, 729–37 ("Myslovice–Braunschweig–Marseilles: The Story of a Hashish Trance," in SW, 2, 386–93). The corresponding radio text is considered lost; what remains is the text published in *Ubu* in November 1930.

34   For the figure of the "vanishing point" with reference to "The Work of Art in the Age of Its Mechanical Reproducibility," see Benjamin's letter to Horkheimer of October 16, 1935 (*The Correspondence of Walter Benjamin*, 509).

In order to present such typologies of vanished life, Benjamin must catalog and read their traces in the present. The problem of the preservation, appearance, and representation of social forms precisely in their moment of evanescence is, of course, hardly novel to Benjamin's work for radio. It is rather the crux of his discussion, in *The Arcades Project*, of the "dialectical image" and "dialectics at a standstill."[35] Yet radio introduces a specific, medially driven problem of presentation: not only how to locate and present the traces of a disappeared past, but how to cite the auditory trace—the past as sound and the past in its historically specific sound forms. Is there a specific audio form for the exemplary remainder? Is there a specifically auditory scene or form of the dialectical image? How does radio, and Benjamin's radio work in particular, confront the much older problem of ekphrasis, or "the verbal representation of visual representation"?[36] How to conceive of the specifically "auditory" remainder in the context of a past that remains silent, a past that precedes the technologies of audio archivization and sound reproduction we have become so accustomed to today? Or, to put such questions, which speak to debates around the definition and nature of medial specificity, in a Benjaminian register: How does radio translate or transpose the dialectical image, which Benjamin argues is found "in language," into language on the radio?[37] Is there such a thing as a recognizable radio language, or language as it sounds and signifies "on radio"? How do Benjamin's well-known arguments in the "Work of Art" essay, in which he names the camera-enhanced visual experience as the scene of the discovery of the "optical unconscious," enable us to ask whether and how new forms of "hearing-matter" might pave the way for

---

35   See Walter Benjamin, *The Arcades Project* [N2a3 and N3,1], trans. Howard Eiland and Kevin McLaughlin, (Cambridge, MA: Harvard University Press, 1999), 462–3.

36   This definition of ekphrasis is from W. J. T. Mitchell, "Ekphrasis and the Other," in *Picture Theory*, (Chicago: University of Chicago Press, 1994), 152. To Mitchell's definition, I would add the "verbal *and sound* representation of visual representation," particularly as radio interests itself in audio-signifiers that are not necessarily words (for instance, the "noises" Benjamin introduces in *Much Ado About Kasper*). Beyond this, however, it is crucial not to presume a fixed understanding of the difference between the "verbal" and the "visual" as objects or modes of presentation. What, after all, is a "visual" object for, presented in the medium of radio? One of Mitchell's key arguments is that we do *not* precisely understand this difference, or the relationship of "otherness" between text and image, especially in relation to the status of speech acts, which are "not medium-specific" and "not 'proper' to some medium or other" (160).

37   "Only dialectical images are genuine images (that is, not archaic); and the place where one encounters them is language" (*The Arcades Project* [N2,3], 462).

something like an "auditory unconscious" to make itself heard?[38] Similarly, we might ask whether and how Benjamin's comments about the effects of technological reproducibility on the appearance and disappearance of aura might carry over to, and be changed by, an attention to the effects of new techniques of sound recording and sound amplification on the experience and spectrum of hearing. Does sound recording bring into focus, or perhaps even into hearing, something like the vanishing of an auditory aura?[39]

Benjamin's radio addresses do not provide us with a direct or simple answer to such questions about the possible medial or sonic specificity of radio. Indeed, where they do foreground the acoustic dimensions of radio as a medium, they also place emphasis on the literary and written text as the mode of transmission of spoken language.[40] Still, the radio texts leave us with questions about how to approach not only the specificity of Benjamin's radio voice, but also

---

38 Benjamin makes note of the psychoanalytic expansion of "our field of perception," comparing Freud's publication of *On the Psychopathology of Everyday Life*, with its emphasis on paying attention to slips of the tongue, with cinema's "deepening of apperception throughout the entire spectrum of optical—and now also auditory—impressions" ("The Work of Art," SW 4, 265). For the phrase "hearing-matter," see "The Work of Art," 278 n. 29, where Benjamin cites Aldous Huxley's disparaging commentary on the proliferation of "trash in the total artistic output" of contemporary culture, an explosive, technologically-enabled multiplication of material that includes not only more "reading- and seeing-matter" but also more "hearing-matter."

39 Adorno, known for his negative assessment of radio and the culture industry, takes up this very problem of analyzing a shift in audio-aura, using Benjamin's essay as a launching point.

40 In "Street Trade and Markets in Old and New Berlin," when Benjamin refers specifically to the *heard* artifact and the specificity of everyday, spoken language, he does not attempt to reproduce the ambient soundscape. Rather, his source is the literature of Adolf Glassbrenner, who permits Benjamin to illustrate his point that the market hall is "as rich and sumptuous for the ear as the image of the market is a feast for the eyes" (11). Benjamin makes similar use of Glassbrenner in "Berlin Dialect" and "Theodor Hosemann," where citations of his work provide something like narrative "images" of an everyday vernacular. In "Theodor Hosemann," Benjamin addresses the problem of radio ekphrasis directly, asking "Is it not a crazy idea to talk about a painter on the radio?—It's out of the question, of course, that I stand here and describe Hosemann's pictures to you," and finally concludes that Glassbrenner's text, as a substitute for the otherwise unpresentable visual object text, has allowed him to present the "speaking" character of a typical Berliner "instead of the drawn version" (69). In other words, if the visual image resists presentation over the radio, a written substitute, featuring not only dialogue but the ever-changing, "living" speech act of a typical Berlin type, can be reproduced through the speaker's citation of that written text. For the problem of "ekphrastic indifference," or the stage of fascination with ekphrasis corresponding to the "commonsense perception that ekphrasis is impossible . . . A verbal presentation cannot represent—that is, make present—its object in the same way a visual presentation can," see Mitchell, *Picture Theory*, 152.

the interactions between the radio texts and his other work. These are questions for future scholarship.

Such scholarship might also consider how Benjamin exploits and plays with the imposed "blindness" of the medium. In both *Much Ado About Kasper* and *The Cold Heart*, Benjamin creates scenes in which fog imposes limitations on sight, forcing the characters to embody the condition of the radio listener, a condition of relative blindness that leads to a kind of amplified call for audio and cognitive attunement, for listening in to both what is said and what cannot be heard. How, if at all, does this attempt to sort out a specific channel for auditory intake support and/or contradict the mixed-media approach of the radio works as a whole?

It is, by now, a truism of media studies that every new medium reinvents those that came before it. If Benjamin's texts for broadcast encourage us to ask how he understood the unprecedented aesthetic potential and political implications of radio, they also compel us to consider how radio reinterprets the very definition of a medium. When adapted for or broadcast over radio, is a "literary" text still literature? What happens to literature "after" radio? How does the shift from the printed page to the airwaves recast notions of popularity and the public? Benjamin takes up such questions and acts of remediation in his radio play, *What the Germans Were Reading While Their Classical Authors Were Writing*, in which he dramatizes the difficulty of pinning down a specifically contemporary definition of "popularity" and "popularization."

It would not be Radio Benjamin if concerns over remediation—the refashioning of old media in the new; ongoing changes to the modes of broadcast, dissemination, and consumption of art—were delimited as exclusively aesthetic or formal. Readers of the works presented in Section IV will quickly recognize a Brecht-inspired attempt to bend radio away from unidirectional transmission in favor of a two-way apparatus, a radio that turns the listener from a passive consumer into an active producer, expanding the public's understanding of its own expertise.[41] In addition to the more explicitly political and theoretical concerns expressed in those essays, Benjamin puts forward a pedagogical approach in the

---

41 See Benjamin, "Reflections on Radio," "Theater and Radio," "Two Kinds of Popularity," and "Listening Models," in this volume. See also Brecht, "The Radio as Communication Apparatus," in *Bertolt Brecht on Radio and Film*, trans. and ed. Marc Silberman (London: Methuen, 2000), 41–6.

children's radio pieces, a mode of storytelling that, for instance, invites his audience to tune into and even to teach their parents a critique of commodity fetishism (see the last paragraph of "Berlin Toy Tour I"). Indeed, the radio stories for children display a range of educational scenes and topics, such as the opening of "The Rental Barracks," where Benjamin offers his audience an architectural history they are unlikely to learn from the usual authorities ("Prick up your ears and I'll tell you something you won't often hear in your German lessons, or in geography, or in social studies ..." [56]).⁴² In "Cagliostro," Benjamin uses a story about a swindler to dismiss any notion of the Enlightenment as inoculation against or triumph over the supernatural. Benjamin's presentations of such "alternative" sources of hearing and learning comingle the high and the low and include sources such as the popular literature of Glassbrenner and the Berlin puppet theater, as well as the works of Hoffmann, Fontane, and Goethe; other, perhaps even more unexpected learning sites include children's books, children's toys, factories and department stores, treatises on witches, the history of the Bastille, folklore, newspapers, and illustrated magazines, to give only a partial list of Benjamin's sources and the situations and stories he draws on.

Perhaps the most unnerving, ambivalent presentation of radio's range and uncertain political import comes in *Much Ado About Kasper*, where Benjamin turns the radio into an apparatus not only of resistance to official channels of power and knowledge, but also of surveillance and unauthorized listening-in. Toward the beginning of the play, when Herr Maulschmidt, the representative of the radio station, eagerly solicits Kasper to speak on the air, Kasper's initial response highlights a playfully naïve point of view, one that gives voice to the non-obviousness of the way and the fact that radio works. Maulschmidt, whose absurd name (something like "mouth-smith" or "snout-forger") satirizes radio as "giving voice," tells Kasper that he has long sought "to place you, Kasper, the age-old and famous friend of children, in front of the microphone" (203). When

---

42 In approaching the radio works for children, it is important not to take for granted the significance of the "child" as a category of addressee for Benjamin. Indeed, in "Children's Literature," he declares that "If there is any field in the world where specialization must invariably fail, it is in the creation of works for children" (254). As Susan Buck-Morss has argued, Benjamin makes no "qualitative distinction" that would offset some topics as "appropriate" for children and others as fitting only for adults ("'Verehrte Unsichtbare!': Walter Benjamins Radiovörtrage," in *Walter Benjamin und die Kinderliteratur*, ed. Doderer, 93–101).

Kasper refuses, his explanation becomes a play on the German for radio, *Rundfunk*:

> HERR MAULSCHMIDT: What's that, Kasper? Do I hear you correctly? You'd turn down the exalted and solemn honor of speaking on the radio?
> KASPER: You bet!
> HERR MAULSCHMIDT: But why?
> . . .
> KASPER: You know, with all those sparks [*Funken*] flying around [*rund*], I might try to catch one and then I'd catch fire myself.
> HERR MAULSCHMIDT: Kasper, you don't even know what radio is. Stick close to me and I'm sure you'll get a better sense of what it's about. (204)

The play makes good on this promise near its end. After escaping the radio station and being chased by Maulschmidt through various other acoustically signaled locations, including a train station, a carnival, and a zoo, Kasper finds himself back at home, where Maulschmidt turns up to inform him that, unbeknownst to Kasper, he has been on the radio after all. Handing Kasper a thousand marks, he explains that it is his fee for speaking on the air:

> KASPER: What's that supposed to mean?
> HERR MAULSCHMIDT: It means that you spoke on the radio, even if you didn't know it.
> KASPER: Well, that must have been in my sleep.
> HERR MAULSCHMIDT: Not in your sleep, but in your bed.
> FRAU PUSCHI: In bed?
> HERR MAULSCHMIDT: He who laughs last, laughs loudest. We at the radio station are even cleverer than you. While you were out in the city perpetrating your scandalous deeds, we secretly installed a microphone in your room, under your bed, and now we have everything you said, on a record, and I just happened to bring one along for you.
> . . .
> KASPER: I've just heard for the first time what radio is. (219)

This scene highlights the structural significance of sound recording and surveillance to radio. Just as the film camera has "penetrated reality," the radio microphone has stealthily entered spaces that might otherwise be thought of as beyond capture or out of (over) hearing range, in this case, the domestic space, the private interior, the bedroom.[43] The hidden microphone, like the omniscient narrator, can travel across otherwise impermeable bounds, picking up voices and gathering material for new forms of acoustic presentation. The mobile location of radio—including its origin and means of recording and transmission—not only expands radio's range of hearing (to, say, new locations including the previously unrecorded zones of private speech, dreams, and the sounds of sleep), but also introduces the possibility of stolen speech and unauthorized audio impressions. The voice is subject to new and unseen forms of expropriation.

Benjamin's most explicit commentary on radio in "The Work of Art" is found in a footnote, where he addresses the acousmatics of the medium, or the technologically enabled "detachability" and "transportability" of the human not only as image but also as voice. Radio and film, Benjamin argues, shift the scope and scene of public presentation for actors and politicians alike, a process that "results in a new form of selection—selection before an apparatus—from which the star and the dictator emerge as victors."[44] Benjamin's more hopeful, affirmative comments on the politics and potential of radio, along with his broadcasts themselves, project a future for radio that would be built from a broader base, one that would be governed not by the "selection" of the interests of capital or the established networks of power, but by a more chaotic, unpredictable stream of voices. That we are finally able to receive the texts of his broadcasts in English is a testimony to his own enduring star power and the chance endurance of his broadcast texts.

A Note on the Compiling of the Texts

In compiling and editing the radio works, we have relied on the *Gesammelte Schriften*, whose editors, despite the dispersed status of the radio pieces, provide detailed notes and introductory comments on the archival history and condition of the extant typescripts. We have also made use of the meticulous and invaluable research of Sabine Schiller-Lerg, whose book on Benjamin and radio remains,

---

43 Here it is worth noting that the representation of such spaces is absolutely "new" only if we discount its appearance in other aesthetic forms, such as the literary representation of the bedroom or even of the mental interior through free-indirect verse.

44 Benjamin, "The Work of Art," 261 and 277 n. 27.

to date, the most important and comprehensive contribution to the subject.[45]

Schiller-Lerg's work provides the most detailed information about the print publications, such as radio journals and their program announcements, which reveal the dates and times of Benjamin's broadcast performances. In some cases, such archival materials also supply the title of the broadcast and the program or series of which Benjamin's work was a part. From such sources we learn, for instance, that most of the radio stories for children, broadcast on Radio Berlin and Radio Frankfurt's Youth Hour, were typically scheduled for a set period of twenty to thirty minutes. We have included all such data about listed broadcast titles, dates, and times at the end of each chapter, in the section following the text of each translation.

The notes to the texts expand on Benjamin's mention of proper names and titles, where we thought such information necessary to illuminate an obscure reference or other relevant contextual information. In addition, and with the help of digital searches, we have been able to provide additional information about possible source materials. Written for broadcast performance rather than publication, Benjamin's typescripts, with very few exceptions, do not give bibliographic details for the texts from which he gathered his quotations; we cannot be certain that he consulted the precise materials or editions to which we direct the reader's attention. However, particularly given the obscurity of some of these sources, the fact of a matched quotation, even without additional verification in Benjamin's own hand, may be enough reason to provide a text and context for follow-up, should the reader be interested. In most instances the reference material is in German, which poses a limitation for the English-speaking audience. Notwithstanding this obstacle, and taking into consideration that Benjamin often modifies or abridges the original, such references indicate to the reader that Benjamin is borrowing from or leaning on a source.

---

45 Schiller-Lerg, *Walter Benjamin und der Rundfunk.* See also Schiller-Lerg, "Die Rundfunkarbeiten," in *Benjamin Handbuch,* ed. Burkhardt Lindner (Stuttgart: Metzler, 2006), 406–20. The scholarship in English is almost nonexistent. The best-known study is Jeffrey Mehlman's *Walter Benjamin for Children: An Essay on His Radio Years* (Chicago: University of Chicago Press, 1993). See also Wolfgang Hagen, "'On the Minute': Benjamin's Silent Work for the German Radio," 2006. Online at whagen.de/vortraege/2006.

Youth Hour: Radio Stories for Children

Benjamin broadcast the radio talks in this section from 1929 to 1932 on Radio Berlin and Southwest German Radio, Frankfurt. They were delivered as part of the stations' youth programming: Berlin Radio's *Jugendstunde* and Radio Frankfurt's *Stunde der Jugend*, or Youth Hour.

The order of the broadcasts is roughly chronological, with further groupings into three overarching Benjaminian concerns: stories related to Berlin; stories about cheats and frauds; stories about catastrophes; and finally "True Dog Stories" and "A Crazy Mixed-Up Day," which do not fit into the preceding categories.

CHAPTER I

Berlin Dialect

Today I'd like to speak with you about the Berlin *Schnauze*. This so-called big snout is the first thing that comes to mind when talking about Berliners.[1] The Berliner, as they say in Germany, well, he's the clever one who does everything differently and better than the rest of us. Or so he would have you believe. That's why people in Germany don't like Berliners, or so they let on. Still, at the end of the day, it's a good thing for people to have a capital they can grumble about now and again.

But really, is this true about the Berlin *Schnauze?* It is and it isn't. Every one of you surely knows lots of stories where Berliners open their big traps so wide that the Brandenburg Gate could fit inside. And later on I'll tell you a few more that perhaps you've never heard. But if you look at it a little closer, much of what you think you know about the big snout isn't actually true. It's quite simple: for example, other peoples and other regions make much of their particular way of speaking; "dialect" is what we call the language spoken in an individual city or area. They go on and on about it; they're proud of it; and they love their poets, like Reuter who wrote in Mecklenburg Low German, Hebel in Alemannic, and Gotthelf in Swiss German.[2] And

---

1 *Berliner Schnauze*, which can be loosely translated as "Berlin snout," refers to both a way of speaking and an attitude. It connotes both the physiological (snout, schnoz, nose, muzzle, gob, or mug) and the linguistic-cultural (insolence, coarseness, lip, sass, wit, yap). It designates a style specific to Berliners, and more exclusively, to working-class Berliners. For more of Benjamin's comments on Berlin dialect, see "Wat hier jelacht wird, det lache ick" [If anyone's laughing here, it's me] in GS, 4.1, 537–42 (first published in the *Frankfurter Zeitung*, May 5, 1929). Both in its stated emphasis on Berlin dialect as spoken, everyday language and in the rhythm and inflections of Benjamin's own syntax (which here includes, even in its typescript form, indications for what some linguists call "filler" words or, in German, modal particles, words such as "so" and "well" and "now"), "Berlin Dialect" stands out, in focus and style, as perhaps the most "spoken" of Benjamin's radio talks for children.

2 Fritz Reuter (1810–1874) was a writer from Mecklenburg in Northern Germany known for his contributions to Low German literature; Johann Peter Hebel (1760–1826)

they're right to do so. But Berliners, as far as "Berlining" is concerned, have always been very humble. In fact, if anything they've been ashamed of their language, at least around sophisticated people and with foreigners. Needless to say, when among themselves, they have a lot of fun with it. And of course they also make fun of Berlining, just as they do of everything else, and there are many pretty stories to show for it. For example: a man sits at the table with his wife and says: "Huh, beans again today? But I et 'em just yesterday." Then his wife one-ups him and says: "It ain't 'I et,' it's 'I ate.'" To which the man replies: "Maybe you call yourself that, but I sure as heck don't."[3] Or the well-known story of a man walking with his son, who points to a sign and asks: "How do you prenounce that word, papa?" And the father corrects him: "'Prenounce' is prenounced 'pronounce.'"

Berliners needed encouragement to own up to their language with outsiders. But this wasn't always the case. One hundred years ago there were already writers creating Berlin characters that would become famous all across Germany. The best known include the Bootblack, the Market Woman, the Innkeeper, the Street Hawker and, above all, the famed Nante the Loafer.[4] And if you've ever had your hands on old issues of the funny pages, you've probably come across the two famous Berliners, one short and fat, the other tall and skinny. They would talk politics, sometimes going by the names Kielmeier and Strobelweber, or Plümecke and Bohnhammel, or Meck and Scherbel, or finally just plain Müller and Schulze, and they came up with some of the greatest lines about Berlin. The newspaper had something new from them each week. But then came 1870 and the founding of the German Reich. Suddenly Berliners had grand ambitions and wanted to become refined. What was missing was a few great, widely respected men to give them back the courage of their own dialect. Strangely enough, two of them were painters, not writers, and we have a slew of lovely stories about them. The first, whom most of you won't know, is the famous

---

wrote in the German dialect of Alemannic; Jeremias Gotthelf (1797–1854) was a Swiss novelist.

3   Our English translation does not pick up the bawdy humor at play in the Berlin dialect. In addition to the comedy of the woman correcting her husband's grammar while making grammatical mistakes of her own, the preterite of the German verb *essen* (to eat) is *aß* (ate), which in Berlin dialect sounds like *Aas*, or carrion, but which also has a slang meaning of "bitch" or "bugger." Her response, in other words, amounts to both "I ate" and "I'm a bitch."

4   The character of Nante the Loafer (*Eckensteher Nante*, or Nante, the man on the corner) is a figure of working-class Berlin, popularized in the work of Adolf Glassbrenner. See also in this volume "Theodor Hosemann."

old Max Liebermann, who is still alive and still feared for his dreadful *Schnauze*. But a few years ago, another painter, one by the name of Bondy took him to task.[5] The two of them were sitting across from one another in a café having a friendly chat, when all at once Liebermann said to Bondy: "You know, Bondy, you'd be a real nice guy and all if your hands weren't so disgusting." Bondy then looks at Professor Liebermann and says: "You got it, Professor, but you see, these hands here, I can just slide 'em in my pockets, like so. What do you do with your face?" And the other great Berliner, whom many of you know by name and who only recently died, is Heinrich Zille.[6] If he heard or observed a particularly good story, he didn't just run out and have it published. Instead he drew a splendid picture of it. These illustrated stories have just been collected after his death, so now you can ask for them as a gift. You'll recognize many of them, but perhaps not this one: A father is sitting at the table with his three boys. They're having noodle soup when one says: "Oskar, look how the noodle's dangling from papa's snout!" Then the oldest, Albert, says: "Gustav, you can't call your papa's mug a snout!" "Nah," says Gustav, "the old buffoon don't mind!" But now the father has had it and jumps up to fetch his cane. The three boys, Gustav, Albert, and Oskar, scurry under the bedstead. The father tries to get at them but can't. Finally he says to the youngest: "Come out from under there, Oskar, you ain't said nothin'. I ain't gonna do nothin' to you." Oskar replies from under the bed: "And face a wretch like you?" Later on I'll tell you a few more stories about fresh little brats.[7]

But don't think Berlinish is just a collection of jokes. It is very much a real and wonderful language. It even has a proper book of grammar, which was written by Hans Meyer, director of the old Gray Cloister School in Berlin. It's called "The True Berliner in Words and Phrases."[8] As much as any other language, Berlinish can be spoken in a manner

---

5 Max Liebermann (1847–1935) was a German-Jewish painter, printmaker, collector, lifelong Berliner, supporter of Impressionism in Germany, and first president of the Berlin Secession. He served as the president of the Prussian Academy of Art from 1920 to 1933. Walter Bondy (1880–1940) was a Jewish painter, editor, art critic and collector. Born in Prague and raised in Vienna, he studied and lived in Berlin, where he was affiliated with the Berlin Secession.

6 Heinrich Zille (1858–1929), German illustrator known for his humorous depictions of working-class life in Berlin.

7 Here Benjamin uses the word *Göre*, or brats, but spelled as it would be pronounced in Berlinish: *Jöhre*. Throughout, his quotations have reproduced the variant spelling of Berlin dialect, but here he has incorporated it into his own language.

8 Hans Meyer, *Der Richtige Berliner in Wörtern und Redensarten* (Berlin: H. S. Hermann, 1904).

that is refined, witty, gentle, or clever, but of course, the speaker must know when and where to do so. Berlinish is a language that comes from work. It developed not from writers or scholars, but rather from the locker room and the card table, on the bus and at the pawn shop, at sporting arenas and in factories. Berlinish is a language of people who have no time, who often must communicate by using only the slightest hint, glance, or half-word. It's not for people who meet socially from time to time. It's only for those who see one another regularly, daily, under very precise and fixed conditions. Special ways of speaking always arise among such people, which you yourselves have a perfect example of in the classroom. There is a special language for school kids, just like there are special expressions used among employees, sportsmen, soldiers, thieves, and so on. And all these ways of speaking contribute something to Berlinish, because in Berlin all these people from all walks of life live piled together, and at a tremendous pace. Berlinish today is one of the most beautiful and most precise expressions of this frenzied pace of life.

Of course, this was not always the case. I will now read you a Berlin story from a time when Berlin was not yet a city of four million people, but just a few hundred thousand.

BRUSHMAKER (*carrying his brushes and brooms, but so drunk that he's forgotten what he's actually selling*): Eels here! Eels here! Get your eels here! Who's got cash!

FIRST BOOTBLACK: Listen up, Sir Scrubber, whoever eats a couple eels gets swept away. (*He leaves the drunkard and runs madly through the streets, screaming.*) Holy cow, this one takes the cake! No more smokin' from the window!

SEVERAL PEOPLE: What are you talkin' about? Really? You can't smoke from the window anymore? Now they've gone too far.

FIRST BOOTBLACK (*running away*): Yep! You gotta smoke from a pipe!—Hah!

BRISICH THE LOAFER (*in front of the museum*): I like this building, it cracks me up.

LANGE THE LOAFER: How come it cracks you up?

BRISICH (*staggering a bit*): Well, because of the eagles on top!

LANGE: What's so funny about the eagles?

BRISICH: Well, they're royal eagles but still they sit there loafin' on the corner! Just think if I was a royal eagle and got to loaf on the corner of the museum just for decoration! I tell you what I'd do. If I was thirsty, I'd quit my decorating for a while and pull out my bottle, take a couple swigs and holler down to the people: "Don't think bad about the museum! A royal eagle's just takin' a break!"[9]

All languages change quickly, but the language of a metropolis changes much more quickly than does language in rural regions. Now, compare the language you just heard to that of a crier in a story from today. The man who wrote it is named Döblin, the same Döblin who told you about Berlin one Saturday not long ago.[10] Of course, he wouldn't have heard it exactly as he wrote it. He often just hung around Alexanderplatz and listened to the people hawking their wares and then cobbled together the best bits of what he heard:

How come the elegant man in the West End wears a tie and the prole wears none? Gentlemen, come closer, you too Fräulein, that's right, the one with the man on your arm, and minors are allowed too, they're for free. Why are there no ties on a prole? Because he can't tie 'em. So he buys himself a tie-holder and once he's got it, it's no good 'cuz he can't tie it. It's a scam and it embitters the masses and sinks Germany into even deeper misery than she's in already. Tell me, for example, why no one wears these big tie-holders? Because no one wants to tie a dustpan around his neck. Not men, not women, not babies if they had a say. It's no laughing matter, gentlemen, laugh not, we don't

---

9 This passage appears in Hans Ostwald, *Der Urberliner in Witz, Humor und Anekdote* (Berlin: P. Franke, 1927), 39, as well as in Adolf Glassbrenner, *Berliner Volksleben*, vol. 3 (Leipzig: Wilhelm Engelmann, 1851), 248–9. In this instance, Benjamin's typescript, rather than giving a full quotation, refers only to "Ostwald, p. 39"; it is unclear whether Benjamin read aloud from this particular passage or from another of Ostwald's many books. As Benjamin's typescript does not provide a full quotation, we follow the editors of the GS, who provided the passage.

10 Alfred Döblin was a speaker on the Berlin Radio Hour from 1925 through 1931, with most of his work for the radio done between 1928 and 1930. Perhaps his most famous contribution to Weimar radio was a never broadcast script, *The Story of Franz Biberkopf*, the radio play for his novel *Berlin Alexanderplatz* (1929); scheduled to go out on September 30, 1930, it was cancelled at the last minute due to fear over Nazi reprisals. As Peter Jelavich puts it, "In the atmosphere of fear and panic in the weeks following the elections of 14 September 1930, when the Nazis emerged as the second strongest party in the Reichstag, the political oversight committee of Berlin's station balked at airing a work by a well-known leftist Jewish author" (*Berlin Alexanderplatz: Radio, Film, and the Death of Weimar Culture*, 93). For Döblin's early contributions to Weimar radio, see ibid., 75–8; and for a reference to Benjamin's reading of the necktie-holder vendor scene from *Berlin Alexanderplatz*, and the political and formal issues raised by its transposition to radio, both in Benjamin's reading and in Döblin's radio script, see ibid., 29–30, 102–3. See also Benjamin's discussion of Döblin's novel—as a new form of epic narration, as well as "a monument to the Berlin dialect"—in "The Crisis of the Novel" [1930], SW, 2, 299–304 (GS, 231–6).

know what goes on in that sweet little baby brain. Dear God, the sweet little head, what a sweet little head, with its little hairs, but what's not pretty, gentlemen, is paying your alimony, that's no joke, that gets a man into trouble. Go buy yourself a tie at Tietz or Wertheim, or somewhere else if you won't buy from Jews. I'm an Aryan man. The big department stores don't need me to pitch for 'em, they do just fine without me. So buy yourselves a tie like I have here and then think about having to tie it every morning. Ladies and gentlemen, who has time nowadays to tie a tie in the morning and give up an extra minute of precious sleep? We need all the sleep we can get because we all work so much and earn so little. A tie-holder like this makes you sleep easier. It's putting pharmacists out of business, because whoever buys one of these here tie-holders needs no sleeping potion, no nightcap, no nothin'. He sleeps safe and sound like a baby at his mother's breast, because he knows there's no hustle in the morning; what he needs is right there on the dresser, tied and ready, just waitin' to be shoved into his collar. You spend your money on so much rubbish. You must have seen the crooks last year at the Krokodil Bar, there was hot sausage in front, and behind lay Jolly in his glass case, with a beard like sauerkraut growing around his mouth.[11] Every one of you saw it—come a little closer, now, I wanna save my voice, I haven't insured my voice, I'm still saving up for the down payment—how Jolly was lying in the glass case, you all saw it. But how they slipped him some chocolate? You didn't see that! You're buyin' honest goods here, not celluloid, but galvanized rubber, twenty pfennigs apiece, fifty for three.[12]

This shows you just how useful the Berlin *Schnauze* can be, and how someone can earn his money with it, drumming up as much interest in his ties as if he were running an entire department store.

Thus a language renews itself every second. All events, great and small, leave their mark on it. War and inflation as much as a Zeppelin sighting, Amanullah's visit, or Iron Gustav.[13] There are even speech fads in Berlinish. Perhaps some of you still remember the famous "to me." For example: if a Berliner is being chatted up by someone

---

11   In March 1926, a "hunger artist" named Jolly sold tickets to an exhibition of himself fasting, setting a new world record of going without food for forty-four days.

12   Alfred Döblin, *Berlin Alexanderplatz* (Berlin: S. Fischer Verlag, 1929), 72ff. The passage, slightly modified from Döblin, is provided by the editors of the GS based on Benjamin's page number reference in the typescript.

13   Amanullah Khan, sovereign of Afghanistan from 1919 to 1929, visited Berlin in 1928. "Iron Gustav" was a coachman who drove his carriage from Berlin to Paris and back in 1928.

he doesn't want to talk to, he says, "That's Kaiser Wilhelm Memorial Church to me," which means "nave." And, as everyone knows, a "knave" is a scoundrel. Or someone is giving an order to a young boy and says to him, "Can you manage it?" And the boy replies, "That's abacus to me." (You can count on me.)

By now you will have noticed that in many of these stories, there's more to Berliners than just the big *Schnauze*. For instance, people can be very impertinent yet also very awkward. Berliners, however, at least the better ones, combine their impertinence with a whole lot of quick wit, spirit, and jest. "A Berliner ain't never taken for a fool," as they say. Take, for example, the nice story of the fellow, who's in a great hurry and riding in a horse-drawn carriage that's going too slow: "My God, driver, can't you move a little faster?" "Sure thing. But I can't just leave the horse all alone." But a true Berliner joke is never only at the expense of others; it's just as much at the jokester's expense. This is what makes him so likable and free: he doesn't spare his own dialect, and there are many wonderful stories to prove it. For example, a man, already a bit drunk, walks into a bar and says: "What ales you got?" And the barkeep replies: "I got gout and a bad back."[14]

And now for the stories I promised you about children. Three boys enter a pharmacy. The first one says: "Penny o' licorice." The shopkeeper fetches a long ladder, climbs to the top step, fills the bag, and climbs back down. Once the boy pays, the second boy says: "I'd also like a penny o' licorice!" Before climbing the ladder again, the shopkeeper, already annoyed, asks the third boy: "You want a penny of licorice, too?" "Nope," he says. So the shopkeeper climbs back up the ladder, and then down again with the full bag. He now turns to the third boy: "And what do you want, lil' man?" And he answers: "I want the licorice for a ha'penny." Or, a man sees a young boy on the street: "Huh, smokin' already? I'm gonna tell your teacher." "Do what you want, you old fool, I ain't big enough for school yet." Or, there's a fifth-grader at school who can't get used to calling his teacher "sir." The teacher's name is Ackermann and he lets it pass for a while until finally he gets angry: "By tomorrow morning you'll write in your notebook 100 times: 'I shall never forget to call my teacher "sir."'" The next day the boy comes to school and gives his teacher the notebook, in which indeed he has written 100 times: "I shall never forget to call

14 The German here is a pun on the verbs *kriegen* (to get) and *kriechen* (to crawl). When the drunkard asks, "Kricht man hier Rum?" [You got any rum here?], the barkeep pretends to have heard "Kriecht man herum?" [Does one crawl around?], and answers "Hier setzt man sich" [In here we sit]. The pun depends on the words being pronounced in Berlin dialect.

my teacher 'sir.'" The teacher counts and, sure enough, there's 100. And the boy says: "What's up, Ackermann, surprised?"

We'll hear some more Berlinish another time if you want, but there's surely no need to wait. Just open your eyes and ears when you're walking through Berlin and you'll collect many more such stories than you've heard on the radio today.

"Berliner Dialekt," GS, 7.1, 68–74. Translated by Jonathan Lutes.

Broadcast on Radio Berlin. The exact date of broadcast has not been determined, but it was almost certainly one of several broadcasts Benjamin gave in November and December of 1929 on subjects related to Berlin; during these months, the Berlin radio journal Funkstunde *[Radio Times] advertised, without specific titles, several broadcasts by Benjamin during the Berlinstunde [Berlin Hour].*

CHAPTER 2

Street Trade and Markets in Old and New Berlin

Are you familiar with the fairy tale, "The Golden Pot"? Do you recall the strange old apple monger whom the student Anselmus runs into as the story begins?[1] Or do you know Hauff's tale "Little Long-Nose,"which begins at a market where a witch touches all the goods with her spidery fingers to pick out the best ones?[2] And when you visit the market with your mother, is it not sometimes thrilling and festive? For even the most ordinary weekly market has some of the magic of oriental markets, such as the Samarkand bazaar. Have you seen the new film shot at the market at Wittenbergplatz?[3] It's more thrilling than most detective films. One thing that's missing in the film—and even books seldom deal with it—is the market talk: the bargaining and trading, all the back-and-forth of goods and money that is, in its own way, as rich and sumptuous for the ear as the image of the market is a feast for the eyes. This is particularly true of the Berlin market. Some months ago I spoke to you here about the dialect of Berlin. The market, and street trade in general, is now one of the places where Berlinish can best be overheard and appreciated in its richness and variation. It's the street trade of old and new Berlin that I'd like to talk to you about today.

Market women were already something very special in old Berlin. Of all merchant women, they were alone in having permission to offer their wares at the weekly market, and were mostly women farmers peddling their own produce. Quite different were the so-called hawker women. They were forbidden to sell the better goods and, as compensation for being permitted to trade, were

---

1 E. T. A. Hoffmann, *Der goldne Topf: Ein Märchen aus der neuen Zeit* (The Golden Pot: A Modern Fairy Tale) (Bamberg: Kunz, 1814).

2 Wilhelm Hauff, "Zwerg Nase" (Stuttgart: Gebrüder Franckh, 1827).

3 Benjamin is likely referring to Wilfried Basse's film *Markt am Wittenbergplatz*, 1929.

forced to spin four pounds of wool per month for the warehouse. As even their purchasing was greatly restricted—they were not allowed to buy directly from farmers, but had to stock up on left-over goods from other vendors at closing time on market days—the hawkers did measly business, eking out only a meager living for their families. This was still the case as late as the eighteenth century. And if a woman of low standing wanted to contribute to the family budget, as so many soldiers' wives did, there was some-times no other option but to become a hawker. For a proper market woman, then, there was no greater insult than to be called a "hawker." So, in one of his best scenes, Glassbrenner depicts a market woman and everything that comes to her mind as she tells off, with her world-famous Berlin *Schnauze*,[4] a customer who has just muttered "hawker" in her direction. "Hawker?" she repeats, standing up, arms akimbo: "Listen here, you old dog, go bark at some other stall or I'll stomp on your paw so hard you'll be whining for eight days." The man says: "Well, well, isn't it remarkable how these hawkers can scold." Hawker: "Scold? Such a daffy beanpole of a guy like you, you can't even be scolded; you're already two or three times worse than anything vile I'd say about you. Such a shadow of a male specimen you are, always trying to get the best of someone. You filthy pedant, you wanna bully us around? Is that it? Why not just hang yourself, so no decent person's forced to commit a crime against you. Go curl up in a ball. Go see the rag man and sell yourself for a quarter pound of rags. Take some gravel and rub yourself clean so there's nothin' left of you. Go hang yourself from the moon so the good-for-nothings can go home early! And steer clear of the choirboys, or they'll start singing: God of my mercy shall preserve me!"[5] It had become an actual sport to lure the market women to rant. And you can see here that it paid off.

To spew insults straight from the heart, and with such persever-ance, is indeed a great talent, one reserved for a privileged few. It requires not only a high degree of crassness and a healthy lung, but also a large vocabulary and, not least of all, great wit. That one attrib-utes such wit to the stall owners and market women is borne out by many wonderful stories. For example this one, which tells of a fruit peddler lying on her deathbed, suffering terribly at the prospect of

---

4 See "Berlin Dialect."

5 See Adolf Glassbrenner, "Die Hökerin: Szene auf dem Spittelmarkte" [The Hawker: Scenes from the Spittelmarkt], in *Berliner Volksleben*, with illustrations by Theodor Hosemann, vol. 2 (Leipzig: Wilhelm Engelmann, 1847), 159.

dying. Her husband stands beside her, not knowing what to say but trying to comfort her: "Don't worry too much that you have to die; everything'll be ok, it'll all work out. We all have to die once in our lives!" "Muttonhead," the poor woman whispers, "that's the whole point. If we had to die ten or twelve times, I wouldn't care so much about this time." The great Berlin catchphrase "Nothing to fear!" was also the motto for this sort of person. As you probably know, Berliners are not particularly impressed by education or refinement. And if they are, they never show it. There's a wonderful Berlin scene from the middle of the last century, back when there were still no funny pages, but bookshops and stationery stores sold individual pictures, with captions and usually in watercolor, by known artists like Hosemann, Franz Krüger, or Dörbeck.[6] Let me tell you about one: somewhere close to the Brandenburg Gate you see a fat fruit seller, and standing next to her is a more refined gentleman with a lady friend, both foreigners. You can tell just by looking at them that they don't know much about Berlin. "My dear lady," says the man, pointing at the Victoria statue atop the Brandenburg Gate, "can you tell me who that is on top of the gate?" Answer: "Yeah, sure, that old thing? Ancient Roman history, the Electors of Brandenburg, the Seven Years' War. That's all." "Aha," says the man, "Thank you kindly."

I do not want to suggest that this sort of Berliner has died out, only that the class divide has become more marked. People stay more and more among their own kind so that, as a customer, it's no longer so easy to get close to these sellers amid the hustle and bustle on market days. So as for the exquisite scoldings like the ones Glassbrenner passed on to us, there's just no more time for them. Today's market women have become more like businesswomen, and the butchers who come to the market have large, refrigerated storerooms where they load up on stock before heading to the market and offload their unsold goods afterwards. This brings us to another spectacle, which was as scrumptious for the eyes as the old Berlin weekly market was a feast for the ears: the market halls. When I was little, it was cause for celebration to be taken to the Magdeburger Platz market halls, where it was always so warm in winter and on hot days so cool. Everything is different there compared to the outdoor markets. First of all, there are huge mounds of one kind of goods, right next to another booth packed with something else. But

---

6   Theodor Hosemann (1807–1875), German illustrator; Franz Krüger (1797–1857), German painter, lithographer, and portraitist; Franz Burchard Dörbeck (1799–1835), a Baltic German illustrator and satirist. For Hosemann, see also "Theodor Hosemann" in this volume.

above all there is the smell, a mix of fish, cheese, flowers, raw meat, and fruit all under one roof, which is completely different than in the open air markets and creates a dim and woozy aroma that fits perfectly with the light seeping through the murky panes of lead-framed glass. And let's not forget the stone floor, which is always awash with run-off or dishwater and feels like the cold and slippery bottom of the ocean. Because I've rarely been to a market hall since I was little, going to one now brings back all the charm of visits long ago. And if I really want a special treat, I go for a walk in the Lindenstraße market hall in the afternoons between four and five. Maybe someday I'll meet one of you there. But we won't recognize each other. That's the downside of radio.

Most of this sort of business has utterly vanished from the streets of Berlin. And with it, the sand wagons, whose drivers, up until around 1900, would holler in front of every house and in every courtyard: "Sand, getcha white sand!" They would come from the Rehberg Mountains in the North, from Kreuzberg in the South and from all over with the white sand that housewives used to scrub their floors clean and white. Or the kipper wagons. Or colporteurs, door-to-door book peddlers who earned meager livings selling pulp novels with colorful pictures and, quite often, sheet music and song lyrics. Before the advent of advertising, publishers had turned to colporteurs to market their books to the people. It's fun to imagine the quintessential book traveler from this time among these social classes, bringing ghost stories and tales of noble knights into servants' quarters in the city and farmhouse parlors in the countryside. He himself featured in many of the stories that he sold. Not as the hero, of course, and not as the young, outcast prince, but rather as the wily old man, the warner, or the seducer. Selling in those days for just a few pennies, these broadsheets, especially the so-called *Neuruppiner Bilderbogen* by Gustav Kühn, have now become very rare and valuable items.[7]

Colporteurs have all but disappeared, at least in today's Berlin, where they have been replaced by the book cart. The bookseller on the streets of Berlin is the only book dealer that can actually be found reading the books that he sells. Often seated on the narrow stone ramp of a garden or on a canvas stool he has brought with him, he is unfazed by people rummaging through his wagon; he

---

7 The *Neuruppiner Bilderbogen* were colorful nineteenth-century broadsheets printed in Neuruppin by the Kühn printing house.

knows that not even one in ten has any real intention to buy. Anyway, were he to depend on people coming with a serious intention to buy, he'd be in sorry shape. But that's the thing with the book carts: people buy books they never would have dreamt of buying when they set out from home in the morning. Casual readers. Casual enthusiasts. Only during the great inflation was it any different.[8] Those who could spare just one extra penny for books could get something worth a hundred or a thousand times its price. The currency devaluation combined with the naïveté of the sellers, who were not all that well informed to begin with, created a situation ripe for collectors to exploit.

The book cart seller is rather quiet. He is, however, an exception; for in general, the Berlin street trade is the elite training ground of the Berlin *Schnauze*, a veritable academy for Berlin dialect. To conclude for today, I will recite for you a masterpiece of Berlinish, something you don't get to hear every day on the street. As you might have noticed, such a speaker gathers momentum, before anyone is listening or paying him any attention, by setting himself up in front of his "Universal Spot Remover," his necktie, or his Crystal Palace glue. Then, in a death-defying manner, he lets loose a diatribe, accompanied wherever possible by gestures, until someone, just anyone, bites. But by "bites," I don't mean "buys." In the street trade, the sale is but the last link in a chain. The first being the enthusiasm of the speaker, and the second, that he draw as many listeners and spectators as possible. The street seller stands in the center. Having learned his speech by heart, he repeats it over and over. His listeners know it just as well as he does. For them, the interesting part is how he always pulls it off, albeit with digressions and slight variations, or how each time at certain critical points he reproduces the exact same intonation with the precision of a gramophone. Should one of the bystanders finally break down and buy something, he must step forward and stand with the seller in the middle of the circle, like two actors sharing the stage in an arena. The allure of being part of the performance, playing a role, and being seen is a key incentive for the buyer.

And so, our man with the collar stiffener: "Ladies and gentlemen! Don't think I want to deceive you into acquiring something that isn't tried and true. A group of experts from the field have analyzed this collar stiffener and put it to the test. Would you like to see it?

---

8   The hyperinflationary period in Weimar Germany during the early 1920s.

Then step right up! My collar stiffener is the best on the market and the most practical of its kind. So simple, so elegant, yet cheap as can be! In these times, when we all have to pinch our pennies before we spend 'em, but if we want to get somewhere in life we must still look clean, this collar stiffener is a saving grace for the whole world. Yes, ladies and gentlemen, you may laugh. But one day you'll see I'm not exaggerating." In the meantime a larger crowd of about twenty or thirty people has gathered around the seller. He picks up his stiffener and explains how it works. "Observe, ladies and gentlemen, you take the flimsy turn-down collar, open it up, put in the collar stiffener, close it up, fasten the collar, and now how's it look? Firm and elegant! Firm and elegant! Even the necktie sits so much better now. Before, the collar used to look dirty after just a few hours, but now you can wear it for eight days! Always firm and elegant! When you are up for a job wearing my product, you'll stand head and shoulders above the rest. The boss will point at you and say: Yes, that man is firm and elegant!"

When you hear a speech like this, there's no need to mourn old Berlin, because it can still be found here in the new Berlin, where it's as indestructible as our speaker's collar stiffener.

"Straßenhandel und Markt in Alt- und in Neuberlin," GS, 7.1, 74–80. Translated by Jonathan Lutes.

Broadcast on Radio Berlin. The exact date of broadcast is not known, but it was likely delivered at the end of 1929 or the beginning of 1930, as one of Benjamin's contributions to the Berlin station's Berlin Hour. As can be gleaned from comments Benjamin makes within the text, it was broadcast after "Berlin Dialect."

CHAPTER 3

Berlin Puppet Theater

Children who want to go to the puppet theater don't have an easy time of it in Berlin. In Munich, there's the famed Papa Schmidt, who performs at least twice a week in a theater of his own, built for him by the city.[1] In Paris there's the ongoing Kasper Theater, several even, located in the Luxembourg Gardens, the equivalent of Berlin's Tiergarten. And in Rome, there's the famous "Teatro dei piccoli," which means "theater of the little ones": not something *for* but rather *by* little ones, namely puppets, and which has certainly become a place for big folks, too. This is what's happened to the puppet theater in general. For a long time puppet theater was mainly for children and common folk. It then gradually deteriorated as it lost popularity, until it was rediscovered and suddenly became something very refined, just for grownups, and very sophisticated ones at that. Only Kasper Theater has always remained for children. During summer, even in Berlin, you can still see an absolutely wonderful rendition of Kasper Theater. At Luna Park, just at the end of the grand entrance way, there's one that goes on all afternoon, even if it is rather short and too often the same thing.

A hundred years ago it was just the opposite. Kasper came in winter. And exactly around this time, just before Christmas. And with him came a bunch of other puppets, mostly under his command. That's the remarkable thing about Kasper: he appears not only in the plays that were written for him; he also sticks his saucy little nose into all sorts of big, proper theater pieces for adults. He knows he can risk it. In the most terrible tragedies nothing ever happens to him. And when the devil catches up with Faust, he has to let Kasper live, even though he's no better behaved than his master. He's just a

---

1 Josef Leonhard Schmid ("Papa Schmidt") (1822–1912) was a founder of the Munich Marionette Theater.

peculiar chap. Or in his own words: "I've always been a peculiar fellow. Even as a youngster I always saved my pocket money. And when I had enough, you know what I did with it? I had a tooth pulled." When Christmas drew near, posters would appear on street corners, red or green, blue or yellow, one of which read:

> The Robber Baron Flayed Alive, or Love and Cannibalism, or Roast Human Heart and Flesh. Followed by a Great Ballet of Metamorphoses featuring several true-to-life dancing figures and transformations that will pleasantly surprise the beholder's eye with their delicate and nimble movements. And finally, Pussel the Wonder Dog will take the stage.[2] For the sake of all attendees, uncivilized young men will not be admitted; and the price: 2 Silbergroschen and 6 Pfennig, for children as well as adult persons.

Such performances were always combined with the so-called "humorous Christmas exhibitions" that took place every year in a few renowned pastry shops. These exhibitions consisted of nothing more than a few colorful figures made from sugar. For example: "On display at Zimmermann's shop in Königstraße are exquisite confections of all kinds, including the Brandenburg Gate made from vegetable gum." But the main attraction was of course the puppet theater. Things were not always very proper or civil in the auditorium. Especially later, when the shows in the pastry shops were replaced by Julius Linde's mechanical marionette theater and Nattke's great Baths-and-Basins Theater Salon, Palisadenstraße 76, which advertised their performances like this: "Entertainment with good humor and tasteful wit of universally recognized quality."[3] The "tasteful" entertainment, however, did not, so we hear, prevent boys of a certain class, ages ten to fourteen, from lounging about there with large pipes and cigars and drinking tall glasses of beer.

Glassbrenner, the famous Berlin writer who described such performances, never failed to mention the music: the quartet, which

---

2 For this reference, see also Benjamin's "Altes Spielzeug," GS, 4.1, 513 ("Old Toys," SW, 2, 99; originally published in the *Frankfurter Zeitung* on March 21, 1928). There, Benjamin mentions the poster as part of his review of an exhibition of eighteenth- and nineteenth-century toys, which he admired for having included "not just 'toys,' in the narrower sense of the word, but also a great many objects on the margins" ("Old Toys," 98), such as this poster, as well as other occasional texts and advertisements.

3 See "Old Toys," where Benjamin makes reference to the display at Zimmermann's Confectionery as part of "a Berlin advertisement from the Biedermeier period" and again to the advertisement for Julius Linde's marionette theater (99).

he said consisted of five men, one of whom accompanied only with brandy or schnapps.

Shall we hear some titles of the shows they put on? "Around the World in Eighty Days," "Murder in the Wine Cellar," "Käthchen von Heilbronn," "The Rogues' Ball or the Ill-Fated Monkey with Fireworks," "The Sharpshooter."

If you ask someone how the puppet theater came about, he would probably say: "Because it's so much cheaper than real theater." And that's certainly true. But it's only one little, welcome side effect of these puppets that they eat nothing and ask for no money. In olden times, the puppet theater was not just something fun, but also something sacred, because the puppets represented the gods. (This is still the case for many peoples of the South Sea Islands, where they make puppets out of straw up to thirty meters high. Then they put a man inside the puppet, and he moves, capering a few steps. When finally he collapses from the weight and the puppet falls, the savages pounce on it, rip it apart, and carry the shreds back home as charms to ward off evil spirits.)

But the way in which the puppet theater later came to Germany is even more remarkable. It was after the Thirty Years' War and masses of mercenaries were wandering about the countryside. They had nothing to do, had no more pay, and were making the roads unsafe. So unsafe that actors, who by trade were often on the road but only knew how to fight with stage guns and swords, were put off from traveling. Then someone had the idea to replace the actors with marionettes, and soon it was widely appreciated what a wonderful theater instrument a puppet was: above all, it never talks back. And although it too has a head, it's much larger and heavier in relation to its body than an actor's; and as for expressiveness, its face is much more stubborn and rigid. But that's what makes it special, as you yourselves have surely observed at the puppet theater. The expressions on such wooden and focused faces seem to suit all the slight and subtle twitching produced in the little body when the proper puppeteer is in charge. A proper puppeteer is a despot, one that makes the Tsar seem like a petty gendarme. Imagine, if you will: he writes his shows alone, paints the decorations himself, carves the puppets any way he likes, and plays five or six roles, sometimes many more, all with his own voice. And he never lets complications, inhibitions, or any kind of obstacle slow him down. On the other hand, he has to get along with his puppets, because for him they're alive. All great puppeteers maintain that the secret of the trade is actually to let the puppet have its way, to yield to it. In his essay on the marionette theater, the great poet Heinrich von Kleist (I say this for the few adults that have snuck in here today and think I don't see them) has even proved that the puppeteer must have the exact skills and demeanor of a dancer if he wants the figures to move as they should.[4] Then comes the most wonderful sight, as the little puppets make as if they're tickling the floor of the stage with their tiptoes, for they, like angels descending from above, are not gravity-bound as real actors are.

But their superiority has already provoked much hate and persecution. First from the church and the authorities, because puppets can so easily mock everything without being malicious. They take the greatest of men and mimic them, as if to say: "What man can do, so can any puppet." In old Austria, for example, they ridiculed the tyrants. But then at times they made for dangerous competition for the proper theater, as in Paris, where the actors didn't rest until they had chased the puppets from the city center to the farthest reaches of the metropolis.

It's widely known that the great puppet-masters were true originals. First off, they live for their puppets; nothing else matters to them. Which is why they live to such an old age. Munich's Papa Schmidt reached ninety-one. And the renowned puppeteer Winter, who ran the Cologne puppet shows where the Kasper figure is called "Hänneschen," lived to be ninety-two.[5] Secondly, to be a puppeteer is to be a member of a kind of secret brotherhood. The skills of the trade are passed from father to son. The routines are learned by imitation and memorization, so the puppeteer always carries all of his stories in his head. Every one of them must swear an oath that he will never commit to paper even one line of the text, so as to prevent it from falling into the wrong hands and jeopardizing their livelihood. At least that's the way it used to be. Today many puppet plays are available in print, but the best ones are surely the unpublished ones that children and puppeteers create themselves. Of course there are exceptions, like the wonderful Kasper comedies by Count Pocci, which are still performed everywhere.[6]

---

4 See Heinrich von Kleist, "Über das Marionetten Theater" (On the Marionette Theater), *Berliner Abendblätter* (December 12–15, 1810).

5 Johann Christoph Winter (1772–1862) founded the Hänneschen puppet theater in Cologne.

6 Franz Graf von Pocci (1807–1876) collaborated with Josef Schmid in founding the Munich Marionette Theater and was one of its writers.

There was once a great puppeteer named Schwiegerling. I saw the Schwiegerling Marionette Theater myself in Bern in 1918, but then it was never read or heard of again. It was more beautiful than anything you could imagine. Schwiegerling invented the so-called "transformation puppets," or "metamorphoses." His marionette theater was actually more of a magician's den. There was only one performance each night. The puppet art was on display prior to the show. I can still remember two of the numbers. Kasper comes dancing on stage with a pretty lady. Then suddenly the music turns very sweet and the lady folds up, transforming herself into a balloon that Kasper, out of love, grasps onto, carrying him off into the sky. For one minute the stage remains empty, and then Kasper falls from above with a frightful crash. The other number was sad. A girl, who looks like an enchanted princess, is playing a sorrowful melody on a barrel organ. All at once the barrel organ folds in on itself and twelve tiny little doves fly out. Then the princess, with her hands held high, sinks dumbfounded into the ground. And just as I'm telling you this, another memory from the show comes to mind. A tall clown stands on the stage, takes a bow and begins to dance. During the dance, out of his sleeve he shakes a small dwarf clown who's wearing the same red and yellow flowery clothes as he is. And then with every twelfth measure of the waltz, a new one slides out, until finally there are twelve identical dwarf or baby clowns dancing around him in a circle.[7] I know this sounds unbelievable, but it's true. On a different puppet stage the main attraction was a soldier, who blew tobacco smoke from his mouth. A rival of Schwiegerling in Hamburg put on *The Beheading of Saint Dorothea*, and, during the applause after the beheading, reattached her head so she could be decapitated all over again. The same Hamburg puppeteer always gave his Kasper a dove, while a rabbit would appear alongside his Viennese Wurstl and a cat with his French Guignol, which is Kasper's name in France.

But now back to Berlin. Another time I'll tell you more about puppets, but meanwhile you can pick up a copy of Storm's *Paul the Puppeteer*, which tells of one of the great original puppet-masters.[8]

7 Benjamin gives a similarly worded account of Schwiegerling's puppet theater in his "Lob der Puppe: Kritische Glossen zu Max v. Boehns 'Puppen und Puppenspiele'" [In Praise of Puppets: Critical Comments on Max von Boehn's "Puppets and Puppet Plays"] (Munich: F. Bruckmann, 1929), in GS, 3, 215–16 (published in *Die literarische Welt* on January 10, 1930).

8 *Pole Poppenspäler* [Paul the Puppeteer], by Theodor Storm, originally published in 1874 in the journal *Deutsche Jugend,* and then in book form in 1875.

We still hear of a puppet show, a silent one, which used to be performed in Berlin around Christmastime. It's actually a secular Berlin variation on the South German nativity scene, and it's called "Theatrum mundi," or "Theater of the World." On stage you would see various, parallel-running depictions of daily life, separated from one another by simple set pieces and continuously moving along invisible rollers. Wild game pursued by hunters and hounds; wagons, riders, and pedestrians; grazing cattle; steamships and sailboats; a train; boys scuffling about—everything came again and went in set intervals. It was a sort of mechanical forerunner to today's cinema.

And finally, *tableaux vivants*, but performed by puppets. For example: "The Three Men in the Fiery Furnace," "The Lisbon Earthquake," "The Battle of Zorndorf," "The Casino in Baden-Baden," "The Discovery of America."

And now, to conclude, let's hear how the compère, a true Berliner of course, explains the scene to the children of Berlin: "Here we have a very interesting group. The song of 'The Three Men in the Fiery Furnace.' This one's exceptionally beautiful and the flames are quite beguiling. In the middle of the furnace stand three men wondering why they're not drenched in sweat; over there in the corner is the cruel King Nebuchadnezzar ordering a basket of peat to be thrown onto the flames, and shouting: 'I'll break you yet!' But the three men take not a bit of notice, and start singing instead: 'Be ever true and constant too, until your chilly grave.' At this bit of impertinence the king becomes nasty and, to anger him even more, one of them sticks his head out the door and yells in a booming voice: 'Be so good as to shut your royal trap!'"

Or here's the discovery of America: "First, we have Christopher Columbus standing before you in the midst of his invention of America. The sky, you may notice, is rather gloomy, but the sea is calm, almost indifferent to the event. Columbus's crew are alternately running around the deck shouting 'Land ho!' and hugging one another, or dropping themselves at his feet. He, however, leans calmly against the mast, pointing in front of him and saying in a serious voice: 'That is America!' Far in the background you'll notice the peaks, the stretch of green where the waves are breaking, and a naked man standing there in a fig leaf. This is America's lookout. As soon as he spots the great ship, he shouts in his mother tongue: 'Who goes there?' To which Columbus replies: 'My good friend, I call myself Columbus.' 'What do you want here?' asks the New Worlder. 'Simply to discover.' 'Look no further' says the native, saluting by placing two fingers on his head. 'Come closer, for a long time now we've wanted to be discovered.' And this is how America was discovered, which is now a republic that for a number of reasons I cannot recommend. As soon as this republic gets a king, it will be a monarchy; that's just the way it is."

And with this nice speech, we're finished for today. Hopefully we can begin next time with one just as nice.

"Berliner Puppentheater," GS, 7.2, 80–6. Translated by Jonathan Lutes.

Broadcast on Radio Berlin, December 7, 1929. Benjamin dated the typescript December 7, 1929, and for this date the Funkstunde *announced an untitled "Youth Hour (Berlin) with Dr. Walter Benjamin at the microphone," from 5:30–6:00 pm.*

CHAPTER 4

Demonic Berlin

I will begin today with an experience I had in my fourteenth year. At that time I was a student at a boarding school. As is customary at such institutions, children and teachers would assemble several evenings each week to make music, or for a recitation or poetry reading. One evening the music teacher gave the "oratory," as these evening assemblies were called. He was a peculiar little man with a grave, unforgettable gaze; he had the shiniest bald pate I've ever seen, and around it lay a half-open wreath of tightly coiled curly dark hair. His name is well-known among German music lovers: August Halm.[1] This August Halm held the oratory that day to read us stories by E. T. A. Hoffmann, the very writer I want to tell you about today. I no longer know what he read and it doesn't really matter, because what I do remember is one single sentence from the introductory speech he gave before reading to us. He elucidated Hoffmann's writing, his predilection for the bizarre, the unconventional, the eerie, the inexplicable. I think what he said was meant to fill us children with suspense for the stories to come. But then he concluded with this sentence, which I have not forgotten to this day: "To what end someone would write such stories, I will tell you sometime soon." I'm still waiting for this "sometime soon," and as the good fellow has since died, this explanation will have to come to me, if it ever does, in such an uncanny way, that I prefer to preempt it and will try today to honor, for you, the promise that was made to me twenty-five years ago.

If I wanted to cheat a bit, I could make it a lot easier on myself. Instead of the words "to what end," I could have said "why," and the answer would be very simple. Why does an author write? For a

---

1 August Halm (1869–1929), German writer, music critic, composer, and music educator. From 1903 to 1906, Halm was an instructor at the Hermann Lietz School in Haubinda. Benjamin attended the school from 1905 to 1907.

thousand reasons. Because he enjoys making things up; or because ideas and images take such possession of him that he can only achieve peace once he has written them down; or because he's burdened with questions and doubts to which he can find a resolution of sorts in the destinies of his invented characters; or simply because he has learned to write; or because, and unfortunately this is very often the case, he has learned nothing at all. Why Hoffmann wrote is not difficult to say. He was one of those writers possessed by his characters. Doppelgangers, monstrous figures of every kind: when he wrote, he actually saw them all around him. And not only when he was writing, but sometimes in the middle of the most innocent dinner-table conversation, over a glass of wine or punch. More than once he interrupted one or another of his dinner companions with these words:

"Pardon me for cutting you off, my dear, but do you not see that accursed little imp creeping out from under the floorboards in the corner, just over there to the right? Just look what the little devil's up to! Over there! Over there! Now he's gone! Oh, don't be bashful you sweet little creature, won't you please stay here with us? And kindly listen to our exceedingly pleasant conversation—You wouldn't believe how much we would appreciate your amiable company— Ah, there you are again—Wouldn't you care to come a little closer?—What's that?—You say you'll stay a while?—Come again?—What's that you're saying?—Eh?—You're leaving?—Your humble servant am I."[2]

And so on. Hardly had he finished speaking such gibberish, his vacant eyes fixed on the corner from where the vision came, when he would reemerge, turn again to his dinner companions and beg them altogether calmly to carry on. Such are the descriptions of Hoffmann by his friends. And we ourselves feel the presence of similar spirits when we read such stories as "The Deserted House," "The Entail," "The Doubles," or "The Golden Pot." Under favorable conditions, these ghost stories can have an astonishing effect. This happened with me, where the favorable condition was that my parents had forbidden me from reading Hoffmann. When I was young, I could only read him in secret, on the evenings when my parents were not at home. I remember one such evening. There was not a sound to be heard in the entire house. I was reading "The

---

2   Benjamin borrows here from the biographical notes by Julius Eduard Hitzig in *Ernst Theodor Amadeus Hoffmann: Ausgewählte Schriften*, vol. 15 (Stuttgart: Brodhag, 1839), 29.

Mines of Falun," sitting alone under the hanging lamp at our giant
dining room table—this was on Carmerstraße—when all the terrors,
such as fish with stubby snouts, gradually gathered in the darkness
along the edge of the table. My eyes clung to the pages of the book,
the source of all these terrors, as if to a life raft. Or another time,
earlier in the day: I still remember standing at our library cabinet, its
door slightly ajar, reading "The Entail" and ready to stuff the book
back onto the shelf at the slightest sound of disturbance, my hair
standing on end, and so wracked with the double horror of the
book's terrifying contents and the fear of getting caught, that I
understood not a word of the entire story.[3]

"Even the devil," Heinrich Heine said of Hoffmann's work, "could
not write such devilish stuff."[4] Indeed, there is something inherently
satanic in the eerie, spooky, uncanny quality of these works. Pursuing
this line further, we proceed from the answer to the "why" of
Hoffmann's stories and arrive at the answer to the mysterious "to
what end." Along with his many other peculiarities, the devil is
renowned for his ingenuity and knowledge. Those who know a little
of Hoffmann's stories will immediately understand when I say that
the narrator is always a very sensitive, perceptive fellow able to sniff
out spirits in all their cunning disguises. In fact, this storyteller
insists with a certain obstinacy that all the reputable archivists,
medical officers, students, apple-wives, musicians, and upper-class
daughters are much more than they appear to be, just as Hoffmann
himself was more than just a pedantic and exacting court of appeals
judge, which is how he made his living.[5] In other words, Hoffmann
did not simply conjure the eerie, ghostly figures that appear in his
stories out of thin air. Like many great writers, he pulled the extraordinary not from his mind alone but from actual people, things,
houses, objects, streets, and so forth. As perhaps you have heard, a
person who can observe other people's faces, or how they walk, or
their hands, or the shape of their head, and can tell from this their
character, their profession, or even their destiny, is called a physiognomist. So, Hoffmann was less of a seer than an observer, which is a

---

3 For a related description of reading texts by the forbidden Hoffmann as a child, see
Benjamin, *Berliner Kindheit um neunzehnhundert*, GS, 4.1, 284–5 (*Berlin Childhood Around
1900*, SW, 3, 402).

4 See Heinrich Heine, *Briefe aus Berlin* [1822], in *Werke und Briefe in zehn Bänden*, vol. 3,
ed. Hans Kaufmann (Berlin and Weimar: Aufbau-Verlag, 1972), 556.

5 Benjamin will make the same comment about Hoffmann's narrator, and about
Hoffmann himself, in his "E. T. A. Hoffmann and Oskar Panizza" (269).

good synonym for physiognomist. And a principal focus of his observation was Berlin, the city and the people who lived in it.

In the introduction to "The Deserted House"—which in reality was a house on Unter den Linden—he speaks with a certain bitter humor about the sixth sense that was conferred on him, that is, the gift of beholding in every phenomenon, whether a person, a deed, or an occurrence, the most unusual things, to which we have no relation in our everyday lives. His passion was to wander alone through the streets, to contemplate the figures he encountered, and even to cast their horoscopes in his mind. For days he would follow strangers who had something unusual about their gait, their clothing, their voice, or their glance. He felt he was in constant contact with the supernatural; even more than he was pursuing the spiritual world, the spiritual world was pursuing him. At noon, in the light of day, it blocked his path in this rational Berlin; it followed him through the noise of Königstraße to the few remaining traces of the Middle Ages in the area around the crumbling City Hall; it let him smell the mysterious scent of roses and carnations on Grünstraße; and for him it cast a spell over the elegant gathering place of refined Berlin, the Linden. Hoffmann could be called the father of the Berlin novel, whose vestiges were later lost in generalities as Berlin became the "capital," the Tiergarten the "park," and the Spree the "river," until our own time, when it has come alive again—Döblin's *Berlin Alexanderplatz* comes to mind. As one of Hoffmann's characters says to another, whom he thinks of as himself:

> You had specific reasons to set the story in Berlin, citing particular streets and squares as you did. In my view it is generally not at all a bad thing to indicate a setting precisely. Not only does it lend the whole story a semblance of historical truth, which aids a sluggish imagination, but, especially for those who are familiar with the setting, the story becomes so much more accessible and alive.[6]

I could easily enumerate the many stories in which Hoffmann proves himself as a physiognomist of Berlin. I could point out the houses that he features in his stories, beginning with his own apartment on the corner of Charlottenstraße and Taubenstraße, followed by the Golden Eagle on Dönhoffplatz, and Lutter & Wegner on

---

6   See E. T. A. Hoffmann, *Die Serapionsbrüder I* [1819–1821], in *Poetische Werke*, vol. 5 (Berlin: Walter de Gruyter, 1957), 165 ("Ein Fragment aus dem Leben dreier Freunde").

Charlottenstraße, et cetera. But I think we'd be better off investigating more closely how Hoffmann studied Berlin and the impression of the city left behind in his stories. Hoffmann was never a great friend of solitude, of nature. Communicating with people, observing them, merely seeing them, mattered more to him than anything else. If he went for a stroll in summer, which he did every evening when the weather was good, it was only to get to public places where he was likely to find people. And while he was out, he could not pass a wine tavern or pastry shop without going in to see if people were there and who they were.[7] But it wasn't just that Hoffmann would look around these spots for new faces to supply him with new and strange ideas: for him the wine tavern was more like a writer's laboratory, or an experimentation chamber where every evening he tested the complexities and effects of his stories on friends. Hoffmann indeed was less a novelist than a storyteller, and even in his books, many if not most of his tales come from the mouth of one of the characters. Of course, in a manner of speaking Hoffmann himself is always this narrator, sitting around a table with friends as each tells a story in turn. One of Hoffmann's friends explicitly recalled that he never sat idly in a bar as people so often do, just sipping and yawning. No, he would look all around with his eagle eye, noticing whatever was ridiculous, striking, or even particularly moving and making it into a study for his writing, or he would draw what he saw with his forceful pen—Hoffmann was a very deft sketch artist. But if ever he was dissatisfied with the company gathered in the tavern, or irked by the narrow-minded, petit-bourgeois guests around him at the table, he could become absolutely insufferable, putting to frightful use his talent for making faces, embarrassing people, even terrifying them. For him, however, the greatest horror sprang from the so-called aesthetic tea societies that were all the rage in Hoffmann's Berlin: gatherings of unlearned, uncouth dilettantes who boasted of their interest in art and literature. In his *Fantasy Pieces* he described one such society to great comic effect.[8]

---

7 Beginning with "Hoffmann was never a great friend of solitude," this passage is an unattributed quotation of Hitzig, in *Hoffmann, Ausgewählte Schriften*, 32–4. Benjamin quotes the same passage, with attribution, in *Charles Baudelaire: Ein Lyriker im Zeitalter des Hochkapitalismus*, GS, 1.2, 551–2 (*The Paris of the Second Empire in Baudelaire*, SW, 4, 28), and *Das Passagen-Werk* [M4a, 2], GS, 5.1, 536 (*The Arcades Project* [M4a, 2], 425–6).

8 See Hoffmann's *Fantasiestücke in Callots Manier: Blätter aus dem Tagebuche eines reisenden Enthusiasten* [Fantasy Pieces in Callot's Manner: Pages from the Diary of a Traveling Romantic] (Bamberg, 1819); and "Die ästhetische Teegesellschaft [The Aesthetic Tea Society]" in *Die Serapionsbrüder 4, Poetische Werke*, vol. 8. [1819–1821].

As we now draw to a close, let us not be accused of forgetting our question, "to what end?" Not only have we not forgotten it, we've already answered it without even knowing. To what end did Hoffmann write these stories? He certainly had no conscious purpose. But we can read them as if he did. And that purpose is nothing other than physiognomic: to show that this prosaic, sober, enlightened, and rational Berlin is full of things to charm a story-teller—not only in its medieval nooks, secluded streets, and somber houses, but also in its working inhabitants of every social rank and from all corners of the city—which can only be teased out by dint of observation. As if Hoffmann set out to teach this to his readers through his work, one of his very last stories, dictated from his deathbed, is nothing less than a seminar on physiognomic seeing.

This story is called "My Cousin's Corner Window."[9] The cousin is Hoffmann, the window is his apartment's corner window overlooking the Gendarmenmarkt. The story is actually a dialogue. The crippled Hoffmann sits in an armchair watching the weekly market below and instructing his cousin, who is there on a visit, how much can be divined, and moreover devised and concocted, from the clothing, pace and gestures of the market women and their customers. After having said so much to Hoffmann's credit, I shall close with something that most Berliners would not suspect: that he is the only writer who made Berlin famous abroad, and that the French loved him and read him at a time when in Germany, even in Berlin, a dog would not eat a biscuit from his hand. Now things have changed. There are a great many affordable editions of Hoffmann, as well as more parents than there were in my day who allow their children to read him.

"Das dämonische Berlin," GS, 7.2, 86–92. Translated by Jonathan Lutes.

Broadcast on Radio Berlin, February 25, 1930. Benjamin dated the typescript, "Radio Berlin, 25 February 1930." For this date, the Funkstunde *announced a "Youth Hour (Berlin), Speaker: Dr. Walter Benjamin," from 6:00–6:25 pm.*

---

9 "Des Vetters Eckfenster" (1822), in *Späte Werke*, eds. Walter Müller-Seidel and Friedrich Schnapp (Munich: Winkler, 1965).

CHAPTER 5

Berlin Guttersnipe

I bet that if you try, you can remember seeing wardrobes or armoires with colorful scenes, landscapes, portraits, flowers, fruits, or other similar designs inlaid in the wood of their doors. Intarsia is what it's called. Today I'd like to present you with some scenes inlaid not in wood, but in speech. I'll be telling you about the childhood of a Berliner, who was a small boy roughly 120 years ago, and about how he saw Berlin, about what kind of games and practical jokes were common back then. Amid all of this, I'd like to inlay the story with a few things that have nothing at all to do with our subject, but will, or so I hope, stand out from the story of Ludwig Rellstab's youth as vividly and colorfully as does intarsia in paneled wood.[1]

Don't worry that you've never heard the name Ludwig Rellstab. And whatever you do, don't ask your parents; they've never heard of him either, and they won't have a clue what to say. This Rellstab is not a famous man. Or rather, to be more precise, in his time he was one of the best-known people in Berlin. The short of it is, little remains of him. Today he is not even known for his greatest accomplishment: his autobiography, parts of which I'll read to you later.

That this autobiography should be so beautiful without there being too much of any importance to say about its author isn't all that surprising. For it is not always the most famous or gifted people who retain the profoundest love and memories of their childhood. Moreover, this is rarer for a city dweller than for someone who has grown up in the countryside. It's hardly common for a child to forge such harmonious and happy connections with a large city so that later, as a mature man, it's a joy for him to recall his boyhood memories. Rellstab knew this joy; you can sense it throughout the book,

---

1   Heinrich Friedrich Ludwig Rellstab (1799–1860), German poet and critic, author of *Aus meinem Leben* [From My Life] (Berlin: J. Guttentag, 1861).

even if he never explicitly says that his childhood was a particularly happy one.

Now let's dive right into the story. What do you say to the fact that his father "took a house in the country with his family every summer"?[2] And where do you think it was? Right there in the Tiergarten. Let's let Rellstab himself tell us how the Tiergarten looked at a time when you could take a summer vacation there:

> As far back as I can remember, I see myself in summer in the green of the Tiergarten, which back then had a more rustic character than it does now. It remains the most beautiful setting of my earliest memories, as well as of those that would come much later. In those days it was even more suited to playing than it is now. The woods provided large areas where everything was left to become overgrown. Except for the road to Charlottenburg, there wasn't a single paved way, only deep sandy paths that crossed the terrain. So there were relatively few wagons even in the larger avenues, and they moved slowly and with difficulty. When I look at the Tiergarten now, I can hardly believe that it once housed genuine wilderness, where raspberry bushes grew between thickets on the moist meadows, and their bountiful fruits would quietly ripen for us, the inhabitants. The strawberries also provided abundant harvest. To us everything seemed far removed from people, and as lonely as a primeval forest. We literally took it over. Each playmate claimed his own rightful plot. We carved out lawns, made rustic lodgings from the dense thickets, and wedged small boards in trees to sit between branches; we even made a border out of little pickets stuck in the ground like a garden fence. All told, we ruled over our lots as if they were our very own. We could go for weeks without visiting our little wilderness colony, but when we did return, nothing was disturbed, so solitary was the forest back then. Today it has been transformed into a garden, terribly noisy and overrun with people.[3]

Thus did an old Berliner describe the Tiergarten of 1815. I find this description very beautiful. But now, time for an inlay. I would like to show you how a friend of mine, born eighty years after Rellstab, described *his* Tiergarten childhood. And, despite the differences, this description shows that the true Berliner never stops loving it.

---

2 Rellstab, *Aus meinem Leben*, 18.
3 Ibid., 18–20.

This new true Berliner is my friend Franz Hessel, who writes in *Spazieren in Berlin* [On Foot in Berlin]:

> In the waning twilight it is still as rough and disorienting today as it was thirty or forty years ago, before the last Kaiser had the nature park transformed into a more open and respectable place. While his orders to clear the undergrowth, widen many of the paths, and improve the lawns are certainly commendable, much of the Tiergarten's beauty has been lost: its charming disorder, branches crackling underfoot, the rustling of leaves along neglected narrow paths. However, he left a few wild spots that managed to survive into the days of our childhood. What I remember most from this time are the tiny sloped footbridges spanning the streams, which were sometimes presided over by vigilant bronze lions, holding in their jaws the chains that served as guard rails.[4]

Hessel goes on to describe the entire Tiergarten up to where it borders the Cornelius Bridge. If we had more time, there would be so much more to say, for example, about this bridge that still today clings to its private, almost rustic appearance. This formerly seldom used and rather isolated bridge now funnels all the city's automobile traffic as it spills toward the west. If you think about it, this bridge's fate is as remarkable as that of many men.

But now back to Rellstab. In the whole of his tale of youth, there's one thing he complains about repeatedly and never seems to have completely got over: the music lessons forced upon him by his father. These after-school lessons were the worst part of his day. He relates how unhappy he was that they forced him to forgo the games and antics his schoolmates would use to prolong the way home from school. Many of these games were rather curious, and we hear about how they were already being diligently prepared during class. "For some time," says Rellstab,

> it was our habit, while still in school during our last class, to make little boats out of paper and bark, and then, and this was especially entertaining after a strong rain, to let them float down the gutter until

---

4 Franz Hessel, *Spazieren in Berlin* (Leipzig and Vienna: Verlag Dr. Hans Epstein, 1929). References to and discussions of Hessel (1880–1941), with whom Benjamin collaborated on the translation of Proust, appear frequently in his work. See, for instance, "Die Wiederkehr des Flaneurs," a review of *Spazieren in Berlin*, in GS, 3, 194–9 ("The Return of the *Flâneur*," SW, 2, 262–7).

they vanished at the corner of Mohrenstraße and Markgrafenstraße, where the runoff feeds into an underground canal. There was nothing more interesting than following the routes of our little boats; we held our breath watching as they disappeared into a little drain tunnel and greeted them with joy as they reemerged on the other side. I had the hardest time tearing myself away in order to head home along my solitary path to my piano lessons.[5]

You can imagine that it was no easier for him to leave when "Zillrad" was the game of the day. But what was this inexpressibly magical game, as he calls it? Thank goodness he explains it to us; otherwise we might wonder forever and never find out. Here's how it works. A bunch of boys—the more the merrier—would climb atop an empty hay wagon, a common sight in the streets back then. One boy, chosen by counting out a rhyme, would run around the wagon trying to tag the feet of the boys above. Whoever was tagged then had to climb down and give it a go himself.[6]

Rellstab's father must have been a very peculiar man. He was an editor of the *Vossische Zeitung*.[7] One evening he was supposed to attend a magic show and then write about it for the newspaper. Having no desire to go and a very busy schedule, he sent his son, who was just twelve years old at the time. When he got home, he had him write down his impressions. Then he fixed the article up a bit and sent it on to the *Vossische Zeitung*. This was Rellstab's first published work. But the visit had a curious effect. After the show the magician explained a few of his tricks to those who had waited around the theater. The young Rellstab heard these explanations and for weeks could think of nothing but magic. He managed to find a shop in Berlin that sold magic supplies, contraptions with secret mechanisms, boxes with double bottoms, playing cards with hidden marks. He also searched out any book that would help him study magic as a science.

Nothing much came of this, he admits. But who knows whether he wouldn't have become a famous magician if back then he had had the splendid book which, as our second inlay, I'd like to tell you about now. Despite technology, cars, electric generators, radio, etc.,

---

5 Rellstab, *Aus meinem Leben*, 38–9.

6 On "Zillrad," see Rellstab, *Aus meinem Leben*, 41.

7 The renowned *Vossische Zeitung* was published in Berlin and was the city's oldest daily newspaper. Rellstab's father, the music publisher and composer Johann Carl Friedrich Rellstab (1759–1813) was a critic for the *Vossische Zeitung* from 1808 to 1813.

it seems that many children are still interested in magic. True, the golden age of magic has passed. There was a time when, every summer in all the big seaside resorts, world-famous magicians, the likes of Bellachini or Houdini, performed before packed houses. Just now a book has finally appeared in which all kinds of magic, including hundreds of tricks and some of the most incredible and astounding things you could ever imagine, are depicted and explained in clear detail. It's called *Das Wunderbuch der Zauberkunst* [The Wonder Book of Magic] and was written by Ottokar Fischer, who calls himself "a formerly practicing artist and director of the Kratky-Baschik Magic Theater in Vienna."[8] One glance at the table of contents and your eyes are popping at the abundance of magic on offer. And don't worry that knowing what's behind the tricks could stop you from enjoying magic shows. To the contrary, only when you know to watch very closely, and no longer let yourself get caught up in the magician's clever patter, always keeping an eye on what's coming next—only then will you appreciate the magician's unbelievable skill and recognize that it is his speed, the result of so much practice and determination, that is oftentimes behind the sorcery. Another time soon we'll speak more about magic, so I'll say nothing more today other than to list a few headings from our book: The Bottomless Punchbowl—The Devil's Target—The Queen of the Air—Schiller's Bell—The Indestructible Cord—The Swami Seer's Wristwatch—Ladies Scorched, Perforated and Cut in Half—The Wonder of Ben Ali Bey—The Disappearance of Twelve Members of the Audience—and many more.

But it is getting late and Rellstab wants to tell us about a few more pranks:

> My Tiergarten pals and I got into all sorts of other mischief: performing daring raids on fruit trees and fruit sheds; driving a fruit seller crazy by fastening a meaty bone, which hung unnoticed behind a fence, to her service bell so that every passing dog was enticed to ring it; holding a string across the path just outside a tavern, where it wasn't rare to see tipsy guests stumbling about in the evening, until a group tripped over it and fell into the wet grass and then, after immediately releasing the string, innocently setting out to find the cause of the stumble. I'll say no more just now, except to mention briefly that

8   Ottokar Fischer (1873–1940), who, from 1898 to 1911, managed and appeared at the Kratky-Baschik Magic Theater in Vienna, wrote *Das Wunderbuch der Zauberkunst* (Stuttgart: F. A. Perthes, 1929).

in this way, too, I was no better than other children, and actually much worse.[9]

And so you can see, from his own words, how a real Berlin gutter-snipe cavorted about the city at a tender age. As later in life we often succeed best at precisely those things we loved and plotted early on, the same was true for Rellstab. His greatest achievements arose not from music criticism, from which he later earned his living, but rather from things intimately associated with Berlin. In addition to these childhood memories, he also has a book, simply titled *Berlin*, a description of the city and its nearest surroundings, including many beautiful steel engravings.[10] On the title pages there's one such engraving that depicts the Tiergarten memorial to Frederick William III. Of all the areas of the Tiergarten, my most beloved is the spot where this memorial is tucked away. I played there as a very small child and to this day I've never forgotten how exciting it used to be to meander along the winding paths to the Queen Louise Memorial, which was even more secluded, hidden among the bushes and separated from the king by a narrow stream. The area around these two monuments was the first labyrinth I would encounter, long before I would sketch them on blotting paper or my desk during school.[11] In this regard I'd say little has changed: your blotting paper doesn't look all that different than mine did.

In any case, for those of you who enjoy labyrinths, I will close with one last inlay. I'd like to reveal the exact location of the most beautiful labyrinths you'll ever see: the home of the bookseller Paul Graupe, a large and wonderful house with an entire hall dedicated to fascinating labyrinths of cities, forests, mountains, valleys, castles, and bridges, each meticulously drawn in pen by the Munich painter Hirth so as to invite you to wander with your eyes.[12] But clean your boots on the way in; Paul Graupe's is a very elegant place. And when

9 Rellstab, *Aus meinem Leben*, 152–3.

10 See Rellstab, *Berlin und seine nächsten Umgebungen in malerischen Originalansichten: Historisch-topographisch beschrieben* (Darmstadt: Gustav Georg Lange, 1852).

11 For Benjamin's memories of the Tiergarten and the motif of the labyrinth, see *Berliner Kindheit um neunzehnhundert*, GS, 7.1, 393–5 (*Berlin Childhood Around 1900*, SW, 3, 352–4).

12 Paul Graupe (1881–1953) was an antiquarian bookseller, auctioneer, and art dealer who, until he fled the Nazis in 1936, was located in Berlin. The "Munich painter Hirth" is Otto Albert Hirth (1899–1969). Benjamin discusses an exhibition at Graupe's featuring works by Hirth in his article "Unterirdischer Gang in Der Tiergartenstrasse" [Underground Passageway in Tiergartenstrasse], GS, 4.1, 563–5, published in *Die literarische Welt* on March 28, 1930, just a few weeks after the broadcast of "Berlin Guttersnipe."

you're standing among the maps, plans, and cityscapes you'll find there, have a look out the window, and right before your eyes you'll see the Tiergarten again; which means our walk today has been rather labyrinthine, leaving us, without ever having noticed, right back where we began twenty-five minutes ago.

"Ein Berliner Strassenjunge," GS, 7.1, 92–8. Translated by Jonathan Lutes.

Broadcast on Radio Berlin, March 7, 1930. Benjamin dated the typescript "Berlin Radio, 7 March, 1930." For this date, the Funkstunde *announced "Youth Hour (Berlin). Speaker: Dr. Walter Benjamin," from 5:30–6:00 pm.*

CHAPTER 6

Berlin Toy Tour I

Are any of you familiar with Godin's book of fairy tales?[1] Of all the children out there listening, perhaps not a single one of you. In the last thirty years of the previous century, however, it could be found in many a nursery, including the one in which the man speaking with you now spent his earliest days. The publisher kept reissuing new editions, each time with a different look, varying the colorful pictures according to the fashion of the time. However, quite a few of the somber images have remained the same since the very first edition. Let's begin with a tale from this book: "Sister Tinchen."[2] Right on the second page of the story is one of these somber pictures. It shows five children miserably huddled together next to a dilapidated hut. They are in a truly wretched state. Their mother died that morning, and it's been quite some time since they had a father. There are four boys and one girl. The girl's name is Tinchen. But this is only the foreground of the picture. In the background one sees a fairy, delicate and doll-like, holding a lily. Her name is Concordia, which means "harmony." She promises the children that she will protect them so long as they always get along. Scarcely upon hearing this, an evil wizard, the fairy's enemy, arrives with a pile of gifts which he promptly throws to the

---

1 Amélie (Linz) Godin (1824–1904), author of *Märchen von einer Mutter erdacht* (1858), *Neue Märchen von einer Mutter erdacht* (1869), and other collections of fairy tales. Benjamin refers to Godin's work as his and his wife Dora's "favorite collection of fairy tales" in a letter to Scholem (letter dated January 13, 1920, in *The Correspondence of Walter Benjamin*, 155).

2 See "Schwester Tinchen," in Godin, *Märchenbuch, 3rd edition, mit 137 Holzschnitten und 6 Bildern in Farbendruck: nach Originalzeichnungen von Otto Försterling, Gustav Süs und Leopold Denus* (Glogau: Carl Fleming, c. 1870–1880), 401–9. The image Benjamin discusses can be found on p. 402. In *The Arcades Project*, Benjamin attributes a version of the story to Friedrich Wilhelm Hackländer (*Das Passagen-Werk* [Z1, 2], GS, 5.2, 847 and 1055; *The Arcades Project* [Z1, 2], 693 and 881), but it has not been found in Hackländer's *Märchen* (Stuttgart: Krabbe, 1843).

children, causing them to quarrel. The boys, as boys will, begin to scuffle. Only the little girl does not join in the fray, so the devils cannot ensnare her in their sack as they did with the boys right away.

So far, you will tell me, this is a rather absurd story. And I would agree. But wait for what happens next. The little girl must, of course, free her brothers from the wicked sorcerer's lair where the devils have taken them. And there, thanks to the good woman who thought up this tale and was otherwise not particularly known as a writer, something wonderful occurs. You're surely familiar with the obstacles that rescuers must overcome in fairy tales. First they have to get through a door guarded by two savages with clubs, as on the former title page of the *Vossische Zeitung*.[3] And then they come to an immaculate, gleaming hall where they must pass between two freshly burnished fire-breathing dragons. And finally, in the last room they encounter a toad, or some other beast, which they have to kiss so that it transforms into a princess. In "Sister Tinchen," whose heroine after all is just a little girl, who no one would imagine capable of such heroic and bloodthirsty deeds, everything is much more civilized. That is to say, she must do absolutely nothing if she is to free her brothers. For her entire journey through the land of the evil sorcerer she can't pause even for a moment—until she reaches his cave. The sorcerer, who of course wants to make this impossible for her, conjures enticing images to coax her to linger. Were she to say, even just once, "Here I'd like to stay," she would fall under his spell.

Now I'll read to you some of the traps he laid for her: Tinchen bravely crosses the border into the magic land, thinking only of her brothers. At first she sees nothing special. But soon she arrives in a vast room filled with toys. Everywhere are little booths laid out with every possible distraction: carousels with ponies and wagons, slides and rocking horses, and above all, the most magnificent dollhouses. Seated in armchairs at a small, decorated table are some large dolls. Upon catching Tinchen's gaze, the largest and prettiest among them stands up, bows gracefully, and says to her in an exquisite little voice: "We've been expecting you for some time, dear Tinchen, come and lunch with us." As she speaks, all the other dolls rise to their feet; even the baby dolls in their cribs lift their little heads to see her, and

3 Benjamin refers to the front page of Berlin's newspaper, the *Vossische Zeitung*, which featured two men holding spiked staffs standing on either side of the king.

Tinchen, enraptured, sits down in the small armchair awaiting her at the table. Tinchen relishes the delectable treats and after lunch, as the dolls begin to dance and more toys begin to stir around her, Tinchen is so beside herself with joy that she claps her hands and cries: "Oh, how beautiful it is here. Here I'd like to . . ." What did she want to say? Of course she wanted to say: "Here I'd like to stay." But she's not allowed to say that if she wants to free her brothers. So, a small blue bird suddenly appears, sits on her shoulder and sings her a little reminder:

> Tinchen, dearest Tinchen mine,
> Think about your brothers thine!

Thus she makes it through all sorts of enchanted lands, with the little bird always appearing just in time. We could follow her everywhere if this weren't the radio station's Berlin Hour and I didn't have to zip back to Berlin through secret underground tunnels while Tinchen stays in the magic kingdom. After all, even while she stands in front of a gingerbread house, Tinchen is coming to Berlin as well. As the door opens, out come two little brown people, who approach her, curtsying daintily: "Welcome to our land." "And who are you, and what is the name of this land of yours?" she asks curiously. "Well now, you've never heard of the Land of Plenty?" said the two little people in unison. "We're the gingerbread man and gingerbread lady. And I'd like to give you my great big heart!" says the little man with a smile, as he pulls from his breast a heart encircled with almonds. "And I give you my pretty white flower," says the little lady as she hands her the tulip she was holding. Then a mob of cakes and chocolates gather around, beckoning her to stay. "Oh, how I'd like to," says Tinchen. But again the bird appears to make sure she doesn't forget.

Perhaps you'll remember this fairy tale in a few years when, in the higher grades at school, you hear some of Goethe's greatest dramas, *Faust* in particular. As you probably know, Faust made a deal with the devil. The devil has to do whatever Faust wants, and in return he gets Faust's soul. But the question is *when* he gets to have it. He's not allowed to take it until Faust is perfectly content and happy and wants everything to remain just as it is. Unfortunately for Faust there's no little blue bird, and sure enough, one day when he's already a very old man he declares:

> To the moment I would like to say:
> Please stay a while, you are so fine![4]

And then and there he drops dead.

You must be thinking, this fellow will never make it to Berlin. But it's like the race between the tortoise and the hare. As is well known, the tortoise is sitting in a ditch when the hare arrives, completely out of breath. The tortoise says: "I'm already here." And sure enough, I'm already here in Berlin, just where you would all like to be. Because just as I've told you about the charmed attractions that little Tinchen has to bravely pass by without lingering, I could tell you of many attractions in Berlin that all of you, just as courageously, have passed by without lingering. Or if your mother had the time, perhaps you were able to stop. By now maybe you've guessed where I'm heading: straight to the middle of Berlin, where we have these long galleries of toys without fairies or sorcerers. In the department stores.

I was thinking, grownups have all sorts of specialized shows on the radio, shows of great interest to them, although, or even because, they understand at least as much about the subject as the speaker. Why shouldn't we make such special shows for children as well? For example about toys, although, or even because, kids understand at least as much about toys as the man who's speaking to you here. So, one day at around noon, when the department stores are as empty as they ever are, I took a leisurely stroll from table to table, as I was never allowed to when I was a boy. I studied everything very closely: the new toys, how the old ones had changed since I was little, and which ones had disappeared altogether. And now I'd like to begin with these, the ones that have vanished. Today we'll only have time to get started; if you enjoy the tour, next week you can hear about its continuation.

I looked everywhere for an old party game called "The Lucky Fisherman." It seems that this no longer exists. I got it for my birthday once. It's so wonderful that I want to tell you about it now. Opening the box, the first thing you see are four cardboard walls glued together. You take them out and set them on a table. The walls are covered with shiny printed paper showing aquatic plants, fish, mussels, and seaweed: everything that swims around in the sea or lies on the ocean floor. In another compartment there are around

---

4 See Goethe, *Faust II*, lines 11581–2 and *Faust I*, lines 1699–700.

twenty or thirty different fish, each of which has a ring in its nose. Why a ring? Something that's usually the privilege of camels? Here's why. The ring is made of iron. And the fishing rods are five or six elegant little sticks, each with a thin red string that, instead of an earthworm, has a pretty little magnet hanging from it. Whoever catches the most fish wins the game. But there are of course rules and the fish in this water are all numbered differently, and when the fishing is over, there's no eating up the catch; there's arithmetic instead. This is one example of what has disappeared. It seems, however, that something much more beautiful has vanished: a special type of music box. Perhaps many of you haven't even seen one: a box that has music inside, a crank on the side, and some kind of landscape or cityscape atop, which, when you turn the crank, starts to move to the music. I got to see all sorts of music boxes on this tour, for example, cows being milked, a dog jumping up in the air, a shepherd stepping out of his hut and walking back in. They're wonderful but not nearly as strange and enthralling as the particular music box I have in mind. I never owned it; I only saw it one day in a shop when I was little. If you wound it, exquisite battle songs would sound from the box, heavy cardboard gates would open onto a dark fortress that you could not see into from above, and a company of soldiers would march out. To the sound of drums they would make a loop through the green grass and then reenter the fortress from behind through a gate, which had since opened, and then wait inside for a short while, in the dark, all the time accompanied by music. The devil only knows how they fared in there before they neatly filed out again.

I've looked for something like it ever since. I can't even find the little books that we used to get at the school bookstore that would sweeten the purchase of arithmetic books—a purchase that was possibly even more despicable than each individual math lesson, because the notebook contained in its empty squares all the lessons added up into one single sum of horrors—flip books, or whatever they were called, sequences of tiny photos showing a wrestling bout or soccer match in all its phases. You had to navigate quickly with your thumb so the images would shoot by, each close on the heels of the next. With such a book cupped in your hand you could easily transform a math lesson into a cinema show. But at least the elaborate toy with the delightful name "Wheel of Life" still exists. It relies on exactly the same trick, only the images aren't bound in a book, but instead are mounted on a disk with the surfaces of the images facing inward. Around the disk is a wall with slits in it. And when you spin the disk quickly—while the wall remains stationary—through the slits you see people as if they were moving and alive, which is why the whole thing is called a wheel of life. I saw this in the "toy" department.

Before I tell you more about it, however, I'd like first to describe the toy gallery in full. By chance I began with the kingdom of dolls, but I'll tell you about that next time. Up next: the animal aisle, which would put any magician to shame. It's hard to describe the sorts of animals I came across there. Blue and pink dogs, horses so yellow that from afar they looked like shapes made of orange peel, apes and rabbits so artificially colored as to resemble the tulips the flower ladies sell at Potsdamer Platz. Not to mention Felix the Cat, who was available in large quantities, and the tiny Bibabo puppets, which you can slip over your fingers as the nice sales lady did before putting on the most indescribable little theater piece. She only stopped once she realized that under no circumstances would I buy what was on offer, which is how I felt in the animal gallery as well. But later on I just couldn't resist and I bought something. It's a very strange game, rather new, I think, but in any case I had never heard of it. It was nothing more than a small box with fifteen or so different rubber stamps. Each stamp had a piece of a landscape on it: houses, figurines, dirigibles, cars, boats, bridges, etc. It also came with an ink pad. With just a large sheet of paper you could spend hours stamping together various landscapes, neighborhoods, events, and stories. But that was already in the "party games" department, which came just after the animals. I nearly forgot to say how many Easter bunnies there are now in the animal gallery. Department stores have now become strategic locations; they would be the first to be occupied by the Easter bunnies if they ever planned an attack.

Cover your ears for a moment. What I have to say now is not for children to hear. Next time I will tell you the conclusion of my tour. I'm worried sick I'll soon be swamped with mail, letters along the lines of: "What? Are you completely mad? You think that kids don't already whine from morning to night? And now you're putting ideas in their heads and telling them about thousands of toys that, up until now, thank God, they knew nothing about, and now they want all of them, and probably things that don't even exist anymore?" How should I answer them? I could just take the easy way out and beg you not to repeat a word of our story, don't let on a thing, and then we can continue next week just like today. But that would be mean. So it's left to me to calmly say what I really think: the more someone understands something and the more he knows of a particular kind of beauty—whether it's flowers, books, clothing, or toys—the more he can rejoice in everything that he knows and sees, and the less he's fixated on possessing it, buying it himself, or receiving it as a gift. Those of you who listened to the end, although you shouldn't have, must now explain this to your parents.

"Berliner Spielzeugwanderung I," GS, 7.1, 98–105. Translated by Jonathan Lutes.

Broadcast on Radio Berlin, March 15, 1930. Benjamin dated the typescript "Berlin Radio, 15 March, 1930," and for this date the Funkstunde *announced a "Youth Hour (Berlin), Speaker: Dr. Walter Benjamin" from 3:20–3:40 pm.*

CHAPTER 7

Berlin Toy Tour II

Many of you will probably want to know where this grand toy store is located, the galleries of dolls, animals, electric trains, and party games that I led you through last time and will continue to lead you through today. Nothing would be easier than to tell you where it is. But advertisements are not permitted on the radio, even subtle ones, so I cannot give you a name.[1] What shall we do? Some children might like to confirm that what I said is true. And since it really is true, I would like nothing more than to do just that. Thus I must be cunning in revealing to you the following: as you have surely figured out by now, I was in a large department store.

Now have a look around, and be sure not to miss the huge metal model of the new Lloyd steamboat, the "Bremen." It's so big, you can see it from afar. The entire thing was made from a mechanical building set. I'm not sure how many of you could rebuild it. To do so you would need the construction kit in size 9, which is the largest, and costs 155 marks. Have you ever heard of the Paris World's Fair, which all of Europe was talking about in 1900? On all the picture postcards made for the exhibition, you could see in the background of the city of Paris a gigantic wheel with maybe sixteen cabins on moving hinges. The wheel turned slowly, and the people sitting in the cabins could look out over the city, the Seine, and the exhibition below until the double motion, from the swaying of the cabin on its hinges and the rotation of the giant wheel, made them feel sick. Even

---

1 Radio advertising in the Weimar Republic was controlled and regulated by the centralized Postal Ministry, and, in contrast to the commercial model of the United States, where advertising paid for broadcasting, the German system was based on subscription, requiring listeners to pay a licensing fee to receive transmissions. While some kinds of commercially sponsored programming were permissible, including the indirect advertisements of programs financed by private companies seeking to promote their products by having them featured on air, advertising was explicitly scheduled and highly regulated.

this wheel has been replicated in a model kit. Its parts move, and the little cabins sway just like the real ones did thirty years ago when your grandparents might have sat in them. All of this was located in the "party games" section. I won't dwell too much on the games I saw there. You're surely familiar with all the different variations of Quartet, this lovely game that teaches you to be sly, mischievous, and polite all at once, and you also know the dice games played on big boards like "Game of the Goose," "Travels Around the World," "Carnival at Schröppstedt," as they used to be called; "In the Zeppelin," "Northern Voyage," and "The Good Copper," as they're called today. I'd rather tell you about an electronic question-and-answer game. It is made up of one little battery, a bulb, and two plugs. You push one of the plugs into a board covered with questions, next to each of which is a little metal rod. Next you look for the answer on a different board. For example, if you stick one plug on the question "Which river flows through Rome?" you then look for the answer with the other plug, and if you find the right spot, the electric bulb lights up. This toy is really quite ingenious, in that the teacher has artfully transformed himself into an electric bulb.

And there are still other, very subtle educational tidbits hidden in toys. I was most impressed with a completely new toy designed for six-year-olds just learning their sums. It is a beautifully polished wooden apple, scented as well, not like a Borsdorfer or Russet apple, but just like wood. Were you to look at it up close, you'd see how cleverly it is constructed, and that it comes apart into six different pieces that can be used to teach arithmetic to the youngest pupils. If only it had a core, it could be used for the older students as well. But is it still a toy? And the so-called activity toys, pearls to be threaded on strings, weaving patterns for kindergarteners, all of which you can find nearby, are these really toys? And decals? And most of all, what about the Oblaten?[2] I don't know. But I'd like to talk to you about the Oblaten. Not just because I liked them as a boy, but also because I put together a very beautiful collection of my mother's Oblaten, which included things that you can no longer get today in stationery stores, such as entire fairy tales: Tom Thumb, Snow White in colorful detail, Aladdin and the Magic Lamp, Robinson Crusoe, and more. I don't know why, but I still see these tiny little images, showing the terrible genie with snarling teeth appearing before

---

2 *Oblaten* were embossed, colorful, small-format images mass-produced in the second half of the nineteenth century. Collected by children as well as adults, they were placed in scrapbooks and cards and were a trend in Germany, Austria, and England.

Aladdin, who's quaking in terror, or Robinson as he nearly drops his parasol with shock when he first discovers the nibbled human bones on the island—these moments, which are depicted in many children's books, are always in my head as if I still had my Oblaten albums open before me today. This is a good counterweight to all those kissing turtledoves, cherubs, flower carts, and ruffled angels; you'll need scissors if you want to remove them from their paper packaging, right next to the manufacturer's name or "UX 798" or some other such business gibberish printed in little red letters.

As far as I'm concerned, nothing is better than a paper toy, starting with the little folding boats or paper caps, which are usually the ones we encounter first, and onto the insert-books I'd like to tell you about now. Imagine a picture book with just a few pages inside. On the first page maybe there's a room, on the second a landscape with mountains, fields, and a forest, on the third a city with its streets, gates, public squares, and houses. Now look a little closer and you'll see that each of these pictures is full of tiny slots: openings between window and windowsill, between threshold and door, between fountain and pavement, between seat and armrest, between river and shore, etc. In the back of such a book there's a little pocket with all sorts of people, furniture, vehicles, ships, food, and plants, each of which has a little ridge that you can slide into the slots on the pictures. So you can furnish the room in a hundred different ways, decorate the landscape with a hundred different sorts of flowers and animals, and show the city first on a market day and then on a Sunday, and, if you feel like it, you can even have deer and squirrels walking down the street. Sure, books like these no longer exist. But it won't be long before they're back again and already you can find some that are just as beautiful. For instance, why not treat yourself to the *The Magic Boat* by Tom Seidmann-Freud, which works almost the same way as the one I just told you about.[3]

Now maybe you're wondering, what does all this have to do with Berlin? In which case I would beg you to put on your thinking caps when I ask you: where in Germany can you imagine taking a tour through the entire kingdom of toys other than here in a Berlin department store? I'm not saying there aren't toy stores where you

3 Tom Seidmann-Freud (pseudonym of Martha Gertrude Seidmann-Freud, 1892–1930), writer and illustrator, niece of Sigmund Freud. Her book, *Das Zauberboot* [*The Magic Boat*] (1929), featured movable parts. Benjamin discusses her work in "Chichleuchlauchra, Zu einer Fibel" (1930) and "Grünende Anfangsgründe, Noch etwas zu den Spielfibeln" (1931), in GS, 3, 267–72, 311–14.

can find just as many things. The big difference is that the department stores simply have more space to put out their giant tables so that nothing remains hidden and anyone with eyes gets to look at everything that would otherwise be stowed away in closets and crates. Mind you, it's been a long road to arrive at these galleries we are wandering through. Most of all, you must not think the toy began as some sort of invention by manufacturers of playthings. On the contrary, the toy emerged gradually from the workshops of wood carvers and tinsmiths. At first, children's toys were actually produced by craftsmen in their spare time, since toys are essentially objects from everyday life recreated in miniature. The carpenter would make, by order, tiny furniture for dollhouses, the tinsmith and coppersmith the pots and plates for the doll kitchens, and a potter would make the tiny ceramic ware. In short: each craftsman was allotted his share in the creation of such miniaturized household items. However, in the Middle Ages, strict regulations enforced by trade guilds set limits on each professional craft, making proper toy manufacturing impossible. Each master craftsman was only allowed to make that which fell in his particular domain. The carpenter was forbidden to paint his wooden dolls himself; he had to leave the finishing work to the "bismuth painters," as they were known, while the chandler had to turn to the carpenter if he wanted his wax dolls or angels to hold some sort of wooden object like a candlestick in their hands. You can imagine how unbelievably laborious it must have been in those days to build a dollhouse when so many different craftsmen had to be involved, and this was true right into the nineteenth century. Hence their great value. Early on, only princes could afford them, and they were used as showpieces in castle nurseries, or sometimes they were on exhibit at fairs for paying customers. We know of one such showing. Around 300 years ago a little old lady came to Nuremberg with the idea of earning some money by illustrating to children the basics of proper homemaking, using a dollhouse in which everything was recreated as true-to-life as possible. I suppose the parents of these kids were taken in by her sales pitch and sent their little girls into her tent. But for the kids it was more fun than anything else. And anyway, in reality the interiors of these houses were not at all true-to-life, but only a series of rooms one after the next, cobbled together just for show. Most dollhouses don't even have stairs to connect the various stories.

You surely know the so-called Nuremberg toys. Remember your Noah's Ark, all the tiny painted animals and human figurines? On my tour I was astounded to see how this biblical and pastoral world of toys has grown to include many modern urban scenes. Alongside Noah's Ark, there are now rental barracks, railway stations, swimming pools, and even Berolina sightseeing cars, complete with dolls dressed as foreign drivers and passengers. In a little while we'll get to why these are called Nuremberg toys. The truth is that today most of them come from the Ore Mountains and Thuringia. These toys have been manufactured there for several hundred years. Their story once again shows how the manufacture and sale of toys back then differed from that of today. It's not by chance that the villages where these toys were created lay deep in the forests of Thuringia and Bohemia, where the long winter days, when traffic on the snowed-over streets and icy passes came to a halt, forced the farmers and craftsmen who lived off this traffic in the warmer seasons to find other work to keep them busy. With wood so readily available, naturally they took up carving. At first it was just wooden spoons, kitchen utensils, simple needle boxes and the like. But those with any talent were not content for long, and soon ventured to carve little dolls, small wagons, and animals they knew from their local surroundings. Merchants passing through the area in the summer would buy up these charming and inexpensive works of art to bring home as gifts for their children. The easy earnings appealed to the carvers who, seeking more than just seasonal sales, packed up their goods in baskets and peddled them across the country. Businessmen then began snapping up these toys and selling them all over the world. The dolls would eventually reach Astrakhan and Archangel, Petersburg and Cadiz, even Africa and the West Indies, as sailors took them overseas to trade the colorful little figures with the natives in exchange for jewels, pearls, bronze, and other such valuable wares.

You must be thinking: what a strange toy tour; we're almost finished and he's yet to mention either dolls or soldiers. And you would be right. But today he's dwelt on the more peculiar and unconventional, and so he will continue until the very end. He will tell you what has surprised him most on this tour. It was not a new discovery, but something he had not thought about in an awfully long time: scaly bath toys. On a piece of soft cotton are ducks and goldfish, and in the middle, a ship that is also scaly and comes with colorful metal sails and a magnetic stick that a child can use to steer the boats while his mother washes his hair. The entire thing was coated in celluloid, which made the fish, ships, and ducks look like they were frozen in ice. It reminded me of the smallest and most exciting of toys, those you can't touch because they're behind glass, like the ships, crucifixes, and collieries enclosed in sealed bottles. Have you ever seen these bottles? Have you ever racked your brains figuring out how those things get in there? I have, for years. And it took years before I learned how they do it, how sea captains, who bring them home after long journeys, go about creating such things. It's not sorcery, just patience that is required, the immense patience possessed only by a skipper who, in his solitude at sea, has nothing to miss out on. All the parts of the ship or crucifix, connected by threads, are movable and narrowly packed together so they can fit through the neck of the bottle. Once they are inside, all the pieces and joints are pulled upright with long pins and tweezers until the ship, crucifix, or whatever else takes its proper form. Finally, colored sealing wax is dripped to make the waves or rocks and to permanently set the little houses or figurines. The inside of the bottle looks like something out of the magical land of Vadutz, as described by the poet Clemens Brentano: "All the magical mountains from storybooks, the world of fables and fairy tales, Himmelaya, Meru, Albordi, Kaf, Ida, Olympus, and the Glass Mountains lie for me in the little land of Vadutz."[4] In his imagination Brentano brought together all the toys that he loved into one country that he called Vadutz. He tells us this in the introduction to his most wonderful fairy tale: *Gockel, Hinkel, and Gackeleia.* Now that our toy tour is finished, you have something to wish for on your next birthday. But what I wish from you is that you remember our tour, if sometime later you happen to read the story of Gockel, Hinkel, and Gackeleia.

"Berliner Spielzeugwanderung II," GS, 7.1, 105–11. Translated by Jonathan Lutes.

Broadcast on Radio Berlin, March 22, 1930. Benjamin dated the typescript "Berlin Radio, 22 March, 1930," and for this date the Funkstunde *announced "Youth Hour (Berlin), Speaker: Dr. Walter Benjamin" from 3:30–3:45 pm.*

4 See Clemens Brentano, *Gockel, Hinkel, und Gackeleia* (Frankfurt: S. Schmerber, 1838).

CHAPTER 8

Borsig

We've already experienced quite a lot of Berlin: we've learned about the markets and street trade, about traffic, about the old Berlin schools, about the uncanny Berlin of a century ago, about the Berliner dialect, even a bit about the construction history of Berlin, not to mention our grand toy tour.[1] However, we have conspicuously avoided touching upon the one thing that has allowed Berlin to become a city of three million inhabitants—of which we are but a few—and it's perhaps to this that we owe our knowing one another as Berliners. This thing is big industry and wholesale trade. Today we won't talk about trade, I'll be showing you an industry instead, just one single company, to be exact, in which you'll find one thousandth of Berlin's three million inhabitants. It's actually even more than that: the workforce at Borsig, which I will tell you about today, is 3,900 strong, plus 1,000 clerks, which leaves you with an operation that in good times employs 5,000 people.

What is Borsig? Many of you have heard the name. And you probably know that Borsig is a machine works. From your Sunday excursions many of you know where it's located. When you head out of Berlin on the street toward Oranienburg and Velten, you pass through Tegel where it's already in plain sight. On your class trips to Tegel, your teacher has surely shown you the villa belonging to the Humboldt family. I mean the two brothers Wilhelm and Alexander von Humboldt, who sit atop the columns in front of the university, as

---

1 In addition to the broadcasts of "Street Trade and Markets in Old and New Berlin," "Berlin Dialect," "Berlin Toy Tour I," and "Berlin Toy Tour II," Benjamin seems to allude here to two broadcasts that are now missing or lost. Based in part on this passage, Schiller-Lerg speculates that Benjamin likely gave broadcasts on the subjects of Berlin Traffic [Berliner Verkehr], Berlin Schools [Berliner Schulen], and Berlin's Building History [Berliner Baugeschichte] (*Walter Benjamin und der Rundfunk*, 141–3).

if they still haven't graduated or they're playing hooky.[2] One of these two Humboldts will appear again shortly, in exactly seventeen minutes. Then there's the prison in Tegel, of which you can see more from the outside than you usually can with prisons; a great number of cell windows face the street. But it seems they're so high that the poor inmates cannot see out. Then walk a few more minutes down the street toward Oranienburg and you're at Borsig. The main gate opens onto a hall, which, like all other Borsig buildings, is constructed of red brick. In this hall there's already something quite startling: a row of posts or stands covered from left to right and top to bottom with numbers, and next to each number a name, and under each name a little slot. Many of these slots have cards peeking out of them, which say, for instance, that employee no. 698 or no. 82 or no. 1014 is currently not at the factory. Each person, upon arrival, must take his card from his slot and stamp it with the automatic time clock, and then, usually after eight hours, have it stamped again when he leaves. Ultimately he gets paid according to the number of hours indicated on this control card.

Walking through the gate, the first thing that would strike you would probably be how difficult it is to find your way around, how foreign the place feels, how someone that doesn't work at the factory has no business being here at all. What are we supposed to make of these more than twenty halls and workshops, sheds and chimneys, randomly connected not so much by streets as by rails? The trains drive right into the factory. The boilers, the ship engines, the steam turbines, the ovens, the chemical contraptions, and the countless other products manufactured here are loaded right on the premises. But they're loaded not only onto freight trains. These large grounds are bordered on the other side, opposite the entrance, by Lake Tegel. From here, the barges, laden with machines ordered from Borsig by overseas customers, begin their slow journey along the Havel and the Elbe until they reach Hamburg, where their cargo is loaded onto ships. The second thing that strikes you is a tower. Twelve stories high and built from beautiful glass bricks, its sixty-five meters made it the tallest structure in Berlin when it was built back in 1923. And by the way, it's still not completely finished, as there's always something more urgent to spend money on at the factory.

---

2 Wilhelm von Humboldt (1767–1835), philosopher, philologist, diplomat, and educational reformer, is considered the founder of the modern university system. In 1810 he founded the University of Berlin (later renamed Humboldt University); Alexander von Humboldt (1769–1859) was a naturalist, geographer, and explorer. Statues of the brothers flank the entrance of the university.

Let's say someone asks you which part of the factory grounds you would like to see, the hall where they make airlift pumps, perhaps, or tempering devices with agitators, or coil-tube boilers, or low-pressure rotators with high-pressure leveraging? You'd stand there with your mouth agape and understand what it is to know German. You could easily realize that you've never in your life heard at least three quarters of the most important words that are used here, year in and year out, from early morning to late at night, and that you can't even guess at the meaning of some, even if you should recognize a couple of the easier ones and know, for instance, what a lathe is, or a milling machine. However, other children, some even younger than you, know all about it, at least those who are apprenticing at Borsig. For up on the fifth floor of one of these factory buildings—I took an elevator up there, a strange feeling, I must say, because it's usually only used to carry chains, machine parts, and other such things—there's a training department where almost 300 apprentices, for the most part children of men who have been employed at the plant for some time, are molded into future workers. They have 100 machine tools up there to help them learn. The company is proud of this department, because it began as a program to hire apprentices not merely on a case-by-case basis when they needed new employees, but instead to systematically train them from the outset. In addition to the apprentice workshop, there's a factory school with classrooms, teachers, a cinema, and proper theoretical training that the youngsters must complete over four years.

But let us not dally any longer with the particular names of machines or the many more I'd like to tell you about; instead let's proceed into one of these halls. Assume we are lucky enough to be there when Borsig is busy building locomotives. Then we could see the various departments, but let's only concern ourselves with the first and the last. And sure enough, we're in luck. Just now Borsig is building seventy locomotives for Serbia, to settle war reparations. The first station is the boiler shop. Let's go in. Every year around 600 locomotive boilers are forged here. The noise that greets us sounds like the 600 are being forged right now and all at once. Forty to fifty people, not more, might be at work in this giant hall. And since it's over 100 meters long, the individual naturally disappears. But that's the remarkable thing: the noise is deafening yet you barely see anyone. At first, until you're accustomed to being here, you move with caution, step by step. Because not only are there rail tracks everywhere below, but there are even more overhead, where large cranes, fixed on wheels, roll from one end of the hall to the other hauling loads, ironware, boiler parts, and wheel halves, since large wheels are always manufactured in halves and then welded together afterwards. You never know when one of these graceful gems might swing back and forth above your head. The boilers are riveted using a so-called hydraulic riveter, a type of pump, with pistons under extremely high pressure. One man alone operates this machine, riveting together parts under 2,000 hundredweights of pressure. But don't think the Borsig manufacturing process begins here. No, the individual parts that are forged to make this boiler are manufactured in a separate shop, located in a different hall, the so-called hammer works, housing twelve forging furnaces and eighteen steam hammers, seven hydraulic presses and whatever else is used to process raw iron into the desired form. Of course Borsig itself does not own the iron ore from which this crude iron is extracted; it is bought in Germany or Scandinavia. But from then on, everything up to the finished product, the locomotive, is handled in-house. The raw iron is not extracted from the ore here, but rather in Borsig's factories on the Polish border in Upper Silesia. Such a system, where everything from raw materials to the finished goods is produced by a single firm, is called vertical integration. One imagines the iron lying in the farthest depths of the Earth and then the production process rising higher and higher, refining itself more and more, until it culminates in the finished product, in this case the locomotive.

You have no idea how wide the variety of locomotives is, all sorts of which are manufactured here: electric locomotives, locomotives that burn coal and those that burn wood (for Brazil, for example, where fuel is so expensive that they have to operate as economically as possible), fireless locomotives, which run on superheated steam, for use in fire-sensitive operations or around stockyards where black soot must be avoided. All these things are made at Borsig. Every country requires something different; every client has his special demands, which sometimes must be met with uncanny speed. When the Spree had to be tunneled under to build the stretch of subway between Spittelmarkt and Alexanderplatz, the head of the completed tunnel section started to collapse. Water began seeping into the tunnel and the entire construction was in danger. At 10 am the site managers had a meeting with Borsig. Borsig proposed installing five giant pumps that together would drain 125 cubic meters of water per minute. At 3 pm the order for the proposed pumps was received at Tegel. Although all the sketches needed to be reworked, by 11 pm all five giant pumps were ready and rolled out to the gate. The next morning they were put into operation and in two hours the subway construction was saved.

But now back to our locomotive. We're skipping over many stations to find it at last in the assembly hall, where it's pieced together from its individual parts and ultimately painted. The painting alone takes about eight days. When I entered the hall it was right at lunch break. It was silent. The workers were sitting on the floor unpacking their lunches. It smelled like paint. In front was a large panel, the locomotive's breastplate, if you will. It was open and you could look inside. Between the rails on which it rested was a deep trench, so people could work on the undercarriage. These locomotive stands are built the same way as dry docks, where the objective is easy access to the underside of the ships. Borsig has thirty-nine such locomotive docks. When these locomotives are finished, they are then driven to Serbia by people from Borsig itself. This is true not only for the locomotives, but for most of the large machines that are ordered, whether it be steam turbines, pumps, oil refining equipment or the like. Sending such merchandise to customers is not as easy as sending, say, an armoire; they must be precisely tuned and fitted at the final destination, and then put into operation. This task requires several workers. These are the construction supervisors, whose job often takes them all around the world. It happens that such people stay away for quite a while, as in the case of one Borsig construction supervisor who left for Lahore, India, in 1925 and stayed for two years in order to install a pipeline, manufactured at Borsig, in a power station there. How do I know this? Well, of course no one in such a factory has the time to sit down for hours and tell people all these interesting things, so I had to make do on my own. Since I knew that at Borsig, as at many other very big factories, there's a newspaper for those affiliated with the firm, I read up a bit on the company news. I found not only the entire Lahore story, but also, notably, all the latest technical engineering inventions. There were also articles by workers, advice columns, and sometimes even complaints. And above all, every issue has a directory of people who have suggested improvements for whatever aspect of the company that they were especially familiar with. These suggestions are reviewed by the front office and sometimes remunerated.

Had you accompanied me to Borsig, right at the start you would have seen something that, in closing, I will tell you about now. Standing quite gracefully in the green grass of the front courtyard, on a small red-brick pedestal and looking rather like memorials, are two Borsig products of special significance. One is a machine with a giant flywheel and the other a small steam boiler. They are among the factory's oldest products. The boiler had been at one company for fifty years until Borsig bought it back for a pretty penny to mount it here as a souvenir of sorts. The firm takes great pride in such relics of times past, and if you stop to consider that in seven years Borsig will celebrate its 100th anniversary, you can understand why. For a factory to reach such a great age is as little a result of chance as for a person. Just as a man, in order to become old, must take the long view, not dwell on the little things, and not snack on everything that suits his momentary desire, so must a large company, if it wants to become old, act with great prudence, caution, and thoroughness. I could tell you just as much about the Borsig of years past as I have about the Borsig of today. Like how the little engine factory, which built Germany's first locomotives in 1841, became the huge factory it is now. Perhaps another time, when I tell you about the different neighborhoods of Berlin. Early on, Borsig was not part of Tegel, but rather Moabit, to which the entire history of industrialization in Berlin was closely linked. But the day is over and now I only owe you Alexander von Humboldt, whom I promised you seventeen minutes ago. How can I fit him into the little time we have left? In a nutshell: no doubt as a relief from the heavy and dull machinery he had to take care of day in and day out, the man who founded Borsig set up greenhouses, which were the most famous in Berlin at the time and showcased many foreign and exotic plants.[3] The great naturalist Alexander von Humboldt studied and marveled at these plants. He was also witness, in 1847, to the great festivities celebrating the completion of the 100th locomotive at Borsig. And because the Borsig Works counts finished locomotives the same way people count years, we will also conclude with a locomotive. The 12,000th, to be exact. It was built by Borsig five years ago as a standard locomotive and as the model for all locomotives of the Deutsche Reichsbahn.

"Borsig," GS, 7.1, 111–17. Translated by Jonathan Lutes.

Broadcast on Radio Berlin, April 5, 1930. Benjamin dated the typescript "Berlin Radio, 5 April, 1930." For this date, the Funkstunde *announced "Youth Hour (Berlin), Speaker: Dr. Walter Benjamin" from 3:20–3:40 pm.*

---

3 Johann Friedrich August Borsig (1804–1854) founded the Borsig Works in 1837.

CHAPTER 9

The Rental Barracks

There is no need to explain to you how the subject of today's talk relates to Berlin. And I need not describe the rental barracks to you either, I'm afraid. You're all familiar with them. And most of you know them from the inside as well. And by that, I don't mean just the apartments and rooms, but also the courtyards, the three, four, five, and even six courtyards of tenements in Berlin. Berlin is the biggest tenement city on Earth.[1] Today I will try to explain to you how over the centuries this gradually became our misfortune. Prick up your ears and I'll tell you something you won't often hear in your German lessons, or in geography, or in social studies, but someday it might be important to you. For you should all understand what is at stake in the great battle against the rental barracks, which has been waged by Greater Berlin since 1925.

They always say Berliners are so critical. And it's true. They're quick-witted, not so easily fooled. They're bright. But it must be said that as far as their buildings and apartments are concerned, for centuries they've gotten the short end of the stick. And if in the beginning they might have blamed the authorities, or the king who dictated what and where to build, things didn't improve even a tiny bit when they later governed the city themselves; in fact, they got worse. Perhaps they were so free with their skeptical humor and wit because they all too seldom thought about putting them to practical use. And the worst of it is that even though Berliners are regarded rather critically within the Empire, and their city is hardly

---

1 Here, Benjamin's language echoes the subtitle of Werner Hegemann's *Das steinerne Berlin: Geschichte der größten Mietskasernenstadt der Welt* [Berlin, City of Stone: The Largest Tenement City in the World] (Berlin: Kiepenheuer, 1930), to which he will refer below. For Benjamin on Hegemann's text, see also "Ein Jakobiner von Heute: Zu Werner Hegemanns *Das steinerne Berlin* [A Jacobin of Our Time: On Werner Hegemann's *Berlin, City of Stone*], GS, 3, 260–5, first published in the *Frankfurter Zeitung* on September 14, 1930.

considered the model for much, their rental barracks have been replicated all over Germany.

Rental barracks—that sounds so military.[2] Not only does the word suggest the military, but the rise of the rental barracks is indeed closely tied to the army. Berlin has been a military city since the Hohenzollerns, and there have been times in which the military, that is the soldiers and their families, has constituted one third of Berlin's entire population. When the Prussian army was not yet so large, the soldiers and their families were often lodged in the homes of townspeople. Fourteen days ago I told you about Berlin's building history under Frederick William I.[3] You heard then how every Berliner was obligated to put up a certain number of soldiers, depending on the size of his house or apartment. This was still possible under Frederick William I; although it was very burdensome for the townspeople, the army was still small and so much was being built that there was no real threat of a housing shortage. When Frederick William I died, Berlin's garrison numbered roughly 19,000. But when Frederick the Great died in 1786, there were some 36,000 men stationed in Berlin. It was no longer possible to house this number of troops in the old way, so Frederick the Great built a whole series of barracks, eight alone during the last four years of his reign. The barracks housed not only soldiers, but also their families. To us, it may seem funny for soldiers to live in barracks together with women and children. The reasons for this, however, were anything but funny. Simply put, Prussian military culture was so dreadfully inhumane that many were driven to desert at the first opportunity. If soldiers were allowed to go home to their families every evening, or even a few times a week, perhaps only half would return the next morning, which is why they were kept with their families in barracks and seldom allowed to leave, and then only with special permission.

Frederick the Great went on to impose this housing remedy, barracking, on Berlin's civilian population. Unlike his father, who

---

2 The term Benjamin uses throughout is "Mietskaserne," which can be translated as both "tenement" and "rental barracks." To emphasize the military history and resonance, as does Benjamin, we use "rental barracks" here and in the title.

3 It appears that this is a reference to a radio broadcast that has gone missing. Perhaps it is the same text Benjamin refers to in "Borsig" when he mentions having previously spoken about "the construction history of Berlin" (see "Borsig," 50). Schiller-Lerg has given this reference the provisional title "Baugeschichte Berlins unter Friedrich Wilhelm I" [The Building History of Berlin under Frederick William I] and dates it as having likely been broadcast on Radio Berlin on March 29, 1930 (*Walter Benjamin und der Rundfunk*, 141–3, 530).

enlarged the capital horizontally, he extended it vertically, up into the air. He used Paris as a model, but this was unwarranted. Paris was a fortress; the city could not expand beyond its forts and bastions. And since its 150,000 citizens made it Europe's largest city, the Parisians had no choice but to construct buildings of many stories. Berlin in Frederick the Great's day, however, was even less of a fortress than it is now. Thus, the city could easily have been extended horizontally. When the Emperor of China at that time was shown images of buildings of such unusual height, he said disdainfully: "Europe must be a very small land indeed if the people have so little space on the ground that they must live in the air." For the Berliners' health, of course, the old building scheme would have been better; instead they were crammed with as many people as possible into tenements that were as high as possible. But the economic effects resulting from these constructions were even more dire than the health risks. Since Frederick the Great, people no longer cared to develop and build on new and inexpensive land along the former city limits; rather, building upon already developed lots, they constructed multi-story buildings and rental barracks where once there had been one- and two-story single-family homes. Because these rental barracks, with their many tenants, brought in much more for their owners than the previous smaller houses, the land on which they stood became more and more valuable. Very soon this influenced the prices of undeveloped lots, which could still be found all across the city. When building lots were sold, sellers could demand prices buyers could only afford if they stuck to the rental barrack scheme and built one apartment piled on top of the next to offset the high property prices with more rent.

A description of Berlin from the year of Frederick the Great's death shows how awful things already looked then. But in those days, of course, the ill-effects of this building style were rarely visible, so that Nicolai, a born Berliner and the writer who gave us this description, is filled with pride that almost half of the apartment blocks had handsome side and rear buildings, which in many areas of the city were almost as densely populated as the front ones. There were buildings in which about sixteen families lived. In most cities, 6,500 apartment blocks would likely house no more than 145,000 residents.[4] That makes for an average of twenty-two occupants per

---

4 Here Benjamin paraphrases a citation of the German writer and critic Christoph Friedrich Nicolai's *Beschreibung der königlichen Residenzstädte* [A Description of Royal Capitals] (Berlin 1786) that appears in Hegemann's *Das steinerne Berlin*.

building. In Berlin today, however, we take it for granted that there are apartment buildings that house well over 500 people. One hundred and twenty years after Nicolai's account, an apartment house on Ackerstraße is home to over 1,000 people. It's at number 132. Go and see for yourselves. If you look from the street down the row of courtyards, it's as if you were looking into a tunnel.[5] In Nicolai's time, the industrialization of Berlin was still in its infancy. The real catastrophe would occur much later, when all attempts by Baron vom Stein to help Berliners through Prussian municipal reforms went awry and, in 1858, the horrific Berlin development plan was executed, making way for the rental barracks to dominate.[6] To understand today's Berlin, we must take a look at this development plan, according to which the average rental barracks had three courtyards. Each of these courtyards was required—it sounds completely unimaginable, but it's true—to be just slightly over five square meters in size. Rental barracks were laid out with twenty meters of street front and extended fifty-six meters deep. If such a house occupied the customary seven stories, including the ground floor, up to 650 people could be crammed inside. You have to wonder how such poor and harmful regulations were possible. And really, the rationale was as convoluted and unhealthy as the homes it produced.

The story begins quite harmlessly. The great development plan was intended to resolve Berlin's problems for many decades to come. The plan was drawn up in the police headquarters. Then it turned out that many of the planned streets crossed land held by private owners. The state, which was executing the development scheme, would have needed to reimburse those private owners. That would have cost a lot of money, especially at a time when there was still no law by which property could be seized in the public interest. If the state wanted to build its streets but not spend any money, it had to win over the property owners. Some crafty public officials said to themselves: We need to allow people to develop their properties, so that they can get much more money from renters than if they were

5   Berlin's largest tenement, Meyers Hof, built by textile factory owner Jacques Meyer, was located at Ackerstraße 132/133. Completed in 1875, it had six courtyards and, at its peak, housed 2,000 tenants. It was demolished in 1972.

6   Heinrich Friedrich Karl, Freiherr vom und zum Stein (1757–1831), Prussian government minister and reformer who helped initiate municipal self-government in Berlin. The Hobrecht Plan, initiated in 1858 by the Prussian Interior Ministry and designed by the urban planner James Hobrecht (1825–1902), was finalized in 1862. It created the master framework for urban development in Berlin.

to sell to us, at such a high price, the little plots of land that we need for our streets. This clever idea would bring about the greatest misfortune. And there was worse. As it happened, the scheme was not carried out according to plan. The plan, originally including only the main roads, was to be expanded to open up side streets that would have provided much air and light. But later on, the thinking changed. The money for the new streets was to be saved, leaving these massive building lots packed with giant rental barracks only occasionally intersected by streets.

The worst came twenty years later, in 1871, with the victory over France that marked the beginning of the so-called Founding Years, in which people all over Germany lost their minds and speculated seemingly at random.[7] At that time the Berlin authorities suffered from delusions of grandeur. An enormous building scheme was hatched, that was supposed to last for centuries, and over the years would have incorporated lands with the goal of housing no fewer than 21 million people. The wild fever of speculation, which rattled Berlin in the Founding Years and, as is well known, ended with the Great Crash of 1873, was to a large extent a result of these bloated plans for expansion. All at once, acres of land, which were still producing grain or potatoes, became building plots and in a few months the sandy soil of the Mark Brandenburg was transformed into fields of California gold for its owners. At the beginning of the 1870s, farmers, some of whom had been born into serfdom, became rich overnight, and sometimes millionaires, without the slightest bit of effort or merit. It was then, during the Founding Years, that the expression Millionaire Peasant was coined. Folks everywhere founded companies, purchased and speculated on land, but almost never developed it. For people at that time, nothing was good enough or expensive enough. When something was actually built, two rules held sway: one, that as many apartments as possible were piled under one roof, and two, that the building looked magnificent from the outside. Especially in the outskirts, so-called boulevards were built that ran from one end of the district to the other and then just fizzled out or terminated in a side street. Even the villas erected there were mostly just disguised rental barracks with basement apartments, cramped sleeping quarters, and scaled-back common areas. The vast and pretentious living rooms overlooked the street

---

7 The *Gründerzeit*, or Founding Years, is a broad term used here to refer to the economic boom period from 1871 to 1873.

regardless of whether it ran north, never allowing sunlight to enter the room.

The egoism, shortsightedness and arrogance that gave rise to the rental barracks was the order of the day almost everywhere in Berlin until the World War. If you have a look around the fringes of Berlin, you'll notice that much has changed since then. And not just the elegant western suburbs with their villas, in Dahlem or in Lichterfelde, but also down in Frohnau by the Stettiner railway, or in Püdersdorf, or closer to Berlin in Britz or Tempelhof. Tempelhof is a particularly good example of what has improved in Berlin since the revolution. You need only compare the houses erected from 1912 to 1914 on the old parade ground with those that lie today in the garden city on Tempelhof Field, each with its own patch of green. More telling than standing in front of the houses is looking at photos taken from a bird's eye view, as if you were peering down on the premises. At first you see how grim, severe, gloomy, and military the rental barracks look in comparison to the peaceful houses of the garden plots, which are so amicably juxtaposed with one another. And you understand why Adolf Behne, who has done so much for this new Berlin, calls the rental barracks the last of the castle fortresses.[8] Because, he says, they arose from a few landowners' egotistical, brutal struggle over the land that they would dismember and divide among themselves. And this is why rental barracks have the shape of fortified and warlike castles, with their walled-in courtyards. As the owners are locked together in hostile confrontation, so too are the residents living in the hundreds of apartments that usually make up these city blocks. Have a look at the April edition of *Uhu* magazine and you'll see images of a completely new form of American skyscraper.[9] Long tenement blocks, so to speak, that are either set on their short end so that they project upward, or that lay on their broad side to make long rows of houses. I'm thinking to myself, this must be *Uhu* magazine's idea of an April Fools' joke. But the joke clearly shows how the rental barracks are on the way out: through the abolition of the somber and monumental stone building that has stood still, immovable, and unchanged for centuries.

---

8   Adolf Behne (1885–1948), Weimar architectural critic. See Adolf Behne, *Neues Wohnen, neues Bauen* [New Living, New Building] (Leipzig: Hesse & Becker Verlag, 1927), which includes a chapter entitled "Die Mietskaserne als letzte Ritterburg" [The Rental Barrack as the Last of the Castle Fortresses].

9   See *Uhu* magazine, vol. 6.7 (April 1930), which features two images of a skyscraper, one in which the building is turned horizontally, "like an apartment block" (59).

The stone is replaced by a narrow frame of concrete and steel, the compact and impenetrable façades by giant glass plates, and the four blank walls by deep-set and exposed stairs, platforms and roof gardens. The many people that will live in such buildings will gradually be transformed by them. They will be freer, less anxious, and also less belligerent. This future image of the city will inspire people at least as much as airships, automobiles, and ocean liners do today. And they will be grateful to those who led the struggle for liberation from the old, fortress-like, and gloomy barrack city. An important person for Berlin in this regard is Werner Hegemann, author of the book *Das steinerne Berlin* [*Berlin, City of Stone*], which offers a history of the city that is very much in favor of this new Berlin and from which you and I have learned all that we now know of the rental barracks.

"Die Mietskaserne," GS, 7.1, 117–24. Translated by Jonathan Lutes.

The precise date of broadcast of "The Rental Barracks" has not been determined. It was most likely broadcast in the spring or summer of 1930. Benjamin's reference to the April 1930 issue of Uhu *magazine suggests a date at some point after the April 5, 1930 broadcast of "Borsig." Bracketing it on the other end is the September 14, 1930 publication of Benjamin's discussion of Werner Hegemann's* Das steinerne Berlin *(GS, 3, 260–5), which almost certainly appeared after the broadcast of "The Rental Barracks." Sabine Schiller-Lerg tentatively concludes that the broadcast took place on April 12, 1930 (* Walter Benjamin und der Rundfunk, *112, 142, 532).*

CHAPTER 10

Theodor Hosemann

Are you familiar with this name? Probably not. You can no longer find him in any of your storybooks. But if one day you dig up an old book that belonged to your father or mother, you might discover this name on the title page, where it might say that he drew the pictures in the book. But because he was a very humble man, he didn't always take credit for all the books he illustrated, so it could be that you know some of his pictures without ever having heard his name.

So, Hosemann was a painter. Why do we talk about him during the Berlin Hour? For starters, he wasn't at all a real Berliner; he was born 123 years ago in Brandenburg, on the river Havel.[1] Moreover, is it not a crazy idea to talk about a painter on the radio? It's out of the question, of course, that I stand here and describe Hosemann's pictures to you. But, even without describing any of his pictures, I can just tell you how he came to paint, draw, and make illustrations, and what people thought of his pictures, and how they were received. You'll soon find out what was special about this man, and you'll quickly grasp why I'm talking about him in the Berlin Hour even though he was from Brandenburg.

Hosemann was not coddled during his lifetime, certainly not by Berliners, among whom he lived and for whom he worked. We will soon learn why this was so. He was quite surprised when one day he received a letter from a professor from his hometown. The man was inquiring about his childhood for a book he wanted to write about Hosemann. Now we'll read some of his reply, written five years before his death: "In 1816, from which point on my memory is quite clear," so he was nine years old at the time,

---

1 Theodor Hosemann (1807–1875). Though he died in Berlin, he was born outside the city, in Brandenburg an der Havel.

we landed in Düsseldorf, on the Rhine, in a miserable little tarpaulin-covered fruit boat. Times were tough, the war against Napoleon and all the moving about had bankrupt my parents, and with prices rising my father's monthly wage of sixteen or seventeen thalers was barely enough for even the most essential provisions. Our first apartment in Düsseldorf was a small, whitewashed room under the roof of a lodging house for sailors. Thanks to my youth I was cheerful, in good spirits and couldn't understand why my mother and sister were crying every day. I took comfort in my box of paints and considered myself lucky if I could get hold of a piece of paper somewhere. But our life grew ever harder. I can still see my poor, sick mother and my sister crocheting curtain fringes from early morning till nightfall, and in winter by the light from a tin lamp. I needed to help earn something, so I went down to the color printing house of Arnz & Winckelmann, where soon I would while away entire days, drawing and painting to my heart's content. I was the happiest child in the world when at the end of the week, on top of everything, I could bring home a few pennies to my tender, beloved mother.[2]

How often Hosemann would later depict such a humble, tranquil family, toiling day after day with busy hands to earn a paltry wage. Often there would also be a sick mother or a feverish child lying in bed, because back then publications for young people, which Hosemann illustrated, loved to appeal to children with rather maudlin stories, hoping to influence their behavior for the better. But that was probably misguided. Kids are naturally interested in everything. If you show them the world only from the good and agreeable side, they'll go out of their way to find out themselves about the other side. And even so, no one's ever heard of kids learning naughty tricks from, say, Max and Moritz and trying to plug their teacher's pipe with powder.[3] But now back to Hosemann. When he wrote this letter, he was already a professor and a member of the Academy of the Arts. But what a hard road it was to get there; the boy was barely twelve years old when he had to start earning his

2 For this passage, see "Briefe von Theodor Hosemann" [Hosemann's Letters], in Lothar Brieger, *Theodor Hosemann, ein Altmeister Berliner Malerei: Mit einem Katalog der graphischen Werke des Künstlers von Karl Hobrecker* [Theodor Hosemann, An Old Master of Berlin Painting: With a catalog of the artist's illustrated works compiled by Karl Hobrecker] (Munich: Delphin, 1920), 103–4.

3 Max and Moritz are the title characters of a popular German illustrated children's book by Wilhelm Busch, *Max und Moritz—Eine Bubengeschichte in sieben Streichen* [Max and Moritz: A Story in Seven Pranks] (1865).

keep. That it wasn't just for fun, that he learned a great deal and that he trained himself very ably is made clear by the fact that when he was just fifteen he became the youngest illustrator employed at his firm, earning a yearly wage of 200 thalers.

We should say a bit more about this Winckelmann firm, as it determined Hosemann's entire life. Having survived for almost exactly a half century, it relocated a few years later from Düsseldorf to Berlin and has only just recently disappeared. Like Hosemann himself, the company grew up with lithography. Lithography is the art of creating a drawing with chemical chalk or a pen on a stone plate, so that after the plate is covered with dye, it can be printed. This technique was invented at the end of the eighteenth century, but it took roughly twenty years before it was applied on a larger scale. Especially in France and Germany, this placed illustration on an entirely new footing. When in 1816 the first beautifully illustrated children's book was published—Hey's *One Hundred Fables*, with pictures by Otto Speckter—the idea came to Winckelmann to make such lithographic children's books his main line of business.[4] To enlarge his firm he went to Berlin. He couldn't have found a better employee than Hosemann. And in turn, Hosemann's work, linked as it was to his publisher, firmly established him in Berlin, where his keen observation and attentive study brought him closer to Berlin life than anyone else of his time. Hosemann had no interest in the grand art tours to Paris and Italy that were common among painters in his day. His travels would take him only as far as Antwerp and Tyrol. But his favorite destinations were Charlottenburg and Schöneberg, right here in Berlin, and in the summer he sometimes traveled with his family to Bad Freienwalde, in the surrounding Province of Brandenburg, which he found very elegant and about whose high prices he sometimes bitterly complained.

His art arose entirely from craft. With Hosemann there are neither grand ideas nor a proper artistic development, other than that he always grew more skillful. But the sobriety of his observations, the precision of his drawings, his sense of the comical, even a certain sentimental quality, entwined him so intimately with his closest subject, Berlin, that in the fifty years he lived here, he made

4 Johann Wilhelm Hey's *"Hundert Fabeln" mit den Bildern von Otto Speckter* ["One Hundred Fables" with Illustrations by Otto Speckter] first appeared anonymously in Hamburg in 1833 as *Fünfzig Fabeln* [Fifty Fables]; the complete edition (*Hundert Fabeln*) was first published in 1884.

pictures and drawings that show us life in Berlin from the widest
range of perspectives: Sunday amusements for the petite bourgeoisie, a country outing or a game of skat in a tavern, as well as the
craftsman at work, the chimney sweep, the bricklayer and the
cobbler, the activities of rag pickers, soldiers and servants, dandies,
Sunday riders, musicians. You would think that Berliners, out of
pride, would have seized on a painter who exhibited such love for
their city by documenting it in minute detail. But that wasn't at all
the case. Their sense of superiority would again rear its head.
Berliners found Hosemann's art to be a bit ordinary, inelegant, lacking in refinement. They were at odds with one another over such
aesthetic questions as: Should one paint historical tableaux, great
battles, scenes from the Reichstag and royal coronations? Or
so-called genre paintings, by which they meant contrived, eccentric,
embellished scenes from everyday life, with no kaisers and no military, but featuring monks, salon-goers, pedants, and dandies. It was
in style to paint, for instance, a portly monk raising his wine glass
and grinning as the sun shines through the wine. Or a young lady
reading a love letter, and behind her, the suitor who wrote it peeking
through a crack in the door, surprising her. Berliners back then were
fond of such nonsense, at least the pretentious ones.

But thank goodness there were others as well. The common
people and the children. It was for them that Hosemann worked.
His love for the people, and especially for Berliners, brought him
into contact with the famous Adolf Glassbrenner, who first brought
the people and dialect of Berlin to literature. In 1834 their first
collaborative work was published: a book in the collection *Berlin,
wie es ist und trinkt*.[5] It was the model for a good many similar series
of publications that were sold in paper shops at the time, as illustrated journals are today. However, these booklets, with titles like
"Berlin in Color" or "Humorous Pictures of Soldiers," "Berlin Town
Gossip," or "Strange Court Scenes," were much smaller. You could
easily fit one into your pocket without bending the lovely color
picture on its front, which each of them had. But there was something else about these writings. Perhaps you know what is meant by
the so-called pre-March period. That was the time before the
outbreak of the March Revolution of 1848. Before the Wars of
Liberation, the king of Prussia famously promised universal suffrage

---

5 Adolf Glassbrenner, under the pseudonym Brennglas, wrote *Berlin, wie es ist und
trinkt* [Berlin, As It Is—and Drinks] (Leipzig: Vetter and Rostosky, 1836), a series to which
Hosemann contributed some of the illustrations.

and then later went back on his promise. Instead, there was what is known as the reaction, during which everyone who wrote was closely monitored to ensure that nothing was written that the government did not approve of. How often in history have there been such times when everything printed was strictly controlled and, if it did not conform, banned; and how often have people who refused to back down searched for ways to say what they thought so that everyone understood them but the police could not hold them accountable. Such was the case of Glassbrenner, who said: "We are separated from the great mass of the people by everything, by eccentric habits and education, by money, by our speech, and by our clothes. Unless we join hands with the people and come to an understanding with them, no freedom is possible."[6] Glassbrenner created his famous Berlin characters to show the power of the common man and of his language, how much can be learned from him and, above all, how he cannot be kept forever at bay. Like Nante the Loafer, who represents the Berlin proletariat, and Buffay Bourgeois, typifying the Berlin citizen, who in his way thinks no differently from Nante when it matters most. And indeed, this was the case when a large portion of the Berlin bourgeoisie stood arm in arm with the workers of Berlin in front of the castle in 1848.

Such were the thoughts of this Glassbrenner, Hosemann's collaborator. Hosemann, however, was a rather careful man, even a bit bourgeois. For instance, when in November 1848 he was reporting to a friend on the unrest in Berlin, his letter read: "I write to you now, my dear Schulz, of events as I myself experienced them, but I take the liberty of offering no further judgment as regards them. And I beg you likewise to please refrain from any judgments and other remarks not concerning the facts at hand. We will surely be able to imagine the rest. Understood?"[7] It seems to have been a cowardly time back then in Berlin, and even our Hosemann had to play along a little. But he only needed to make pictures. And in principle he was most certainly at one with his friend Glassbrenner when he depicted, for instance, Nante the Loafer, as the Berliner who stood up for himself and even prevailed when facing an official endowed with significant authority. And now I will conclude, not by describing a picture by Hosemann, but by reading part of a court

6   See Glassbrenner, *Unterm Brennglas: Berliner politische Satire, Revolutionsgeist und menschliche Komödie* [Under Glassbrenner's Magnifying Glass: Berlin Political Satire, Revolutionary Spirit, and Human Comedy], ed. Franz Diederich (Berlin: Paul Singer, 1912), 75.

7   Hosemann, letter dated November 15, 1848, in Brieger, *Theodor Hosemann*, 109–10.

trial against Nante presided over by a court clerk. "Approach the bench," says the clerk. "Great," says Nante, as he approaches, brushing the hair from his face and assuming an imposing stance. "There. Now you can truly appreciate me, Herr Justice."

CLERK: The defendant's name?

NANTE: You.

CLERK: What's that supposed to mean?

NANTE: Well, that's what I say when I'm talking to myself. I wouldn't call myself "Herr Nante."

CLERK: I wish to know the defendant's name. Is it not Nante the Loafer?

NANTE: Yes, I flatter myself with such a name. And don't pretend you don't know me. Who else would I be if not Nante? Nante remains Nante, the one and only.

CLERK: Born?

NANTE: Yep. Born I am. *Je suis.* Pardon me if I sometimes pour a little French into my talking.

CLERK: I'm asking where the defendant was born.

NANTE: I see, *where!* On Horse Street, but as a human. Before I was born I lived at my mother's. After that I moved out and cried, because I grew two legs, and then ate.

CLERK: Eight legs?

NANTE: Ate, I said. With these teeth right here. But it's bad luck that a guy gets teeth and nothing good to bite on.

CLERK: Religion?

NANTE: Religion?

CLERK: What religion are you?

NANTE: I see. I thought I was supposed to repeat after you. Protestant!

CLERK: Have you been under investigation once before?

NANTE: Heaven forbid, no! Twice! Once, when I was out of work, I investigated whether I could live on the wind, and then a little bit later I was under investigation here because I'd borrowed a couple rolls from a baker without telling him about it. Oh, and a third time I was also under investigation here, because I'd found a horseshoe.

CLERK: Investigated for that? Had they gone crazy?

NANTE: Crazy? Heaven forbid. Not as crazy as you . . . would think. I found a horseshoe in the street and when I took a good look at it at home, there was a horse on it. That was some bad luck.

CLERK: Enough, enough.

NANTE: Great. (*He turns around and starts to leave.*)

CLERK: Stop, you are not even close to being finished.

NANTE: I see, I thought you'd had enough of my chatter. Guess not, so much the better! Because I still have a couple stories to tell you. If you like gruesome ones, I'll tell you about something that happened to yours truly along with my wife and three kids. How we were thrown out of our house just because we couldn't pay our three thalers of rent.

CLERK: Very sad, but I don't have time to hear your stories. I can't go on any longer listening to you.

NANTE: Can't go on any longer? I can't go on any longer than I am, either. Whatever I do I'm just as long as nature intended me to be, and no longer. But I'm hungry and I ain't getting served around here. The only thing served around here is justice and I ain't biting. Well, so long, Herr Justice Server.[8]

So now I've just shown you the speaking Nante instead of the drawn version. No matter that at the end of today Hosemann has crept a bit into Glassbrenner's shadow. Because one day we'll talk some more about Glassbrenner and then Hosemann will emerge again from behind him.

"Theodor Hosemann," GS, 7.1, 124–30. Translated by Jonathan Lutes.

Broadcast on Radio Berlin, April 14, 1930. Benjamin dated the type-script "Berlin Radio, 14 April, 1930," and for this date, the Funkstunde *announced "Youth Hour (Berlin), Speaker: Dr. Walter Benjamin," from 5:45–6:10 pm.*

---

8 See *Unsterblicher Volkswitz: Adolf Glaßbrenners Werk in Auswahl* [Immortal Joke-Lore: Selected Works by Adolf Glassbrenner], eds. Klaus Gysi and Kurt Böttcher (Berlin: Das neue Berlin, 1954), vol. 1, 95ff. In this passage, Nante's parts are written in Berlin dialect, whereas the court representative speaks in standard High German.

A Visit to the Brass Works

I can imagine that upon hearing something like "A Visit to the Brass Works" on the radio, a listener might think: "Oh dear, another of those harebrained topics. You have to see something like that, you can't describe it." If that listener did not turn off his radio a few seconds ago, then I beg him to be good enough to give me just a few moments more, because it is precisely to him that I wish to speak.

One thing I would admit to him right away: one can really describe only the smallest part of all that meets the eye there. The writer or poet has yet to be born who is capable of describing a three-high rolling mill or a rolling shear or an extrusion press or a high performance cold rolling mill so that others can imagine them. An engineer could hardly do that. He simply draws the things. But what of the observer? I mean, for instance, what if one of you went into the Hirsch-Kupfer Brass Works near Eberswalde, and walked from one of those machines with the almost unpronounceable names to the next? What would you see? Very simple: just about as much as I can describe here with words. That is: next to nothing. And what would be the point of describing such a machine purely by its appearance? It is not made to be looked at, unless perhaps by someone who has first grasped its structure, its functional performance, its purpose and because of that knows what he should pay the most attention to as he observes it. One can only correctly comprehend something from the outside if one knows it on the inside; that is true for machines just as it is for living things.

But of course, you cannot get to know a machine from the inside, even if you are directly in front of it. Let's assume you are standing in one of the giant halls: it would be fascinating to see how the mixture that is melted to brass is poured into the ovens, how the brass plate comes out of the ovens, how the fat, short metal plates go into the rolling mill and come out the other end all thin and long, how the short, round cylindrical rods get pushed automatically into the pressing mill and appear again as long, delicate, narrow tubes. You would see all of that. But you would not see how it was done, and what with the deafening racket of the machines at work, the rolling cranes, the dropping of loads, no one could explain it to you either.

Thus one can say that the closer one wants to get to what is going on in such an immense plant—should one witness such an operation some day—and the more one longs to understand a little bit of it, the further one has to distance oneself from it. And we should think of our few minutes here on the radio as if they were the gondola of a tethered balloon from which we can see into the whole operation down there in the Hirsch-Kupfer Brass Works, and can single out the points that must first be grasped in order to master the whole. Even then it will be difficult enough for us. For are there not many such crucial points? First we have the whole science, everything that physics and chemistry can tell us about brass. What is brass? What is its melting point? What is its hardness grade? How does it expand when it is warmed? What is its specific weight? And so on. Not one of these questions would be unimportant to the technical operations in a brass works. Or we could approach it from a completely different angle: What does such a plant have to produce in order to sell its products well? What is produced there? We'll hear later, for example, that it's none of the brass objects we normally handle. None of the things that were made there 200 years ago, when the Brass Works was founded by the Great Elector. Neither kettles nor ornamental coverings, neither candlesticks nor cutlery. All of these are made by specialized factories, and it is precisely to these specialized factories that the Hirsch-Kupfer Brass Works delivers its material. That means that it is here that the semi-finished products are made: metal plates and bands, rods, bars, wires of all sorts of different lengths, qualities, and sizes that are then further processed in other metalware factories or electro-technical businesses.

Or another point: How did such an enormous business, employing about 2,000 workers and 400 administrators, emerge? Naturally not from one day to the next. And this Hirsch-Kupfer Brass Works, the biggest of its kind in Europe, is also one of the oldest businesses. It dates back to the year 1697. It would be another story in itself to tell how it came about. But the only thing that matters to me now is that, as you contemplate the innumerable parts, conditions, and difficulties of such an enormous factory, you have your breath taken away exactly as if you had unexpectedly stepped into one of its roaring halls. So there are ever more such points that one has to keep in mind in order to even begin to understand the whole. For example, the power industry. Where does the mighty power, harnessed to the metal works day and night, come from? It comes from the Mark Brandenburg's electric power plant, which lies only a kilometer away from the Brass Works. The electricity alone costs the Brass Works approximately 100,000 marks a month. Naturally, such huge customers pay the electric power plant at a special rate. There, too, every detail is given the sharpest consideration, and is subject to the most exact accounting. For such an operation must make sure to have as constant a power consumption as possible, day in, day out, even at any given hour, because the power plant will demand more payment the more irregular the use of power.

I could go on this way for quite a while, explaining one point after another, and still it would be only the most important and necessary ones. We haven't said a word about the workers yet, about their training, or the complicated calculation of their wages. We also still haven't said a word about the calculations, the responsibilities of the management, who not only have to organize the work procedure but also have to simultaneously keep an eye on the world markets, who have to see to it that they don't buy at too high a price and that they always get enough orders to keep the plant running at full capacity, who have to ensure that the stock is never too great, because that costs interest, and never too small, so that the most urgent orders can be filled quickly.

If you now know how infinitely much there would be to say, to ask about all of this, and if you remember that we only have twenty minutes for our conversation, then you will see that there is no point running ahead in our seven-league boots, and that we should rather take our time at a few, individual stations. I suggest we start with the hall where the casting is done. What is brass? Brass is an alloy of copper and zinc. Some of you will surely know the difference between a compound and an alloy. Two elements must always form a chemical compound in a specific manner according to their atomic weights. You learn about it in school as Dalton's Law. They can be alloyed physically by smelting them in very different proportions. The average proportion of copper and zinc in brass is sixty-three parts copper to thirty-seven zinc for the plates, and fifty-eight to forty-two for the rods. So there are different kinds of brass, and very different kinds are cast in the individual ovens, of which there are twenty-three in all. Which kind depends on the orders that have been received at the time. But it is not as if copper and zinc are simply weighed out in specific proportions and then poured into the ovens. If one were to proceed like that, a very poor, irregular brass would be the result. Zinc melts at about 600° C and copper only at about 1100° C. The solid bits of copper would swim around for a long time in the liquid zinc and would then, when they finally began to melt, dissolve only very irregularly in it. Therefore a balancing, as it were, mediating mass is added, namely old brass waste. It melts at about 900° C, and thus makes the melting process constant. Not very long ago, such a casting could not be heavier than thirty kilograms. However, in the new ovens that the Brass Works put into operation in 1920, blocks of up to 600 kilograms can be produced. When the casting is done, the receptacles—they are called coquilles—that contain the blocks open, like a book, and one can see the brass inside. It is not, however, yellow and shiny but unsightly; there is a black, pitted skin from the casting process covering it, and that first needs to be scraped off. Then each block gets marked with its own special symbol, indicating what combination of metals the brass has and from which oven it came. Before it can be further processed, the casting is tested in the laboratory, not only for its purity but for its strength, ductility, hardness, elasticity, et cetera. For all these tests, there are special devices, among them a so-called tensile testing machine, which utilizes its 40,000 kilogram weight to test the plates or tubes. It is only in the laboratory that one can see how different the interiors of the individual kinds of brass look, because each of them presents a different image under the microscope depending on whether it was cast, or hard-rolled, or heated after its rolling.

Now the brass is there. But the immense work process is only just beginning. The massive blocks, the heavy cylinders that come from the foundry must be transformed into millimeter-thin sheets, fine-as-a-hair threads, narrow bands. These manufactured products, which are very long, naturally demand to be processed in much bigger rooms than the products of normal mechanical workshops. Years ago, the situation was remedied by building one factory hall next to the other when needed. But during the course of the war, the Brass Works started enlarging and transforming its entire operation, and it was clear from the start that the entire rolling process had to be housed in a single, great hall. And in the year 1920, the 215-meter-long rolling-mill hall was inaugurated. The history of its construction was a long chain of difficulties. Wherever the ground was probed for its suitability to support such a big building and the enormous load created by the machines, groundwater was discovered, and in the end, nothing could be done except anchor all the iron posts and all the machines' bases in deep, extra-thickly sealed concrete troughs. Thus every single press, every single rolling mill had to have its own, very exact, unchangeable spot in the blueprints even before the hall was built. In addition, because no above ground electric lines could be tolerated due to the danger they posed to operations, a blueprint for the distribution of electric cables had to be worked out from the start. A blueprint for the distribution of electric cables at the same site, and for the same Brass Works, where 150 years earlier the operations had been powered by charcoal made by charcoal burners in the kilns around Eberswalde.

If we now enter the rolling-mill hall, we must take our leave of the beautiful, bright flames of the smelting furnaces and the golden mountains of brass waste. It gets grayer and more monotonous. All the more strange and lively, therefore, is what we see disappearing into the machines and then gliding out of the machines, transformed. There are the hydraulic presses, which seize hold of a short, massive brass cylinder with a pressure of more than 1,000 metric tons and then release a bundle of glowing tubes, as soft as an animal's viscera, at the other end. Outside, at the mouth, workers stand already waiting for them with tongs, and stretch them the entire length of a ten- to fifteen-meter-long trough like a canal. After that, they are put in a corrosive bath in which they are cleaned; and here at these corrosion machines, as in a few other places, one can still see the old manual operation next to the new automatic one and make comparisons. Some of you have heard talk of rationalization. This is the technical escalation of the work process, which is thereby made cheaper through savings in the workforce and work time. The bigger and more modern a workplace is, the better it can be used to gauge what rationalization means. In the Brass Works there are now thirty ovens, or muffle furnaces as they are called, to reheat the metal that has cooled in the rollers, and two workers are needed to service these thirty ovens, whereas in the old factory no less than twenty-eight were employed for fifteen ovens. These muffle furnaces are necessary because the rods and plates get very hard in the rolling process and, to soften them up again, they need to be constantly reheated so that they can continue to be formed. Perhaps you can get an idea of the rollers, which are staggered in three rows behind one another, when I tell you that just one of them cost 500,000 marks and that it took eight weeks to set it up.

If you ever have the opportunity to see this Brass Works or a similar gigantic enterprise, then you must first have a good night's sleep, keep your eyes open, and, especially, have no fear. That is necessary because otherwise you would stumble over the tracks and workpieces that cover the floor of the hall; you would have no eye for the work and instead would constantly look up in case one of the ton blocks, which are being swung through the air by cranes, was about to fall on your head; you would see only an impenetrable linkage, a network that seems to flicker, and not the clear, sharp division of the hall, where every worker has his specific place and every machine has, in a way, its own small office, from which the manager, with his eye on the automatic electricity, pressure, and temperature gauges, directs it. But if you then step outside, your head spinning from so much noise, so many great impressions, some understood and some not, and think that now you are in open nature, which has nothing to do with the labor and the racket going on inside, then the factory guide, who hopefully will explain everything to you as clearly and in as much detail as he did to me, will tell you that a large part of this countryside depends on the fate of the factory. Because this fate is closely tied to transportation. The Brass Works could not have become what it is without the now aging Finow Canal and without the new, modern Hohenzollern Canal, on which freight barges bring its raw materials, copper from Chile and Africa and brass waste from German factories, and export its products to India, China, Australia, et cetera, via Hamburg. The land between the Brass Works and the Hohenzollern Canal is still open. Yet, because nowadays industries spread out in ten years as much as they used to in a hundred, it is possible that later one of you, when he enters the Brass Works as a visitor, a worker, or an engineer, will step into new halls and factories that are mirrored in the water of the Hohenzollern Canal.

"Besuch im Messingwerk," GS, 7.1, 131–7. Translated by Lisa Harries Schumann.

Broadcast on Radio Berlin, early July 1930, most likely on July 12, 1930. Benjamin dated the typescript, "Radio Berlin, 11 July, 1930." The Funkstunde *announced what was probably a related broadcast for July 1, 1930, and for the Youth Hour on July 12, 1930: "'A Walk through a Brass Works [Gang durch ein Messingwerk].' Speaker: Dr. Walter Benjamin," from 3:20–3:45 pm.*

CHAPTER 12

Fontane's *Wanderings through the Mark Brandenburg*[1]

Some of you may know this, but many will be astounded when I tell you: the beauty of the Mark Brandenburg was discovered by the youth of Berlin.[2] By their vanguard, the *Wandervogel*.[3] The *Wandervogel* movement is now about twenty-five years old, and it's been just as long since Berliners ceased being ashamed of "The Good Lord's Sandbox," as the Mark is commonly known. And still it took some time before they really started to love it. For in order to love it, you have to know it. In the last century, however, that was something quite rare. Earlier on, only craftsmen and the more well-to-do hiked in the Alps. It occurred to very few people to do so in Germany, and especially in the Mark, until just around 1900 when this great, important movement began among students in Berlin: the *Wandervogel*. They had had enough, not only of the city, but also of the ritualistic Sunday stroll with their parents; they wanted something more than the same, over-grazed patches of the city; they wanted something new, to walk free in the open air among themselves. They didn't have money so they couldn't stray far, and they only had Sundays off. If they really wanted to make use of the short time they had, they needed to find places where they were safe from Berlin's petite bourgeoisie. Areas without train access or hotels. You know how many such hidden locations still exist today in the Mark, despite the ever-tightening web of light railways across the

---

1 This title was provided by the editors of the GS. Benjamin's typescript does not have a title.

2 The Mark Brandenburg is a German state surrounding Berlin. It is sometimes translated as the March or Margraviate of Brandenburg, from Markgrafschaft Brandenburg.

3 The *Wandervogel* ("wandering bird") was a popular German youth movement started at the turn of the century. It promoted excursions in nature as a salutary, community-building alternative to urban life.

countryside. But *before* the train and *before* the students, individual
poets and painters always loved the Mark. Caspar David Friedrich
and Blechen were two famous Brandenburg painters from the last
century.[4] Among the poets, however, none has done more for this
landscape than the Berliner Theodor Fontane, who published his
Wanderings through the Mark Brandenburg in 1870.[5] Far more than
tedious descriptions of landscapes and castles, these books are full of
stories, anecdotes, old documents, and portraits of fascinating
people. Let's hear from Fontane himself how he felt about these
wanderings, and how he got to know the Mark so well.

"Only foreign lands teach us what we have at home." I learned this
first-hand, and my first inspirations for these "Wanderings through
the Mark Brandenburg" came to me on excursions in a foreign land.
The inspirations became desire, the desire became resolve. It was in the
Scottish county of Kinross, whose prettiest point is Loch Leven. In the
middle of the loch lies an island, and on the middle of the island, half
hidden behind ash trees and black firs, rises an old Douglas castle, the
Loch Leven Castle of song and legend. On returning to land by boat,
the oars rapidly engaged, the island became a strip, finally disappearing
altogether, and for a while, only as a figure of the mind, the round
tower remained before us upon the water, until suddenly our imagination receded further into its memories and older images eclipsed the
images of this hour. They were memories of our native land, an unforgotten day. It was the image of Rheinsberg Castle that, like a Fata
Morgana, hovered over Loch Leven, and before our boat reached the
sand of the shore, a question posed itself: beautiful was this image that
Loch Leven and its Douglas castle unfurled before you. And that day
when you journeyed in your flatboat across Lake Rheinsberg, was it
actually less beautiful than the imaginings and memories of a splendid
time that engulfed you here? And I answered: no. The years gone by
since that day on Loch Leven have returned me to my native land, and
the resolutions from that time remain unforgotten. I traversed the
Mark and found it richer than I dared hope. Each footbreadth of earth
came alive, taking on shapes, and if my descriptions do not satisfy, I
must forgo an apology that it was meager surroundings that I was
forced to ameliorate or embellish. To the contrary, I was confronted

---

4   Caspar David Friedrich (1774–1840), German Romantic painter known for his
desolate, haunted landscapes; Carl Blechen (1798–1840), German landscape painter.

5   Fontane's *Wanderungen durch die Mark Brandenburg* was originally published in five
volumes from 1862 to 1889.

with abundance, leaving me with the certain feeling of never being able to take it all in. And free of care, I gathered it in, not as someone approaches the harvest with sickle in hand, but rather as a rambler, plucking individual ears from the affluent fields.[6]

So goes Fontane's preface. Now we will see how he describes a small village in the Mark, about which there seems nothing particularly noteworthy. But one can't describe something one only sees and knows nothing about. It is not always necessary to know what the experts know. A painter who is painting an apple tree, for example, does not need to know what kind of apples grow on it. He only knows how the light falls through the various types of leaves. How it changes its appearance at different times in the day. How strongly or gently the shadows fall on the grass, stones, or soil. But while it can be seen, it can only truly be seen with experience, with repeated viewings, and with comprehension. So it is with Fontane. There aren't many lyrical descriptions of nature, and no moonlight rhapsodies, no fancy speeches on the solitude of the forest and other such things you sometimes struggle with at school. Fontane simply wrote what he knew, and that was a lot; not only about kings and castle owners, fields and lakes, but also about simple people: how they live, what they care about, and what sorts of plans they have. Most of you are familiar with Caputh, so you can easily judge for yourselves the description I'll read to you now.

Caputh is one of the largest villages in the Mark, and certainly one of the longest; it easily measures a half-mile. Its name points to the fact that it's Wendish. There are too many theories as to what the name actually means for any to have much merit. As certain as the meaning of the name is uncertain was the poverty of its residents in the old days. Caputh has no fields, and the large expanse of water at its doorstep, the river Havel, along with Lake Schwielow, was jealously guarded and exploited by the local Potsdam fishermen, whose time-honored dominion stretched over the entire middle Havel until Brandenburg. So, things were bad for the people of Caputh; farming and fishing were equally unavailable. But necessity being the mother of invention, ultimately the people of this narrow strip of coastline

---

6 Fontane, *Wanderungen,* eds. Gotthard Erler and Rudolf Mingau, Part 1: "Die Grafschaft Ruppin" [County Ruppin] (Berlin: Aufbau, 1976), 1–3. For this passage, as well as for the subsequent references to Fontane, Benjamin's typescript does not provide full quotations. We follow the editors of the GS, who provided the passages based on Benjamin's notations.

found a way to survive. They devised a two-pronged scheme to make ends meet; men and women divided to attack the problem from two sides. The men became *boatmen* while the women took up *gardening*.

Proximity to Potsdam, and above all the rapid growth of Berlin, favored the Caputher's transformation from day laborer into boatman or boat-builder, perhaps even evoked it. Brickworks sprung up all along the Havel and Schwielow, and the millions of bricks baked year in and year out on the shores of these lakes and their inlets required hundreds of boats to ferry them to the Berlin market. For this the Caputhers lent a hand. An entire fleet arose, and at this very moment more than sixty vessels, all built at village wharves, are plying Schwielow, the Havel, and the Spree. The usual destination, as already implied, is the capital. A fraction, however, also sails down the Havel to the Elbe and ultimately does business in Hamburg.

However, Caputh—the Chicago of Lake Schwielow—is not merely the great trade emporium of this region, not merely a point of arrival and departure for the Zauche-Havelland brick districts, no, it is also a port that all Havel traffic must pass through. The detour through Schwielow is unavoidable; for the time being there is only this *one* navigable strait. A shortened route through the North Canal has been planned but not yet carried out. And so, Caputh, home to a fleet of boats made from its own resources, would fare perfectly well on its own if it ever *needed* to. At the same time it has become an all-around maritime and trading center, a harbor for ships from other regions, and, were disaster to strike or hurricanes to loom, the flotillas of Rathenow, Plaue, and Brandenburg could descend and drop anchor here. But the strait through Caputh is most exciting when there's some big festival and custom dictates closing it to traffic. Pentecost is a particular highlight, when everything converges here; on either side of the strait lie a hundred ships or more, banners waving, and high atop the masts, a delightful sight: one hundred May bushes saluting the horizon.

This is the grand side of Caputh life, but there's also a small side. The men possess the recklessness of the seafarer; their money acquired over months of work is spent in just a few hours, when it then falls to the women to bring the accounts into order through their industriousness and the earnings brought by their *small* labors.

As we already mentioned, they are gardeners; nurturing the soil requires meticulous care, and individual crops are so skillfully cultivated that the Caputhers can even compete with their neighbors in

Werder. Chief among their crops is the strawberry, which also reaps benefits from the close proximity of the two capitals: there are small-scale gardeners who in three to four weeks, with a half-acre garden plot, take in 120 thalers for their pineapple-strawberries. However, these ventures remain small-scale, and even here in Caputh it is apparent that the more sophisticated crops don't add up to much and that fifty acres of wheat is still the best and easiest option.[7]

It's always nice when what's in a book is not just what the title promises, but all sorts of wonderful things you never would have imagined when you picked it up. Such is the case with these *Wanderings*. Not only does Fontane talk about the Mark and its inhabitants in his day, he also tries to imagine what it looked like in earlier times. He is especially intent on discovering the peculiarities and quirks of the former inhabitants of the Mark. Among the strangest stories he happened upon concern the conspiracies circulating in this region before 1800, especially among the Potsdam aristocracy. These plots and secret alliances were not so much about people as about nature, from which they hoped to wrest the secret of gold. If you could synthesize gold, so people thought, you would know all of nature's secrets. In those days only very fanciful people believed it was possible to make gold. Today, even great scholars no longer hold it to be impossible. But people no longer pride themselves on having nature in their grasp. We are continually working on an infinite number of technical problems whose solutions would be much more significant in a practical sense than making gold. In those days no one ever dared dream of such things as power generation, transportation systems, radio photography,[8] the manufacture of synthetic medications, and so on, which is why people were so interested in making gold. Potsdam was home to several societies intent on the pursuit of the "philosopher's stone," the name for the magic that would materialize gold and whose possessor would become not only rich, but also wise and all-powerful.

Fontane tells us of one such society. From a letter found in an old book we learn of an order in whose ceremonies the harmonica plays an important role. The letter, from a harmonica virtuoso, reads as follows:

The address you gave me has provided me with a very interesting

---

7 Ibid., Part 3: "Havelland. Die Landschaft um Spandau, Potsdam, Brandenburg" [Havelland: The Region around Spandau, Potsdam, Brandenburg], 1977, 437–9.

8 Radio photography (*Bildfunk*) was a term used for an early form of television. It could be translated more broadly as the transmission of images.

acquaintance in Herr N.....The harmonica meets with his utmost approval; and he speaks as well of *various special attempts*, which at first I did not properly grasp. Only yesterday did things become clear to me: —Yesterday evening we drove to his country estate, which leaves an extraordinarily handsome impression, especially the garden. Various temples, grottoes, waterfalls, labyrinthine pathways, and underground vaults, etc., treat the eye to such manifold diversity that the observer is left transfixed. Only the height of the all-encompassing wall would I do without; it robs the eye of a terrific view. —I had the harmonica and had to promise Herr N. that I would play it, on his cue, for just a few moments at a specific location. While waiting for this moment, he led me into a large room in the front part of the house and left me there, explaining that his presence was required to arrange the details and lighting for a ball. It was already late and just as sleep was upon me, I was roused by the arrival of several carriages. I opened the window but saw nothing conspicuous, understanding even less of the soft and mysterious whispering of the arriving guests. Shortly afterwards I once again succumbed to my weariness and fell sound asleep. I must have slept for an hour when I was awoken by a servant, who at once offered to carry my instrument and beseeched me to follow him. Because he was moving at a hurried pace, I could only follow at some distance, which allowed me the opportunity to indulge my curiosity and pursue the muffled sounds of several trombones that seemed to be coming from the depths of the cellar.

Imagine my astonishment when, halfway down the cellar steps, I spied a crypt in which, amid funeral music, a corpse was being laid into a coffin and a man, dressed in white but spattered all over with blood, was having the veins in his arm bandaged. But for the assistants, everyone was cloaked in black robes with unsheathed swords. At the entrance lay a heap of skeletons and the crypt was lit by torches whose flames appeared to emanate from burning wine-spirits, making the spectacle all the more gruesome. I hurried back so as not to lose my guide, who was just coming in from the garden as I arrived at the very same door. Impatiently, he grabbed me by the hand and dragged me away with him.

Entering the garden was like something from a fairy tale: everything lit by green fire; countless flaming lamps; the murmuring of distant waterfalls. Nightingales singing, the scent of blossoms, in short, everything seemed supernatural, as if nature had given way to magic. I was assigned my spot behind a garden house with a lavishly adorned interior. Moments later an unconscious man was carried in, presumably the same fellow who had had his veins opened in the crypt. But I don't know for sure because now the color and cut of everyone's garments were refined and glamorous, so they were all new to me. Then and there I received the sign to begin playing.

As I now needed to focus more on myself than on the others, I must admit that I missed a lot. This much I'm certain is true: the unconscious man revived after hardly a minute of my playing and asked in amazement: "Where am I? Whose voice am I hearing?"

Exultant cheering and trumpets and kettledrums were the reply. All at once everyone reached for their swords and hurried deeper into the garden where whatever happened subsequently was lost to me.

I am writing this to you now after a short and fitful rest. Only yesterday, before I went to bed, I certainly would not have recorded this scene in my journal, as I would have been more inclined to think it all a dream. Farewell.[9]

Let us hasten to return from this uncanny nocturnal rite to the light of day. We will now hear something of the inspection conducted by Frederick the Great in the vicinity of Rathenow on July 23, 1779, around the same time this ghost story takes place. The setting was the Dosse floodplain, which after years of work was finally drained. 1,500 settlers were moved there and twenty-five new villages were established. We have the precise transcript of how the king made the head magistrate, Fromme was his name, follow along beside his carriage for hours as he delivered his full report. You can see how sometimes it must not have been all that much fun to answer him.

The carriage was readied and the journey continued. Just as we passed the canals dug in the Fehrbellin marsh at His Majesty's expense, I rode up to the carriage and said: "Your Majesty, here are two new canals, realized with Your Majesty's grace, that are keeping the marsh dry for us."

KING: Tell me, has canalizing the marsh helped you much here?
FROMME: Oh yes, Your Majesty!
KING: Are you rearing more cattle than your ancestors?
FROMME: Indeed, Your Majesty! On this estate I keep forty, on all estates another seventy cows more!

9 Fontane, *Wanderungen*, Part 3, 335–7.

KING: That's good. But there's no cattle plague here in this area?

FROMME: No, Your Majesty.

KING: Have you had the cattle plague here before?

FROMME: Oh, yes!

KING: Just use plenty of rock salt and you won't have the cattle plague again.

FROMME: Yes, Your Majesty, I use that, too; but table salt works almost as well.

KING: I don't believe that! You mustn't grind the rock salt, but hang it up so the cattle can lick it.

FROMME: Certainly, it shall be done!

KING: Are there other improvements to make here?

FROMME: Oh yes, Your Majesty. Right here are the Kremmen lakes. If they were canalized, Your Majesty would gain 1,800 acres of meadow where colonists could be settled, and this entire region would become navigable, which would help the town of Fehrbellin and the city of Ruppin tremendously; and many things could come from Mecklenburg to Berlin via water.

KING: That I believe! Indeed, such a thing would help you considerably, and spell ruin for many, certainly for the local landlords, would it not?

FROMME: With all due respect, Your Majesty, the lands belong to the royal forest, where there are only birch trees.

KING: Oh, if there's nothing more than birchwood, then it should be done! However, you mustn't make such plans without first checking with the landlord that the costs do not exceed the benefits.

FROMME: The costs will most definitely not exceed the benefits! Firstly, Your Majesty is certain to gain 1,800 acres from the lake; that would be thirty-six colonists, each with fifty acres. Then add a small, reasonable tariff on the lumber and on the ships passing through the canal and the capital will yield good interest.

KING: Well! Take it up with my privy councilor Michaelis! The man will understand and I should advise you to turn to him on all matters, including when you know where to put the colonists. I don't demand entire colonies right away; but if there are just two or three families, you can always arrange it with him!

FROMME: It shall be done, Your Majesty.[10]

---

10   Ibid., Part 1, 430ff.

Whoever has heard this conversation will also have a picture of the landscape unfurling like a gleaming, freshly laundered tablecloth. There is something extraordinarily broad and expansive in the landscape of the Mark, which comes across vividly in its endless succession of villages and settlements. Its sandy, marly soil does not lend itself to strong shapes; however, one is occasionally surprised to come across a steep precipice, or a gorge ripped into the earth. But the plain of the Mark, with its birch forests and vast acres of fields stretching to the horizon like a broad sea of gray and green, is the landscape's most beautiful feature. It is so shy, subtle, and unobtrusive that sometimes, at sundown, on the water amid pillars of pine, you think you're in Japan, and other times, in the limestone hills of Rüdersdorf, you imagine yourself in the desert, until the names of the villages here call you back to reality. Fontane strung some of these names together in a few light and airy lines, which we close with today.

> And on this tapestry's flourishing seam
> the laughing villages prosper and teem:
> Linow, Lindow,
> Rhinow, Glindow,
> Beetz and Gatow,
> Dreetz and Flatow,
> Bamme, Damme, Kriele, Krielow,
> Petzow, Retzow, Ferch am Schwielow,
> Zachow, Wachow and Groß Behnitz,
> Marquardt-Uetz at Wublitz-Schlänitz,
> Senzke, Lentzke, and Marzahne,
> Lietzow, Tietzow, and Reckahne,
> And lastly a garland of lively haunts:
> Ketzin, Ketzür, and Vehlefanz.[11]

"Fontanes 'Wanderungen durch die Mark Brandenburg,'" GS, 7.1, 137–45. Translated by Jonathan Lutes.

The exact date of broadcast is unknown, but the text appears to belong to Benjamin's broadcasts for Radio Berlin's children and youth programming on the Berlin Hour, and was most likely produced in 1929 or 1930.

---

11 Ibid., Part 3, 8.

CHAPTER 13

Witch Trials

The first time you heard about witches was in "Hansel and Gretel." What did you take away from it? An evil and dangerous woman who lives a solitary and purposeless life in the forest and from whom you'd better steer clear. You certainly didn't rack your brains about her being in league with the devil or with God, or about where she comes from, or what she does and doesn't do. For centuries people thought exactly as you do about witches. Most people back then believed in witches just like little children today believe in fairy tales. But in the same way that few children, no matter how small, live their lives as if they were fairy tales, people in those centuries thought just as little about incorporating their belief in witches into their daily lives. They were content with simple tokens for protection: a horseshoe above the door, a picture of a saint or, at most, a charm worn under their shirt.

So it was in ancient days, and when Christianity arrived things didn't change all that much, at least not for the worse, because Christianity was opposed to believing in the power of evil. Christ had defeated the devil, he had descended into hell and his followers had nothing to fear from evil powers. At least that was the old Christian belief. People back then certainly knew of disreputable women, but these were mostly priestesses and pagan goddesses and their magical powers were seldom taken seriously. Instead they were to be pitied, because the devil had fooled them into believing that they possessed supernatural powers. Over the course of a few decades, roughly around the year 1300 A.D., all of this completely yet imperceptibly changed. And no one can explain to you with any certainty how. But there is no doubt that it did indeed change: after belief in witches had coexisted alongside all other superstitions for centuries, while causing no less but no more harm than the others, around the middle of the fourteenth century people began seeing

witches and sorcery left and right and soon enough they were carrying out witch-hunts everywhere. All of a sudden there was a formal
doctrine on the doings of witches. Suddenly everyone wanted to
know exactly what they did in their gatherings, what sort of witchcraft they were practicing, and whom they were out to get. As
mentioned before, we'll probably never fully understand how it all
came about. But the little we do know is all the more astounding.

Nowadays superstition is mostly found among the simpler folk,
where it takes root most firmly. The history of believing in witches
shows us, however, that this was not always the case. The fourteenth
century, when this belief displayed its most rigid and threatening
face, was a time of great scientific progress. The Crusades had begun,
which brought to Europe the latest scientific theories, above all
those concerning the natural sciences, a realm in which Arabia was
far ahead of other countries. Improbable as it sounds, these new
natural sciences strongly promoted the belief in witchcraft, and
here's how: in the Middle Ages the purely speculative and descrip-
tive natural sciences, which we now call theoretical science, were not
yet distinct from applied sciences, such as technology. For their part,
applied sciences in those days were the same as, or at least very
closely associated with, magic. People knew very little about nature.
Investigating and using its secret forces was considered sorcery. But
sorcery was permitted, if it were not put to evil purposes; to differ-
entiate from the Black Arts, it was simply called the White, or
White Magic. Thus new discoveries about nature contributed
directly, or in a roundabout way, to beliefs in sorcery, the influence of
the stars, the art of making gold, and other such notions. However,
alongside the proliferation and popularity of White Magic came
interest in the Black.

But the study of nature was not alone among the sciences encouraging the terrifying belief in witchcraft. Belief in and the practice of
Black Magic gave rise to a great number of questions for the philosophers of the time—who were all clergymen in those days—questions
we no longer understand so easily today; and if we do grasp them, it
makes our hair stand on end. People wanted to distinguish, in no
uncertain terms, the sorcery practiced by witches from other forms of
evil magic. It had long been understood that all evil sorcerers were
heretics, that is, they did not believe in God, or did so in the wrong
way; the popes had often preached exactly that. But now people
wanted to know how to distinguish witches and warlocks from other
practitioners of the Black Arts. To this end scholars deliberated at

length, which would perhaps have been more absurd and curious than horrific if, 100 years later, when the witch trials had reached their high point, two men had not, in all seriousness, taken these vagaries and compiled them, compared them, and drawn conclusions from them, formulating meticulous instructions for determining precisely which acts of sorcery would be incriminated. This book is the so-called *Witches' Hammer*;[1] I dare say that nothing else ever printed has brought more harm to people than these three thick volumes. So, according to these scholars, how could witches be identified? Above all, they had made a formal pact with the devil. They had renounced God and promised the devil to do his bidding. In exchange the devil promised them all things good—for their earthly life, of course—but since he is the father of lies, he almost never kept this promise, at least not in the end. There was an interminable list of witches' deeds accomplished by the power of the devil, with explanations of how they were done and the practices they were forced to observe. Those of you who have seen the Witches' Dance Floor and Walpurgis Hall near Thale, or have held a volume of Harz legends in your hands, will know a bit about it. But I won't tell you now about Blocksberg, where witches allegedly assembled every May 1, or about riding on broomsticks from chimney to chimney.[2] Instead I want to tell you a few strange things you've maybe not read about, even in your books of legends. Strange for us, that is.

Three hundred years ago it went without saying that if a witch walked into a field and raised her hand to the sky, hailstones would shower down on the crops. With a glance she could bewitch a cow, so that blood instead of milk would come from her udder. She could bore into a willow tree in such a way that milk or wine would flow from its bark. She could transform herself into a cat, a wolf, or a raven. Once suspected of witchcraft, people could go about their lives as they wished, but there was nothing they could do that wouldn't strengthen the suspicion they were under. So, at home or in the fields, in word or deed, at church or at play, there was nothing back then that malicious or stupid or crazy people couldn't somehow link to witchcraft. And still today certain terms remind us of how the most innocent and naturally occurring things were associated with this belief: witches' butter (frogspawn), witches' ring (the circular

---

1 The *Hexenhammer*, or *Malleus Maleficarum*, by Heinrich Kramer and James Sprenger, first published, as Benjamin mentions below, in 1487.

2 The Witches' Dance Floor [*Hexenplatz*], the Walpurgis Hall, and Blocksberg, situated in the Harz mountains, are legendary sites associated with witchcraft.

formation of mushrooms), witches' mushroom, witchweed, and so on. But if you would like to read a very short summary, a sort of guide to the life of witches, ask for the play *Macbeth* by Shakespeare. There you will also see how people thought of the devil as a severe master, to whom every witch had to answer, and in whose honor they committed their evil tricks and misdeeds. Even the simplest of men knew as much about witches as you will after reading *Macbeth*, while philosophers knew a good deal more. They advanced evidence for the existence of witches that was so illogical, a ninth-grader today would not get away with it in an essay for school. In 1660 one of them wrote: "He who denies the existence of witches also denies the existence of spirits, because witches are spirits. But he who denies the existence of spirits also denies the existence of God, because God is a spirit. Therefore, he who denies witches denies God."

Fallacy and nonsense are bad enough. But they become very dangerous when order and logic are added to the brew. Such was the case with those who believed in witchcraft; the stubbornness of the scholars caused much greater misery than superstition had. We have already mentioned the scientists and philosophers. But there were worse culprits: the jurists. Which brings us to the witch trials—save for the plague, the most horrible scourge of its time. They spread like an epidemic, jumped from one land to the next, reached their apogee only to diminish temporarily, and seized on young and old, rich and poor, jurists and mayors, doctors and naturalists. Church elders, ministers, and clergymen were burnt at the stake alongside snake charmers and carnival actors, to say nothing of the women of all ages and social standing who suffered in even far greater numbers. We can no longer count how many people in Europe perished as witches and warlocks, but it's certain to have been at least 100,000, perhaps many times more. I have already mentioned that frightful book, *The Witches' Hammer*, published in 1487 and reprinted countless times. Written in Latin, it was a handbook for inquisitors. Inquisitors, interrogators really, were monks who had been invested, directly by the pope, with special powers to combat heresy. Since witches were always seen as heretics, they were targeted by the inquisitors. While one might think that no one would covet such a wretched task, there were still other jurisdictions burning to join in the fight against witches. There were both the regular ecclesiastical court of bishops and the regular secular court, the latter being harsher.

The burning of witches was not a part of old Church law, so for a long time, punishment for witches consisted merely of excommunication and prison. In 1532 Charles V introduced his new book of laws, the so-called Carolina, or "Procedure for The Judgment of Capital Crimes," which called for those practicing witchcraft to be burned at the stake. But there was still the stipulation that actual harm must have occurred. Many jurists and princes found this law to be too mild and preferred to follow Saxon law, under which all wizards and witches could be burned, even if they had inflicted no harm. These multiple jurisdictions resulted in such terrible confusion that there was no longer any question of law and order. On top of all this came the notion that witches were possessed, inhabited by the devil; thus, people believed that they were contesting the superiority of the devil and that in this fight everything was allowed. Nothing was too horrible or too nonsensical for the jurists of the day to be at a loss for a Latin word to describe it: witchcraft was deemed a *crimen exceptum*, an exceptional crime, meaning a crime for which those accused could hardly ever defend themselves. They were treated as guilty from the very start. Even if they had counsel, there was not much the latter could do, because the suspicion was that any advocate who too eagerly defended those accused of witchcraft was probably a wizard himself. Jurists tended to see witchcraft cases purely as matters of professional expertise, which they alone possessed. The most dangerous principle they espoused was the following: in crimes of witchcraft a confession would suffice, even if no proof were found. For those who know that torture was the order of the day in witch trials, it's plain to see how little such confessions were worth. One of the most astonishing things about this story is that over 200 years went by before it occurred to jurists that confessions given under torture have no value. Perhaps because their books were so jammed full of the most unlikely and dreadful, hairsplitting minutia, they couldn't entertain the simplest of thoughts. And what's more, they believed they were staying wise to the devil and his tricks. If, for example, the accused was keeping silent, because she knew that every word she said, however innocent, would get her deeper into trouble, the jurists would claim this was "Devil's lockjaw," meaning that the Evil One had hexed her, leaving her unable to speak. So-called witch tests, used when occasionally the proceedings needed to be shortened, were equally effective. For example, the test of tears. If someone did not cry under torture, it was considered proof that she was being aided by the devil; it would again be 200 years before doctors made the observation, or dared to utter the fact, that people suffering extreme pain do not cry.

The fight against the witch trials is one of the greatest liberation struggles in the history of man. It began in the seventeenth century and took 100 years to succeed, in some countries even longer. It began, as such things very often do, not with a realization, but out of necessity. Over the course of a few years individual princes saw their lands grow desolate as their subjects accused one another under torture. One single trial could spawn hundreds more, taking up years. Some princes started to simply forbid these trials. People gradually dared to reflect. Clergymen and philosophers discovered that belief in witches never existed in the early Church, that God would never grant the devil so much power over men. Jurists came to understand that slander and confessions provoked under torture could not be relied upon as evidence. Doctors reported that there were illnesses that made people think they were wizards or witches even when they weren't. And finally, healthy common sense prevailed as people acknowledged the countless contradictions in the case files of individual witch trials and in the belief in witchcraft itself. Of the many books written at that time against the witch trials, only one became famous. It was written by a Jesuit named Friedrich von Spee. In his younger years he was a confessor at the deaths of condemned witches. When one day a friend asked him why he had gray hair at such a young age, he replied: "Because I've had to accompany so many innocent victims being burned at the stake." His book, *Cautio Criminalis, or a Book on Witch Trials*, is not particularly subversive.[3] Friedrich von Spee actually believed in the existence of witches. But he outright refused to believe in the horrific, erudite, elaborate, fantastical evidence used for centuries to brand just about anyone a witch or a wizard. In this one work he confronted all the ghastly Latin-German gibberish in thousands upon ten thousands of case files, letting his anger and emotion spew forth. His work and its impact proved how necessary it is to place humanity above scholarship and subtlety.

"Hexenprozesse," GS, 7.1, 145–52. Translated by Jonathan Lutes.

Broadcast on Radio Berlin, July 16, 1930. The Funkstunde announced for July 16, 1930, from 5:30–6:00 pm, "Youth Hour, 'Witch Trials.' Speaker: Dr. Walter Benjamin."

3   Written in Latin and first published in 1631, Friedrich Spee's *Cautio Criminalis, or a Book on Witch Trials*, was a critique of contemporary legal proceedings against witches, including the use of torture.

CHAPTER 14

Robber Bands in Old Germany

If robbers had nothing else over other criminals, they would still be the most distinguished of them all because they alone have a history. The story of the robber bands is an integral part of the cultural history of Germany, and indeed of Europe as a whole. Not only do they have a history, but for a long time at least they also possessed the pride and self-assurance of a profession with ancient traditions. A history of ordinary thieves or crooks or murderers cannot be written; they are just individuals, from families where the art of thievery has been passed down only once, if at all, from father to son. With these robbers it is altogether different. Not only were there great robber families that propagated over several generations and great stretches of land, and, like royal families, forged ties between lineages; not only were there individual bands that remained intact for up to fifty years, oftentimes with more than 100 members, but they also had old customs and traditions, their own language, Rotwelsch, and their own notions of honor and rank, all of which persisted as legacies among their kind.[1]

I was thinking of telling you today about some of the thoughts, customs, and convictions of the robbers. After all, it's hard to form a clear picture of such bands from story after thrilling story about figures with names like Schinderhannes, Lips Tullian, or Damian Hessel.[2] However, more interesting and more important than knowing the life stories of a few robber captains is understanding how the bands arose, which principles they upheld among themselves, how they waged their battles against kaisers, princes, and commoners,

---

1 Rotwelsch is the thieves' cant or argot in Southern Germany and Switzerland that developed as early as the thirteenth century. A "secret language," it functioned both to protect criminals and to identify them to each other.

2 Schinderhannes (nickname of Johannes Bückler, c. 1778–1803), Lips Tullian (c. 1675–1715), and Damian Hessel (1774–1810) were legendary German bandits.

and later against the police and law courts. In this vein I must reveal one of the best and most important of the robbers' secrets, which we'll talk about later, namely the language of the robbers and their robber script, their so-called *Zinken*, or secret signs. This Rotwelsch language alone tells us a quite a lot about the origin of the robbers. Next to German, Rotwelsch contains more Hebrew than anything else, evidence of the close ties the robbers had with the Jews from early on. Later, in the sixteenth and seventeenth centuries, some Jews themselves became feared leaders. At first their involvement with the bands had been mainly as fences, or buyers of stolen loot. Since they had been barred from most honest trades in the Middle Ages, it's not hard to see how this came about. After the Jews, it was the Gypsies who played the greatest role in the emergence of robber bands. It was from the Gypsies that these crooks learned their peculiar brand of artistry and cunning, along with how to commit a myriad of brash and daring misdeeds. From them they learned to turn crime into a profession, and eventually absorbed a number of their artful expressions into Rotwelsch. From both Jews and Gypsies the rogues and robbers also adopted quite a few unusual superstitions as well as hundreds of magic spells and recipes of the Black Arts.

Early in the Middle Ages, the robber bands' main business was highway robbery. Because the princes were unable to keep the roads safe for travel, banditry, under certain conditions, became almost a proper occupation. This is indeed rather the way we view the robber bands, with whom the great merchant caravans often had to negotiate a certain sum to secure free passage through an otherwise perilous region. So it's no wonder that very early on the robber bands developed a sort of gallant or martial disposition. I will read to you now a genuine robber oath from the seventeenth century, which goes like this:

On the head and soul of our robber captain, I swear: 1. that I will obey all of his commands; 2. that I will remain faithful to my comrades in all their undertakings and ventures; 3. that I will attend any such gathering that the captain may appoint, here or at any other location; my absence must otherwise be authorized; 4. that I will be on call and eagerly awaiting orders at all hours of the day or night; 5. that I will never leave my comrades in danger, but will stand with them until the last drop of blood; 6. that I will never flee before an equal number of adversaries, but will fight bravely to the death; 7. that we will readily offer a helping hand to anyone who may be captive or sick, or who has suffered some other misfortune; 8. that I will never leave one of my comrades, be he wounded or dead, in enemy hands if I can do otherwise; 9. that, should I be captured, I will confess nothing and, most importantly, will not reveal or betray the location or dwellings of my confederates, even should it cost me my life. And were I to break this oath, may I be beset by and succumb to the greatest of plagues, the most horrible punishments in this world or the next.[3]

Such chivalrous oaths are consistent with the information we have about other bands, namely, that they had their own administration of justice, the so-called *Plattenrecht*, or gang law—in Vienna today crooks are still called *Plattenbrüder*, or gang brothers. We even know of several bands that had elaborate hierarchies. There were privy councilors, senior magistrates, governing councils; some robber captains were even given titles of nobility. The leaders of one famous Dutch gang carried crowbars in their hands as a sign of prestige. The strong loyalty within a single band was in proportion to the low cunning of the tricks sometimes played by one band against another. One of the strangest was the trick the robbers Fetzer and Simon played on Langleiser and his associates, when he wouldn't let them take part in the planned heist of a banker in Münsterland. In revenge, Fetzer and Simon and their companions committed a string of daring robberies in that area just before Langleiser's, so that everyone was on the lookout for trouble and the planned hold-up could not be risked.

Betrayal was the worst crime of which a robber could be found guilty. The power of the robber captains was often so great that captured comrades who had only just informed against them retracted the accusations before the captains had even been confronted. In my interrogations, said a famous policeman, I witnessed the incredible power that a robber's mere presence, his mere intake of breath exerted over others tempted to confess. Nevertheless, there were always some gang members who would betray their comrades in order to be treated more mercifully. The strangest such offer came from a famous robber, the Bohemian Hans, who promised, in exchange for his freedom, to write a compilation of crime lore that could be used to prevent crime in the future.

---

3   See Friedrich Christian Benedict Avé-Lallemant, *Das Deutsche Gaunerthum in seiner sozial-politischen, literarischen und linguistischen Ausbildung zu seinem heutigen Bestande* [German Thiefdom: Its Socio-Political, Literary and Linguistic Development into its Current State] (Leipzig: F. A. Brockhaus, 1858), 91.

This friendly proposal was not accepted; in those days there were already many similar books. The most famous was the *Liber Vagatorum*, or the *Book of Vagabonds and Beggars*, which was first published in 1509 and included a preface written by Luther,[4] part of which I will read to you now.

> This little book on the villainy of beggars was initially published by someone who, without giving his name, referred to himself simply as a man experienced in the art of deceit. He needn't have told us so; the booklet bears it out. It's a good thing that such a book should be not only printed but widely read, so that people can see and grasp how mightily the devil rules over this world, and perhaps will become wiser and learn, once and for all, to tread warily. However, the Rotwelsch language that appears in the book comes from the Jews, as it's filled with Hebrew words; anyone who knows Hebrew will notice this.

Then Luther goes on to describe other advantages of the book: one learns that it's better to fight beggars with charity and compassion instead of forfeiting, having fallen for their roguish tricks, five or ten times as much money as one would voluntarily give. Of course, these beggars, as they appear in the book, were not genuine beggars as we conceive of them today, but very dangerous characters who moved about in hordes and, like swarms of locusts, infested the city, often feigning illness or frailty. Not for nothing did cities in the Middle Ages appoint so-called beggar bailiffs, whose job was nothing more than to oversee the unending influx of vagrant beggars, thus minimizing any harm to the city. There were many fewer resident beggars than tramps from foreign lands, and to distinguish between them and the robbers was often as difficult as telling the difference between some tradesmen and robbers. Some pretended to be peddlers, lugging around their wares only in order to deceive people as to their true profession, thievery. As we have already said, the business of being a crook has changed over the course of time. The artful feigning of illness, a common practice in the Middle Ages, vanished over time as the influence of the Church weakened and alms grew more scarce. We can no longer fathom the number of

---

4 The *Liber Vagatorum*, which discusses the varieties of beggars' tricks and dodges as well as their language, was published anonymously c. 1509. Luther's edition and preface first appeared in 1528.

tricks people used back then to prey on the sympathy of their fellow men. Such false afflictions had the advantage of giving the most dangerous burglars and murderers a semblance of harmlessness. There were people who attended church and, during the benediction, made themselves foam at the mouth by chewing soap, as though they were suffering convulsions. They then collapsed to the floor right before everyone's eyes, ensuring that they would receive donations from the devout. The steps of the church were strewn with such riff-raff. You would find people there showing off arms painted with false shackle wounds: they made people believe they had been on a crusade, had fallen into the hands of heathens, and had languished for years as galley slaves. Others would shave the top of their heads, claiming they were priests on a pilgrimage and that robbers had stolen their belongings. Still others shook rattles, as lepers did in those days, so that people would not draw near but could leave them alms from a distance. To get a better sense of these wild and dangerous mobs, one can look to the secluded square where the same sort of riff-raff gathered in Paris at the time. Bleak and desolate, it was popularly known as the Court of Miracles because it was where the blind would regain their sight, the lame walk, the deaf hear and the dumb speak once more. There was no end to the list of ruses they attempted. Besides pretending to be deaf, which made it so easy for the crooks to overhear the location of things to steal, a particular favorite was acting the imbecile. For instance, if a hoodlum had the misfortune to be caught keeping lookout, he simply played the idiot and acted like he didn't know how he got there or why.

But now, back for a moment to what Luther wrote in his preface to the *Book of Vagabonds and Beggars*. He says that the book shows how the devil rules the world, and this is to be taken much more literally than we would take it today. In the Middle Ages people were quick to assume that the most skilled and courageous robber captains had made a pact with the devil. This awful and, for them, almost always fatal misconception was strengthened by all sorts of supposed evidence, as well as by the fabulous superstitions prevalent among the robbers themselves. Everyone with an unsteady profession dependent on thousands of contingencies tends toward superstition, and doubly so if the profession is a dangerous one. Robbers were convinced they possessed hundreds of charms to make themselves invisible during a break-in, to lull people to sleep in the house they wanted to burgle, to ward off pursuers' bullets, to find especially lavish treasures where they were targeting a heist. This was greatly enhanced by the misunderstood fragments of Hebrew the robbers had picked up from the Jews, and further still by the so-called demon seals, small squiggles, and dashes painted on parchment to ensure the blessing of evil spirits while committing crimes. After all, their cunning and bravery aside, most of these robbers were poor and ignorant, mostly of peasant origin. Only very few could read and write; but if the mysterious magic symbols in letters from Schinderhannes are any indication, even those who could read and write were not exempt from superstition. Many, however, knew as little about their religion as about math. There is a poignant utterance by a poor imprisoned robber who sought guidance from the divine, but received no answer: "We are told that our dear Lord and Holy Mother will provide such great assistance and intervention; but they never help us find where the money is in a farmhouse, tavern, or town hall." There may even have been robbers who believed themselves to be wizards, in league with the devil. But bear in mind that in those days torture was still practiced, forcing the poor fellows to confess to all sorts of things they had never heard of before.

When torture was abolished in the eighteenth century, by and by people emerged who attempted to treat the captured robbers more humanely, not only trying to rehabilitate them with edifying principles and threats of hell, but also trying to understand them. One of them left us an elaborate account of the so-called Vogelsberg and Wetterau bands, in which he precisely depicts each one of these robbers. Should we think that the man whom he describes with the following words is a dangerous gang leader? "He is sincere, truth-loving, valiant, frivolous, passionate, easily excitable but stands firm behind a decision. Gracious, effervescent, vengeful, blessed with a lively imagination, a good memory and generally good humor. Of clear mind, naïve, witty at times, somewhat vain and even musical." Those who have read *The Robbers* by Schiller will perhaps remember this description of Karl Moor. So there really were noble robbers. Of course, people made this discovery only when the robbers began to die out altogether. Or did they perhaps begin to die out as a result of this discovery? The ruthlessness with which they were pursued and punished up until that point, oftentimes by execution for mere theft, prevented a robber from easily returning to the life of a peaceful citizen. The cruelty of the old criminal law played just as big a role in the emergence of professional crime as the more humane law did in its disappearance.

"Räuberbanden im alten Deutschland," GS, 7.1, 152–9. Translated by Jonathan Lutes.

Broadcast on Southwest German Radio, Frankfurt on September 23, 1930, and on Radio Berlin on October 2, 1930. Benjamin dated the typescript, "Frankfurt and Berlin Radio, September, October, 1930." The Südwestdeutsche Rundfunk-Zeitung *[Southwest German Radio Times], the Frankfurt station's program guide, announced the broadcast for September 23, 1930, from 3:25–3:50 pm; the* Funkstunde *advertised it for October 2, 1930, from 5:30–5:50 pm.*

CHAPTER 15

The Gypsies

You've probably never had the courage to climb the wheel spokes of a Gypsy wagon and look inside. But I'm sure you've all been tempted to; I know I have, whenever I see one creeping down a country road from afar. By the way, do you know where in Germany you're most likely to come across one of these wagons? In East Prussia. Why? Because the region is sparsely populated and it's much too far for people to go to the cities for distraction. The traveler folk know this, and that's why you run into them so often in these areas. Of course these travelers are not all Gypsies, but there are quite a few who are; these days, however, we only encounter Gypsies in small groups of tightrope walkers, fire-eaters, or bear tamers. It was a good 500 years ago, during the rule of Emperor Sigismund, that they invaded Germany in large mobs almost like an armed tribe; since then, even as they held fast to their language and customs, their cohesion has grown ever weaker. Now there are hardly any more large bands of Gypsies, but mostly just large individual families.

These families are large because Gypsies have lots of children. They do not, thank goodness, rely on stealing small children from strangers. Over centuries, of course, this sort of thing has happened now and again. But one can rightfully accuse the Gypsies of enough dirty tricks that there is no need to denounce them for things of which they're innocent. All the same, they've earned their bad reputation. When they crossed the German border in large hordes in 1417 they were initially received quite well. Emperor Sigismund granted them a letter of protection, which was occasionally given to foreigners in those days. Perhaps you know that now and again the Jews also received such letters of protection from the German Emperor. Whether these always helped is another matter. In any case, such letters provided their bearers with a number of important rights: they could not be deported, they were answerable directly to the Emperor and they had their own jurisdiction. And so it was for the Gypsies. Their kings, or voivodes as they were called, administered justice over their people and enjoyed safe passage. Just think of the tall tales they had to invent to obtain this. As for their origins, they said they hailed from Little Egypt. Not a word of it is true. But people believed them for hundreds of years, until the nineteenth century, when a great linguist—a friend of the brothers Grimm, a name familiar to you—spent many years studying the Gypsy language. He figured out that they came from Hindustan, in the highlands of West Asia. They must have suffered terribly in ancient times, for not a trace of this history remains in their lore. To this day they have—and this is rather puzzling—an immense pride in their national character, yet virtually none of their historical memory has been preserved, not even in legends. And why did they say they came from Little Egypt? The answer is very simple: in those days Europeans generally believed that Egypt was the birthplace of magic. And from the beginning it was magic that the Gypsies used to gain respect. It must be remembered that despite outward appearances they were a weak and unwarlike people; they needed some other way to assert themselves besides the threat of violence. Thus, deception through magic was not only a way to make a living, but also a recourse to their instinct for self-preservation. The centuries-long campaign against the Gypsies by the German police would not have been so drawn-out, and largely so futile, if not for the patronage of uneducated people, especially peasants. A house where a Gypsy child was born was alleged to be safe from fire; if a horse became so ill that it could no longer work, a Gypsy's help was sought; if a peasant heard talk of treasures buried in a field, a nearby wood, or the ruins of a castle, he was likely to consult a Gypsy, for they were known as highly skilled at unearthing hidden treasure. This of course gave them opportunities for many lucrative schemes. Upon arriving in a new region, a favorite trick was to make a horse or ox artificially sick, and then to promise the desperate peasants an immediate cure in return for a good reward. And because they knew the cause of the illness they could cure the animal in no time at all, thereby further establishing their reputation for magical powers.

However, when it came to dealing with important people concerning the affairs of their tribe, they used altogether different methods. They cited letters stating they had originally lived in Egypt as Christians but had turned apostate, upon which the pope forced them to roam the world for seven years as penitence. Thus they were forbidden to settle in one place. Some contrived even more elaborate tales: because their forefathers had refused to harbor Mary when she fled to Egypt with the baby Jesus, they are forced to wander the Earth without peace. You may be wondering about the Gypsies and their Christian beliefs. They were just an invention to stir sympathy or, as in the story of King Herod, dread among Westerners.[1] Although doubtless the Gypsies once had a religion, its features are difficult to glean from their dark practices and even harder to ascertain from their folk legends, for, while their customs have remained fairly undiluted, their legends are a ragbag of their own fables and those invented by others. The greatest proof that they no longer have a religion is the ease with which they conform to others' customs when expected to do so. For instance they attach very little significance to being married by a preacher, and even allow him to baptize their children. Old police circulars recall that baptisms of Gypsy children required close monitoring, as Gypsies would often have their children baptized multiple times to receive more of the gifts handed out on such occasions.

The letter of protection the Gypsies received from the Emperor did not remain valid for long. They became a burden, and in 1497 an expulsion decree was issued that called for all Gypsies to leave Germany by a certain date; any Gypsy who stayed was declared an outlaw and could be punished by anyone with impunity. Such orders were issued frequently over the years, sometimes for all of Germany and sometimes just for particular regions. As recently as March 31, 1909, the German parliament discussed how best to deal with the Gypsies. The public threats and bans had proved ineffective. Policemen, missionaries, and teachers considered the possibility of attaining better results with milder and more humane methods. Their idea was to move family groups of Gypsies into permanent settlements that lay far from one another. This plan began well, but when the first Gypsy schools were established, it was next to impossible to get the adult Gypsies to return home after walking their children to school. They were intent on remaining in class and learning along with the children. It also proved futile to get them to settle in one place. If they were given a hut, they would abandon it straightaway for a tent right next to it, provided the weather was not bitter cold. They stubbornly clung to this freedom of movement.

---

1 Benjamin refers here to a version of the previously mentioned legend whereby the Gypsies, having tried to prevent Joseph, Mary, and the baby Jesus gaining refuge from King Herod in Egypt, were punished with eternal homelessness by God.

They're not lazy; in a pinch they can earn their living as tinkers, cobblers, sieve makers, and wire workers. But under no circumstances will they be persuaded to farm. Emperor Joseph II of Austria came to understand this as well. He was the first to attempt to improve life for the Gypsies in a more humane way. It was the 1760s, in Hungary, during a time of frightful persecution of the Gypsies. The rumor had arisen that secretly the Gypsies were cannibals. Many of them had been captured and executed before Joseph II intervened. But he wanted to do more: with the hope of encouraging them to become more sedentary, and above all to work the land, he forbade the Gypsies from performing magic or street entertainment anywhere in the empire, except in bad weather when the fields could not be farmed. But this didn't help at all. The Gypsies stuck to their ways and continued to roam. The government tolerated them all the less for having acted as spies for invading troops. Their feel for the terrain and their extraordinary knowledge of the land often proved helpful for generals of enemy armies; Wallenstein had used their services during the Thirty Years' War. So everything remained as before; even in winter, the Gypsies opted for any sort of shelter other than a house. Mostly they lived in earthen caves, shielding themselves from the elements with planks or large cloths carefully arranged to ensure that no fresh air would enter their abodes. In the middle there was a fire; around it lounged a group of half-naked figures. The talk was not of washing, cleaning, or mending; at most there was a flat cake cooking in the ashes, not in a pan, of course. Their only activities were cooking, roasting, eating, smoking tobacco, chatting, and sleeping. Or so claims a schoolmaster from Langensalza, who in 1835 wrote a very unfriendly book about the Gypsies to encourage the authorities to crack down on them more harshly.[2] But not all that he wrote should be taken as fact. No one could understand less about the Gypsies than this old breed of schoolmaster. And he's certainly wrong about their idleness.

I don't know whether Gypsies have ever offered you one of those funny wire-mesh contraptions they piece together in the quiet of their winter caves. You don't see them very often any more, but they are little works of wonder. With a flick of the wrist a fruit bowl is transformed into a bird cage, the bird cage into a lampshade, the lampshade into a bread basket, then the bread basket again becomes

---

2 See Theodor Christian Tetzner, *Geschichte der Zigeuner: ihre Herkunft, Natur und Art* [History of the Gypsies: Their Origins, Nature and Ways] (Weimar and Ilmenau: B. F. Voigt, 1835), 93.

a fruit bowl. But their main craft, their national art, is music. One might say that they've conquered entire countries with their fiddle. It's impossible, especially in Russia, to imagine a large banquet or wedding without Gypsy music, and it just so happens that Gypsy women, through marriage with the Boyars, have ascended to the highest circles of court society. Every Gypsy is a born violinist, but in most cases can't read a note. Their musical instinct makes up for everything; people say that no one plays the fiery Hungarian melodies like they do. Gypsies are never more proud than when they are holding their violins. There's a story of a Gypsy who appeared in the council chambers at the castle of a Hungarian duke, and asked the assembled company if they would like to hear him play. Although it was a difficult matter they were discussing, the Gypsy's offer was so proud and so irresistible that they couldn't turn him away. The chronicler of this story claims that it was only while the Gypsy was playing his music that the duke arrived at the solution to the problem that had previously vexed him and his councilmen.

Gypsy music is rather melancholy. They are generally a melancholy people. Their language has no word for joy or exuberance. Perhaps this melancholy comes not only from having suffered in so many different places, but also from the dark superstitions that pervade their everyday lives. Have you ever watched a Gypsy woman cross the street? Have you noticed how tightly she gathers her skirts around her body? She does this because, according to the Gypsies, anything that comes into contact with a woman's clothing can no longer be used. This is why cooking utensils in Gypsy wagons are not placed on tables or shelves, but are hung from the ceiling where they won't accidentally be brushed by a piece of women's clothing. Similar superstitions surround the Gypsy's silver cup, his most prized possession. Imbued with magical powers, this cup must never fall to the ground, because the Earth is sacred. If the cup touches the ground even once, it is cursed by the Earth and can never be used again. But the strangest manifestation of the Gypsies' inherent melancholy is found in their expressions of love: the silent, eloquent, and serious signs they use to communicate important feelings to each other. For example, if a couple has separated and the man wants to make up, upon seeing her he throws a card, or just a piece of paper, up into the air. Her reaching out to catch it signals that they're reconciled. If she doesn't move her hand, however, everything is over between them. And there would be many more such customs to tell. When Goethe was studying in Strasbourg as a young man, he took a passionate and solicitous interest in the most foreign and uncouth of tribes, including the Gypsies. He spoke about them in *Götz von Berlichingen*. At the same time he was writing the eerie, sad, and rather savage "Gypsy Song," which you will find among his poems.[3] Look it up sometime; reading it aloud would sound so scary that I will refrain from doing so now. But it will remind you of much that I've told you today.

"Die Zigeuner," GS, 7.1, 159–65. Translated by Jonathan Lutes.

Broadcast on Radio Berlin, October 23, 1930. The Funkstunde announced for October 23, 1930, from 5:30–5:50 pm, "Youth Hour, 'The Gypsies.' Speaker: Dr. W. Benjamin."

---

3 Goethe's early drama, *Götz von Berlichingen mit der eisernen Hand: ein Schauspiel* [Gottfried von Berlichingen with the Iron Hand: A Play] (1773), contained, in a previous version, the "Zigeunerlied," or "Gypsy Song" [in *Geschichte Gottfriedens von Berlichingen mit der eisernen Hand, dramatisiert*, or the "Urgötz," 1771, published posthumously]. See Goethe, *Nachgelassene Werke* (Stuttgart: J.G. Cotta, 1833), 173.

CHAPTER 16

The Bastille, the Old French State Prison

On the French calendar, July 14 is marked in red. It's the national holiday. On this day, for almost 150 years, they have celebrated the storming of the Bastille, which took place on July 14, 1789, and was the first great visible act of revolutionary destruction. The building was seized without much of a struggle. Yet it was a strong fortress; built over the course of fourteen years, from 1369 to 1383, it was protected by massive towers and surrounded by a moat. We still have many images of it. Gloomy and squat, it stood on the edge of the giant city. Its walls were over 400 years old when they fell. Though poorly armed, an enormous mob succeeded in forcing the commandant to surrender it in no time at all. When they stormed through the wide corridors, ransacking the fortress from its cellar vaults up to its rafters, many may have been surprised to find only sixteen poor prisoners inside this house of terror. And this was in proportion to the military presence in the Bastille at the moment of the assault, when the governor had no more than forty Swiss Guards and eighty old soldiers at his disposal. How can we comprehend the immense hatred the people of Paris had for this building, a hatred so savage that the revolutionaries who had granted the governor safe passage could not prevent him from being slain by the people? This is something I hope you'll understand in a half hour.

First and foremost, the Bastille was no ordinary prison. Only people accused of violating the security of the state were sent there. Some were prisoners of the state, while others were prisoners of the police. Prisoners of the state were those convicted of alleged or actual crimes, conspiracies, treason or the like; the many more prisoners of the police were writers, booksellers, engravers, and even bookbinders who were in some way involved, allegedly or in actuality, with books unpopular with the king and his minions. The Bastille was indeed an unusual prison. On holidays, especially when the weather was good, carefree Parisians could be seen strolling on its embankments and behind the battlements of its towers. Elegant carriages bearing guests of the governor rolled across the drawbridges; musicians arrived to play at gala dinners given by the governor, that is, the director of the prison. Meanwhile, however, the picture inside its mighty towers and dark cellars was quite different. Those outside were as little aware of those inside as those inside were aware of their fellow citizens who were free. Narrow window guards, which are still found in many penitentiaries today, ensured that most prisoners saw no more than just a small corner of sky. Not to mention the dungeons, where a ray of light shone through one tiny slit in the wall, illuminating the cockroaches with which the prisoners had to share their cells. In Paris there were only rumors concerning who was actually held inside the Bastille. No one could prepare for his own arrest. Officers would suddenly appear and pack the captive into a carriage, which was just an ordinary cab, so as not to draw attention. When it arrived in the courtyard of the Bastille and the detainees were let out, the guards held their hats in front of their faces, for no one besides the governor was allowed to know who the prisoners were. Within the Bastille, of course, news traveled fast. Outside, though, not a soul knew who was there, and in a moment I'll tell you the story of the man in the iron mask, whose identity remains a mystery to this day.

The arrests happened so quickly that people used to say it was fortunate to be arrested during the day, for at night one was hardly given time to dress. So quickly that we know of a servant who, when his master disappeared into one of these cabs, unsuspectingly jumped in after him and had to spend the next two years in the Bastille for the sole reason that his release would have been a nuisance. The warrant for the arrests were so-called sealed letters— *lettres de cachet* in French—which bore no marks except the name of the person to be arrested. The prisoner was often not informed of the reason for the arrest until weeks later, sometimes months, sometimes never. When I tell you that some cronies of the king obtained letters of arrest of this kind on which the name of the detainee was not filled in, so that they could add one at their discretion, you will guess that abuse became the rule. How things were generally done in the Bastille can best be learned from the story of the man in the iron mask, which I'll read to you now.

Thursday, September 18, 1698, at three o'clock in the afternoon, M. de Saint-Mars, governor of the Bastille, arrived here for the first time from Sainte-Marguerite Island (home to another large prison). In his sedan he brought with him a prisoner whose name was kept secret and who was always masked. He was initially placed in the Bazinière tower—all the towers of the Bastille have special names; at nine o'clock, once it was dark, I was ordered to take him to the third room of one of the other towers, which I had carefully furnished with all conceivable necessities.[1]

That is all we have in writing to attest to the man in the iron mask until the news of his death, which we find entered in the diary of the same lieutenant five years later, on Monday, November 19, 1703: "The unknown prisoner, always veiled in a black velvet mask, whom the governor brought with him on coming from Sainte-Marguerite Island, felt a bit unwell yesterday after Mass and then died today, at around ten o'clock at night, without ever having been seriously ill . . ."[2] He was buried the very next day; the lieutenant dutifully recorded in his diary that the interment cost forty francs. It is also known that the body was buried without its head, which, upon being cut off, was chopped into several pieces, ensuring that it was fully unrecognizable, and then buried in a number of different locations. In sum, the king and the governor of the Bastille feared that, even after his death, the identity of the man in the iron mask might still be discovered. They went so far as to order that every last thing he might have used be burned: underwear, clothes, mattresses, bedding, et cetera; the walls of his room were to be carefully scraped and whitewashed. Precautions included even loosening and removing all the stones in the walls one after the other, lest he had hidden a note somewhere or left some other sign by which he could be identified. His mask was not made of iron, though that is how he got his name, but of black velvet reinforced with fish bones. It was fastened at the back of his head with a sealed lock and constructed such that it was impossible for him to remove; indeed, no one could free him without the key to the lock. However, he could eat with it on with relative ease—the order was to kill him immediately were he ever to make his identity known. He was given everything he requested.

---

1   See Frantz Funck-Brentano, *La Bastille et ses secrets* (Paris: Jules Tallandier, 1979), 126.
2   Ibid., 127.

Judging by the respect he was shown, as well as by his fondness for fine linens, his expensive clothes, his skill at playing the zither, and many other indications, it was clear he was a nobleman. His table was always supplied with the most exquisite dishes; the governor only seldom ventured to sit in his presence. An old doctor in the Bastille, who occasionally would see and examine this remarkable man, later stated that he never saw his face. The man in the iron mask was very attractive physically, displayed good comportment, and captivated everyone with the mere sound of his voice. For all his apparent humility and subjection, however, it is believed that he was able to send a message to the outside world. The story goes that one day he threw out the window a wooden plate on which he had carved the name Macmouth. This tale has played a large role in the many attempts to discover the truth behind this mysterious man. Since the beginning, researchers have agreed that this prisoner of the state could only have been a scion of one of the noblest houses, indeed, in all probability a royal house. At the time, King James II ruled England and a son of Charles II rose up against him as anti-king. This anti-king was the duke of Monmouth. He was defeated and apparently executed on July 15, 1685. Almost at once, however, rumors arose that the executed man was an officer of the duke of Monmouth, who saved his master's life by being executed in his place. The actual duke escaped to France, where he was arrested by Louis XIV. The man in the iron mask was alleged to have been this duke. I wanted to tell you this, but you should know that a great many explanations, hardly less plausible than this one, have emerged over the centuries. To this day, none of the many historians researching the case has found any conclusive evidence.

I told you how everyone released from this prison had to sign an oath never to speak a single word of what he had seen and heard in there. If today not all regulations are as strict as they're made to seem, this was even more true back then, for we know a lot about the Bastille. And from whom should we have learned it, but from the prisoners themselves? The guards certainly had no interest in relating for posterity all the cruelty and harassment of which they were guilty. Of the many aristocratic or educated people who had been incarcerated in the Bastille, a good number published memoirs much later, or at least recollections of their years in the prison. But not in France, of course. Manuscripts in those days had to be smuggled to a foreign country, usually Holland, or if they were printed in France, the place of publication was given as Holland, usually The

Hague. I will now read you a page from one of these memoirs, written by Constantin de Renneville, who was jailed in the Bastille under Louis XIV. The passage shows just how diverse the means of communications actually were among the prisoners, among whom all interactions were forbidden.

I was always eager to converse with someone. Man is born to be social; and this natural urge was sharpened even more by the solitude in which I lived. While the prisoners below me never answered me, those above finally did so by way of signals; but it was impossible, or at least very dangerous, to bore a hole in the ceiling through which to pass a note. It was very white and smooth; the slightest nick would easily have been noticed by the guard. After much contemplation, however, I found a way of communicating my thoughts to those above. It was admittedly slow and demanded much attention, but as such it occupied us longer and shielded us from the boredom of our insomnia. I contrived an alphabet in my head, which I performed by striking the wall with a stick and the chair. For A I tapped once, for B twice, C three times, and so on. A short pause indicated the transition from one letter to the next, a longer one the end of a word. After much repetition, those above me grasped it, and I was happily surprised when, in the same manner, they asked me who I was, why I was there, and so forth. When I was later privileged to be given a cellmate, I gave up this tiresome way of communicating. For five years I heard nothing more of it, and I was more than a little surprised when I later heard other prisoners speaking in the same manner with great fluency. My invention had been perfected; it came to be called "the art of speaking with the cane." By necessity, others invented even stranger systems. There was an officer who was not acknowledged as the nobleman he truly was. In an attempt to validate his claim, he falsified a document that had been lost. Now he sat in the Bastille and to converse with his fellow prisoners, he took a piece of coal and drew very large, single words on the table in his room. He then dragged this table to the window and tipped it on end so that the table top appeared in the opening of the window. The words were written so large that one could discern them from the distant windows of opposing towers, and other prisoners answered him in like fashion. —For a while, one of the governors kept a dog, which often ran around the courtyard of the Bastille. The prisoners passed the time by teaching the dog to fetch; they would throw a wad of paper into the courtyard and the dog would pick it up and bring it back. When they had finally trained him to the point that he would drop the ball of paper in front of specific cells, they began to write messages on the paper before crumpling it up and throwing it. Messages were thus conveyed from one prisoner to the next by the retrieving dog. One day, however, the governor caught on and had the windows barred so narrowly that no one could throw anything out of them.[3]

As harshly as the prisoners were treated, nobody wished to see an inmate die in the Bastille. It was very seldom that people incarcerated there had been condemned to death at their trial, and if this were the case, they were transferred to an ordinary prison shortly beforehand. For the Bastille was held to be a house of the king, in which there should be no scandal. Therefore, in the famous discharge book, which I have already mentioned, even those who had been executed were recorded as having died of some disease. However, if one of the inmates actually became sick, unless he were an especially noble prisoner he was taken to the barber for bloodletting; only if he grew much worse was a doctor called. The doctor never hurried to the Bastille, as he lived very far away, and furthermore, wasn't paid for the visit—he merely received a general stipend for his duties at the prison. If, however, the prisoner eventually became so sick that his life was in danger, he was either set free or taken elsewhere. As I said before, the ministry did not like to see well-known people die in the Bastille. There was much to consider. Everyone knew that many of the prisoners confined to the Bastille were innocent, sent there, for example, because they were owed money by an aristocrat who wanted them out of the way. But sometimes an enemy was so powerful that locking him in the Bastille was not enough; one day he might be released. So there were prisoners in the Bastille who lived in constant fear for their lives, not knowing whether their enemy might one day bribe a kitchen boy to mix some lethal powder into their food. The ministry was sufficiently aware of this potential crime that it ordered a sentry to be posted in the kitchen, to prevent anyone from coming too close to the kitchen boys and the pots.

One of the most astounding things for us today is how the prison meals depended on the prisoner's class. Fifty francs a day were allotted for a prince—then the sums became drastically smaller: twenty-six francs were budgeted for the meal of a French marshal;

---

3 See Constantin de Renneville, *L'inquisition françoise ou L'histoire de la Bastille* (Amsterdam: Étienne Roger, 1715), 120–2, 131–3.

for a judge or a priest, ten francs; the food for the common people—workers, servants, peddlers, etc.—cost no more than three francs. If I were to read you the whole list, you would see how the Bastille was equipped for visitors of all classes. As with other matters, however, here too the differences were often greater on paper than in reality. But there was one way in which all prisoners of the Bastille were equal: from the governor down to the lowliest prison guard, everyone wanted to make money off of them. There was never a chance that the money paid by the king for the nourishment of his prisoners would actually be used for its intended purpose. And it was no secret. Everyone knew exactly how much could be earned from administering the Bastille, and that the sums one governor had to pay to another to assume his post or to be named by him as his successor could be raised only by rich people.

The injustice committed during the arrests and interrogations of the prisoners of the Bastille was not alone in embittering the people to the point that the destruction of this fortress became the slogan of the first day of the Revolution. Even more galling was the singular brazenness with which, behind the walls of the Bastille, rampant excess stood side by side with the deepest misery. The chief of the Paris police conducted an inspection of the prison two or three times a year to be sure that everything was in order. In reality, however, this inspection consisted of a grand formal dinner, hosted by the governor of the Bastille for the chief of police. Only once all the finest wines, coffee, and the best liqueurs had been washed down, and enough time had been spent at the banquet table, did the chief get up from his chair and amble leisurely over to the towers and along the cells, peeking into one here and there; before long he was back in the governor's reception rooms.

All of these things show how much the Bastille was a tool of power and how little a means of justice. Even cruelty and hardship can be tolerated if people feel that there's an idea behind it, that the severity is not merely a matter of the rulers' convenience. The storming of the Bastille is a turning point not only in the history of the French state, but also in the history of life under the law. People have not always been of one mind about inflicting punishment upon their fellow human beings. The oldest view, from the Middle Ages, was that every wrong should be expiated, not for the sake of human beings but to establish divine justice. The idea of reforming the guilty through punishment had caught on among bright minds long before the French Revolution. Later, in the nineteenth century, this doctrine competed with the so-called doctrine of deterrence, according to which punishments should above all serve a preventive purpose: punishments exist to dissuade those with bad intentions from carrying them out. The people in charge of the Bastille did not trouble themselves with such questions. Whether they were right or wrong was of no consequence to them, and for this reason they were swept aside by the French Revolution.

"Die Bastille, das alte französische Staatsgefängnis," GS, 7.1, 165–73. Translated by Diana K. Reese.

Broadcast on Southwest German Radio, Frankfurt, April 29, 1931. The Südwestdeutsche Rundfunk-Zeitung *announced for April 29, 1931, from 3:20–3:50 pm, "Youth Hour, 'The Bastille, the Old French State Prison,' presented by Dr. Walter Benjamin, Berlin (for children ten years old and above)."*

CHAPTER 17

Kaspar Hauser

Today, for a change, I'm simply going to tell you a story. But before we start there are three things you should know. First, every word of it is true. Second, it's just as exciting for adults as it is for children, and children will understand it just as well as adults. Third, although it concludes with the death of the main character, this story has no real ending, so it has the advantage that it continues on, and that perhaps someday we'll learn its ending.

Once I begin the story, try not to think: but it starts like some kind of story for adolescents, with pictures. I'm not the one starting the story in such a roundabout and slow-paced way, after all; it's the chief court of appeals judge Anselm von Feuerbach, who, God knows, did not write for adolescents; he intended his book about Kaspar Hauser to be for adults. It was read all over Europe, and just as people breathlessly followed this tale for five years, from 1828 to 1833, you will listen to this story for twenty minutes, or so I hope. It begins:

The second day of Pentecost is one of Nuremberg's most festive holidays. The greater part of its residents retreat to the countryside and neighboring villages, particularly in fine Spring weather, leaving the city, already sparsely populated for its considerable size, so quiet and free of people that it looks more like an enchanted city in the Sahara than the bustling center of commerce and trade that it is. On such a day, especially in those areas just outside the center of town, secret things can happen right out in the open while remaining secret nevertheless. And so it occurred on the second day of Pentecost, the 26th of May, 1828, between four and five in the evening: a townsman, who lived along Unschlitt Square, was lingering for a moment in front of his house before heading to the so-called New Gate when he turned around and caught sight of a young man nearby. He was dressed like a farmhand, and with a most awkward posture, not unlike a drunkard, he struggled to move forward, unable to stand upright and lacking proper control of his feet. The townsman approached the stranger, who reached out to him with a letter bearing the address: "To the noble cavalry captain of the 4th Squadron of the 6th Regiment of Chevaux-Légers Nuremberg."[1]

I must interrupt the story here, not only to explain that a Chevaux-Légers regiment is what we call a cavalry regiment today, but also to tell you that this French word was written entirely wrong, as if it were spelled just as it sounds. This is important because you will have to imagine the spelling in the letter that Kaspar Hauser had with him and that I will read to you in a bit. Once you have heard this letter, you will have no problem imagining why the cavalry captain didn't tarry with the boy, but tried to be rid of him the quickest way possible, which was to call the police. You know that the first thing that happens when something is brought to the attention of the police is that they open a file. And on that day, when the cavalry captain, not knowing what he should do with Kaspar Hauser, turned him over to the police, the first file was created of what would become the massive collection of "Kaspar Hauser" files, which are preserved today in forty-nine volumes in the state archives in Munich.

This first file clearly states that Kaspar Hauser came to Nuremberg as a savage idiot, whose vocabulary consisted of no more than fifty words, who understood nothing that was said to him, and had only two answers to all the questions he was asked: "Wanna be a rider" and "Dunno." But how did he come to have the name Kaspar Hauser? That's a strange story in itself. When he was brought to the police station by the cavalry captain, most of the policemen were divided over whether he should be considered an imbecile or a half-savage. However, they all agreed that this young fellow might be concealing a sophisticated fraud. The following circumstance at first lent a certain credibility to this suspicion. The police came up with the idea of seeing whether or not he could write, so they gave him a quill with ink, laid a sheet of paper in front of him, and told him to write. He grew very excited, adeptly placed the quill between his fingers and, to the astonishment of all who were present, in firm, legible letters wrote the name: *Kaspar Hauser*. He was then asked to

1 Anselm Ritter von Feuerbach, *Kaspar Hauser: Beispiel eines Verbrechens am Seelenleben des Menschen* [Kaspar Hauser: A Case of a Crime against the Soul of a Human Being] (Ansbach: Dollfuss, 1932), 1–2. Feuerbach's book was greatly influential in making Kaspar Hauser and his case famous throughout Europe and beyond.

write the name of where he came from, upon which he did nothing but garble his "Wanna be a rider" and "Dunno."

What these good policemen never succeeded in doing, and no one else has managed to do to this day, was to learn where Kaspar Hauser came from. But what people in the police station first whispered to themselves back then—that perhaps this fellow was a very skilled impostor—continues today as a rumor, or even a firmly held belief. Later on you will hear quite a few curious things that lend credence to this claim. All the same, I, the storyteller, won't keep from you that I hold this to be untrue. The deceit that triggers this story is not to be found in the young man himself, but somewhere else entirely, which brings us to the letter Kaspar Hauser carried to Nuremberg.

"Noble Herr Cavalry Captain! I send you a young man who seeks loyal service to his king," the letter begins.

> This young man was given to me—let's say foisted on me, secretly passed to me—in 1812, the 7th of October, and being a poor laborer myself, and having ten children on top of it all, I got enough to do just to take care of my own, and I couldn't ask his mother. And I did not tell the court that the boy was foisted on me the way he was; I just figured I had to take him on as my own son. I raised him Christian and never let him take a step out of the house since 1812, so no one knows where he was raised; not even he knows what my house is called, or even what village it's in. You can go ahead and ask him but he can't tell you. Dear Herr Cavalry Captain, badger him all you like but he doesn't know the place where I'm at. I took him away in the middle of the night and he doesn't know his home any more. And he has not got any money on him because I got none myself. If you don't keep him, you ought just strike him dead or hang him from the chimney.[2]

Accompanying this letter was a small note written not in German script, like the letter, but in Latin script instead. The note was also on different paper and appeared to be in completely different handwriting. It was supposed to be the letter left by the mother upon abandoning the small child sixteen years before. It explained that she was a poor girl. She couldn't support the child. The father was in the Nuremberg Regiment of Chevaux-Légers, and the child, upon reaching his

---

2 Feuerbach, *Kaspar Hauser*, 12–14.

seventeenth year, should be sent along to join him. But here in the handwriting we encounter the first bit of deception to play a part in this mysterious affair: a chemical analysis revealed that both letters, the one from 1828 written by the laborer and the one from 1812 allegedly from the mother, were written with the same ink. You're probably thinking that immediately upon this discovery, neither one of the letters would be trusted, and that no one would believe in the existence of the supposed laborer or the supposed poor girl.

Although Kaspar Hauser was initially put in the Nuremberg municipal jail, he was there less as a prisoner than as an object of interest, becoming one of the attractions for visitors to see in the city. Among the many genteel people whose interest in this extraordinary case led them to Nuremberg was the chief court of appeals judge Anselm von Feuerbach, who met Kaspar Hauser and several years later wrote a book about him, the beginning of which I just read to you. With Feuerbach the story took its decisive turn, for he was the first to not only marvel at Kaspar Hauser, but also study him with genuine interest. He very quickly noticed that the helplessness, idiocy, and ignorance of the boy stood in glaring contrast to his exceptional gifts and noble disposition. His particular nature and exquisite talents, as well as certain superficial details like the presence of vaccination marks at a time when only the finest families had their children vaccinated—all this led Feuerbach to the conclusion that the enigmatic foundling must be the child of a very well-off family whose relatives disposed of him to eliminate an heir. The family of the Grand Duke of Baden came to Feuerbach's mind. Veiled references to the same suspicions even appeared in newspapers back then, increasing public interest in the boy. It's easy to see how much all this must have upset those who had thought Kaspar Hauser would be discreetly banished to some Nuremberg poorhouse or hospice. But this was not to be. Feuerbach, who as a high state official had something to say in the matter, saw to it that the boy was placed in an environment that would satisfy his now immense thirst for knowledge.

Kaspar Hauser became like a son in the family of a Nuremberg professor named Daumer, a good and noble man, but a rather odd bird.[3] Daumer left us with not only a large book on Kaspar Hauser, but also an entire library full of curious works on oriental wisdom,

---

3 Georg Friedrich Daumer (1800–1875) played host and teacher to Kaspar Hauser and wrote several books about him.

secrets of nature, miracle cures, and magnetism. He conducted experiments of this kind on Kaspar Hauser, though in a very gentle and humane way. According to descriptions he gave, Kaspar Hauser seems to have been a creature who displayed great tenderness, clarity of thought, sober-mindedness, and purity during his stay in the Daumer household. In any case, he made enormous progress and soon came so far as to undertake to tell the story of his own life.[4] It is through this endeavor that we have learned what we know today about the time before his appearance in Nuremberg. He seems to have spent many years in an underground cell where there was no light and no other living soul. Two little wooden horses and a wooden dog were his only companions, water and bread his only nourishment. Shortly before he was led out of the dungeon, an unknown man made contact with him, entered his dungeon and, standing behind Kaspar Hauser so he couldn't be seen, took the boy's hand in his and taught him to write. There's no need to explain why these stories, written in awkward German to boot, created much cause for doubt. But here things get strange again: the fact is, during his first months in Nuremberg, Kaspar Hauser took only bread and water; he couldn't digest anything else, not even milk. Furthermore he could see in the dark. The newspapers didn't pass up the opportunity to report that Kaspar Hauser had begun to work on his life story, and it nearly spelled his doom. Shortly after it became known, he was found unconscious in the Daumers' cellar, his forehead bleeding. He claimed that an unknown man hit him from above with a hatchet while he was beneath the stairs. The unknown man was never discovered. But around four days after the incident, an elegant gentleman was said to have conversed with a townswoman before the city gates, pressing her for news on the life or death of the wounded Hauser. He then walked with the woman up to the gate, where a police notice had been posted concerning the attack on Hauser. After reading this, he very suspiciously went on his way without entering the city.

If we had enough time—which I and hopefully you as well would appreciate—I could introduce you to another strange personage who appeared at this point in Hauser's life, the distinguished gentleman who adopted him. We cannot explore this man's role in the story just now, but suffice it to say that people were concerned for

4 For Kaspar Hauser's autobiography, see Jeffrey Moussaieff Masson, *Lost Prince: The Unsolved Mystery of Kaspar Hauser* (New York: The Free Press, 1996), 187–95.

Kaspar Hauser's safety and he was taken from Nuremberg to Ansbach, where Anselm von Feuerbach himself held the post of presiding judge. That was in 1831. Kaspar Hauser would live for two more years, until he was murdered in 1833. How, I will tell you now in closing. In the meantime he had undergone a striking transformation. After some time, as quickly as his mental faculties had developed in Nuremberg and his finer talents likewise, his development suddenly came to a halt, his character dimmed and ultimately, at the end of his life—he was no older than thirty-one—he had become an average, even mediocre person, who made an honest living as a court clerk and with paper crafts, at which he was very skilled. But apart from this, he displayed neither industriousness nor any great love of the truth.

It happened on a December morning in the year 1833. A man came up to him in the street with the words: "I bear greetings from the court gardener, who inquires as to whether this afternoon you might not like to be shown the artesian well in the park, at such-and-such a time." Around four o'clock Kaspar Hauser showed up at the court gardens. Not seeing anyone at the artesian well, he continued on another hundred steps. A man then emerged from the bushes and gestured to him with a violet bag, saying: "I give you this bag as a gift!" Kaspar Hauser had hardly touched it when he felt a stab, the man disappeared, Kaspar let the bag fall to the ground and then dragged himself home. But the wound was fatal. He died three days later, but not before being questioned. Whether this unknown man was the same that had tried to kill him in Nuremberg four years earlier remained as murky as everything else. There were even people who claimed the stab wound was inflicted by Kaspar Hauser on himself. But the bag was found, and with it something quite extraordinary. It contained only a folded note, with a message written in mirror script: "Hauser will be able to reveal to you exactly what I look like and whence I come. To spare Hauser the trouble, I will tell you myself where I am from. I come from the Bavarian frontier. I will even tell you my name." But what followed were just three capital letters: M L O.

I've already told you that there are forty-nine volumes of files in the Munich State Archives. King Ludwig I, who took great interest in the affair, is said to have examined them all. And many scholars have since followed suit. The dispute over whether or not Kaspar Hauser was a Baden prince is still unsettled. Every year there's some new book claiming to solve the riddle at last. We can wager a hundred to one that when you're all grown up, there will still be people unable to tear themselves away from this story. If such a book falls into your hands, perhaps you'll read it, to see whether it holds the resolution that the radio station still owes you.

"Caspar Hauser," GS, 7.1, 174–80. Translated by Jonathan Lutes.

Broadcast on Radio Berlin, November 22, 1930, and on Southwest German Radio, Frankfurt, December 17, 1930. The broadcast was announced in the Funkstunde *for November 22, 1930, from 3:20–3:40 pm, and in the* Südwestdeutsche Rundfunk-Zeitung *for December 17, 1930, from 3:25–3:50 pm.*

CHAPTER 18

Dr. Faust

As a boy I learned history from the Neubauer, which is still used in many schools, I believe, but perhaps now looks different than it did in those days.[1] Back then what especially struck me about the book was that most of its pages were divided into large and small print. The parts in large print covered princes, wars, peace treaties, alliances, dates, etc., which we had to learn, though I did not enjoy doing so. The parts in small print dealt with so-called cultural history, including the habits and customs of people in earlier times, their convictions, their art, their knowledge, their buildings, and so on. Learning these things wasn't required. We only had to read them over, and this I enjoyed greatly. As far I was concerned, there could have been even more of it, no matter how small the print. There wasn't much discussion of it during class. Our German teacher would say: "We'll hear about that in history class," and our history teacher: "We've already heard about that in German class." In the end, we heard almost nothing about it.

About Faust, for instance, maybe they told us that Goethe's great drama is based on more than 200 years of lore concerning the arch-magician Johann Faust and his eternal pact with the devil; they told us that his life is depicted in ten or twenty books, which all trace back to two in particular, the first published in 1587 and the second in 1599;[2] and perhaps they even told us that Dr. Johann Faust had indeed been a real person. But that was the

---

1 Friedrich Neubauer was the author of the history textbook, *Lehrbuch der Geschichte für höhere Lehranstalten* [History Textbook for Higher Learning], (Halle: Verlag der Buchhandlung des Waisenhauses, 1897).

2 The first "Faust Book," *Historia von D. Johann Fausten*, was compiled anonymously and published in 1587 in Frankfurt by Johann Spieß. Many subsequent retellings were to follow. The date of 1599 suggests the Hamburg edition by Georg Rudolf Widmann.

extent of it. We didn't hear what the first books said of the many magic stories, journeys, and adventures that filled his life, although not only are they important in order to understand Goethe's *Faust*, they're also fun.

To plunge right into it, I'll tell you one of the most savage magic stories there is, which bears no resemblance to anything I've found in other books of legends. Admittedly, it's not the only tale in which a magician knocks off someone's head and then miraculously puts it back on. Now let's hear the story:

> Once when Faust was being fêted in a tavern by a few spirited fellows, they requested that he perform the magical decapitation of a man and the reattachment of his head. The houseboy offered himself as the subject of this endeavor and Faust proceeded to knock his head off. But when he wanted to place it back on, it wouldn't go, leading Faust to conclude that one of the guests was interfering with magic of his own. Faust admonished the guests and, since the guilty party would not lift his spell, he made a lily sprout up from the table and cut off its blossom with the knife. At once, the head of the guest who had obstructed Faust's magic fell from the trunk of his body. Faust then restored the houseboy's head to his torso and went on his merry way.[3]

In those days such performances were referred to by the scholarly term *magia innaturalis*, meaning unnatural magic, as opposed to *magia naturalis*, or natural magic, which was what we today call physics and chemistry and technology. The Faust we hear of in the first Faust book dealt more in the first type of magic—blatant, shameless magic that he exploited to obtain bags of money, good meals, expensive wine, trips to faraway lands on a magic coat, and other such things. However, the Faust from the theater, and also from the puppet play you will hear a little of later, as well as in Goethe's drama, is not a rogue, but simply a man who consecrates himself to the devil in order to partake in the secrets of nature, and thus in natural magic. Indeed, the puppet play starts right off with the devil conversing in hell with his minister Charon, telling him how dull it's getting being surrounded by all the miserable wretches that land in hell. I'd like, he says, to get just one great man down

3 For a similar passage, see *Das Volksbuch vom Doktor Faust: Nach der ersten Ausgabe, 1587* [The first Faust Book, based on the edition of 1587], ed. Robert Petsch (Halle: Max Niemeyer, 1911), 144–5.

here. The devil Mephistopheles then seeks out Faust in order to seduce him.[4]

To summarize, this Faust was born in southern Germany probably around 1490. He would later scrape by as a student, giving lectures and teaching school, as was common at that time. In Heidelberg on January 15, 1509, as we know from the university register, he received his doctorate. After this he began the gay life of the adventurer. In 1513 he came to Erfurt, where he called himself "Faust, the Heidelberg Demigod." His path then most likely led him to Krakow, and finally to Paris, where he served King Francis I of France. He was also in Wittenberg. A passage in Luther's *Table Talk* even makes reference to Faust.[5] But he had to flee Wittenberg when his magic caught up with him, and finally, as we know from the Zimmern Chronicle, he died in 1539 in a village in Württemberg.[6]

This chronicle from Count Christof of Zimmern, the same from which we have the only notice of Faust's death, contains something else of great interest. It is written in the chronicle that Faust left behind a library, which came into the possession of the Count of Staufen, on whose territory Faust died. Apparently people often came to the Count of Staufen to buy books from Faust's estate for a hefty price. Indeed, we know from a seventeenth-century necromancer that he paid 8,000 guilders for a so-called *Höllenzwang*.

Now, what is a *Höllenzwang*? It is a collection of the incantations and magic symbols used to supposedly summon the devil or other spirits, both good and evil. I don't know how to describe them to you. These symbols are neither letters nor numbers; at best they resemble sometimes Arabic, sometimes Hebrew, and sometimes convoluted mathematical figures. They make absolutely no sense except as a way for a master sorcerer to explain to his students why their incantations failed: they simply didn't draw the figures precisely. This must have often been the case, because they are so convoluted that they can really only be traced. And the words in a *Höllenzwang*, a gobbledygook of Latin, Hebrew, and German, sound very bombastic and also make no sense.

---

4 Modified by Benjamin from *Das Puppenspiel vom Doktor Faust* (Leipzig: Höfer, 1914), 5–6.

5 See Luther, *Tischreden* (1566), in *Martin Luthers Werke: Kritische Gesamtausgabe: Tischreden*, vol. 1 (Weimar: Hermann Böhlaus Nachfolger, 1912), no. 1059, 534–5.

6 The *Zimmern Chronicle*, quoted in Johann Scheible, *Das Kloster*, vol. 5: *Die Sage vom Faust* (Stuttgart: J. Scheible, 1847).

You can imagine that people back then had a different opinion on the matter. Indeed, the *Höllenzwang* was considered so dangerous that the Frankfurt typographer Johann Spieß, who in 1587 printed the first book about Faust and wrote the foreword to it, remarked that after much deliberation he left out everything that could have caused offense, that is to say the incantations that would have been found in the magic library. You should think of this magic library, of which there were actually quite a few in the Middle Ages, less as a collection of books, for they were not even printed, and more as a pile of handwritten notebooks, almost like chemistry or math notebooks. People were not altogether wrong if they saw possession of such books as dangerous; it was, though not because the devil would come into their houses through the chimney, but because the Inquisition, were they to get wind of it, imprisoned those possessing magic books and accused them of sorcery. History attests to cases in which just owning the book of folk tales about Dr. Faust had dire consequences. Indeed, all sorts of things could have the most dreadful consequences. When later you read Goethe's *Faust*, you will learn how Faust takes in a stray dog he finds while on an Easter stroll by the city gate. Afterwards, while he is studying in his room, the poodle disturbs him with its noisy antics, prompting Goethe's Faust to say:

> If you wish to share this cell with me,
> poodle, stop your yowling;
> bark no more.
> A nuisance such as you
> I cannot suffer in my presence.
> One of us must leave this room;
> I now reluctantly suspend
> the law of hospitality.
> The door is open, you are free to go.
> But what is this?
> Is this a natural occurrence?
> Is it shadow or reality?
> How broad and long my poodle waxes!
> He rises up with mighty strength;
> this is no dog's anatomy!
> What a specter did I bring into my house!
> Now he's very like a river horse
> with glowing eyes and vicious teeth.
> Oh! I am sure of you!

> For such a half-satanic brood
> the key of Solomon will do.[7]

This poodle is a shape-shifting demon. The magic books refer to him as Praestigiar, which can be roughly translated as magical deceiver. The old books state that on Faust's command, this poodle could turn white, brown, or red, and that upon his death Faust bequeathed him to an abbot in Halberstadt, who was none too pleased to own the poodle; in fact, his life would end very soon thereafter. Just how firm was the popular belief in such nonsensical ghost stories can be seen in the fact that a great scholar—Agrippa von Nettesheim was his name—had to be defended by one of his students expressly against accusations of sorcery, based in part on the fact that Agrippa was always seen in the company of a black poodle.

There were passages in the first Faust stories that people accepted, as we do today, as strange, sometimes spooky, sometimes amusing ghost stories that they didn't fret about too much. But there were also other passages, and other readers. As shown by the use of the term "natural magic" for physics and chemistry, these sciences were not thought to be as distinct from magic as they are for us today. For example, when in several stories Faust shows curious princes or students images of the ancient Greeks, Homer, Achilles, Helen of Troy, etc., it was considered magic, and even if some of the readers of such stories had already seen or heard of the *laterna magica*, such knowledge confirmed rather than refuted the magic of Dr. Faust. As far as these people were concerned, the ability to use the *camera obscura*, upon which the principle of the *laterna magica* is based, counted as magic, hence the name *laterna magica*, or magic lantern; similarly, the difference between the first attempts at flying, which were undertaken using air balloons, and Faust's flights on his magic coat was not as clear-cut as it is for us today. What's more, many medicinal prescriptions, which we may now consider natural and sensible, were seen as magical.

In those days there was a fine line between being considered a sorcerer or a scholar. The sorcerer was abhorred for being in league with the devil, while the scholar was revered as a higher being; this later became of great importance for Goethe's *Faust*. The puppet play conveyed the same message in its own way: even the least

---

7 This translation is from Goethe, *Faust I*, trans. Peter Salm (New York: Bantam, 1985), lines 1238–48, 77–9.

sophisticated spectators could recognize what an unusual man this Faust was when they were presented with Hanswurst as a foil, who also had a pact with the devil; he remains as silly and foolish as before yet eventually manages to break loose from the devil.[8] The best passage in the puppet play is at the end of Faust's life, when the poor, haunted Faust meets the dull, boring Hanswurst. The devil has long since lost interest in Hanswurst, but plans to fetch Faust in two hours. Let me read it to you:

> FAUST: Nowhere do I find rest and repose, everywhere it follows me, the vision of hell. Oh why was I not steadfast in my scheme, why did I let myself be swayed? The evil spirit knew to grasp me at my weakest point; I have irrevocably slid into hell. Even Mephistopheles has abandoned me, just now at my unhappiest hour, when I am most in need of diversion. Mephistopheles, Mephistopheles, where are you?
>
> *Mephistopheles appears as the devil.*
>
> MEPHISTOPHELES: Faust, how do you like me now?
>
> FAUST: What's gotten into you? Have you forgotten that you are obliged to appear to me in human form?
>
> MEPHISTOPHELES: No, not anymore, because your time has expired. Three more hours and then you're mine.
>
> FAUST: Eh? What is that you say, Mephistopheles? My time has expired? You must be lying. Only twelve years have elapsed. Therefore twelve years remain that you must serve me.
>
> MEPHISTOPHELES: I've served you for twenty-four years.
>
> FAUST: But how is that possible? You changed the calendar?
>
> MEPHISTOPHELES: No, that I can't do. But listen to me carefully. You are demanding twelve more years.
>
> FAUST: Indeed I am—our contract says four-and-twenty years.
>
> MEPHISTOPHELES: Indeed it does, but we didn't account for me serving you day and night. And you harried me day and night, so, add on the nights and you'll see that our contract is coming to an end.
>
> FAUST: Father of all lies! You've betrayed me.
>
> MEPHISTOPHELES: No, you have betrayed yourself.
>
> FAUST: Let me live just one more year.
>
> MEPHISTOPHELES: Not even a day.

---

8 Hanswurst, a traditional jester character in German-speaking comedy and a predecessor figure for Kasper (see "Berlin Puppet Theater"), appears in the seventeenth- and eighteenth-century German puppet plays based on the story of Dr. Faust.

FAUST: Just one more month.

MEPHISTOPHELES: Not an hour longer.

FAUST: Just one more day, so I can take leave of my good friends.[9]

But Mephistopheles has nothing more to say on the matter. He has served long enough: "We meet again at twelve o'clock." And with these words he takes leave of Faust.

You can imagine the excitement and suspense when the audience suddenly sees Hanswurst enter the puppet stage, slow and steady as a night watchman, leisurely calling out the top of each hour. Three times.

"Listen all and count alike, now the clock doth ten times strike," and so on: the old German night watchman song.

Thus Faust has two more hours to live, two hours until twelve. In his final quarter of an hour he meets Hanswurst. So that, for all his mistakes, we don't feel sorry for Faust when the devil finally comes for him, and so that we may palpably feel his utter desperation, the writer of the old puppet play has Faust try to save himself by means of a pathetic scam, which fails. Let's hear how:

Hanswurst catches sight of Faust and says: "Well, good evening, my dear Sir Faust, good evening. Still out on the street?"

FAUST: Why yes, my servant, I haven't a moment's peace, on the street or at home.

HANSWURST: And rightly so. You see, I'm having a rough go of it myself at the moment—and you still owe me last month's pay. Be so kind as to give it to me now—I really need it.

FAUST: Alas, my servant, I have nothing—the devil has made me so poor, I don't even own myself anymore. (*Aside.*) I must try to use this fool to wrest myself free from the devil. (*To outwit Hanswurst.*) Yes, my dear servant, although I have no money, I'd hate to leave this world without first paying you. Here's what I propose: take off your clothes and put on mine. That way you get your payment and I lose my debt.

HANSWURST (*shaking his head*): Oh no, then the devil would be likely to nab the wrong guy. No, before any great mistake occurs, I'd prefer just to forget the money. And in exchange, you can do me a favor.

FAUST: Gladly, what is it?

HANSWURST: Say hello to my grandmother. She's in hell number eleven, just to the right when you walk in.

---

9 See *Das Puppenspiel vom Doktor Faust*, 60–1.

Hanswurst hurries off. We hear him singing from behind the stage:

> Listen all and count alike,
> now the clock doth twelve times strike.
> Guard the fire and guard the coal
> The devil comes for Dr. Faust's soul.[10]

The clock strikes twelve, and with thunder, brimstone, and lightning, an entire company of devils emerges from hell to fetch Faust.

Goethe saw this puppet play as a young boy. He began composing *Faust* before he was thirty years old, and he was eighty when he finished writing it. His Faust similarly made a pact with the devil, and the devil also comes to fetch him at the end. But in the 250 years between the appearance of the first Faust book and the completion of Goethe's *Faust*, mankind had changed. More and more, it was understood that what had previously drawn people to magic was often not greed, depravity, or sloth, but rather thirst for knowledge and elevation of mind. Goethe demonstrated this in his *Faust*, forcing the devil to retreat at last before a legion of angels filling the entire stage.

"Dr. Faust," GS, 7.1, 180–8. Translated by Jonathan Lutes.

Broadcast on Radio Berlin on January 30, 1931, and on Southwest German Radio, Frankfurt on March 28, 1931. The Funkstunde *announced the Berlin broadcast for January 30, 1931 from 5:30–5:50 pm. In Frankfurt, the* Südwestdeutsche Rundfunk-Zeitung *advertised it for March 28, 1931, from 3:20–3:50 pm, under a variant title: "Youth Hour: 'Der Zauberkünstler Dr. Faust' [The Conjurer Dr. Faust] by Walter Benjamin, Berlin (for children ten years old and above)."*

---

10   Ibid., 65–6.

CHAPTER 19

Cagliostro

Today I want to tell you about a great swindler. By great I mean not only that the man was hugely unconventional and brazen in his swindling, but also that he carried it out flawlessly. His prowess for fraud made him famous across all of Europe; he was revered by tens of thousands, almost as a saint; during the years 1760 to 1780, his portrait could be found everywhere—on engravings, paintings, busts. He performed his séances, miracle cures, alchemies, and rejuvenation treatments in the so-called Age of Enlightenment. This was an epoch when, as you know, people were particularly skeptical of all forms of irrational tradition, claimed to want to follow only their own free minds, and, in short, should have been especially well protected from men such as this Cagliostro. At the end of the broadcast we'll say a few words about how he managed to be so successful in spite of this, or rather because of it.

To this day no one knows exactly where Cagliostro came from, but one thing is certain: he did not come from where he claimed he did, namely Medina, or, for that matter, anywhere in the Orient; most likely he hailed from Italy, or perhaps Portugal. Of Cagliostro's youth, one thing is clear: he was first trained as a pharmacist while, on the side, he taught himself all sorts of useless skills such as grave digging, counterfeit handwriting, panhandling, and the like. He never lingered anywhere for too long. He ended his life just as he began it: as a wanderer. Of all his stops, none was more important than London, where he arrived for the first time around 1750. It was there that he learned of the Freemasons and was most likely admitted to the order. His experiences in London, the strange and mystical tests to which he was subjected—some of you are perhaps familiar with the "Magic Flute," with its fire trial and water trial, two masonic rituals—left a lasting impression on his fantasy worlds and his works of imagination. Cagliostro's life goal was to do something extraordinary with Freemasonry. The actual Freemasons were a society that had nothing at all to do with magic, instead pursuing goals that were part humanitarian and part political. These were closely related, as their political activities were directed against the vicious tyranny of many European rulers of the time, as well as, of course, against the pope. But these comparatively prosaic ambitions could not satisfy Cagliostro. He wanted to found a new Freemasonry, a so-called Egyptian Freemasonry, a sort of magic society whose laws he plucked out of thin air. Yet his goals were more ambitious. As opposed to the hostile approach of the real Freemasons, Egyptian Freemasonry was meant to treat the pope in a friendlier manner. Cagliostro wanted to reconcile the Freemasons with the pope, and thereby acquire, as the arbiter of these two forces, the highest power in Europe.

As successful as this extraordinary man was all over Europe with his various schemes—which these days couldn't get him from Magdeburg to Berlin—he occasionally ran into people who were not so easily fooled. And I don't mean the physicians, who, wherever he showed up, would vigorously hound him, not so much because they knew he was a fake, but out of professional jealousy. Cagliostro operated according to an old charlatan's trick; that is, wherever he settled for a while, he made sure it was known that he would treat the poor for free. And he kept his promise without fail. But on the sly he let on to the many genteel people who also sought his medical help just how impoverished he was by his selfless philanthropy: the prosperous and the high-born were positively honored when he accepted their gifts. When I speak of people who could see through him, I don't mean just the doctors or the countless esteemed scientists and philosophers he encountered in his life who saw through his tricks. No, in order to speak frankly of Cagliostro, and wholly without reservation, it took a very pragmatic man, and it's surely no accident that one of the most hostile, but also sharpest and most insightful portraits that we have of Cagliostro's appearance and demeanor comes from a well-traveled salesman:

> I've never seen such a shameless, pushy, self-important charlatan. He's a short, plump, extremely broad-shouldered, round-headed fellow with black hair, a neck that's fat and stiff, a thick forehead, bold and finely curved eyebrows, black, glowing, milky and constantly rolling eyes, a somewhat bent, finely curved and broad nose, round, thick, disjointed lips, a strong, round, protruding chin, a round, steely jaw: an

auburn-skinned thoroughbred with a forceful and resounding voice. He is the miracle man, the spirit conjurer, the humanitarian doctor and helper who has lived lavishly in these parts for many years without anyone ever knowing where he gets his money. One cannot help but wish that all the transfixed adulators who surround him could witness a man take the trouble to adopt the same shameless character with him and to treat him as despicably as he does others; they would soon perceive what a miserable creature the empty braggart really is, as he has neither the natural gifts nor the education to hold his own against such a man for even a few minutes. And of course the man would have to be physically strong, in case it should be necessary to suspend the monstrous knave out the window with one hand and hear his final confession before he plummets to the ground.[1]

You see that this honest salesman does not mince his words. But he's taking it a bit too far; for it's no accident that during the first forty years of his life Cagliostro never met his match. There has been a great deal of speculation as to the cause of this superiority. Many believe it was the power of his gaze; no one he looked at could resist it. And there's also the fact that people back then were fundamentally hungry for such experiences. The more they distanced themselves from the Church, the clergy and all the rest, the more interested they were in any form of natural magic power, which in those days was thought to derive from a so-called magnetism found in people, and even more in animals. And what Cagliostro lacked in knowledge and education, he made up for with an exceptional knack for the theatrical. Hearing a description of just one of his lectures, delivered in all the cities he visited, is enough to make us understand the huge audiences he attracted.

In an almost pitch-black hall with walls covered in black velvet, he stood on a type of throne under a brocade canopy, wearing a black robe and a black hat with an enormous brim. Before stepping onto the dais, however, he strode through the so-called Street of Steel, a corridor created by two rows of his most distinguished followers, crossing their raised swords over the central aisle. The candles, which only dimly lit the room, stood on candelabras in

---

1 From "Der Pseudo-Graf Cagliostro (Aus dem Tagebuch eines Reisenden, Straßburg, 1783)" [The Pseudo-Count Cagliostro (From the Diary of a Traveler, Strasbourg, 1783)], *Berlinische Monatsschrift* 4 (December 1784), 536–9. See also: *Der Erzzauberer Cagliostro: Die Dokumente über ihn nebst zwölf Bildbeigaben*, ed. Johannes von Guenther (Munich: G. Müller, 1919), 185–7.

groups of seven or nine—numbers to which Cagliostro attached particular significance. Then there was the smell of incense wafting from copper vessels, and the play of lights in a large water-filled carafe from which Cagliostro himself foretold the future, or where he delivered prophecies through a child. The lectures themselves began with him producing an esoteric parchment roll from which he read off a hodgepodge of incantations, ways of turning coarse cloths into silk, methods for transforming small gems into jewels the size of a hen's egg, and so forth.

You might be wondering, what did Cagliostro want from all this? It is unlikely that someone who merely wanted to live the good life, to eat and drink well, would be able to muster the power and imagination to captivate Europe for twenty years with ·his fabulous inventions. Cagliostro attached at least as much importance to the imaginary eminence of the Freemasons and to power as he did to money. But that's not all. No man can live for decades under the spell of fantastical ideas, holding forth about eternal life, the philosopher's stone, the seventh book of Moses, and other kindred secrets that he claimed to have discovered, without believing them at least to some degree himself. Or, better put: Cagliostro certainly didn't believe what he told people, but you can be sure that he believed that his power to make his fantastical lies seem credible was in reality worth as much as the philosopher's stone, eternal life, and the seventh book of Moses put together. And that's the crux at which his lies contain a kernel of truth. Cagliostro's enormous strength actually derived from his belief in himself, his belief in his powers of persuasion, his imagination, his knowledge of human nature. This faith in himself must have grown so strong that it became something like a secret religion, quite different from the one he taught his students.

This is precisely what Goethe found so very interesting about the man; as you have learned in school or soon will, he wrote a play about him, *Der Großkophta* [The Grand Cophta]. But what you probably haven't heard is that Goethe himself once played the role of Cagliostro, and not for the public, but for Cagliostro's family. In his *Italian Journey* he recounts how he was sitting in a tavern in Palermo when the conversation turned to Cagliostro and his poor relatives; how he, Goethe, expressed his wish to meet the family of this extraordinary man; how this proved difficult and, indeed, only possible if Goethe pretended to have seen Cagliostro himself and to be carrying greetings from him to his loved ones; how this encounter awakened great hope in the family, causing Goethe to reproach himself for his little game; and how finally, to alleviate his bad conscience, after returning to Weimar, he sent a large sum of money to the poor family, which everyone believed to have been a gift from Cagliostro.[2]

You will notice that I have not told you much about Cagliostro's actual life. And this is how I'd like it to remain, because every single one of his stops involves so many entanglements that telling his life story would take a great tome. In any case, his life ended like the jug of the story, which went to the well so often that it broke. After thirty years Cagliostro had reached the point that wherever he went, old and very unpleasant stories lay dormant, waiting only for his arrival to be reawakened on people's lips. His stops grew shorter and shorter, and by the end he was constantly on the run. A respected newspaper, *The European Courier*, played an important and curious role in this decline, as I will now relate in closing.[3] Among the multifarious medicinal and chemical absurdities that Cagliostro sought to promote was the story of the pig. He wrote somewhere that in Medina, where famously he claimed to be from, the people got rid of the lions, tigers, and leopards by fattening up pigs with arsenic and then shooing them into the woods where they were devoured by the wild animals, who died from the poison. Morande, the publisher of *The European Courier*, took up the matter and ridiculed it. This infuriated Cagliostro, who then presented Morande with a peculiar challenge. On September 3, 1786, he printed a leaflet inviting Morande to a feast on November 9, where together they would eat a piglet fed as they were in Medina, while betting 5,000 guilders that Morande would die from it, but he himself would remain healthy. Now, it's quite a lot to propose to someone that he will die and on top of that lose 5,000 guilders on a bet. As you can imagine, Morande had no interest in taking up the offer. Instead he compiled a collection of disparaging facts and rumors about Cagliostro and published it in his *European Courier*. In the end

2 For Goethe's account of Cagliostro and meeting his family, see *Italienische Reise*, in *Goethes Werke*, vol. 10 (Gera: C. B. Griesbach, 1897), entry for 13 and 14 April, 1787, 312f (*Italian Journey*, trans. W. H. Auden and Elizabeth Mayer [London: Penguin, 1992], 247f). Goethe's play *Der Großkoptha* [The Grand Cophta], a satire on Cagliostro's life and his involvement in the so-called Affair of the Diamond Necklace, was completed in 1791.

3 *Le Courier de l'Europe* was a bilingual political bi-weekly published in London and Paris between the years 1776–1792. From 1784–1791, it was edited by Charles Théveneau de Morande (1741–1805), who famously engaged in an exchange of accusations and counter-accusations with Cagliostro.

Cagliostro fled to Rome, although because of his connection to the Freemasons, he couldn't have chosen a place where he would have felt less safe. His friends were quick to inform him of the Inquisition's intention to jail him, but Cagliostro was tired and stayed put. In 1789, Pope Pius VI had him arrested and imprisoned in the Castel Sant'Angelo while he was tried by the Inquisition. Most of what we know today about Cagliostro derives from this trial, which seems to be have been conducted with great accuracy but also with astounding leniency. Nevertheless, it concluded unsurprisingly with a death sentence for heresy. In 1791, however, the pope reprieved Cagliostro and his sentence was commuted to life imprisonment. A few years later, although it's unclear exactly when, he died in the San Leo prison in Urbino.

There's much to learn from this story if you are so inclined. You could take the easy way out and simply say: there's a fool born every minute. But on closer examination, the essence of Cagliostro's story holds a more important truth.

At the beginning I spoke of the Enlightenment, an age in which people were very critical of the traditions of government, religion, and the Church, and indeed, we can be thankful for the great strides made during this period in terms of freedom and culture. It was precisely during this free and critical Age of Enlightenment that Cagliostro was able to turn his artistry to such advantage. How was this possible? Answer: precisely because people were so firmly convinced that the supernatural world did not exist, they never took the trouble to reflect upon it seriously and thus fell victim to Cagliostro, who led them to believe in the supernatural with a magician's finesse. Had their convictions been weaker and their powers of observation stronger, they wouldn't have succumbed. This is another lesson from the story: in many cases, powers of observation and knowledge of human nature are even more valuable than a firm and correct point of view.

"Cagliostro," GS, 7.1, 188–94. Translated by Jonathan Lutes.

Broadcast on Southwest German Radio, Frankfurt on February 14, 1931. The Südwestdeutsche Rundfunk-Zeitung *announced the broadcast, with a variant title, for February 14, 1931, from 3:20–3:50 pm: "Youth Hour, 'Der Erzzauberer Cagliostro [The Arch-Magician Cagliostro].' Talk by Walter Benjamin."*

CHAPTER 20

Postage Stamp Swindles

Today I'd like to speak about something that even the most learned and clever postage stamp experts have not been able to keep up with: fraud. Postage stamp fraud. In 1840 Rowland Hill, a mere schoolteacher at the time, invented the postage stamp, for which the British government would later appoint him postmaster general of England, knight him, and award him a gift of 400,000 marks. Since his invention millions upon millions have been earned with these little scraps of paper, and many individuals have made their fortunes with them as well. From your Senff, Michel, or Kohl catalogs you certainly know how much a single one of them can sometimes be worth.[1] The most valuable of them all is not, as most believe, the twopenny "Post Office" from Mauritius, but rather a one-cent stamp from British Guiana, a provisional stamp from the year 1856, of which, evidently, only one specimen remains. It was printed at the local newspaper with the same crude printing plate used for shipping company advertisements. This single remaining specimen was discovered years ago by a young Guianese collector among some old family documents. It then found its way into the La Renotière collection in Paris, which was the largest stamp collection in the world. No one knows how much its owner paid for this stamp, but its catalog price is now 100,000 marks. Already by 1913 the collection it joined comprised over 120,000 stamps, and was estimated to be worth well over 10 million. Of course, only a millionaire could afford to amuse himself compiling such a collection. Whether or not it had been his intent, he earned millions more from his collection. Its beginnings go back to the year 1878.[2] However, the

---

1 Benjamin refers to three stamp catalogs and reference works of the period: *Senfs Illustriertes Briefmarken Journal*, *Michel Briefmarken Katalog*, and *Paul Kohls Briefmarken Handbuch*.

2 The German mistakenly gives 1778 as the date here. The La Renotière collection,

beginnings of stamp collecting itself date back another fifteen years. In those days collecting was easier than it is today, not only because there were many fewer stamps; not only because things that are prohibitively expensive now were much easier to come by back then; and not only because one could much more easily collect them all, but also because there were no forgeries in those days, or at least, none perpetrated in order to deceive collectors. Those of you that read stamp journals surely know that new forgeries are written about as something quite ordinary, even expected. And how could it be otherwise? Stamps can be so lucrative and the world of stamps has become so vast that no one can keep track of it all. In 1914, before the countless war and occupation stamps appeared, there were no less than 64,268 different stamps.

So, forgery. You know that whenever anything is collected it will be forged, without exception. While forgeries intended to fool the more dim-witted can be rather coarse and haphazard, others are too intricate even for the greatest experts to spot, and still others are so well executed that it takes decades to reveal them as forgeries, if they're ever uncovered at all. Many collectors, especially beginners, think they're safe from forgery if they concern themselves only with used stamps. This is because a number of states, particularly the Papal States, Sardinia, Hamburg, Hanover, Heligoland, and Bergedorf, reprinted rare sets of stamps that were no longer in use, and delivered them directly to collectors. These reprints, or, if you will, forgeries are all characterized by the fact that they're not post-marked. But this is a special case that does not hold true across the board. There is nothing more preposterous than to say, "This stamp is counterfeit, because it's not postmarked." It would be much more accurate to say: this stamp is postmarked because it's counterfeit. For there are in fact many fewer counterfeit stamps that are not postmarked: for the most part, only those where the forger, if we can use this word, is the state. The private forger who dares to counter-feit an intricately designed stamp can surely replicate a simple postmark as well. And when he has finished his forgery, he looks it over once more, very closely, searching for any irregularity that he can then obscure by covering it with a postmark. In short, collecting only postmarked stamps would protect you from some reprints but not from the great majority of counterfeit stamps. Very few

owned by Philipp Ferrari de la Renotière (1850–1917), was bolstered by his 1878 purchase of the one-cent stamp, "Black on Magenta" of British Guiana. This stamp was valued in 2014 at $20 million.

collectors know which country enjoys the greatest reputation among stamp forgers, in other words, where the most successful counterfeits are made. That would be Belgium. Not only do Belgians counterfeit their own postage stamps—most famously the Belgian five-franc stamp—but they're equally willing to forge foreign stamps, such as the one-peseta German Morocco.

To offload their goods, the forgers have found a great trick that both earns them more revenue and ensures they don't get caught. They explicitly advertise their products as what they are: fakes. In marketing the counterfeit stamps as non-genuine, they of course forgo the huge profits of other forgers. But because their buyers, for the most part, intend to do just the opposite with these newly acquired stamps, that is, to sell them on as real, the fabricators can ask considerable prices for their wares, which they state are not counterfeits but rather stamps reproduced for scholarly purposes. They send their offerings to small stamp dealers along with literature boasting of the flawless replication of their out-of-circulation stamps, their admirable execution of a brand-new technique, the stamps' painstakingly faithful imagery, overprints, colors, paper, watermarks, perforations, and—let's not forget—postmarks. To guard against such goods, large stamp dealers have proposed a sort of guaranty, or mark of authenticity, that clearly indicates which respectable firm has vouched that a given stamp is genuine. Yet others have quite reasonably objected, asking why the image on an original stamp should be disfigured with a company's seal, no matter how small. Instead, valuable stamps discovered to be counterfeits should be marked with a seal of forgery, or branded, in other words. Furthermore, not everything sold as a "replica" is necessarily intended as forgery. The famous 1864 Penny Black from England, for example, was reproduced a couple of times by the state printing office for the collections of a few English princes. Those of you who remain stamp collectors later on will have your own problems related to forgery, which will teach you more than I've told you today, and you will gradually find means to help you in the struggle against counterfeits. Today I'll mention the title of a single but very important book, the *Handbuch der Fälschungen* [Handbook of Forgeries] by Paul Ohrt.[3]

There are many cases of collector fraud, including the private and state exploitation of stamp collectors, that do not involve forgery.

---

3 A work with this title by Paul Ohrt has not been found. Ohrt is the author of *Handbuch aller bekannten Neudrucke* [Handbook of All Known Reprints] (1906–1938).

Above all there are the countries that, so to speak, live off the postage stamp trade. In earlier times especially, quite a few smaller states relied on the deep pockets of stamp collectors to improve their finances. The discovery of this peculiar source of income can be credited to an inventive resident of the Cook Islands. Not long ago the 10,000 to 12,000 inhabitants of this island were cannibals. Along with the first objects and tokens of civilization to reach these people came postage stamps ordered from New Zealand. They were very simple stamps, made of gummed paper outlined in block letters. Nevertheless, the big stamp dealers in America and Europe took great interest in these editions and paid handsomely for them. No one was more surprised than the people of the Cook Islands when such an easy and lucrative source of income suddenly presented itself. They immediately printed new sheets of stamps in Australia, which were different from the first ones in design and color. There are similar stories from many South American countries, especially Paraguay, and even from the little Indian principalities of Faridkot, Bengal, and Bamra. Even shrewder than the sovereigns who profited in this way were private individuals, like the engineer who delivered two million new stamps to Guatemala for free, in return asking only for all the series of old stamps that could still be found in the state printing office. It's not hard to imagine how much money he would later make from selling them. When things were going badly for Germany at the end of the war, even the German Reichspost followed the example set by these exotic kingdoms and principalities, and quickly sold their supplies of colonial stamps to private collectors.

Shall I now tell you an entirely different sort of swindle story, not directly related to stamp collecting? It's one of the cleverest you could ever imagine. And it centers around a stamp collection, so maybe I'll chance it. The story takes place in Wilhelmshaven in 1912. A well-to-do resident of the city sold his beautiful stamp collection, compiled over years of hard work, to a gentleman in Berlin for 17,000 marks and sent it cash-on-delivery. In the meantime the buyer had sent a crate, allegedly filled with books, to the man in Wilhelmshaven. Shortly afterwards he telegraphed to have this crate sent back to Berlin. Both crates arrived safely at the Berlin freight office. The swindler then succeeded in claiming the crate holding the stamp collection, without paying the cash due, by passing it off as the crate he himself had sent. The crate allegedly filled with books contained only scraps of paper, and the Berliner disappeared without a trace.

So much for postage stamp fraud insofar as the stamp collector is concerned. There is another, much greater entity with a vested interest in postage stamp fraud, and especially in counterfeit stamps: the post office. Each year the postal service sells roughly 6 billion stamps, that is, 6,000 million; worldwide, the total is 30 billion. This works out as people in Germany annually spending around 5 billion marks on stamps. Therefore, each year the postal service makes and sells 5,000 million marks worth of small paper money, if you will. Postage stamps can be thought of as small bank notes, as they're used not only to send letters, but often for payments up to a certain amount. In fact, stamps differ from paper money in one single way: printing counterfeit ten-mark or 100-mark notes requires tremendous knowledge and skill, as well as expensive and complicated equipment; whereas reprinting postage stamps is extraordinarily simple, and the rougher the original print, the more difficult it is to distinguish it from a forgery. A few years ago it so happened that several German ten-pfennig stamps were declared counterfeit by some very experienced stamp collectors, while the Reichspost was of the opinion that they were genuine. The frequency of this kind of stamp forgery—why not call it "banknote counterfeiting," as the law punishes it just as harshly—is hard to determine, because the postal service keeps an annual tally of the millions of marks it earns selling stamps, but doesn't record the values of the many millions of stamps it postmarks each year. There are people who claim that the postal authorities lose hundreds of millions of marks annually through fraud. As mentioned, this can't be confirmed, but if one considers that the post office can be bilked even more easily than through counterfeit stamps, that is, by cleanly removing a stamp's postmark, there's no reason to doubt this claim. Some even maintain that there is a predilection for certain types of swindle depending on the region. For example, large-scale printing forgery seems most prevalent in Southern Europe, while washing and cleaning stamps on a smaller scale is more popular in the North. I'm telling you all this because what these people are driving at concerns all stamp collectors. They want to abolish stamps and replace them with simple postmarks. You've probably all noticed that postmarks, not postage stamps, are already in use for bulk mail. Enemies of the postage stamp think this procedure should also be used for private mail, which would require the automation of mailboxes. There would be five-, eight-, fifteen-, and twenty-five-pfennig mailboxes and so on, a different box for each amount of postage demanded for a letter. For the mail slot to open, the sender would first need to insert the corresponding amount in coins. But this idea is still fresh and quite a few obstacles remain, especially the fact that the Universal Postal Union acknowledges only stamps, not postmarks. However, the age of mechanization and technology will most probably spell the end of the postage stamp. Those of you eager to prepare for this eventuality would be wise to think about how to put together a postmark collection. We can already see how postmarks are becoming more and more diverse and intricate, even showing advertisements with words and pictures, and to win over stamp collectors, the enemies of the postage stamp have promised that postmarks will be adorned with historical images, coats of arms, etc., just like before with stamps.

"Briefmarkenschwindel," GS, 7.1, 195–200. Translated by Jonathan Lutes.

The precise date of broadcast for this text has not been determined. It was most likely written during the second half of 1930. A catalog, found in the Benjamin archive, of an exhibition entitled "Die Alt-Berliner Post" [The Mail in Old Berlin], which took place between May 23 and August 3, 1930, suggests the end of May as the earliest "Postage Stamp Swindles" could have been created.

Schiller-Lerg speculates that "Postage Stamp Swindles" might have been broadcast from Berlin on January 16, 1931, a date for which the Funkstunde *announced an untitled broadcast by Benjamin (*Walter Benjamin und der Rundfunk, *165).*

CHAPTER 21

The Bootleggers

Bootleggers—we'll hear a bit later about the literal meaning of this word. The radio gazette was right to add "or the American alcohol smugglers" to its program announcement, otherwise you would have had to ask your parents.[1] They know what sort of people bootleggers are; they've recently read a lot about the infamous Jacques Diamond, the rich bootlegger who fled to Europe to escape his enemies, but was arrested in Cologne and shipped back to America. Perhaps the few adults who have wandered into this show for children are interested in such people, these smooth customers who are always on the run. And maybe they're interested in something else, too, such as the question: Should children even hear these kinds of stories? Stories of swindlers and miscreants who break the law trying to make a pile of dough, and often succeed? It's a legitimate question. It would weigh on my conscience if I were to sit here and fire off one tale of villainy after another without first saying a few words about the laws and grand intentions that create the backdrop for the stories in which alcohol smugglers are heroes.

I'm not sure if you've heard about the alcohol debate. But you've all seen a drunk person before, and just one look at such a creature is all it takes to understand why men came to ask themselves whether the state should prohibit the selling of alcohol. People in the United States did just that in 1920, by adding an amendment to the constitution. Ever since, what they call Prohibition has been in force, which means it's illegal to provide alcohol without a medical purpose. How did this law come about? There are lots of reasons, and if you were to look into them, you would learn all sorts of important things about the Americans. On a December day 300

---

1 The *Südwestdeutsche Rundfunk-Zeitung* advertised Benjamin's broadcast ahead of time as "Youth Hour: 'The Bootleggers, or the American Alcohol Smugglers,' read by Dr. Walter Benjamin."

years ago the first European settlers, the ancestors of the white Americans, landed their small ship, the Mayflower, on the rocky shores of what is now called the state of Massachusetts, where the town of Plymouth lies. Today they are called the 100-percenters, referring to their unwavering convictions, their austerity, and the imperturbability of their religious and moral principles.[2] These first immigrants belonged to the Puritan sect. Their effects are still clearly noticeable in America today. One of the traces of Christian Puritanism is Prohibition. The Americans call it the noble experiment. For many of them Prohibition is not only a matter of health and economy, but something downright religious. They call America "God's Homeland" and say that the country is obligated to have this law. One of the law's greatest proponents is Ford, the automobile king, but not because he would have been a Puritan. He explains: Prohibition allows me to sell my cars more cheaply. Why? The average worker used to spend a good part of his weekly wage in bars. Now that he can no longer drink his money away, he has to save. And, according to Ford, once the worker has begun to save, he will soon have enough for a car. Prohibition has multiplied my car sales, he says. And many American manufacturers think the way he does, not only because big American companies sell more as a result of Prohibition, but because the alcohol ban makes manufacturing cheaper as well. A worker who doesn't drink is of course much more productive than one who does so regularly, even if he doesn't drink much. Thus, over the same time period the same manpower produces more than before, even if this increase is very small: for a country's economy, this tiny bit of improved efficiency among individuals is multiplied by the total number of workers and all their work hours over the course of ten years.

Enough, you're thinking. Now you know what Prohibition is, now you know why it became law. Now let's hear about the bootleggers. The term "bootlegger" harks back to the gold rush in Klondike, where every man stuck a bottle of booze in his bootleg. If I tell you a few of the many tricks people use to sneak alcohol in, you mustn't conclude it's all that easy to find wine, beer, or any other kind of liquor. American law punishes not only alcohol sellers, but consumers as well. The punishment for the former, however, is certainly more severe. In fact, the cruelty of these punishments is one of the

---

2 During the 1920s, the "100 percent Americanism" movement promoted a nationalist, anti-immigrant, anti-communist, traditionalist ideology.

reasons why opponents of Prohibition are turning against this law. It has fomented a certain type of elite among the unscrupulous, as only the most intrepid and audacious become bootleggers. Let's first track them on the sea, where their operations begin. The law specifies that no ship carrying alcohol may come closer than fourteen miles to the American coast. This is where America's so-called territorial waters begin; at this demarcation, even ordinary passenger liners coming from Europe must seal off their supplies of alcohol. The big export companies wanting to sell their liquor in America don't even consider facing the perils of smuggling. They order their freighters to drop anchor just outside the territorial waters, where American customs ships can see them but can do nothing to them. But more importantly, the bootleggers can see them; day and night their little smuggling boats zip across "Rum Row," the name given to this border in honor of rum smuggling. The challenge is to transport the cargo to a secret unloading point on the mainland while evading the attention of customs ships and exploiting every advantage to do so: fog, moonless nights, bribes to customs officials, and, above all, stormy seas, which make pursuit more difficult. Police and smugglers must constantly try to outwit one another with their cunning.

Here are two little tales in which first the smugglers and then the customs wardens got the upper hand, using a similar ruse. One day a Coast Guard cutter was pursuing a petroleum boat whose cargo seemed suspicious. When the cutter had almost reached the boat, whose engines were not so powerful, the smugglers came up with a novel idea: they threw one of their own into the water. While the cutter slowed down to rescue the man, the boat disappeared in a flash, leaving behind a terrific wake.[3] As I said, however, the customs authorities do not always lose out. There's the story of a steamer, the *Frederic B.* from Southampton, which had been loaded with 100,000 cases of liquor and champagne worth 180 million francs. This ship, whose mysterious captain went by the name of Jimmy, was the cause of many a sleepless night for customs officials. The American government promised a great reward to whoever captured Jimmy. A very young man, first name Paddy, took on the adventure, and off he sailed with a few dollars and a handshake on behalf of the entire customs authority of the United States. A few days later a very large

---

3 See Pierre Mac Orlan's fictionalized account in *Les pirates de "l'avenue du rhum": reportage* [The Pirates of "Rum Row"] (Paris: Sagittaire, 1925); *Alkoholschmuggler*, trans. Paul Cohen-Portheim (Berlin: Die Schmiede, 1927), 26ff.

cargo steamer, the same *Frederic B.* of Southampton, which would often hang around Rum Row not far from the Bahamas, collided with a fishing boat. The steamboat naturally took on board the castaways, four men and a cabin boy named Paddy. The four fishermen were taken ashore as they requested, but the cabin boy asked to stay on board and work, and his wish was granted. Before the second night had barely passed, the cabin boy lowered a rope overboard, and four brawny men grabbed it and climbed on deck. Revolvers in hand, they seized the rudder, then the telephone, and the game was won. The men in the engine room believed they were following orders from Captain Jimmy, and the *Frederic B.* of Southampton pulled into Miami Harbor, where it was greeted by the customs authorities, who proceeded to pour the 180 million francs of cargo into the sea.[4]

Rum Row, permanently policed by around 400 coastal vessels, is just one of the fronts on which the battle between alcohol bandits and the state unfolds. In the American interior, at the border between Canada and the United States, are the Great Lakes. Here, events typically play out in the following manner. The customs authorities have, let's say, three ships. The smugglers then employ twelve. In the best case, the three can hold in check, or pursue, four or five boats. When things become dangerous, the boats being followed turn around halfway and peacefully head back to Canada, whereas the seven or eight others dock unmolested somewhere on the shores of the State of Illinois. "OK. Then why don't the customs authorities use twelve cutters as well?" I asked the American friend who told me this story. He looked at me, smiling, and explained: "Then the smugglers would use thirty-six." In other words, they earn so much, there's no expense they would spare. Even so, don't think their position is such an easy one. Sure, if the customs authorities were their only adversaries, they would have it made. But I've yet to mention their truly feared enemies: hijackers, the name for the type of bandits who get their alcohol supplies not off of ships like the bootleggers do, but off of the bootleggers themselves. Only they don't pay for them, they steal them. For years the conflict of interests between smugglers and robbers—because that's fundamentally what it's about—has governed the infamous and storied underworld of Chicago. Most murders on the open streets are handled as private affairs between these two kinds of gentleman.

---

4 Mac Orlan, *Alkoholschmuggler*, 29ff.

Chicago is also the scene of an interesting story told by an American journalist, a certain Arthur Moss. He was just walking into his club when he noticed a crew of respectable-looking fishermen unloading an entire shipment of small sharks from a truck smelling like sea salt. Although shark fins are a popular delicacy, they're hardly common, and Mr. Moss wondered to himself since when had sharks been in such high demand. While he was pondering this, it struck him how gingerly each of the little sharks was being rolled from the truck down a ramp and then lifted and carried with careful hands. Then a seemingly mild, unassuming man approached the truck and, despite the rather discourteous, even ornery reaction of the seamen, insisted on prodding one of these delicately handled fish. It turned out that the man was with the police, and inside each fish was a bottle of whiskey.[5]

The tricks bootleggers have devised to deliver their booze defy the imagination. Dressed as policemen, they cross the border with whiskey stowed in their helmets. They organize funeral processions, just to get coffins packed with liquor over the border. They wear rubber underwear filled with alcohol. They hire people to sell restaurant-goers dolls or fans with bottles of liquor inside. Almost any object, no matter how harmless—an umbrella, camera, or boot tree—can make the customs police suspect that there may be whiskey inside. The police, and ultimately the Americans as well. There's a wonderful story of a train station near New Orleans. Little Negro children[6] walk along the train that stops there, hiding under their clothing variously shaped containers with large labels that read "Iced Tea." One passenger gives a nod and for the price of a suit buys the container, which he then cleverly conceals. Then another one, then ten, twenty, fifty. "Whatever you do, ladies and gentlemen," implore the Negro children, "drink the tea only once the train is under way." Everyone winks knowingly ... The whistle blows, the train drives off, and right away the passengers put the containers to their lips. And then their expressions turn to disbelief, as what they are drinking is actually real tea.[7]

When American elections to the House of Representatives occurred a few weeks ago, Prohibition played a role. The elections revealed that it has many opponents. These opponents are not only,

---

5   Ibid., 28ff.

6   Benjamin uses the German "kleine Negerlein." "Negerlein" is the diminutive form of "Neger," an offensive term with connotations between "Negro" and "Nigger."

7   Mac Orlan, *Alkoholschmuggler*, 26.

as you might think, those who want to get drunk, but also very intelligent, sober, thoughtful people, who are against laws that are broken by half the residents of a country, laws that make adults act like naughty children, who do something only because it's forbidden, laws whose enforcement costs the state a tremendous amount of money, and whose violation costs many people their lives. Wholeheartedly for the retaining of these laws are the bootleggers, who have become rich as a result of them. But viewing this matter from afar, we Europeans will wonder whether Swedes, Norwegians, or Belgians, who have fought alcohol consumption less radically and with much milder laws, haven't made more progress than the Americans with their violence and fanaticism.

"Die Bootleggers," GS, 7.1, 201–6. Translated by Jonathan Lutes.

Broadcast on Radio Berlin, November 8, 1930, and on Southwest German Radio, Frankfurt, December 31, 1930. Benjamin dated the typescript "Radio Berlin, November 8, 1930," and the Funkstunde *announced the broadcast for this date from 3:20–3:40 pm. For December 31, 1930, the* Südwestdeutsche Rundfunk-Zeitung *announced its Youth Hour, from 3:00–3:25 pm, as "Die Bootleggers oder die amerikanischen Alkoholschmuggler' [The Bootleggers, or the American Alcohol Smugglers], read by Dr. Walter Benjamin."*

CHAPTER 22

Naples

When someone says Naples, what first comes to mind? I would say, Vesuvius. Will you be very disappointed if you hear nothing at all from me about Vesuvius? If I were granted my greatest wish—an ugly wish, but I had it all the same—it would be to experience an eruption of Vesuvius. That would really be something. I was in the region for eight months, and I waited and waited.[1] I even climbed Vesuvius, and looked into its crater. But the only exciting thing I got to see in Naples was a fiery red glow that occasionally flashed in the night sky as I sat in a tavern garden beside the city's highest point, the Castel Sant'Elmo. And by day? You think there's lots of time in Naples to look around and admire Vesuvius? You're happy if you emerge unscathed from the hustle of the cars, cabs, and motorbikes, or if your nerves are still intact from the din of all the barkers, car horns, rattling sounds of electric trams, and the shrill, drawn-out cries of the paperboys. It's not so easy to get around. When I arrived in Naples for the first time, the subway had just opened. I thought to myself: great, with my luggage I can ride straight from the train to the neighborhood where my hotel was located. But I didn't know Naples so well yet. As the subway train pulled into the station, hanging on all the windows and doors, and sitting and standing on all of the seats, were Neapolitan street urchins. It was fun for them that the subway had just opened two or three days before. They didn't care whether it was meant for them or the serious adults going about their workdays. They saved up a few soldi and then were happy just to zip back and forth between stations. If it hadn't been for the fact that these new trains were so overrun with people, anyone in a hurry might actually have reached their destination.

---

1 In a letter to Scholem, Benjamin refers to having visited Pompeii, as well as Naples, during his stay on Capri in 1924 (letter of September 16, 1924, *The Correspondence of Walter Benjamin*, 250).

Neapolitans can't imagine existence without swarms of people. Here's an example: when old German artists painted the *Adoration of the Magi*, they had Melchior, Caspar, and Balthasar, and sometimes their entourage, approaching the Baby Jesus with gifts. The Neapolitans, however, depict the *Adoration* with giant mobs of people. I mention this because these images are famous throughout the world, like the Neapolitan manger scenes, which are more beautiful than any others. January 6, Three Kings Day, has always been the occasion for an enormous procession through the streets, where each manger scene outdoes the next in size and in the true-to-life quality of its figures. However, you mustn't imagine seeing the ancient Jews: the Neapolitans are much more interested in the faithful and vibrant depiction of what they see in front of them every day. So, in terms of the costumes and goings-on of the common folk, these manger scenes are more an animated portrayal of the city of Naples than of the Orient. Sure enough, there are water vendors, peddlers, and jugglers. But the macaroni dealers, mussel sellers, and fishermen that accompany the manger scenes are true Neapolitan characters. You're thinking to yourselves, why should such a throng of people be made up only of angels or good role models? But if you want to know what the really dangerous people look like in Naples, don't imagine wild, black-bearded bandits, or Rinaldo Rinaldinis.[2] No, the worst Neapolitan villains come across as honest middle-class folks, and often have a rather harmless trade. They are not outright criminals, but rather members of a secret society that comprises only a few active thieves and murderers and whose other affiliates have nothing to do but protect the true criminals from the police, shelter them, warn them when there's danger, and let them know of opportunities for new reprehensible deeds. In exchange they receive a share of the spoils. This wide-ranging criminal association is called the Camorra.

While we're discussing the Neapolitans' faults, let's see how they fare against other Italians. There's an old list of the seven deadly sins, where each sin matches up with one of the seven most important cities in Italy. Have you ever heard of the seven deadly sins? You're about to hear what they are, for the Italians have spread them over all of Italy. Each large city has its share: pride is said to live in Genoa, greed in Florence, lust in Venice, anger in Bologna,

---

2 A reference to the once popular main character and emblem of the "noble robber" in Christian August Vulpius, *Rinaldo Rinaldini: der Räuberhauptmann* [Rinaldo Rinaldini: Robber Captain] (Leipzig: Gräff, 1799).

gluttony in Milan, envy in Rome, and in Naples, sloth. The laziness in this city is indeed manifest in strange ways. It's not just that the poor people, who have nothing to do, lie in the sun and sleep and, when they wake up, head to the harbor or tourist areas to beg for a few centimes. Sometimes a poor devil even gets work. And what does the Neapolitan do then? He spends two thirds of his earnings to hire someone else to do the work for him, as he would prefer to lie in the sun for five lire than to earn fifteen. Perhaps laziness also explains the passion for lotto in Naples, which is greater here than almost anywhere else. And by lotto, I don't mean picture lotto: in Italy, lotto is what we call lottery in Germany. At four o'clock every Saturday people gather outside the house where the numbers are drawn.[3] Time and again they try their luck, and repeatedly fail, despite all the fortune tellers' prophecies and their superstitions about lucky numbers.

Maybe it's not just the climate that makes the Neapolitans lazy. After all, it's only physical work they find so unappealing. When they're bargaining, however, or transacting business, they're very much in their element. The Neapolitans are great tradesmen, and the Bank of Naples is over 500 years old, making it one of the oldest in Europe. But what I wanted to say was this: the Neapolitans shy away from physical labor not only because the weather allows them to get along fine without a roof over their heads for part of the year, and not only because there's always something to be made of the overabundance of fruits and sea creatures found on the street, but also because the work, at least in the factories, is particularly hard. Industry in Naples is very much behind the times, especially now, although the city must have almost one million residents. Don't picture Naples with the new, clean, light factory buildings found in lots of big German cities. Take a look at the desolate shacks in Portici, Torre Annunziata, Biscragnano, and Nocera, in short, in any of Naples's countless suburbs, or walk in the blazing sun down the endless dusty streets where they're located, or try just to navigate your way through one of them, and you'll understand why many Neapolitans prefer even the most miserable idleness to industrial labor in such conditions.

Food is the main product of Naples. Most importantly, the

---

3   Here, Benjamin borrows from his previously published essay, "Naples," cowritten with Asja Lacis, with whom he had spent time in Capri during the visit in 1924. See "Naples," in SW, 1, 418; "Neapel," GS, 4.1, 312–13, first published in the *Frankfurter Zeitung*, August 19, 1925.

Neapolitans process and can the many fruits that ripen on the slopes of Vesuvius, along with tomatoes. They also produce macaroni in all shapes and sizes. These goods go mainly to India and America, because the other countries on the Mediterranean produce and sell similar foods. And then there are the big textile mills, but they manufacture only the cheapest fabrics. These mills were created not by Neapolitans, but by foreigners. After just a day in Naples, however, one thing stands out as made locally, because it's everywhere in the streets, and that's furniture, beds in particular. The other merchandise is grouped by specialty in certain streets, where there are ten or twenty stores selling the same thing. It might seem that it would hurt the traders to be so close to one another, but it clearly doesn't, because this is also the case in other cities. There are streets where nearly all the shops sell leather goods, others where every third shop sells old books, and then some with one proprietor after the next, each making watches.

The goods from all these stores overflow onto the streets: books lie in little crates in front of bookstores; beds and tables stand halfway on the pavement; hosiery and clothing hang in doorways and on the exterior walls of shops. But a good portion of Neapolitan business is transacted without premises, making do just with the street. I remember a man who stood at a street corner on an unhitched carriage. Crowds swarmed around him. The carriage box had been swung open and the hawker pulled something out of the box while extoling the item in one continuous sales pitch. I couldn't make out what it actually was, because before you could see it, it disappeared into a small piece of pink or green paper. He then held the thing high over his head and instantly it was bought for a few soldi. I asked myself whether there were perhaps prizes in the paper, or little cakes with coins hidden inside, or fortunes from soothsayers. The mysterious expression on the man's face was like that of a peddler from *1001 Nights*. But the most mysterious thing was not, as I would soon find out, what was for sale, but rather the artistry of the seller, who sold it so quickly. What was in the colorful paper? What was he twisting into it? Just toothpaste. Another time, when I was up very early, I saw a street peddler unpacking his things from a suitcase. But how he did this was true theater. Umbrellas, shirt fabrics, shawls, each piece he presented individually to his audience, and warily, as he first had to examine each of the goods himself. Then, seemingly out of wonder and surprise at how beautiful his things were, he began to heat up, spread out a scarf, and asked for

500 lire—which would be about eighty marks. Then all of a sudden he folded up the scarf, lowering the price with each successive fold, and finally, once it had become just a small bundle in his arm, he delivered his final price: fifty lire.[4]

If this is the scene on just any corner in Naples, you can imagine what a market must look like. And the fish market is the strangest of them all. Starfish, crabs, polyps, snails, squid, and all sorts of other slithery things—just one look at them will give you goose bumps—are gobbled up like treats. I must say, it wasn't easy for me to scoop that first squid out of the red, peppered broth in which it swam. I've always thought that in foreign countries, one should do more than just look around and, when possible, speak the language; one should go further and adapt to the customs of the country, as in the way people live, sleep, and eat. After a while, even squid tastes wonderful. And why shouldn't it? The Neapolitans are great culinary experts. Only in Germany's finest restaurants do diners get to see the meat, fish, etc., before it's prepared. In Naples, this happens even in the most humble eateries; the few provisions a tavern has bought for the day are displayed in the window. Every September 7, Naples is host to great gluttonous feasts: the Piedigrotta, an old Roman fertility festival still celebrated by the Neapolitans. And how do the poor make sure they and their families have something good to eat on this day? All year long, week after week, they pay the shopkeeper twenty or thirty soldi more than they owe. During the days of Piedigrotta, this extra money is added up and then the people have their joint of roast goat, their cheese, and their wine. Thus, in Naples, people insure themselves for the national feast the way we insure ourselves against old age and accidents.

In other respects, what happens during Piedigrotta defies description. Imagine that in a city with one million residents, all the boys and girls have conspired to make the most outlandish and infernal commotion, up and down the street, in front doors, on public squares, under bridges and arches, starting at nightfall and not letting up until dawn. Then imagine that most of them have bought one of the wretched, garish horns on offer at every street corner for five centimes. And that they run around in mobs with no other purpose than to assail innocent people, blocking their way, surrounding them on all sides and blasting into their ears until their victims either collapse half dead in the street or somehow manage to escape. To make up for this,

---

4   For a similar account, see Benjamin and Lacis, "Naples," 419; "Neapel," 313.

elsewhere in the city there is something sweet and agreeable for the ears: on this day a competition for songwriters is held in Naples. Most of the songs heard every day in the streets on accordions and small pianos have their debut during the Piedigrotta festival, and judges award prizes to the best. Naples showers renown on a gifted singer nearly as much as America does on a talented boxer.

But the great holidays are just part of it. Almost every day there's something happening in this city. Each neighborhood has its own guardian saint, and on the saint's name day, the festivities get under way early. In fact, they begin a few days beforehand, when posts are erected to which green, blue, or red light bulbs are attached, and when paper garlands are strung from one side of the street to the other. Paper of all colors plays an essential role in these street scenes; its radiance, its mobility, and how quickly it wears out perfectly reflect the lively and temperamental character of the Neapolitans. Red, black, yellow, and white fly-whisks, altars made of bright, shiny paper abutting the city walls, green paper rosettes on the raw and bloody cuts of meat: such sights are everywhere to be seen. The traveler folk—they're everywhere here in the streets— quickly scout out which neighborhood is hosting festivities and head over there at once. And what characters I came across! The fire-eater, calmly surrounding himself with bowls of fire on a wide sidewalk, and then gobbling up the flames from one bowl after another; and the silhouette-cutter, perched in the shade of a city gate, placing his models in the glaring sun and, for one lira, cutting a strikingly accurate profile in shiny black paper. I won't speak of the soothsayers and athletes, as we see these sorts at fairs here in Germany. But I would like to tell you about a type of painter I've never observed anywhere but in Naples. At first I didn't see him, the painter, at all, only a crowd encircling what seemed to be an empty space. I moved closer. And there, kneeling in the middle of this cluster of people was a small, nondescript fellow drawing a Christ-figure on the cobblestones with colored chalk, and under it the head of the Madonna. He takes his time. He is obviously working with great precision, contemplating where to apply the chalk in strokes of green, yellow, or brown. After a long while he gets to his feet and waits beside his work. Fifteen minutes pass, maybe a half hour, until gradually the limbs, head, and torso of his drawing are covered with copper coins, two or three each thrown from every one of his admirers. He then gathers up his money and soon the drawing disappears under people's footsteps.

Every festival is capped off with fireworks over the sea. Or I should rather say *was*, at least back in 1924 when I was first there. Then the government thought better of the great sums of money flying into the night sky year after year, and ordered the fireworks to be scaled back. But in the early evenings back then, from July to September there was one single trail of fire running along the coast between Naples and Salerno. Sometimes over Sorrento, sometimes over Minori and Praiano, but always over Naples, fireballs filled the sky. Every parish sought to trump the festival of its neighbors with new kinds of light shows.

I've told you a bit about everyday life in Naples, and a bit about the festival days, but what's remarkable is how the two blend into each other, how every day the streets have something festive, full of music and idlers, and laundry flapping in the wind like flags; and how even Sunday has something of a workday feel to it, because every little storekeeper can keep his shop open into the night. To really get to know the city, you would probably have to transform yourself into a Neapolitan postman for a year; you would become acquainted with more cellars, attics, backstreets, and recesses than there are in many other cities combined. But even the postmen never really get to know Naples, with so many tens of thousands of people living there who don't receive one single letter in a year, who don't even have a place to live. There's great misery in the city, in the whole region, which explains why most Italian emigrants hail from there. As steerage passengers aboard American steamers, tens of thousands have cast their last glance on their hometown, so beautiful in parting, lying there with its countless flights of staggered stairs, its nestled courtyards, its churches disappearing amid a sea of buildings. We leave you today with this vision of the city.

"Neapel," GS, 7.1, 206–14. Translated by Jonathan Lutes.

Broadcast on Southwest German Radio, Frankfurt, on May 9, 1931. The broadcast was listed in the Südwestdeutsche Rundfunk-Zeitung *for May 9, 1931, from 10:30–10:50 am: "Schulfunk: 'Von einer Italienreise: Neapel' [School radio: On an Italian Journey: Naples]. Talk by Dr. Walter Benjamin."*

CHAPTER 23

The Fall of Herculaneum and Pompeii

Have you ever heard of the Minotaur? He was the hideous monster that dwelt in a labyrinth in Thebes. Every year a virgin was sacrificed by being thrown into this labyrinth, whose hundreds of meandering, branching, and crisscrossing paths made it impossible for her to find her way out, so she was eventually eaten by the monster; that is, until Theseus was given a ball of thread by the Theban king's daughter.[1] Theseus fastened one end of the thread at the entrance, so he was sure to find his way out, and then slew the Minotaur. The Theban king's daughter was named Ariadne. People visiting modern-day Pompeii could certainly use one of Ariadne's threads: it's the largest labyrinth, the largest maze on Earth. Wherever the eye wanders, it finds nothing but walls and sky. Even 1,800 years ago—before Pompeii was buried alive—it mustn't have been easy to find one's way; for old Pompeii, like Karlsruhe for us, was composed of a complex network of perpendicular streets. But the landmarks that helped people orient themselves in those days—shops and tavern signs, raised temples and buildings—have all disappeared. Where stairs and walls once lent order to buildings, gaps everywhere now create paths through the ruins. How often it happened that, while walking through the dead city with one of my friends from Naples or Capri, I turned to him, pointing out a faded painting on a wall or a mosaic underfoot, only to find myself suddenly alone; then anxious minutes would pass as we called out each other's name before finding each other again. You mustn't think that you can stroll through this defunct Pompeii as if it were a museum of antiquities. No, there in the mugginess that often fills the air, in the wide, monotonous, shadeless streets, where the ear encounters not a sound and the eye only dull colors, the visitor soon

---

1 The Minotaur and the palace in which he lived were not in Thebes, but rather in Crete, in the Palace of King Minos of Knossos. The Athenians annually had to send seven virgins and seven young boys as a tribute.

enters a strange state. The simple sound of footsteps startles him, as does the unexpected appearance of another solitary walker. And the uniformed guards with their villainous Neapolitan faces make the whole experience even less pleasant. Ancient Greek and Roman houses almost never had windows; light and air entered through an atrium, an opening in the roof with a basin beneath into which rainwater fell. The windowless walls were always rather austere, but became even more so once their color disappeared, making the streets doubly severe. But Vesuvius, with its forests at the base and its vineyards above, never looks prettier or more charming than when it appears here over the city's stark walls or through the opening of one of Pompeii's three or four gates that still stand today.

For centuries the volcano appeared simply beautiful, and not at all ominous to the Pompeians whose city it would one day destroy. There was an ancient tradition according to which the entrance to the underworld could be found here in Campania, the region where Pompeii and Herculaneum lie. Yet, since the beginning of written history there had been no account of an eruption by Vesuvius. For many centuries Vesuvius lay dormant; shepherds grazed their livestock in its green crater, and the slave leader Spartacus hid his entire army under its rim. There were always earthquakes in Campania, but people had grown accustomed to them. For some time they seemed to have been weak, and limited to a narrow area. This centuries-long peace that the Earth seemed to have made with men—among one another, men were as far removed from peace in those days as they are today—was disrupted for the first time by a horrific earthquake in the sixty-fourth year after the birth of Christ. Pompeii was thus in large part already destroyed. So, sixteen years later, when the city disappeared from the face of the Earth for several hundred years, it was not an ordinary city. At the time Vesuvius erupted, Pompeii was in the midst of a complete renovation and transformation, because it never happens that people rebuild a destroyed city as it was before. They always want to turn their misfortune into at least some kind of gain by rebuilding the old, only better, more secure, and more beautiful. And so it happened in Pompeii. In those days it was a medium-sized rural city of about 20,000 residents. The Samnites, a small Italian tribe, lived there completely on their own until shortly before the birth of Christ. When the Romans subjugated the region, 150 years before the city's demise, Pompeii did not suffer all that much. It was not conquered, and was only occupied by a few Roman subjects with whom the Samnites had to share their fields. These

Romans soon settled into the city and began adapting it to their own customs and habits. Since they were already in the process of modifying and rebuilding, they were well positioned to take advantage of the earthquake. In short, not much remained of the Samnites when Pompeii was destroyed, and there are scholars who would have preferred that there hadn't been an earthquake, so that the old Samnite city would have been buried by Vesuvius and as much of it would have been preserved as remains today of Roman Pompeii. While we know quite a bit about Roman cities, we know nothing at all about those of the Samnites.

It can be said that as much is known about the fall of Pompeii as if it had happened in our time, thanks to two letters written to the Roman historian Tacitus by an eyewitness of the Vesuvius eruption. These letters may be the most celebrated in the world. They tell us not only about the events that transpired, but also about how they were understood. They were written by Pliny the Younger, a great naturalist who, when the disaster happened, was eighteen years old and living with his uncle in Misenum, just next to Naples. His uncle, Pliny the Elder, commander of the Roman fleet, was killed in the eruption. I will now read to you from one of the letters:

> By now it was dawn, but the light was still dim and faint. The buildings round us were already tottering, and the open space we were in was too small for us not to be in real and imminent danger if the house collapsed. This finally decided us to leave the town. We were followed by a panic-stricken mob of people wanting to act on someone else's decision in preference to their own (a point in which fear looks like prudence), who hurried us on our way by pressing hard behind in a dense crowd. Once beyond the buildings we stopped, and there we had some extraordinary experiences which thoroughly alarmed us. The carriages we had ordered to be brought out began to run in different directions though the ground was quite level, and would not remain stationary even when wedged with stones. We also saw the sea sucked away and apparently forced back by the earthquake: at any rate it receded from the shore so that quantities of sea creatures were left stranded on dry sand. On the landward side a fearful black cloud was rent by forked and quivering bursts of flame, and parted to reveal great tongues of fire, like flashes of lightning magnified in size.[2]

---

2   This translation is from *The Letters of the Younger Pliny*, ed. and trans. Betty Radice (London: Penguin Books, 1963), Book Six, Letter 20, 171.

So writes Pliny, from whom you'll hear more in a moment. But as I said, he watched the event from afar. The fiery cloud he describes was over Vesuvius; it didn't directly affect Pompeii. Pompeii did not perish as the island of Martinique did at the beginning of our century, when it was devoured by a glowing cloud.[3] Fire did not engulf Pompeii. Not even lava flows, which had proved so devastating in previous eruptions of Vesuvius, reached the city. No, Pompeii was actually buried by rain. But it was a strange rain. In another part of his letter, Pliny tells how the cloud over Vesuvius looked sometimes black, sometimes light gray. The excavation of Pompeii has shown us the cause of this spectacle: the volcano ejected by turns black ash and massive amounts of gray pumice stone. These layers are clearly discernible in Pompeii, to particular effect. To the layers of ash we owe something never to be found again on Earth: the perfectly clear and lifelike forms of people who lived 2,000 years ago. It happened as follows. While people were literally battered to death by the falling pumice, even as they tried desperately to protect themselves with towels and pillows, they were suffocated by showers of ash. The corpses covered in pumice rotted, and upon excavation, only skeletons remained. But in the layers of ash, something entirely different was discovered. Whether because the ash from inside the crater was wet, as many have suspected, or because cloudbursts after the eruption dampened the ash—whatever the reason, ash managed to insinuate itself into every wrinkle of clothing, every whorl of the ear, and everywhere between people's fingers, hair, and lips. The ash then congealed much faster than the corpses decomposed, bequeathing us a series of lifelike human casts: of those who had just fallen to the ground and were struggling against death, and others such as a young girl, who lay down peacefully, with her arms cradled under her head, waiting for the end to come. Of Pompeii's 20,000 residents, just over ten percent were killed in the catastrophe.

We see that for many, the primary concern was saving their possessions, leaving them too little time to save themselves. They locked themselves in cellars with their gold and silver treasures, and by the time the eruption came to an end, they were buried alive; there was no way to open the door and they starved to death. Others burdened themselves with sacks of jewelry and silverware and collapsed under their weight. Many, such as the uncle of

---

3 On May 7, 1902, Martinique's Mount Pelée erupted, burying the city of Saint-Pierre and killing over 30,000 people.

Pliny—more of whose letter I shall presently read—opted not to flee inland, but rather to wait on the shore for the first opportunity to row out to sea. But the water was still too turbulent from the earthquake, and these would-be escapees were entombed on the beach. "Soon afterwards," writes Pliny,

> the cloud sank down to earth and covered the sea; it had already blotted out Capri along with the mountains on the mainland. I looked round: a dense black cloud was coming up behind us, spreading over the earth like a flood. "Let us leave the road while we can still see," I said, "or we shall be knocked down and trampled underfoot in the dark by the crowd behind." We had scarcely sat down to rest when darkness fell, not the dark of a moonless or cloudy night, but as if the lamp had been put out in a closed room. You could hear the shrieks of women, the wailing of infants, and the shouting of men; some were calling their parents, others their children or their wives, trying to recognize them by their voices. People bewailed their own fate or that of their relatives, and there were some who prayed for death in their terror of dying. Many besought the aid of the gods, but still more imagined there were no gods left, and that the universe was plunged into eternal darkness for evermore. A gleam of light returned, but we took this to be a warning of the approaching flames rather than daylight. However, the flames remained some distance off; then darkness came on once more and ashes began to fall again, this time in heavy showers. We rose from time to time and shook them off, otherwise we should have been buried and crushed beneath their weight. I could boast that not a groan or cry of fear escaped me in these perils, had I not derived some poor consolation in my mortal lot from the belief that the whole world was dying with me and I with it.[4]

From this letter we can see that during the disaster, no one guessed its cause. Many thought the sun was about to fall to Earth, others that the Earth was flying off into the heavens. Some even believed, as a later historian would tell us, that they saw giants among the fiery clouds and thought that the ancient gods were rebelling against the reigning ones. Ash from the monstrous eruption reached as far as Rome, Egypt, and Syria, while accounts of the natural phenomenon took much longer to arrive. The survivors returned, not to

---

4 *Letters of the Younger Pliny*, 171–2. Benjamin has slightly altered the first part of the passage.

reestablish their lives there—with ash between fifteen and thirty meters deep, this would have been impossible—but on the off-chance of digging for and finding their belongings. Many more would lose their lives in the process, as they were buried alive under avalanches of debris. Over hundreds of years the city vanished from memory. In the last century, however, as the city reemerged from the Earth with its shops, taverns, theaters, wrestling schools, temples, and baths, the Vesuvius eruption of 79 A.D., which destroyed the city two millennia ago, appeared in a whole new light: what for its contemporaries meant the destruction of a flourishing city, for us today means its preservation. A preservation so precise and so detailed that we can read the hundreds of small inscriptions that covered Pompeii's public walls the same way leaflets and posters cover ours, affording us a look into their day-to-day life: their city council disputes, their animal fights, their spats with superiors, their trades, and their taverns. Of these hundreds of inscriptions, we will conclude with one, which we can well imagine was the last; as the menacing, fiery glow fell over Pompeii, a Christian or Jew well versed in such matters must have scrawled this final and uncanny inscription: "Sodom and Gomorrah."

"Untergang von Herculanum und Pompeji," GS, 7.1, 214–20. Translated by Jonathan Lutes.

Broadcast on Radio Berlin, September 18, 1931. The broadcast was announced in the Funkstunde *(issue dated September 11, 1931) with an accompanying image of the excavation of Pompeii.*

CHAPTER 24

The Lisbon Earthquake

Have you ever had to wait at the pharmacy and noticed how the pharmacist fills a prescription? On a scale with very delicate weights, ounce by ounce, dram by dram, he weighs all the substances and specks that make up the final powder. That is how I feel when I tell you something over the radio. My weights are the minutes; very carefully I must weigh how much of this, how much of that, so the mixture is just right. You're probably saying, But why? If you want to tell us about the Lisbon Earthquake, just start at the beginning. Then go ahead and tell us what happened next. But I don't think that would be much fun for you. House after house collapses, family after family is killed; the terror of the spreading fire, the terror of the water, the darkness and the looting, the wailing of the injured, and the cries of the people searching for loved ones—no one wants to hear just this and nothing more, and besides, these things are more or less the same in every natural catastrophe.

But the earthquake that destroyed Lisbon on November 1, 1755, was not a disaster like thousands of others. In many ways it was singular and strange, and this is what I'd like to talk to you about. To begin with, it was one of the greatest and most devastating earthquakes of all time. But it was not only for this reason that it moved and preoccupied the entire world in that century as few other things did. At the time, the destruction of Lisbon was comparable to the destruction of Chicago or London today. In the middle of the eighteenth century, Portugal was still at the height of its colonial power. Lisbon was one of the wealthiest commercial cities on Earth; at the mouth of the Tagus river, its harbor, full of ships year in and year out, was lined with trading houses belonging to merchants from England, France, and Germany, and above all from Hamburg. The city had 30,000 dwellings and well over 250,000 inhabitants, roughly a quarter of whom died in the earthquake. The royal court was famed for both its austerity and its splendor. The many accounts of Lisbon published before the earthquake reveal the strangest details of the court's rigid formalities, how, for instance, on summer evenings courtiers and their families would rendezvous in the main square, the Rucio, where they chatted for a short spell without ever leaving their carriages. People had such an elevated notion of the king of Portugal that one of the many leaflets conveying detailed descriptions of the calamity all across Europe could not fathom that such a great king could also have been affected by it. "Just as the extent of a catastrophe can only be grasped once it has been overcome," writes this particular chronicler, "the dire ramifications of this frightful case can only be felt once one considers that the king and his wife, altogether abandoned, spent an entire day in a carriage under the most wretched conditions." Leaflets featuring such passages functioned as newspapers do for us today. Those with the capacity to do so collected detailed eyewitness accounts and had them printed and sold. Later on I will read to you from another such report, one based on the experiences of an Englishman residing in Lisbon at the time.

Yet there's another, special reason that this event affected people so strongly, that it inspired countless leaflets to be passed from hand to hand, and that almost 100 years later new accounts of the catastrophe were still being printed: the impact of this earthquake was greater than any ever heard of before. It was felt all over Europe and as far away as Africa, a colossal area calculated at two and a half million square kilometers if one includes the farthest reaches where it was detectable. The strongest tremors ranged from the coast of Morocco on one side to the coasts of Andalusia and France on the other. The cities of Cadiz, Jerez, and Algeciras were almost completely destroyed. According to one eyewitness, the cathedral towers in Seville trembled like reeds in the wind. But the most violent tremors traveled through the water. Massive groundswells were felt from Finland to the Dutch East Indies; it was calculated that ocean convulsions progressed from the Portuguese coast to the mouth of the Elbe with tremendous speed, in only a quarter of an hour. But so much for what occurred at the moment of the calamity. The weeks leading up to it saw a series of strange natural phenomena that, after the fact and perhaps not wholly without reason, people looked back on as omens of the impending calamity. For example, in Locarno, in southern Switzerland, two weeks before the catastrophic day, vapor suddenly began rising from the ground. In two hours it had changed into a red mist, which around evening precipitated as purple rain. From then on frightful hurricanes, combined with cloudbursts and floods, were reported across western Europe. Eight days before the quake, the ground around Cadiz was covered with masses of worms emerging from the earth.

No one was more preoccupied with these strange events than Kant, the great German philosopher whose name some of you may already have heard. When the earthquake occurred he was a man of twenty-four, and neither before nor after did he ever venture beyond his hometown of Königsberg; yet he collected all the accounts of this earthquake he could find, with tremendous enthusiasm. The short works he published on the phenomenon constituted the beginnings of scientific geography in Germany.[1] The beginnings of seismology, at any rate. I'd like to tell you something about the path this discipline took from that portrayal of the 1755 earthquake up until today. But I must be careful that our Englishman, whose account of his experiences during the earthquake I would still like you to hear, does not get lost in the shuffle. He has been waiting impatiently; after 150 years of being ignored, he'd like once more to have his say, and has allowed me to share only a few words concerning what we now know about earthquakes. But one thing first: they are not what you think. If I could pause for a moment and ask how you would explain earthquakes, I bet the first thing you'd think of is volcanoes. It's true that volcanic eruptions are often linked to earthquakes, or at least heralded by them. So, for 2,000 years, from the ancient Greeks through to Kant and on until about 1870, people believed that earthquakes were caused by fiery gases, steam from the Earth's interior and suchlike. But once people began to use measuring instruments and to make calculations, whose subtlety and precision surpass anything you might imagine—and that goes for me as well—in short, once people could verify the matter, they

---

1 In 1756, Kant wrote three essays on the subject of the earthquake, emphasizing the nature of its physical dynamics rather than theological justifications: "Von den Ursachen der Erderschütterungen bei Gelegenheit des Unglücks, welches die westliche Länder von Europa gegen das Ende des vorigen Jahres betroffen hat" ("On the Causes of Earthquakes, on the Occasion of the Calamity that Befell the Western Countries of Europe toward the End of Last Year"); "Geschichte und Naturbeschreibung der merkwürdigsten Vorfälle des Erdbebens, welches an dem Ende des 1755sten Jahres einen großen Teil der Erde erschüttert hat" ("History and Natural Description of the Most Noteworthy Occurrences of the Earthquake that Struck a Large Part of the Earth at the End of the Year 1755"); "Fortgesetzte Betrachtung der seit einiger Zeit wahrgenommenen Erderschütterungen" ("Continued Observations of the Terrestrial Convulsions that have been Perceived for Some Time"). See translations by Olaf Reinhardt in Kant, *Natural Science*, ed. Eric Watkins, (Cambridge, UK: Cambridge University Press, 2012).

found something altogether different, at least for large earthquakes like the one in Lisbon. They do not originate from the deepest recesses of the Earth—which we still think of as liquid, or more exactly muddy, like molten sludge—but rather from events in the Earth's crust. The Earth's crust is a layer roughly 3,000 kilometers thick. This layer is in perpetual upheaval; the masses within it are constantly shifting in an ongoing attempt to find equilibrium. We know some of the factors that disturb this equilibrium, and ceaseless research is being conducted to discover others.

This much is certain: the most significant shifting is a result of the continuous cooling of the Earth. This subjects the masses of rock to enormous tension, ultimately causing them to break apart and then to seek a new equilibrium by rearranging themselves, which we experience as an earthquake. Other shifting results from the erosion of mountains, which become lighter, and from alluvial deposits on the ocean floor, which becomes heavier. Storms, whirling about the Earth, especially in autumn, do their bit to rattle the planet's surface; and finally, it remains to be determined just how the pull of celestial bodies exerts force on the Earth's surface. But you might be thinking: if this is true, then the Earth's crust is actually never at rest, so there must be earthquakes all the time. And you'd be right, there are. The incredible precision of the earthquake-monitoring instruments available today—in Germany alone we have thirteen seismological stations in various cities—is such that they are never completely still, which means that the Earth is always quaking, only most of the time we don't feel it.

When, out of a clear blue sky, this quaking suddenly becomes noticeable, it's even worse. And literally out of a clear blue sky. "Because," writes our Englishman, who now finally gets his say,

the sun was shining in full splendor. The sky was impeccably clear, giving not the slightest sign of any natural phenomenon to come, when, between nine and ten in the morning, I was sitting at my desk and the table began to move, which was rather surprising as there was no reason at all that it should have. While I was still pondering the cause of what had just happened, the house started to shake from top to bottom. From beneath the ground came a shuddering boom, as if a storm were raging in the distance. I quickly set down my pen and jumped to my feet. The danger was great but there was still hope that it would all pass without harm; the next moment, however, would erase any uncertainty. A horrible crackling noise was heard, as if all the buildings in the city were falling down at once. My building was so jolted that the upper floors caved in, and the rooms in which I resided swayed so much that everything was turned upside down. I expected to be struck dead at any moment; the walls were crumbling, large stones fell from their cracks and the roof beams appeared to hover in midair. But at this time the sky became so dark that people couldn't make out what was in front of them. Pitch-dark prevailed, either as a result of the immense amount of dust caused by the collapsing houses, or because of the volumes of sulfurous vapor escaping from the earth. Finally the night brightened again, the violence of the shocks relented; I collected myself as best I could and had a look around. It became clear to me that I owed my survival thus far to a small bit of luck; that is, had I been dressed I most certainly would have fled to the street and been struck dead by collapsing buildings. I quickly threw on some shoes and a coat, rushed outside and headed to St. Paul's cemetery, where I thought I would be safest given that it sits on a hill. People no longer recognized their own streets; most could not say what had happened; everything was destroyed and no one knew what had become of their loved ones and all that they owned. From the hill of the cemetery I was then witness to a horrific spectacle: on the ocean, as far as the eye could see, countless ships surged with the waves, crashing into one another as if a massive storm were raging. All of a sudden the huge seaside pier sank, along with all the people who believed they would be safe there. The boats and vehicles so many people used to seek rescue fell equal prey to the sea.[2]

As we know from other accounts, it was about an hour after the second and most devastating seismic shock that the massive swell, twenty meters high, which the Englishman saw from afar, came tumbling over the city. When the tidal wave receded, the Tagus riverbed suddenly appeared completely dry; its recoil was so powerful that it took all the river's water with it. "When evening lowered over the desolated city," the Englishman concludes, "it looked like a sea of fire: the light was so bright, you could read a letter by it. The flames soared from at least a hundred different points and raged for six days, consuming whatever the earthquake had spared. Petrified in anguish, thousands stood mesmerized before the city, as wives

---

2 Benjamin borrows from an account of the earthquake by Rev. Charles Davy. For Davy's text, see "The Earthquake at Lisbon," in *The World's Story: A History of the World in Story, Song and Art*, ed. Eva March Tappan, vol. 5 (Boston: Houghton Mifflin, 1914), 618–28.

and children beseeched all saints and angels for help. All the while the earth continued to quake with greater or lesser force, often for a quarter of an hour without cease."

So much for this fatal day, November 1, 1755. The disaster it brought is one of the very few before which mankind is as powerless today as it was 170 years ago. Here, too, technology will find a way out, albeit an indirect one: through prediction. For the time being, however, it seems that the sensory organs of some animals are still superior to our finest instruments. Dogs in particular will exhibit unmistakable agitation for days before the onset of earthquakes, which is why they are deployed to provide assistance to earthquake stations in vulnerable regions. And with that, my twenty minutes are up; I hope they didn't go by too slowly for you.

"Erdbeben von Lissabon," GS, 7.1, 220–6. Translated by Jonathan Lutes.

Broadcast on Radio Berlin, October 31, 1931, and on Southwest German Radio, Frankfurt, on January 6, 1932. The Funkstunde *announced the broadcast for October 31, 1931, from 3:20–3:40 pm (see Schiller-Lerg,* Walter Benjamin und der Rundfunk, *173). The Frankfurt broadcast was advertised in the* Südwestdeutsche Rundfunk-Zeitung *as taking place on January 6, 1932, with a variant title: "'Das Erdbeben von Lissabon 1755' [The Lisbon Earthquake of 1755], read by Dr. Walter Benjamin, Berlin." The talk was the second of two broadcasts on the Youth Hour, from 3:15–4:00 pm.*

CHAPTER 25

Theater Fire in Canton

I have told you about the eruption of Vesuvius, which buried old Pompeii, and last time I told you about the earthquake that destroyed the capital of Portugal in the eighteenth century. Today I would like to talk about an event that took place in China almost 100 years ago. If I had simply wanted to tell you about any old catastrophe set in China, I could have—as you know all too well—chosen other, more recent incidents than this theater fire in Canton. You need only think about the battles that now fill the newspapers day after day or about last year's floods of the Yangtze, about which we have far more detailed reports, naturally, than about this long-ago theater fire.[1] But what matters to me is to speak about a subject through which you can really get to know the Chinese a little, and for that there's nowhere better than a theater, perhaps. I don't mean the plays that are performed, or the actors—them, too, but that will come later—but chiefly the audience and the space itself: the Chinese theater, which bears no resemblance to anything we imagine when we think of a theater. When a stranger draws near, he would believe himself to be anywhere but in front of a theater. He hears a formless din of drums, cymbals, and squeaking stringed instruments. Only after he has seen such a theater or heard one of the gramophone recordings of Chinese theater music does the European believe he knows what caterwauling is. If he then steps into the theater, he will feel like someone who enters a restaurant and first has to walk through a dirty kitchen: he will stumble upon a sort of laundry room in which four or five men stand bent over steaming tubs, washing hand towels. These towels play the biggest role in Chinese theater. People wipe off their face and hands with them before and after

---

1 In 1931, the Yangtze River valley flooded in a catastrophe that killed millions and that has been called the worst natural disaster of the twentieth century.

every cup of tea, every bowl of rice; servants are constantly taking the used towels out and carrying fresh ones in, often flinging them skillfully over the heads of the theater audience. Eating and drinking is rife during the performance, and that makes up for the lack of everything that provides us with comfort and a ceremonious atmosphere in a theater. The Chinese do not demand comfort, because they have none at home either. They come from their unheated apartments into the unheated theater, sit on wooden benches with their feet on flagstones, and it does not concern them in the slightest. Nor do they give a hoot about ceremony. That's because they are much too great theater authorities not to demand the freedom to make their opinion of the performance known at any time. If they were to express it solely at the premiere—as we do here—then they would wait a long time, because there are plays in China that are presented over and over again for four or five hundred years, and even the newest are mostly versions of stories that everyone knows and has half-memorized in the form of novels, poems, or other plays. So ceremoniousness does not exist in the Chinese theater, and suspense doesn't exist either, at least not with regard to the denouement of a plot.

Instead there is another sort of suspense, which we can best compare to what we feel when we see circus acrobats swinging on a trapeze, or jugglers balancing a whole stack of plates on a stick they perch on their nose. Actually, every Chinese actor must simultaneously be an acrobat and juggler and on top of that a dancer, singer, and fencer. You will understand why when I tell you that there are no sets in the Chinese theater. The actor not only has to play his role, but he must also act out the set. How does he do that? I will explain it to you. If he has to cross a threshold, for example, going through a door that is not there, he will lift his feet a little above the floor as though stepping over something. In contrast, slow steps while lifting his feet high, for example, indicate that he is going up a flight of stairs. Or if a general has to ascend a hill to observe a battle, then the actor who portrays him will climb on a chair. One can recognize a rider by the whip the actor holds in his hand. A mandarin being carried in a sedan-chair is portrayed by an actor who walks across the stage surrounded by four other actors, who walk with their backs bent, as if they were carrying a sedan chair. But if they suddenly make a jerky movement, it means that the mandarin has gotten down. Naturally, actors who have to be able to do so much have a long apprenticeship, usually almost seven years. During this time they learn not only singing, acrobatics, and all the rest but also the roles for about fifty plays, which they are expected to be able to perform at any time. This is necessary because it is rarely enough to perform just a single play. Instead, one scene is taken from one play, another from another, and they are all put together in a varied sequence, so that on a single evening there are often more than a dozen plays performed. On the other hand, a single play, if one wanted to perform it in its entirety, would often take two or three days, that's how long they are. There are, however, some that are very short in which only one man performs, and I will now read you one of these. It is called "The Dream." The speaker is an old man.

I would like to tell you a beautiful story. It is regrettable how unfair the sky is; it lets rain and snow fall down but no silver bars. Yesterday evening I was lying on my hearthside bed of clay; I tossed and turned and could not fall asleep. I lay awake from the first night-watch to the second and then again from the second until the third was sounded. As the third night-watch sounded, I had a dream. I dreamed of a treasure to the south of the village. So I took a spade and a hoe and went out into the field to dig up the treasure. I was really lucky; after a few strokes with the spade and hoe, I dug it up. I dug up a whole cellar of silver shoes; it was covered by a big mat of rushes. I lifted it up and looked under it. Oh, I had to laugh: there was a coral branch fifteen meters high, real red carnelian and white agate. Then I took seven to eight sacks of diamonds, six big baskets full of cat's eye agates, thirty-three chiming clocks, sixty-four women's watches, beautiful boots and caps, beautiful jackets and cloaks, beautiful new-fangled little bags, seventy-two gold bars and 33,333 silver shoes in addition. I had so much gold and silver, I didn't know where I should put it. Should I buy land and build something to house it? But I was afraid of droughts and floods. Or should I open up a grain business? Then the mice could eat everything. Should I lend money and charge interest? There were no guarantors. Should I open up a pawn shop? I was afraid I would have to shell out money; what if the manager runs off with the money, where would I look for him? All those thousands of difficulties made me so irritated, I woke up from the irritation: it was only a dream! I had groped around the hearthside bed with both hands; while doing so I had touched the lighter—that was the silver shoes! Then I had touched the brass pipe: that was the gold bars! After groping here and there for quite a while, I came across a big scorpion with a green head, and it stung me so that I howled loudly.[2]

Of course, it is only the most superb actors who appear alone in front of the audience in such small plays. The reputation of such actors is immense. Wherever they appear, they are received with the greatest honor. Wealthy businessmen or officials frequently invite them with their troupe to perform in their houses. And yet probably no European artist would want to trade places with them. So great is the ambition and passion of Chinese actors that the acknowledged masters among them live in continual fear of the attacks that jealous rivals plan against them. It's impossible to tempt an actor or an actress to ingest the smallest morsel outside of their apartment. They are convinced that the slightest inattentiveness could turn them into the victim of a poisoning. The tea they drink during the performance is purchased secretly and in a different store every time. The water it is boiled with is brought in their own teakettle from home, and only one of their entourage is allowed to make it. The great stars would never think of performing if their own bandmaster was not conducting, because they are afraid of the malice of their rivals, who could set traps for them during the performance by faulty conducting or misleading movements. The audience pays hellishly close attention, and dishes out scorn and mockery at the smallest gaffe. And they are not above throwing teacups at the artists if they are not satisfied with their achievements.

Now, the fire that I want to tell you about on this occasion was the biggest theater fire of all time. It happened in Canton on May 25, 1845. The theater was built, as was common, of bamboo posts interwoven with mats. It had been built for the special celebratory performance in honor of the war god Guan Yu. The performance was supposed to last two days. The theater stood in the middle of a great square among hundreds of similar but much smaller stalls. It held 3,000 people. On the afternoon of the second day, when everything was overcrowded, the stage was supposed to represent a temple of the war god. But because, as I have already explained, there are no sets in China, this was only identifiable because of a sacrificial fire that flickered in the middle of the stage. Then an actor left one of

---

2 See "Der Traum" [The Dream], in *Chinesische Schattenspiele*, compiled and trans. Wilhelm Grube and Emil Krebs, ed. Berthold Laufer (Leipzig: O. Harrassowitz, 1915), in *Abhandlungen der Königlich Bayerische Akademie der Wissenschaften, Philosophische-Philologische und Historische Klass*, vol. 28 (Munich, 1917), 440.

the two doors in the background open as he exited, and a strong gust of wind swept inside the theater, causing a pair of mats lying near the fire on stage to ignite. In the blink of an eye, the whole stage was in flames, and a few minutes later the fire had engulfed the entire structure. Now, the terrible thing was that in the whole theater there was only one single exit. Whoever just happened to be near it could save themselves; whoever sat closer to the front was lost. Hardly had a few hundred people reached the open air when the door began to burn. In vain they tried to douse it with hoses and water buckets. After a quarter of an hour had passed, it was impossible to get near the center of the fire because of the heat, and thus more than 2,000 people perished.

The European who hears about such things naturally thinks with pride and satisfaction about his own great stone theaters, which are under the strict supervision of the building control departments, in which there are firemen present at every performance, and where everything is done for the safety of the spectators. If there was ever a disaster at some point, it would hardly take the same terrible form, even if only because our theaters hold far fewer spectators. But that's just it: in China all big events, whether work or celebrations, are tailored for enormous masses of people. And the feeling of being one of the masses is much stronger in the Chinese than it can ever be in the European people. Hence the humility, unimaginable to us, that is the main virtue of the Chinese and in no way implies low self-esteem; rather it is simply the constant awareness of the enormous size of the mass of people they belong to. This humility has a strong foundation in the rules for living and educational books of their great wise men Confucius and Lao Tzu, where it is cloaked in very particular codes of conduct that everyone can learn and understand. And at the same time, these great teachers of the Chinese, by instructing their fellow citizens in this humility, have taught them to act in such a way that they make the life of the great mass they belong to easier; they have instilled in them enormous respect for the state and especially for civil servants, whom we must not imagine to be like European civil servants. The exams that the Chinese civil servants take require not only specialized knowledge, such as our exams require, but also close familiarity with the whole corpus of poetry and literature, and especially the wise men's instructions I spoke about. One might go so far as to say that it is these convictions of the Chinese that make their theaters so shabby and such fire hazards. At least that is what a Chinese man with whom I once discussed these matters told me:

"In China we are convinced that the most long-lasting and impressive house in every city must be the government building. After that come the temples. But places of amusement should not draw attention to themselves, because then one would think that in such a city order and work are only a minor matter." And now, as you know, in many cities in China they really are a minor matter. But we must hope that the theater of blood, in the face of which they have retreated, will soon come to an end.[3]

"Theaterbrand von Kanton," GS, 7.1, 226–31. Translated by Lisa Harries Schumann.

Broadcast on Radio Berlin, November 5, 1931, and on Southwest German Radio, Frankfurt, on February 3, 1932. Benjamin inscribed on the typescript: "Berlin and Frankfurt." The Frankfurt broadcast was announced in the Südwestdeutsche Rundfunk-Zeitung *for February 3, 1932, as the second of two broadcasts on the Youth Hour, which was scheduled to air from 3:15–4:00 pm.*

---

3 Given the dates of the broadcasts (November 1931 and February 1932), Benjamin is most likely referring to the Sino-Japanese conflicts surrounding the Mukden incident of September 1931—during which Japan almost certainly staged an attack on its own railway lines in Mukden, in Northern China, and used the explosion as a pretext for occupying Manchuria—followed by the Battle of Shanghai in early 1932.

CHAPTER 26

The Railway Disaster at the Firth of Tay

When, at the beginning of the last century, iron foundries began their first trials with the steam engine, it was something altogether different than when modern technicians and scientists work on a new airplane, a space rocket, even, or some other such machine. Today we know what technology is. These scientists and engineers have the whole world's attention. Newspapers report on their work. Large businesses give them money for their research. But when at the turn of the last century men were creating the inventions that transformed the face of the entire world—the mechanical loom, gas lighting, the iron foundry, the steam engine—no one really knew what these great technicians and engineers were making. Indeed, even they didn't know the import of their work. It's hard to call one of these inventions more significant than any other. People today can hardly conceive of them as separate from their use. Nevertheless, it can be said that the most conspicuous changes to the globe over the course of the last century were all more or less related to the railroad. Today I'll be telling you about a railroad catastrophe, but not only because it's a horrible and frightening story. I also want to place it within the history of technology, specifically of railroad construction. The story is of a bridge. This bridge collapsed. It was certainly terrible for the 200 people who lost their lives, for their loved ones, and for many others. Even so, I want to present this accident as only one minor incident in a great struggle, a struggle in which humans have been victorious and will remain victorious if they do not once more destroy the fruits of their own labor.

When I was considering what to talk to you about today, I returned to one of my favorite books. Published around 1840, it's a thick book containing pictures and, really, just a collection of silly stories and pranks. But what people considered jokes back then makes for curious reading today. In a nutshell, it's about the adventures of a fantastical little goblin finding his way around outer space. As he's nearing the planets, he comes across a long cast-iron bridge connecting the myriad celestial bodies:

> A bridge so long that you cannot see both ends of it at once, whose supports rest on planets, and which conveys wonderfully smooth asphalt from one globe to the next. The three hundred and thirty-three thousandth support touches Saturn. There our goblin sees that Saturn's famous ring is nothing but a balcony running all around the planet, on which its inhabitants catch a little fresh air come evening.[1]

Now you see what I meant when I said that people back then didn't really know what to make of technology. For them there was still something amusing about it. Now that things were to be built only using molds and calculations, as was particularly true with iron construction, people found it very funny. Thus there was a playful element to the first constructions of this kind. Iron construction began with winter gardens and arcades, that is, with luxury buildings. But very quickly it found a more appropriate, technological field of application, enabling entirely new constructions to emerge that were, until then, without precedent. Not only did they rely on this new technology, they also catered to entirely new needs. It was then that the first exhibition palaces were built, the first covered markets, and above all, the first railway stations. At that time they were still called "iron railway stations," and people associated them with the most outlandish ideas. Around the middle of the century one particularly bold Belgian painter, Antoine Wiertz, even petitioned to be able to paint the walls of these first train stations with large ceremonial images.[2]

Now, before we look at the Firth of Tay, the great 3,000-meter-wide estuary of the River Tay in central Scotland, let's first take a look back. In 1814 Stephenson built his first locomotive;[3] but only in 1820, once the rails could be effectively rolled, was the rail-*road*

---

1 J. J. Grandville, *Un autre monde* (Paris: H. Fournier, 1844), 138–9. For further references by Benjamin to the image of Saturn in Grandville, see *The Arcades Project*, 8, 18, 64–5 [B1a, 2], 151 [F1, 7]; and "The Ring of Saturn, or Some Remarks on Iron Construction," also in *The Arcades Project*, 885–7, where Benjamin mentions the railway catastrophe at the Firth of Tay, and which might be an early draft of what eventually became the radio broadcast; *Das Passagen-Werk*, in GS, 5.1, 51, 66, 112–13 [B1a, 2], 212 [F1, 7], and GS, 5.2, 1060–3.

2 Antoine Joseph Wiertz (1806–1865), Belgian painter and sculptor.

3 George Stephenson (1781–1848), the English engineer known as the "Father of the Railways," is credited with building the first public railroad line powered by steam locomotive.

possible. Do not think, however, that everything went according to some systematic plan. No indeed: right away a quarrel broke out over the rails. Under no circumstances, so people thought, would it ever be possible to scrape together enough iron for the English rail network—and back then, of course, people were only imagining a tiny one. Many experts honestly believed that the "steam carts" should be run on granite tracks. In 1825 the first railroad line was opened, and "Locomotive No. 1" is still on display today at one of its terminals. You can be sure that if you're ever there, at first glance it will look more like a steamroller for flattening pavements than like a real locomotive. In Europe, on the Continent, only very short routes were laid out, which could have just as easily been traveled by post coach or even on foot. Perhaps you've heard that Nuremberg and Fürth were the first two German cities connected by the railroad; then came Berlin, Potsdam, etc. For the most part, people saw it as a curiosity. And when the medical professors at the University of Erlangen were asked for their expert opinion of the Nuremberg railroad, they concluded that on no account should the service be permitted: the rapid motion would scramble people's brains; indeed, the mere sight of these speeding trains was enough to cause people to faint. At a minimum, three-meter-high wooden barriers were required on either side of the tracks. When the second German railroad started running from Leipzig to Dresden, a miller filed a lawsuit claiming it obstructed his wind, and when a tunnel was required, the doctors again weighed in against the railroad: older people might suffer from the shock of the sudden change in air pressure. How people initially thought of the railroad is perhaps most clearly seen in what a great English scholar, who in other matters was no fool, had to say about railroad travel: he didn't regard it as traveling at all; it was like "being sent somewhere, and very little different from becoming a parcel."[4]

Alongside these battles over the benefits or ills of the railroad were those related to its construction. It is difficult for us today to imagine the perseverance of those first railroad engineers, the enormous amount of time they had to devote to their work. When work began in 1858 on the twelve-kilometer-long tunnel through Mont Cenis, it was expected to take seven years to complete. And it was no different with the bridge over the Tay. But here there was an

---

4   See John Ruskin, *Modern Painters*, vol. 3 [1856], in *The Works of John Ruskin*, eds. E. T. Cook and Alexander Wedderburn (London: George Allen, 1903–1912), vol. 5, 370.

additional hurdle. The engineers had to consider not only the load that this bridge would have to sustain, but also the terrible storms that raged along the Scottish coast, especially in autumn and spring. During construction of the bridge, which lasted from 1872 to 1878, there were months when the hurricanes hardly let up, preventing the men from working more than five or six days over the course of four weeks. In 1877, when the bridge was nearly finished, a gale of unimaginable force tore two forty-five-meter-long iron girders from their stone piles, destroying years of work in an instant. Thus all the more triumph when, in May 1878, the bridge was inaugurated with great fanfare. There was but a single voice of warning, albeit that of J. Towler, one of England's greatest bridge-construction engineers.[5] He believed that it wouldn't withstand severe storms for long, and that only too soon would the world hear once more of the bridge over the Tay.

A year and a half later, on December 28, 1879, at four in the afternoon, a crowded passenger train left Edinburgh on schedule for Dundee. It was Sunday; the train's six cars held 200 passengers. It was another one of those stormy Scottish days. The train was due to arrive in Dundee at 7:15 in the evening; it was already 7:14 when the watchman in the south tower of the bridge signaled the train. To recount the final moments of the train after this final signal, I will turn to the words of Theodor Fontane, in a passage from a poem called "The Bridge on the Tay."[6]

> There! The train! At the south tower
> Gasping on despite the storm's power.
> And Johnny speaks: "The bridge is due!"
> But so it is, we press on through.
>
> A rugged boiler, twice the steam,
> Victors they with such a team,
> It races, churns, does not relent,
> Yet will succumb: the element.

---

5   This is almost certainly a reference to Sir John Fowler (1817–1898), an English engineer who devoted his career to railway construction in Britain and abroad. After the collapse of the Tay Bridge, which had been designed by Victorian engineer Sir Thomas Bouch, Fowler was one of the engineers appointed to review and redesign Bouch's plan for another bridge in Scotland, the Forth Rail Bridge.

6   See Theodor Fontane, "Die Brück' am Tay" [1880], in *Werke, Schriften und Briefe*, eds. Walter Keitel and Helmuth Nürnberger, vol. 6 (Munich: Hanser, 1978), 286.

Our bridge: our pride. I laugh and sigh
As I ponder times gone by,
All the sorrow, grief; emote!
That miserable old ferry boat!

Many a precious Christmas night
Spied I would our window light
While lingering in the ferry shack
Wishing I would soon be back.

The bridgehouse waits, north of the mouth,
With all its windows facing south,
The bridgemen pacing to and fro'
All southward staring, full of woe;

The wind grew furied, high but high.
And now, like fire from the sky,
It plummets, glory glowing bright,
Into the Tay. Again, it's night.

There were no eyewitnesses to what happened that night. Not one passenger was saved. To this day it is not known whether the storm had already torn away the middle of the bridge before the convoy reached it, leaving the train to simply hurl itself into the void. Be that as it may, the storm is said to have made such an awful commotion that it drowned out all other sounds. However, other engineers at the time, especially those who had built the bridge, maintained that the storm must have blown the train off its tracks, causing it to hurtle against the guard rail. They insist that the train broke through the parapet and the bridge itself must have collapsed only much later. Thus the first indication of the disaster was not the crash of the tumbling train, but rather a fiery glow noticed at the time by three fishermen, who didn't suspect it was caused by the plummeting locomotive. When these men alerted the south bridge terminal and communication was then attempted with the north terminal, no contact could be made. The wires had been ruptured. The Tay stationmaster was informed, who immediately set out in a locomotive. In a quarter of an hour he was on the scene. Carefully he drove out onto the bridge. But after roughly a kilometer, upon reaching the first middle support, the engine driver braked so suddenly that the locomotive almost jumped off the tracks. In the moonlight he had detected a gaping hole. The middle portion of the bridge was gone.

When you open the *Funkstunde* [Radio Times], you'll see a picture of the collapsed bridge published around that time in the *Leipziger Illustrierte Zeitung*.[7] Even in its iron construction, it bears similarities to a wooden bridge. Iron construction was still in its infancy and had yet to gain confidence in itself. But you all must know, at least from pictures, the structure in which iron first proudly declared its self-assurance, the structure that also stands as a monument to the calculations of the engineer: the tower completed by Eiffel for the Paris World's Fair, just ten years after the collapse of the Tay Bridge. The Eiffel Tower, when it was built, had no function whatsoever; it was just a landmark, a wonder of the world, as they say. But then came the invention of radiotelegraphy. All of a sudden the soaring structure had found a purpose. Today the Eiffel Tower is the radio transmitter for Paris. Eiffel and his engineers built the tower in seventeen months. Every rivet hole was prepared in workshops with tenth-of-a-millimeter precision. Each of the 12,000 metal parts was specified in advance, down to the millimeter, along with every one of the two and a half million rivets. Not a chisel could be heard in the workshops. Even at the site, as in the draftsman's studio, thought prevailed over physical strength, which was transmitted to sturdy scaffolds and cranes.[8]

"Die Eisenbahnkatastrophe vom Firth of Tay," GS, 7.1, 232–7. Translated by Jonathan Lutes.

Broadcast on Radio Berlin, February 4, 1932, and on Southwest German Radio, Frankfurt, on March 30, 1932. The Berlin broadcast was announced in the Funkstunde *for February 4, 1932, from 5:30–5:50 pm; the Frankfurt broadcast was announced in the* Südwestdeutsche Rundfunk-Zeitung *as taking place March 30, 1932, as the first of two broadcasts on the Youth Hour, which was scheduled to air from 3:15–4:00 pm.*

---

7 The *Illustrierte Zeitung* (Leipzig), Germany's first illustrated newspaper, was a popular weekly published from 1843 to 1944. This image was featured in the *Funkstunde*'s announcement of Benjamin's broadcast. See *Funkstunde* 5 (January 29, 1932), 106.

8 For the last three sentences, see Alfred Gotthold Meyer, *Eisenbauten: Ihre Geschichte und Ästhetik* (Esslingen: P. Neff, 1907), 93. For this passage elsewhere in Benjamin, see *The Arcades Project*, 160–1 [F4a, 2]), 887; *Das Passagen-Werk*, GS, 5.1, 223 [F4a, 2] and GS, 5.2, 1063.

CHAPTER 27

The Mississippi Flood of 1927

When you open a map of middle America and look at the Mississippi—that giant-sized 5,000-kilometer-long current—you'll see a somewhat sinuous and meandering line, with frequent bends but still clearly heading from north to south, a line on which you might think you could rely, just as you would on a boulevard, or on a railroad line. The people, however, who live on the banks of this current—the farmers, the fishermen, and even the city folk—know this appearance is deceptive. The Mississippi is continuously moving: not only its waters, flowing from source to mouth, but also its banks, which are forever changing. Within ten to fifty miles of the present-day watercourse lie countless lakes, lagoons, swamps, and ditches whose forms reveal themselves to be nothing other than segments of the former riverbed that has since shifted to the west or to the east. As long as the river flows through solid rock, roughly until the southern tip of the state of Illinois, its path is pretty straight. Further down, however, it enters into the flood plains and in this loose ground its restlessness and unreliability are revealed. Never is it satisfied with the bed it has made for itself. And on top of all this, every spring, great volumes of water from the lower Mississippi's swollen tributaries, such as the Arkansas, the Red River, and the Ouachita, descend upon the flanks of the glutted Mississippi and their waters not only force out those of the main river but also create, so to speak, a barrier that congests the Mississippi, further contributing to the flooding of its adjacent states. And so it was that every year, for centuries, all the land within hundreds of miles was flooded. The plantations, fields, settlements, primeval forests, and gardens rested under a meter of water such that the area surrounding the river resembled an ocean whose islands were the summits of trees. At the beginning of the last century people began to secure individual segments of the shore against the annual mood changes of the river.

In those days levees were paid for by the owners of the river-front where they were built. These embankments, of course, protected the land that lay behind them, but only at the expense of other neighbors who stood to suffer even more. It was in this way that most of the lower-lying plantations protected themselves over time. In order to lighten the burden of the planters, the American Congress gave them the marshland behind their fields as compensation. Now, imagine what it must have meant to these planters, who owned nothing but their land, when one day they were ordered to tear down the embankments with their own hands and expose their plantations to the destructive violence of the water. But this is precisely what happened, which brings me to the most appalling and miserable episode of the great flood of 1927.

At the mouth of the Mississippi lies, as perhaps you know, the big and important trading city of New Orleans. In less than two weeks the water had climbed so high that this critical port appeared poised for destruction. If New Orleans were to be saved, people would have to take every last and desperate measure: the protective levees upriver from the city would have to be torn open to give the water an outlet onto the fields. This set off a series of bitter civil wars that only increased the horrors of the natural catastrophe. The farmers whose land was to be sacrificed to save the metropolis were among the poorest in the country. To prevent the levees from being blown up, they formed armed militias under the direction of one of America's many sect leaders. Thousands of farmers resolved to fight rather than pay for saving the city with the destruction of their own fields. As a last resort, the government appointed a general to act as dictator of the flood regions and declared a state of siege. As for the farmers, they armed themselves with machine guns in order to resist the military. There was an assassination attempt against today's president of the United States, Hoover, who, as a government secretary at the time, was visiting the flood regions.[1] But the government would not allow itself to be intimidated, and proceeded with the detonations. New Orleans was saved but 100,000 square miles of land were underwater. The number of those made homeless in the region reached a half million.

---

1   Herbert Hoover, then secretary of commerce, was appointed by President Coolidge to lead the federal, state, and private flood relief efforts. He called for the appointment of state flood commissions, to be headed by a single "dictator" in each of the affected states of Louisiana, Arkansas, and Mississippi.

The flood walls that were blown up—provided the current hadn't already swept them away—rank among the largest public projects in American history. These levees stretch for 2,500 kilometres on both sides of the river leading to the Gulf of Mexico. They often measure fifty meters in width and are ten meters high. Thousands upon thousands of workers have to toil year after year to build new levees while maintaining the old ones. An electrical monitoring network connects all stations with one another. The levees are inspected each week, and millions are spent annually on their upkeep. For more than ten years these constructions had provided complete reassurance to those living in the area, until the high waters came in the spring of 1927.

On April 16 the telegraph reported for the first time that the river had overrun its banks. These first reports sounded fairly innocuous, and Washington hoped that the minor disturbances would amount to little else. This proved ill-founded, however. Two days later, parts of seven states were entirely flooded. Large parts of Missouri, Arkansas, Kentucky, Tennessee, Louisiana, and Texas were underwater. Water seven to eight meters deep flowed over the fields. Dozens of cities and hundreds of small towns had to be evacuated, and woe to those who hesitated or failed to heed the warnings. And so we come to the story of three brothers, small farmers from the area around Natchez. They thought they had time to save their cattle; while others abandoned everything and ran for their lives, the brothers were making their way to the stalls. Before they knew it a powerful surge of water had blocked their path: they were cut off and would remain so. Only one of the three would escape with his life, and from him we have the hair-raising description of the hours spent on the peak of their roof, staring into the rising waters with ever-dwindling hope. Here's a bit of the story from the survivor:

> The water had left us with only a small strip of the pitched roof. One of the chimneys had already been ripped away. Around us there was nothing left to see of the destroyed town. Only from the church tower soaring heavenwards undamaged, could we hear the ringing voices of the rescued. From far off we could hear the rushing of the water. The sound of collapsing houses had ceased. It was like a shipwreck in the middle of the ocean, thousands of miles from the shore. "We're drifting," murmured John, clinging to the roof tiles with all his might. It actually felt as if the roof had transformed itself into a raft carried

along by the current. But when we looked over at the steeple just standing there, unmoving, we saw that it had only been our imagination. We were still at the very same spot amid the roaring swells.

Now the real battle began. At first the river followed the street but now the rubble blocked its way and drove it back. It was a downright assault. The current gathered every beam or tree trunk in its way and fired it like a missile against the house. And even then the current wouldn't let it go, sweeping it up again and firing it off anew. The walls were shaking under these unrelenting and steady attacks. Before long we were bombarded in this way by ten or twelve beams. The churning water masses raged and roared and the foam splashed round our feet. From the house beneath us we heard what sounded like a dull moan; we heard its joints creak. Sometimes when a beam would strike with frightful force, we thought it was over and the walls would give in, delivering us to the wild river. Sometimes when we saw a bundle of hay or an empty barrel drift by, we would wave our handkerchiefs excitedly until we realized our mistake and sank back into our silent fear. "Hey, look over there," cried John suddenly, "a big boat!" With outstretched arm he pointed to a dark spot in the distance. I couldn't see anything, neither could Bill, but he carried on. And it really was a boat. It rowed closer and closer until we could finally make it out. It glided slowly forward, seeming to encircle us but not coming any closer. I can only say that at this point we were like mad men. We flailed our arms about, yelling at the top of our lungs. We hurled insults at the boat, calling it a coward as it drifted by, silent and sinister. Was it really a boat? I still don't know to this day. When we finally saw it disappear, our last hopes went with it.

From that point on we expected the house to cave in at any moment and to swallow us whole. It seemed that the house must already have been completely undermined save for one especially strong wall, and if that gave way everything else would go down with it. I trembled at the thought that the roof would no longer carry our weight. The house might have lasted the whole night, but the roof began to give way under the constant barrage of beams. We had fled to the left side of the roof, where the rafters were still more or less intact. But then they, too, began to sway and it was plain to see that they would not hold much longer if all three of us stayed huddled together in the same spot.

My brother Bill had, very mechanically, placed his pipe back in his mouth. Grumbling to himself, he curled his moustache and furrowed his brow. The rising danger he saw before him, against which all his courage amounted to nothing, began to make him impatient. He spat a few times into the water with angry disdain. Then, as the timber beneath him continued to give out, he made his decision and climbed from the roof.

"Bill, Bill," I called. I sensed, with horror, what he was doing. He turned himself around and said, peacefully: "Farewell, Louis . . . You see, it's taking too long. I want to make room for you two."

First he threw his pipe and then himself into the flood. "Farewell," he said again, "I've had enough." He never resurfaced. He was a bad swimmer and he probably didn't even try to save himself. He didn't want to survive our ruin and the death of our loved ones.

And so it ends, the tale of the third brother, the only member of this family to be rescued by one of the boats combing the water.

More than 50,000 ships, motorboats, and steamers had been mobilized. The government even requisitioned luxury boats for the rescue operations. Entire aircraft squadrons were deployed day and night, as they were last year when, under the command of Charles Lindbergh, food and medical supplies were brought to the Chinese in the Yangtze River valley after they had been completely cut off from all other forms of contact. And on the banks of the Mississippi hundreds of thousands of refugees camped under the open sky, lacking shelter and warm clothing, exposed to hunger, rain, and the horrific tornadoes that further devastated the flood regions at that time.

So much for the raging elements of the Mississippi. On some other occasion we'll return to its banks during times when the river flowed peacefully in its bed, but there was little peace to be found on its shores. For a long time now I've planned to tell you the story of America's greatest and most dangerous secret society, next to which all bands of whiskey smugglers and criminal gangs are child's play: the Ku Klux Klan. Once again we'll find ourselves on the banks of the Mississippi, but this time facing the raging elements of human cruelty and violence. The dams that the law has built to contain them have held up no better than the actual ones made from earth and stone. And so, stay tuned for the Ku Klux Klan and Judge Lynch and the other unsavory characters that have populated the human wilderness of the Mississippi, and still populate it today.

"Die Mississippi-Überschwemmung 1927," GS, 7.1, 237–43. Translated by Jonathan Lutes.

Broadcast on Radio Berlin on March 23, 1932. The Funkstunde *announced the broadcast under the title "Die Überschwemmung des Mississippi" [The Mississippi Flood] for March 23, 1932, from 5:30–5:50 pm.*

CHAPTER 28

True Dog Stories

You probably think you know dogs. By this I mean, when I read you a famous description of dogs, you will have the same feeling I did when I first read it. I said to myself: if the word "dog" had not appeared in the description, I wouldn't have guessed which animal it was about; things look so new and special when a great scientist looks at them, as if they had never before been seen. The name of this scientist is Linnaeus, the very same Linnaeus you all know from botany and the man responsible for the system we still use today to classify plants. Here's what he has to say about dogs:

Feeds on meat, carcasses, farinaceous grains, but not leaves; digests bones, vomits up grass; defecates onto stone: Greek white, exceedingly acidic. Drinks by lapping; urinates to the side, up to one hundred times in good company, sniffs at its neighbor's anus; moist nose, excellent sense of smell; runs on a diagonal, walks on toes; perspires very little, lets tongue hang out in the heat; circles its sleeping area before retiring; hears rather well while sleeping, dreams. The female is vicious with jealous suitors; fornicates with many partners when in heat; bites them; intimately bound during copulation; gestation is nine weeks, four to eight compose a litter, males resemble the father, females the mother. Loyal above all else; house companion for humans; wags its tail upon master's approach, defends him; runs ahead on a walk, waits at crossings; teachable, hunts for missing things, makes the rounds at night, warns of those approaching, keeps watch over goods, drives livestock from fields, herds reindeer, guards cattle and sheep from wild animals, holds lions in check, rustles up game, locates ducks, lies in wait before pouncing on the net, retrieves a hunter's kill without partaking of it, rotates a skewer in France, pulls carts in Siberia. Begs for scraps at the table; after stealing it timidly hides its tail; feeds greedily. Lords it over its home; is the enemy of beggars, attacks strangers without being provoked. Heals wounds, gout and cancers with tongue. Howls to music, bites stones thrown its way; depressed and foul-smelling before a storm. Afflicted by tapeworm. Spreads rabies. Eventually goes blind and gnaws at itself.[1]

That was Linnaeus. After a description like that, most of the stories frequently told about dogs seem rather boring and run-of-the-mill. In any case, they can't rival this passage in terms of peculiarity or flair, even those told by people out to prove how clever dogs are. Is it not an insult to dogs that the only stories about them are told in order to prove something? As if they're only interesting as a species? Doesn't each individual dog have its own special character?

> No single dog is physically or temperamentally like another. Each has its own good and bad tendencies, which are often in stark contradiction, giving dog owners precious conversation material. Everyone's dog is cleverer than his neighbor's! When an owner recounts his dog's silly tricks, he is illuminating its character, and when the dog experiences some remarkable fate, it becomes something greater, part of a life story. It is special even in its death.[2]

Now let's hear about some of these peculiarities. It must also be true of other animals that they possess many unique qualities that are not found in the species as a whole. But humans make this observation so readily and definitively only with dogs, with whom they have a closer bond than with any other animal, except perhaps horses. It all began thousands of years ago with man's great victory over the dog, or more precisely, over the wolf and the jackal; yielding to man, allowing themselves to be tamed, these wild animals became dogs. However, the most ancient dogs, which first appeared around the end of the Stone Age, were far removed from our pets and hunting dogs of today. They were more similar to the half-wild dogs of Eskimos, which have to fend for themselves for

---

1 Linnaeus as quoted in A. E. Brehm, *Die Haushunde: mit einem Anhang: Zur Stammesgeschichte der Haushunde* [Household Dogs: With an Addendum on the Phylogeny of Household Dogs] (Leipzig: Reclams Universal Bibliothek, 1923), 33ff. For this passage as well as those that follow from Brehm and Czibulka, Benjamin's typescript refers to the text he wanted to cite by title but does not give the full quotation, which was supplied by the editors of the GS, who also note that Benjamin was unlikely to have had time in the twenty-minute broadcast to read these passages in full (GS, 7.2, 584).

2 Brehm, *Die Haushunde*, 43.

months at a time and resemble the Arctic wolf in every respect, as well as the fearful, treacherous, and currish dogs of Kamchatka, which, according to one traveler's account, haven't the slightest love for or loyalty to their master—in fact, they constantly try to kill him. The domesticated dog must have arisen from such a beast. It is truly regrettable that later on, some dogs, especially mastiffs, returned to their old savagery as a consequence of breeding, becoming even more dreadful and bloodthirsty than they had been in their primitive state. Here is the story of the most famous of all bloodhounds, named Bezerillo, whom the Spaniards of Fernando Cortez came upon while conquering Mexico, and then trained most hideously.

In earlier times the Mexican bulldog was used in the nastiest way. It was trained to catch people, tackle them to the ground, and even kill them. During the conquest of Mexico, the Spaniards deployed such dogs against the Indians and one of them, by the name of Bezerillo, became famous, or rather, infamous. It can no longer be said whether or not he was an actual Cuban mastiff, which is considered to be a mongrel of a bulldog and a bloodhound. He is described as medium-sized, red in color, but black around the nose and up to the eyes. His audacity and intelligence were equally extraordinary. He enjoyed the highest status among the dogs and received twice as much food as the others. When on the attack he would hurl himself against swarms of Indians while taking care to lock onto an arm so he could drag away a captive. If they complied, the dog would inflict no further harm; if they refused to accompany him, in a flash he would pin them to the ground and strangle them. He could tell exactly which Indians had capitulated and let them be, focusing instead on the resisters. Although so cruel and so fierce, he sometimes showed himself to be much more humane than his masters. One morning, so the story goes, Captain Jago de Senadza wanted to have a little barbarous fun by letting Bezerillo rip to shreds an old captive Indian woman. He gave her a letter and ordered her to deliver it to the governor of the island; the letter instructed that the dog be let loose on the old woman to rip her apart. When the poor, defenseless Indian woman saw the ferocious dog storming after her, she fell to the ground in fear, desperately begging him for mercy. She showed him the letter, explaining that she had brought it to the commander on orders. The ferocious dog hesitated at these words, and, after a moment's contemplation, approached the old woman tenderly. This incident astounded the Spaniards, appearing to them as something mystical, or supernatural, which is probably why the governor set the old Indian free. Bezerillo met his end in a skirmish with Caribs, who felled him with a poison dart. It's easy to see how the unfortunate Indians saw such dogs as four-legged abettors of the two-legged devil.[3]

The following story tells of a breed of wild mastiff that roams in packs about Madagascar:

On the island of Madagascar, large hordes of dogs roam wild. Their bitterest enemy is the caiman, which would frequently devour them as they swam from one riverbank to the next. Over the years of struggle against the beast, the dogs have invented a trick that enables them to stay clear of the caiman's jaws. Before diving into the water, they gather in a large group by the shore and bark as loudly as they can. Drawn to the noise, all the alligators in the vicinity raise their giant heads out of the water just below the spot on the bank where the pack is waiting. At this point the dogs gallop along the bank and then swim across the water unmolested, as the ungainly alligators are not able to keep up. It is also interesting to observe that dogs brought to the island by new settlers fall victim to the caiman, while their offspring later save themselves from certain death by employing the trick invented by the indigenous dogs.[4]

We have seen that dogs know how to help one another. Now let's see how helpful they've been to humans. I'm thinking of age-old human activities such as the hunt, the night watch, trekking, war, in all of which dogs have cooperated with humans, spanning various epochs of world history and the most remote corners of the Earth. Some ancient peoples, like those from Colophon, waged wars using great packs of dogs, who would attack first in all their battles. But I'm thinking not only of dogs' heroism throughout history, but also of their roles in society, and the assistance they give people in count-less aspects of everyday life. There is no end to the number of stories, but I will tell only three very short ones, the Boot Dog, the Coach Poodle, and the Death Hound.[5]

3 Ibid., 96–8.
4 Alfons von Czibulka, *Der Hundespiegel: Eine Auswahl* [Reflections on Dogs: A Selection] (Munich: Drei Masken Verlag, 1923), 299.
5 See Czibulka, *Der Hundespiegel*, 302ff.

At the Pont-Neuf in Paris there was a young bootblack who trained a poodle to dip her thick hairy paws in the water and then tread on the feet of passersby. The people would cry out, the bootblack would appear and thereby multiply his earnings. As long as he was busy shining someone's shoes, the dog behaved, but when the footstool became free, the game would begin anew.

Brehm tells us about a poodle he knew whose intelligence brought great amusement. He was trained in all sorts of things and, in a manner of speaking, understood every word. Whatever his master sent him to fetch, he was sure to deliver what was asked. He would say: "Go fetch a carriage!" and the dog would run to the spot where the cabs wait, jump into a coach and keep barking until the carriage drove off; if the coachman took a wrong turn, the dog began barking again, and in some cases would even run along ahead of the wagon until they reached his master's home.

An English newspaper reports: In Campbelltown in the province of Argyllshire, every funeral procession, with very few exceptions, makes its way from the church to the cemetery accompanied by a quiet mourner in the form of a huge, black dog. He always takes his place beside those immediately following the casket and escorts the funeral cortege to the grave. Once there, he lingers until the final words of the eulogy have come and gone. With much gravitas he then turns around and exits the graveyard at a solemn pace. This remarkable dog seems instinctively to know when and where a funeral will occur, as he always shows up just at the right moment. Because he has been shouldering this freely chosen obligation for years, his presence has become more or less expected, such that his failure to appear would be conspicuous. At first the dog was always chased from the open grave, his preferred spot to sit, but he would always return to accompany the mourners at the earliest opportunity. Eventually people gave up chasing away the quiet sympathy-bearer, and he has since had an official role in every funeral procession. However, the most remarkable thing was when a chartered steamer pulled into the harbor, carrying a recently deceased man and his attendant mourners: the dog waited right where the ship would dock and then accompanied the funeral procession to the cemetery in his usual way.

Incidentally, did you know there's an encyclopedia of famous dogs? It was made by a man who busied himself with all sorts of obscure things. For instance, he compiled a lexicon of famous shoemakers, and wrote a whole book titled *Soup*, as well as other, similarly esoteric works. The dog book is very handy. Every dog known to man is in it, including some that the writer has conceived of himself. It was in this book that I found the wonderful and true story of Medor the dog, who took part in the Paris Revolution of 1831 and the storming of the Louvre, but lost his master there. I'll tell it to you now in closing, just as its author Ludwig Börne wrote it.[6]

I left Napoleon's coronation for another spectacle that was more after my own heart. I visited the noble Medor. If virtue were rewarded with a title on this Earth, Medor would be the emperor of all dogs. Consider his story. After the storming of the Louvre in July, those who died in the battle were buried in the square in front of the palace, on the side where the delightful columns stand. When the bodies were laid onto carts to carry them to the grave, a dog jumped with heartrending sorrow onto one of the wagons, and from there into the large pit into which the dead were thrown. Great efforts were made to pull him out; he would have been scorched by the scattered lime even before being buried under the dirt. That was the dog people would later call Medor. During battle he always stood beside his master. He was wounded himself. Since his master's death he never left the graves, moaning day and night before the door to the narrow cemetery, or howling while running back and forth in front of the Louvre.

No one paid much attention to Medor, because no one knew him or could guess his pain. His master must have been one of the many foreigners that came to Paris in those days, fought unnoticed for the freedom of his homeland, bled there, died there, and was buried anonymously. Only after several weeks did people begin to take notice of Medor. He was emaciated about the ribs and covered in festering wounds. People gave him food, but for a long time he refused it. Finally the persistent compassion of a good townswoman succeeded in alleviating Medor's grief. She took him in, bandaged and healed his wounds, and made him strong again. Medor was more content, but his heart lay in his master's grave, where his caretaker took him after his recovery and where he would stay for the next seven months. A few times greedy people sold him to rich curiosity seekers; once he was taken thirty hours from Paris, but he always found his way back.

---

6 Karl Ludwig Börne (1786–1837) was a German-Jewish writer, journalist, and satirist.

Medor is often seen unearthing a small piece of fabric; he becomes excited upon finding it and then sadly reburies it. It's probably a piece of his master's shirt. If he's given a piece of bread or cake, he buries it in the ground, as if wanting to feed his friend in the grave, and then retrieves it, repeating this process several times a day. For the first few months the national guardsman at the Louvre would invite Medor into the guardhouse every night. Later on the guard saw to it that a hut was built for Medor beside the grave.

Medor quickly found his Plutarch, his rhapsodists, his painters. When I visited the square in front of the Louvre, peddlers offered me Medor's life story, songs of his exploits, his portrait. For ten sous I purchased Medor's immortality. The little graveyard was surrounded by a thick wall of people, all poor folks from the street. Here lies buried their pride and joy. This is their opera, their ballroom, their court, their church. They're thrilled to get close enough to pet Medor. I too managed to edge my way through the crowd. Medor is a large, white poodle. I bent down to pet him, but he took no notice of me; my jacket was too fine. But when approached and stroked by a man in rough clothes, or a ragged woman, he responded warmly. Medor knows very well where to find the true friends of his master. A young girl, all in tatters, came to him. He jumped up to greet her, clung to her and wouldn't let go. He was so happy, so at ease with her. To ask something of the poor girl, he didn't need to first bend before her and touch the hem of her skirt as with a groomed and genteel lady. Wherever he bit at her dress was a rag that fit snug in his mouth. The child was very proud of Medor's familiarity with her. I crept away, ashamed of my tears.[7]

And with this we are through with dogs for the day.

"Wahre Geschichten von Hunden," GS, 7.1, 243–9. Translated by Jonathan Lutes.

Broadcast on Radio Berlin, September 27, 1930. Benjamin dated the type-script "Berlin Radio, September 27, 1930." The Funkstunde *announced the broadcast for this date from 3:20–3:40 pm.*

---

7 See Czibulka, *Der Hundespiegel*, 225–7, and Ludwig Börne, *Briefe aus Paris 1830–1831, Gesammelte Schriften*, vol. 2 (Hamburg: Hoffmann and Campe, 1832), 138ff.

CHAPTER 29

A Crazy Mixed-Up Day:
Thirty Brainteasers

Perhaps you know a long poem that begins like this:

> Dark it is, the moon shines bright,
> a car creeps by at the speed of light
> and slowly rounds the round corner.
> People standing sit inside,
> immersed they are in silent chatter,
> while a shot-dead hare
> skates by on a sandbank there.

Everyone can see that this poem doesn't add up. In the story you'll hear today, quite a few things don't add up either, but I doubt that everyone will notice. Or rather, each of you will find a few mistakes—and when you find one, you can make a dash on a piece of paper with your pencil. And here's a hint: if you mark all the mistakes in the story, you'll have a total of fifteen dashes. But if you find only five or six, that's perfectly alright as well.

But that's only one facet of the story you'll hear today. Besides these fifteen mistakes, it also contains fifteen questions. And while the mistakes creep up on you, quiet as a mouse, so no one notices them, the questions, on the other hand, will be announced with a loud gong. Each correct answer to a question gives you two points, because many of the questions are more difficult to answer than the mistakes are to find. So, with a total of fifteen questions, if you know the answers to all of them, you'll have thirty dashes. Added to the fifteen dashes for mistakes, that makes a total of forty-five possible dashes. None of you will get all forty-five, but that's not necessary. Even ten points would be a respectable score.

You can mark your points yourselves. During the next Youth Hour, the radio will announce the mistakes along with the answers to the questions, so you can see whether your thoughts were on target, for above all, this story requires thinking. There are no questions and no mistakes that can't be managed with a little reflection.

One last bit of advice: don't focus on just the questions. To the contrary, keep a lookout for the mistakes above all; the questions will all be repeated at the end of the story. It goes without saying that the questions don't contain any mistakes; there, everything is as it should be. Now pay attention. Here's Heinz with his story.

What a day! It all started early this morning—I had hardly slept a wink, because I couldn't stop thinking about a riddle—anyway, the doorbell rang early. I opened the door and there was my friend Anton's deaf housekeeper. She handed me a letter from Anton.

"Dear Heinz," writes Anton, "yesterday, while I was at your house, I left my hat hanging by the door. Please give it to my housekeeper. Best regards, Anton." But the letter continues. Below he writes: "I just now found the hat. Forgive the disturbance. Many thanks for your trouble."

That's Anton for you, the absent-minded professor type. By the same token, he's also a great fan and solver of riddles. And when I looked at the letter, it occurred to me: I could use Anton today. Perhaps he knows the solution to my riddle; I made a bet that I would figure out the riddle by this morning. The riddle goes like this (*Gong*):

The peasant sees it often, the king only seldom, and God never at all. What is it?

Yes, that's it, I thought to myself, I have to ask Anton. I was hoping to ask his housekeeper whether he was already at school—Anton is a teacher—but she had already left.

I thought to myself, Anton must be at school. I put on my hat and just as I was heading down the stairs, it occurred to me that summer daylight saving time began today, so everything starts an hour earlier. I pulled out my watch and set it back one hour. When I reached the street, I realized that I had forgotten to shave. Just around the corner to the left I saw a barbershop. In three minutes I was there. In the window hung a large enamel sign: "A shave today ten pfennigs, a shave tomorrow free." (*Gong*): A shave today ten pfennigs, a shave tomorrow free. The sign struck me as odd. I wish I knew why. I went in, took a seat and got a shave, all the while looking in the large mirror hanging before me. Suddenly the barber nicked me, on my right cheek. And sure enough, blood appeared on the right side of my mirror image. The shave cost me ten pfennigs. I paid with a twenty-mark note and got back nineteen marks in five-mark coins, along with five groschen and twenty five-pfennig coins. Then the barber, a jolly young man, held open the door and said to me as I went out: "Say hello to Richard if you see him." Richard is his twin brother who has a pharmacy on the main square.

Now I'm thinking: the best thing is to go straight to Anton's school and see if I can't track him down. On my way there, walking down a street, I saw a large crowd of people standing around a carnival magician performing his tricks. With chalk he drew a tiny circle on the sidewalk. He then said: "Using the same center point, I will draw another circle whose circumference is five centimeters greater than the first." After doing so he stood up, looked around with a mysterious smile and said (*Gong*): "If I now draw a gigantic circle, let's say as big as the circumference of the Earth, and then I draw a second one whose circumference is five centimeters greater than that of the giant circle, which ring is wider: the one that lies between the tiny circle and the one five centimeters larger, or the ring between the giant circle and the one five centimeters larger?" Yes, I would like to know this, too.

I'd finally managed to push my way through the crowd, when I noticed that my cheek still hadn't stopped bleeding, and as I was on the main square, I went into the pharmacy to buy a bandage. "Greetings from your twin brother, the barber," I said to the pharmacist. He's old as the hills and a bit of an odd bird to boot. And more than anything, he's terribly anxious. Whenever he leaves his ground-floor shop, not only does he double-lock the door, he also walks around the whole building, and if he sees he's left a window open somewhere, he reaches inside to close it. But the most interesting thing about him is his collection of curiosities, which he'll show to anyone who comes into his shop. Today was no exception and, before long, I was left to admire everything at my leisure. There was a skull of an African Negro when he was six years old, and next to it a skull of the same man when he was sixty. The second was much larger, of course. Then there was a photograph of Frederick the Great, playing with his two greyhounds at Sanssouci. Next to it lay a bladeless antique knife that was missing its handle. He also had a stuffed flying fish. And hanging on the wall was a large pendulum clock. As I paid for my bandage, the pharmacist asked (*Gong*): "If the pendulum on my clock swings ten times to the right and ten times to the left, how often does it pass through the middle?" This, too, I wanted to know. So, that was the pharmacist.

Now I needed to hurry if I wanted to make it to the school before lessons were over. I jumped onto the next streetcar and just managed to get a corner seat. A fat man was seated to my right and on my left was a small woman talking to the man across from her about her uncle (*Gong*): "My uncle," she said, "has just turned one hundred years old, but has only had twenty-five birthdays. How can that be?" This, too, I wanted to know, but we had already reached the school. I went through all the classrooms looking for Anton. The teachers were very annoyed at being disturbed.

And they asked the oddest questions. For example, I walked into a math class where the teacher was getting cross with a young boy. He had not been paying attention and the teacher was going to punish him. He said to the boy (*Gong*): "Add up all the numbers from one to a thousand." The teacher was more than a little surprised when, after a minute, the boy stood up and gave the right answer: 501,000. How was he able to calculate so fast? This I also wanted to know. First I tried it with just the numbers one through ten. Once I came upon the quickest way to do this, I had figured out the boy's trick.

Another class was geography. (*Gong*): The teacher drew a square on the blackboard. In the middle of this square he drew a smaller square. He then drew four lines, each connecting one corner of the small square with the nearest corner of the large square. This resulted in five shapes: one in the middle, this was the small square, and four other shapes surrounding the small square. Every boy had to draw this diagram in his notebook. The diagram represented five countries. Now the teacher wanted to know how many different colors were needed so that each country was a different color than the three, or four, countries that it bordered. I thought to myself, five countries need five colors. But I was wrong, the answer was smaller than five. Why? This, too, I wanted to know.

I then entered another class, where students were learning to spell. The teacher was asking very strange things, for example (*Gong*): "How do you spell dry grass with three letters?" And (*Gong*): "How can you write one hundred using only four nines?" And (*Gong*): "In your ABC's, which is the middlemost letter?" To conclude the lesson he told the children a fairy tale (*Gong*):

"An evil sorcerer transformed three princesses into three flowers, perfectly identical and planted in a field. Once a month, one of them was allowed to return to her house for the night as a human. On one of these occasions, one of the princesses said to her husband just as dawn broke and she had to return to her two friends in the field and become a flower again: 'If you come to me this morning and pluck me, I will be redeemed and can stay with you for evermore.' This came to pass. Now the question is, how did her husband recognize her, since the flowers looked identical?" This, too, I wanted to know, but it was high time for me to get hold of Anton, and because he wasn't at school, I headed to his home.

Anton lived not far away, on the sixth floor of a building on Kramgasse. I climbed the stairs and rang the bell. His housekeeper, who had been at my house in the morning, answered right away and let me in. But she was alone in the apartment: "Herr Anton is not here," she said. This irritated me. I thought the smartest thing to do was to wait for him, so I went into his room. He had a gorgeous view onto the street. The only hindrance was a two-story building across the way, which obstructed the view. But you could clearly see the faces of passersby, and on looking up, you could see birds fluttering about in the trees. Looming nearby was the large train station clock tower. The clock read exactly 14:00. I pulled out my pocket watch for comparison and sure enough, it was 4 pm on the nose. I had waited for three hours when, out of boredom, I started browsing the books in Anton's room. (*Gong*) Unfortunately a bookworm had gotten into his library. Every day it ate through one volume. It was now on the first page of the first volume of *Grimm's Fairy Tales*. I thought to myself, how long will it need to reach the last page of the second volume of *Grimm's Fairy Tales*? I wasn't concerned about the covers, just the pages. Yes, this is something I wanted to know. I heard voices outside in the hallway.

The housekeeper was standing there with an errand boy, who had been sent by the tailor to collect money for a suit. (*Gong*) Because the errand boy knew the housekeeper was deaf, he had handed her a piece of paper with one word written on it in large capital letters: MONEY [*GELD*]. But the housekeeper had no money with her, so to convey her request that he be patient, she drew just two more letters on the piece of paper. What were these two letters?

I had had enough of waiting. I headed out to find a little something to eat after such a tedious day. As I reached the street the moon was already in the sky. There had been a new moon a few days prior, and by now it had waxed to a narrow crescent that looked like the beginning of a capital German "Z" hovering over the rooftops. In front of me was a small pastry shop. I went in and ordered an apple cake with whipped cream. (*Gong*): When the apple cake with whipped cream arrived, it didn't appeal to me. I told the waiter I would prefer a Moor's Head.[1] He brought me the Moor's Head, which was delicious. I stood up to go. As I was just on my way out, the waiter ran after me, shouting: You didn't pay for your Moor's Head!—But I gave you the apple cake in exchange, I told him.—But you didn't pay for that either, the waiter said.—Sure, but I didn't eat it either! I retorted, and left. Was I right? This, too, I'd like to know.

As I arrived home, imagine my astonishment at seeing Anton, who had been waiting there for five hours. He wanted to apologize for the silly letter he had sent to me early this morning via his housekeeper. I said that it didn't matter all that much, and then told Anton my whole day as I've just told it to you now. He couldn't stop shaking his head. When my story was over he was so astounded that he was speechless. He then left, still shaking his head. As he disappeared around the corner, I suddenly realized: this time he really has forgotten his hat. And I—of course I had forgotten something as well: to ask him the answer to my riddle (*Gong*): The peasant sees it often, the king only seldom, and God never at all.

But perhaps you've found the answer by now. And with this, I say goodbye.

Repetition of the fifteen questions:

1. The first question is an old German folk riddle: The peasant sees it often, the king only seldom, and God never at all. What is it?

2. What's fishy about a barber who hangs an enamel sign in his window reading, "A shave today ten pfennigs, a shave tomorrow free"?

3. If I have a small circle and then around its center point I draw a circle whose circumference is five centimeters greater than that of the original, this creates a ring between the two circles. If I then take a giant circle, one as big as the circumference of the Earth, and around the same center point I draw another one, whose circumference is five centimeters greater than that of the first giant one, there is then a ring between those two circles. Which of the two rings is wider, the first or the second?

---

1 "Moor's Head," a direct translation of Benjamin's *Mohrenkopf*, is rarer in English as a name for this chocolate-coated marshmallow pastry. The English term for this dessert is usually "mallomar," and the modern-day German is *Schokokuss*, "Chocolate Kiss."

4. If the clock pendulum swings ten times to the right and ten times to the left, how often does it pass through the middle?

5. How can a man who is 100 years old have had only twenty-five birthdays?

6. What is the quickest way to add up all the numbers from one to 1,000? Try it first with the numbers from one to ten.

7. A country is surrounded by four other countries, each of which borders the middle country and two of the others. What is the fewest number of colors needed so that each country has a different color than its neighbors?

8. How do you spell dry grass with three letters?

9. How can you write 100 using only four nines?

10. In your ABC's, which is the middlemost letter?

11. There are three identical flowers in a field. In the morning, how can you tell which of them has not been there overnight?

12. If each day a bookworm eats through one volume in a series of books, how long will it take for it to eat its way from the first page of one volume to the last page of the next, provided he eats in the same direction in which the series of books is arranged?

13. You have a piece of paper with the word "money" [*Geld*] written on it. Which two letters can you add to convey a request for patience [*Geduld*]?

14. What's wrong with the logic of a man who orders a piece of cake, exchanges it for another once it arrives, and then won't pay for the new piece because he claims he traded the old piece for it?

15. The old riddle once more, whose solution is worth four points because it has now appeared twice: The peasant sees it often, the king only seldom, and God never at all.

Answers to the fifteen questions:

1. His equal.

2. If the barber were serious about his offer, he wouldn't have made a permanent sign out of enamel, because "tomorrow," when shaves are free, will never come.

3. The two rings are of equal width.

4. The pendulum passes through the middle twenty times.

5. The man was born on February 29.

6. Calculate: 999 + 1 = 1,000; 998 + 2 = 1,000; 997 + 3 = 1,000; there are 500 such pairs. Then all that's left is 1,000 at the high end, and 0 at the low end; so adding 1,000 to 500,000 gives a total of

501,000. Using the same method, the numbers from 1 to 10 add up to 60.[2]

7. Three colors are needed: one for the country in the middle, one for the two countries above and below the one in the middle, and a third color for the two countries to the left and the right of the one in the middle.

8. Hay.

9. 99 9/9.

10. B.

11. The flower that was not there overnight is the one with no dew on it.

12. The bookworm needs only a moment to get from the first page of the first book to the last page of the second, because in a properly arranged library, the first page of the first book is right up against the last page of the second.

13. Inserting the letters "du" into the middle of the German word for "money" [*Geld*] spells the German word for "patience" [*Geduld*].

14. The first piece of cake, which he did not pay for, does not belong to him, so he should neither eat it nor exchange it for the second piece.

15. His equal.

List of the fifteen mistakes:

1. Heinz realizes that summer daylight saving has just begun and sets his watch back one hour. He should set it one hour forward.

2. If the barbershop is just around the corner and it would take him as long as three minutes to get there, it would be impossible for him to see it.

3. If Heinz is cut on his right side, the wound will be on the left side of his reflection.

4. Nineteen marks cannot be disbursed in five-mark notes.

5. Five groschen and twenty five-pfennig coins equals 1.50 marks. Heinz should have received only ninety pfennig in addition to the nineteen marks, because he gave the barber twenty marks for a shave that cost ten pfennig.[3]

---

2 Benjamin has made a mistake here. There are only 499 number pairs adding up to 1,000, giving a subtotal of 499,000. Adding the two remaining numbers, 1,000 and 500, gives a correct total of 500,500. Correspondingly, the sum of the numbers between 1 and 10 is 55. Benjamin's mistake was first corrected in the GS, 7.2, 649–50.

3 There were ten pfennig in one groschen, and 100 pfennig in one mark.

6. If the barber, the pharmacist's twin brother, is a young man, then the pharmacist cannot be an old man.

7. A window cannot be closed from the outside.

8. Even if he is dead, a man has only one skull, not two.

9. One could not yet take photographs in the time of Frederick the Great.

10. A bladeless knife missing its handle is simply not there.

11. Someone with a corner seat cannot have neighbors to the right and the left.

12. If Anton's housekeeper is deaf and alone in the apartment, she wouldn't know to open the door after Heinz rings the bell.

13. If someone lives on the sixth floor, a two-story building cannot block his view and he cannot see the faces of passersby.

14. If the train station clock reads 14:00, it's 2 pm, not 4 pm.

15. The crescent of a waxing moon looks like the start of a German uppercase "A," not "Z."

"Ein verrückter Tag, Dreißig Knacknüsse," GS, 7.1, 306–15. Translated by Jonathan Lutes.

Broadcast on Southwest German Radio, Frankfurt, probably on July 6, 1932. The Südwestdeutsche Rundfunk-Zeitung *announced for the Youth Hour on July 6, 1932, at 3:15 pm, "Denksport' [Mental Exercise], by Dr. Walter Benjamin (for children ten years and older)." "A Crazy Mixed-Up Day" was most likely the text Benjamin prepared for this broadcast.*

SECTION II

Radio Plays for Children

Much Ado About Kasper and *The Cold Heart* (with Ernst Schoen) are Benjamin's radio plays for children.

CHAPTER 30

Much Ado About Kasper
A Radio Play

Dramatis personae
KASPER
HERR MAULSCHMIDT, RADIO MAN[1]
FOOD SELLER
CAROUSEL MAN
BOOTH OWNER
SHOOTING GALLERY MAN
LION KEEPER
PUSCHI, KASPER'S WIFE

Also with
HERR MITTMANN AND HERR GERICKE FROM THE RADIO
   STATION
TRAIN STATION MASTER
LIPSUSLAPSUS, A SPIRIT
THE FIRST AND SECOND SHOOTER
CHILDREN AND ANIMALS

The sound of whistles and horns from a ship.

KASPER: Sure is a foggy morning.
   More horns.
KASPER: They're trying to break our eardrums with that racket. But

---

1 The name Maulschmidt, when broken down into its components in German, can be understood literally as *Maul*, "snout," "mug," or "muzzle," and *Schmidt*, or the common "smith." Together they create a satirical proper name that is not common in German. An English equivalent might be something like: mouth-smith, mug-maker, or snout-forger.

it's not easy going for ships in this fog. Just today my wife Puschi sent me to the market. She wants a flounder, a flounder eight centimeters long. Can't forget that. And it's gotta be fatter than last time. Eight centimeters, by golly, and I forgot my tape measure at home—I'd just got to the market. The market, where is it anyway? Yikes, I pretty near marched right into the water with all this fog. You can't see a thing.—But if you can't see anything, how do I see the fog? It seems to me, you can't even see the fog on account of all the fog.—Do I see the fog or don't I!—If I can't see it then I must be seeing somethin' else.—And if I do see it, then I see it, and it can't be foggy.

HERR MAULSCHMIDT: Darn it all! Can't you just open your eyes? Do you have to barrel into people?

KASPER: How can I barrel into people? I can't even find 'em in this fog.

HERR MAULSCHMIDT: That's an interesting take, YOU knock ME in the belly and YOU get cross!

KASPER: Why don't you buy a foghorn like the other guys?
Another horn from a ship.

HERR MAULSCHMIDT: Is there something wrong with you?

KASPER: Just open your ears! Can't you hear the man blowing his horn? That'll stop it from happening.

HERR MAULSCHMIDT: You must be out of your mind. That was a steamboat.

KASPER: For all I care, you can jump in the water too, old pal.

HERR MAULSCHMIDT: Who are you anyway? You impertinent fellow!

KASPER: Pardon me, but to whom do I have the honor of introducing myself?

HERR MAULSCHMIDT: Maulschmidt.

KASPER: Come again?

HERR MAULSCHMIDT: Maulschmidt.

KASPER: I have to ask, old pal, how do you smith a mouth? I thought at best they were stuffed.

HERR MAULSCHMIDT: You scoundrel, you! I'm not a mouthsmith, it's my name.

KASPER: Sure, old pal, but I just asked who you were.

HERR MAULSCHMIDT: What do you think you are?

KASPER: What you are, who you are, now I don't give a damn.

HERR MAULSCHMIDT: How dare you say such a thing! I'm an upright person.

KASPER: For an uptight person, you seem pretty loose to me.

HERR MAULSCHMIDT: I don't intend to waste my time with you any longer. March! Give me your name and then it's off to the precinct with you! Now listen, buster, where do you come from?

KASPER: I come from my native country.

HERR MAULSCHMIDT: And how do you write the name of this country?

KASPER: It's written with ink on paper.

HERR MAULSCHMIDT: Enough, my patience is wearing thin. Will you tell me your name, or won't you?

KASPER: If it weren't so foggy, old pal, you'd know it by now.

HERR MAULSCHMIDT: What's that supposed to mean? Do you wear your name painted on your chest?

KASPER: No sir, but I have a colorful skirt.

HERR MAULSCHMIDT: So you're a soldier, are you?

KASPER: Not exactly.—But you know what, old pal, I'll let you guess my name.

HERR MAULSCHMIDT: How can I guess your name? This is monkey business.

KASPER: Hang on, old pal. Here it is, for last names I write Spar. And my first name starts with a K.

HERR MAULSCHMIDT: Your first name I don't care to know. So let's go, off to the precinct, Mr. Spar!

KASPER: So take him in. I'm not Mr. Spar.

HERR MAULSCHMIDT: Rogue! But you just said you were.

KASPER: But you do need my first name.

HERR MAULSCHMIDT: This is a devilish game. (*Spoken with increasing excitement, and finally as a joyful cry of discovery.*) Kay Spar . . . Kas-par . . . Kasper!!!

KASPER: Bravo, old pal, I'm Kasper indeed.

HERR MAULSCHMIDT: What luck, Kasper! This is truly a happy day. I've been looking for you for quite some time.

KASPER: You were looking for me, old pal? Whatever for?

HERR MAULSCHMIDT: Kasper, I have to tell you a happy little secret: I'm actually a radio announcer.

KASPER: Well, well, you don't say!

HERR MAULSCHMIDT: And for a long time it's been my goal to place you, Kasper, the age-old and famous friend of children, in front of the microphone.

KASPER: That ain't gonna happen.

HERR MAULSCHMIDT: What's that, Kasper? Do I hear you correctly? You'd turn down the exalted and solemn honor of speaking on the radio?

KASPER: You bet!

HERR MAULSCHMIDT: But why?

KASPER: You know, old pal, if you really wanna know, I can tell you.

HERR MAULSCHMIDT: Oh Kasper, do tell!

KASPER: But do I understand you correctly, old pal? You're in radio?

HERR MAULSCHMIDT: Most certainly.

KASPER: You know, with all those sparks [*Funken*] flying around [*rund*], I might try to catch one and then I'd catch fire myself.[2]

HERR MAULSCHMIDT: Kasper, you don't even know what radio is. Stick close to me and I'm sure you'll get a better sense of what it's about.

KASPER: Let me think about it on the way.

Street noise.

KASPER (*after a while*): See this iron fence? The one we're walking along? I wanna count the stakes.

The sound of him striking each of the stakes.

KASPER: I'll speak—I won't speak—speak—won't speak—speak— won't speak—speak—won't speak—speak—won't speak—speak.

HERR MAULSCHMIDT: Look around you, Kasper, we've arrived!

KASPER: Huh? This ugly box?

HERR MAULSCHMIDT: The Radio Palace.

KASPER: There must be more windows than you can count. Is that where they're locked up and forced to hear radio?

HERR MAULSCHMIDT: Follow me, Kasper, and I'll explain everything to you.

Pause.

KASPER (*softly*): So much quiet makes me uneasy.

HERR MAULSCHMIDT: Shhh, you're not allowed to speak here.

KASPER: I thought you brought me here to speak.

HERR MAULSCHMIDT: In here, Kasper!

KASPER: Funny place. What are all these cages for? Do you keep mice in there?

HERR MAULSCHMIDT: Those are the microphones, Kasper. You're

---

2 The German for radio and broadcasting, *Rundfunk*, is made up of the words *rund*, which means round, and *Funke*, spark. The English "radio" carries a similar connotation of dissemination outward, as in radiality. Kasper's humor depends on the embedded German connotation of radiating fire or disseminating sparks, which cannot be conveyed in the English.

now about to speak into such a microphone.

KASPER: Then what happens?

HERR MAULSCHMIDT: Then people hear you all over the world.

KASPER: Even in Putzingen? (*Aside.*) That's where Seppl lives, I've wanted to give him a piece of my mind for some time.

HERR MAULSCHMIDT: Of course, now we'll switch it on.

KASPER: If I had my druthers, I'd like to listen for a bit first.

HERR MAULSCHMIDT: Certainly, Kasper, with pleasure. Dresden, Posen, Brno, Milan, Brussels, Kassel, Linz, London, Vienna, Riga, Breslau—whatever you want. Just turn this knob and then you hear it!

Good Lord, Kasper, not like that!

We hear a minute of fading noises.

KASPER: It seems to me it's all the same. It's a mess. (*More fading noises.*) This is a wreck, I can't make anything out.

HERR MAULSCHMIDT: Herr Mittmann, Herr Gericke, come quick! Switch it on. Kasper's speaking.

KASPER: Now Seppl in Putzingen is hearing this.

HERR MAULSCHMIDT: I should think so.—Everything ready, Herr Mittmann?

Voices: Quiet, Kasper's speaking.

KASPER: If only it weren't so far, I'd be in Putzingen now, where I'd wet my whistle so Seppl would hear me loud and clear.

HERR MAULSCHMIDT: If you get stuck, I'll head right down to the cafeteria and get you a tall one.

KASPER: That would be just fine. Now seems to me the perfect moment. (*He clears his throat.*) You miserable wretch, you! Sorry creature! You hear me? Who bought you to play the snitch? Just as I was sitting pretty. There'll be payback, my friend. You cursed lout, you scum! Lemme get my hands on you just once! I got something for you that'll suit you just fine—

A telephone rings.

Woman's voice: Long distance service. Yes, sir. I'll connect you.

New voice: Putzingen police. Is that the radio station?

HERR MAULSCHMIDT: Oh my! Switch it off! Disconnect! Kasper, the menace, the rascal. I turn my back for just a second ... Herr Mittmann! Herr Gericke! Get him! Get him! Dead or alive, I must have him, that Kasper.

Sounds of doors slamming, things breaking. Another telephone rings. Cars honking.

Shouts: That way! Around the corner!

HERR MAULSCHMIDT: He's gone, but we'll get him. That'll be a laugh.

Pause.

KASPER: Whew! That'll leave you gasping for air. Thank heavens I found a peaceful, out-of-the-way place to rest. Finally I can have a breather. A breather? Well put, Kasper. I gotta high-tail it for home. It's a miracle I've still got the fish. And Puschi, she must be starving by now. No, really, I gotta hop the fast train. (*He repeats in a pondering tone.*) Train, train, train . . . Just as I say it, there it is. And that's the station. Damn. Damn. Half past two. The train to Tuntenbühl must be leaving soon. Let's have a look at who all's going to Tuntenbühl today.

We hear commotion and the patter of feet.

What's all that scampering? Someone's scared to miss the train. And now here comes a whole slew of people? And I know that guy leading the pack. Why, if it isn't Herr Maulschmidt himself.

HERR MAULSCHMIDT: Hey! Hey! That's him, walking over there. That's just like him, off to Munich and then out of sight.

Other voices: But this time we've got him. We're gonna nab him. Let's make tracks!

KASPER: This is looking a bit dicey to me. If I knew my way around the station, I could surely hide away somewhere. I'll have a look at the luggage lockers.

HERR MAULSCHMIDT: And check under the bags to make sure he hasn't holed up in there.

KASPER: Alas, not much hope with the luggage. How about the waiting area?

HERR MAULSCHMIDT: And you, Herr Gericke, go to the waiting room! And look under all the tables!

KASPER: Not much luck in the waiting room either. The best would be if I stood here behind these columns.

HERR MAULSCHMIDT: And you, Herr Mittmann, look behind all the columns!

KASPER: I've whistled my last tune.

The whistle of a locomotive.

KASPER: I've really blown it. How about if we try knocking? Maybe this glass door will help?

He knocks.

KASPER: No answer.

He knocks harder, everything remains quiet. We hear the sound of a creaking door.

KASPER: The people in this station are so nice. They don't even lock the doors.

Pause.

Hey, what's this cap here on the table? A beautiful red cap with a visor. Just like the one Xaverl had, the station master in Hutzelheim.—That cap doesn't look so bad on you, Kasper. If only they cleaned the mirrors. And that beautiful stick lying on the table, we'd like to take that along as well. Kasper, the teacher always used to say, you need the stick more than anyone.

Again, voices of the pursuers: Kasper's gone. Vanished. Must be on the train. But this time he won't get away.

Noises of the train station.

THE STATION MASTER: My cap, my cap! Has anyone seen my cap? Just have a little patience, it's sure to turn up. Thank God there's still ten minutes until I have to announce the departure.

KASPER: All aboard!

HERR MAULSCHMIDT: What? We're leaving already? Herr Gericke, have you found Kasper?

HERR GERICKE: I'll go now and search the café car. If he's not there, we'll have to get off the train again fast.

KASPER: The train is leaving the station!

We hear the whistle of the locomotive and the sound of the train pulling away.

KASPER: So, the coast is clear. What do we say to a little relaxation, Herr Kasper, how about a leisurely stroll?—A fine idea.—That's nice. I knew it, I always agree with myself. It's not every day you find someone who always agrees with you. So I'll take this opportunity to talk with myself a bit more. Beautiful weather we're having, Kasper, isn't it?—

The answers are always from the same speaker, but in a deeper voice.

—Very beautiful.

—I wouldn't have thought so after such a foggy morning. Would you?

—It would never have occurred to me that today would become so beautiful.

—You see, I was just thinking to myself that you were not thinking that.

—And I was just thinking to myself that you were just thinking that I would never have thought that.

—What, are you making fun of me?

—Who do you think you are? I have one thing to say to you.

For a long time now I've been fed up with always agreeing with myself.

—You're getting a slap. One, two, three.

The sound of someone being smacked. The same voice that just spoke cries:

Ow!—That slap I just gave myself? It's not good to argue with yourself. Be sensible, Kasper, and just listen to the music coming from over there.

Noises from the fair. From the sounds of the barrel organ, the voices of the criers and the bells of the carousel, the voice of a Chinese food seller stands out. He is delivering his pitch as an elaborate performance with a discreet musical accompaniment of flutes and castanets.

THE FOOD SELLER: I'm a Chinese food seller. I come from China. I haven't made much of myself since I was a child. But now I have a wine and food store at the fair. I'm not after profits or loss, only the happiness of my customers. I've got all kinds of food here. Listen up and I'll tell you what I have: chicken boiled in water, meat dumplings baked in oil, hard and crispy and sprinkled with lots of sugar, smoked ham, sea cucumbers, swallow's nests, large pieces of mutton with five different delicious spices; and then there's the rice dishes. You want rice or flour? If you want dishes with flour, I can make those, too. There's also dry rice, and when you're done eating, I'll give you a cup of tea.—Dear customers, whether you've got money or not, step right on up. Just leave a piece of clothing for deposit and I'll write you a bill.

KASPER: Oh my, I've been dying for that for ages. Finally, Chinese food. But the Chinese eat rotten eggs and earthworms. Mister cook, please take my cap. And for that I'd like a great meal of Chinese wedding food.

THE FOOD SELLER: My dear man, I can't take your cap. The cap you have there is worn neither in Europe nor China. And as far as I've traveled the world, I've never before seen a cap with bells.

KASPER: No hard feelings, old pal, you can also take my jacket for a meal of great Chinese food.

THE FOOD SELLER: Sure, but don't you see my sign hanging there? We don't take things that have been patched.

KASPER: Then you'll get something you're sure to take.

THE FOOD SELLER: And what would that be, sir?

A cracking sound.

KASPER: A slap.

THE FOOD SELLER (*breaking into a long elaborate wail*): Ow-ow-ow-ow-ow-ow-ow!

KASPER: Such a beautiful language, Chinese.

We hear the bells of the carousel.

Excuse me, I just wanted to ask how much a ride costs.

THE CAROUSEL MAN: One ride costs five cents.

KASPER: And then afterward I can get out?

THE CAROUSEL MAN: Of course, then you have to get out.

KASPER: But if I sit in a ship . . .

THE CAROUSEL MAN: . . . you still have to get out.

KASPER: But if I'm on an elephant, I can stay?

THE CAROUSEL MAN: If you pay for two rides.

KASPER: But then I'll really not want to get out.

THE CAROUSEL MAN: So how long do you want to ride?

KASPER: I was thinking an hour or so.

The occasional sound of carousel music and bells ringing.

THE CAROUSEL MAN: Then you have to take nine tickets.

KASPER: And how much would that cost, old pal?

THE CAROUSEL MAN: I reckon that'd cost nine times five cents.

KASPER (*pausing, a bit baffled*): So it would, old pal, so it would.

THE CAROUSEL MAN: So, what don't you get?

KASPER: I just wanna write it out.

THE CAROUSEL MAN: Please, be my guest.

KASPER: How would I go about starting to write that, old pal?

THE CAROUSEL MAN (*impatient*): Five times nine is forty-five. Right?

KASPER (*slowly*): Forty-five, I'm writing it down, starting with an F.

THE CAROUSEL MAN: Go ahead and just write "4" and "5."

KASPER: Sure, four, I know how to write that.

THE CAROUSEL MAN: Here you go, let me tell you how: a line from top to bottom, then one from left to right, and then one more from top to bottom makes 4.

KASPER: Makes three.

THE CAROUSEL MAN: Makes four.

KASPER: Makes three.

The exchange of words accelerates. Kasper counts off: One line, and then another line, and then another makes three.—Makes four. (*Etc.*)

THE CAROUSEL MAN: But I'm telling you, it's a four. Didn't you learn anything in school?

KASPER: It may suit you to make fun of people. First you say one line, then you say another, and then finally a third. That makes three. And you're about to see how that makes three.

The sound of three slaps to the face.

One slap, and then another slap, and then another slap. That makes three slaps. And with that we conclude our counting.

The exchange devolves into a brawl. After a pause:

KASPER: I don't like the carousel any more. Instead, let's listen to what we have next door.

The voice of a booth owner is heard over the sounds of the fair.

THE BOOTH OWNER: Treasured guests, gather round! Ladies and gentlemen, step right up! What does this tent say to you, my honored listeners? Do you imagine something upon looking at my modest hut? And please, ladies and gentlemen, don't mistake it for the infamous swindle booths you see around you. Because this, ladies and gentlemen, this simple tent houses the earthly presence of the supernatural spirit Lipsuslapsus, the invisible, all-knowing, and great magician who will have the honor and pleasure of predicting your precious and happy future. Ask his advice, ladies and gentlemen, and Lipsuslapsus will discover lost objects, teach you foreign languages while you sleep, explain your dreams, and do your schoolwork.

KASPER: For years I've wanted to lead a more honorable life. Maybe this invisible spirit can help me.

THE BOOTH OWNER: Bravo, young man! Be certain he can help you. To the left, please, enter to the left! And please, don't forget your twenty cents for my humble tent.

Pause.

KASPER (*softly*): It's a bit damp in here. Actually, it feels more like a basement. I'm beginning to feel a bit uneasy, but I think I have to check it out.

The following play of echoes should be enacted with ceremony and solemnity. The answers especially must seem as if echoes from afar.

KASPER: If you would be so kind, Lipsuslapsus, I have questions about my future that I would like to ask.

LIPSUSLAPSUS (*the echo*): Ask!

KASPER: What should I do with my life so that later on I will regret nothing?

LIPSUSLAPSUS: Nothing!

KASPER: How do I begin to assess my abilities?

LIPSUSLAPSUS: Tease!

KASPER: Should I not perhaps study philosophy? For what is a man without wisdom?

LIPSUSLAPSUS: Dumb!

KASPER: But that's a difficult life. Can you live just from the things you know?

LIPSUSLAPSUS: No!

KASPER: So I need to find a lucrative line of work?

LIPSUSLAPSUS: Work!

KASPER: The law is a tough road. I'm not sure I would pass.

LIPSUSLAPSUS: Pass!

KASPER: I think becoming a doctor would be fruitful.

LIPSUSLAPSUS: Fool!

KASPER: You don't think medicine would be a decent life course?

LIPSUSLAPSUS: Of course!

KASPER: With not too much pressure?

LIPSUSLAPSUS: Sure!

KASPER: Perfect. Is there nothing about life that a doctor doesn't enjoy?

LIPSUSLAPSUS: Joy!

KASPER: Then I'll be a statesman. Do you have anything to say against diplomacy?

LIPSUSLAPSUS: Messy!

KASPER: Right you are, Lipsuslapsus, many more capable men have had little success.

LIPSUSLAPSUS: Yes!

KASPER: So I guess I'll find a rich widow.

LIPSUSLAPSUS: Uh-oh!

KASPER: But then I'd have money. What's stopping me from being fulfilled?

LIPSUSLAPSUS: Guilt!

KASPER: Then what should I do to make money with merit?

LIPSUSLAPSUS: Inherit!

KASPER (*By his tone of voice and from the background noise, it's clear that he's left the tent.*): This spirit is no help at all. That just wasn't right. I've got a hunch, in fact I believe it was the booth guy. I'd like to knock his spirit for a loop.

Again, the voices of the pursuers:

FIRST VOICE: I just saw him whizz by, Herr Maulschmidt.

SECOND VOICE: This time we'll get that scoundrel.

Other voices: To the left, Herr Mittmann! And you cut him off from the right! Quick, Herr Gericke! Look! There he goes!

Shots are heard.

VOICE OF THE SHOOTING GALLERY OWNER: Here, here, gents, step right up, ladies and gentlemen! I'm offering you a one-time chance to put the world to rights with a single shot. Please have a gander at my tableau here, where you'll see original human dummies and other wonders: this father here, hit him on the bull's-eye and just like that, he kicks into motion this little cradle where his youngest babe is asleep. And at back right, the violinist: hit him square on and he starts to play the fiddle, the sight and sound of which defies description. And have you seen the Moor behind the locked gate? Shoot him in the pinky toe, gentlemen, and watch the gate spring open in front of your unbelieving eyes to reveal the inside of the sultan's palace in all its splendor and glory. But, gentlemen, if you want to do a noble deed and free a prisoner from the dungeon, you just have to hit his dungeon window and in a trice he's out and about. This, ladies and gentlemen, is the eighth wonder of the world, Doctor Crackbang's world-famous shooting gallery.

The speech is interrupted by more rumbling voices of the pursuers.—Now and again we hear the sound of shots, as during the speech by the shooting gallery owner.

FIRST SHOOTER: Okay, Gustav, I'm aiming at the bear. He dances when you hit him.

SECOND SHOOTER: Hey, wait a sec, that one in the back is swell. I've never seen one like that in a booth.

FIRST SHOOTER: And he looks so real. I'd swear he wasn't painted.

SECOND SHOOTER: I just can't find the bull's eye we have to shoot at.

FIRST SHOOTER: But wait, Gustav, what do you think he'll do if you hit him?

SECOND SHOOTER: Well, we're about find out.

The sound of the gun being cocked.

KASPER: Mercy, gentlemen. Please don't shoot. Take pity on old Kasper.

FIRST SHOOTER: Well, you don't say! The dummy can talk.

KASPER: Gentlemen, may I take the liberty to point out, in all sincerity: I'm no dummy. Under pressing circumstances I was unfortunately compelled to pose here as a dummy.

THE SHOOTING GALLERY OWNER (*very loudly*): Silence! This is no place for chit-chat! How dare you bring disorder into my establishment. Who are you, anyway?

KASPER (*aside*): The coast is clear. The mob has moved on.

Voices of the pursuers: He's nowhere. Foiled again.

KASPER: I beg you, Herr Shootout Director, I just wanted to show off my skills. Take a nickel. And give me a rifle.

THE SHOOTING GALLERY OWNER: Please, be my guest.

KASPER: Do you have something with music?

THE SHOOTING GALLERY OWNER: But of course. Right here we have a little radio orchestra. If you hit the conductor, you hear the overture from the opera "Plimplamplasko or the Enchanted Monkey Prince."

The sound of a shot, followed by the playing of a cheery music box, which is eventually drowned out by the noises of the fair.

KASPER: Everything would be just fine if only I hadn't lost my flounder talking to that Lipsuslapsus. What do I do now? The market's been closed for ages. Where can a guy get a fish at this hour? There's no way I can go home to Puschi without a fish. But here's an idea! How about it, Kasper? You've long been wanting to visit the zoo, now, haven't you? Don't think twice! One leap and we're over the wall.

He claps his hands.

No time to lose. At the bottom of the pond we're gonna catch ourselves a fish!

CHILDREN'S VOICES: Hey Kasper, hello, hello, can't you hear us? Over here!

FIRST CHILD: Kasper, what are you doing here?

KASPER: Oh, good day. Hello, Hans. Well, you know, I . . . actually I wanted to . . . You know what? I came to study a little animal language.

FIRST CHILD: What? You're here to learn language?

KASPER: No, you see . . . actually, I already know them all. It's just that with the guinea pigs there are still a few words I have to learn. That's really why I came.

FIRST CHILD: Oh, Kasper, if you know animal language, you have to come with us and tell us what all the animals are saying.

CHILDREN'S VOICES: Come with us! Come with us! First the apes! No, the rhino! No, wait! He should start with the big birds!

LITTLE GIRL: Kasper, pretty please can you come see the antelopes?

KASPER: Kids, kids, easy now. One at a time. How about we start with the foxes and wolves?

CHILDREN'S VOICES: Yes, good, let's! Let's!

Sound of wolves howling and foxes baying. After a pause:

CHILDREN'S VOICES: Now, Kasper, what are they saying? Tell us, Kasper!

KASPER: So, they're saying ... You want to know what they're saying, huh? Well, they're talking about what each of them wants done with his fur once he's dead.

CHILDREN'S VOICES: We don't understand, Kasper. What does that mean?

KASPER: OK, look over there. That little fox with the torn and shabby fur, he's saying: later, when he's dead, he'd most like to be on a soldier's satchel going off to war.

CHILDREN'S VOICES: And the wolf over there, what's he saying?

KASPER: That wolf? Ideally he'd like to become a doormat at a hunter's cottage in the middle of the woods.

CHILDREN'S VOICES: And the cute little blue fox? What does he say?

KASPER: All his life he's wished just once to meet the people from the neighborhood. Now he thinks he'd like to later become a muff that a little girl sticks her hands in.

CHILDREN'S VOICES: Next, Kasper! Over here, Kasper! To the apes! What are they saying?

Grunting sounds and children screaming.

KASPER: You have to be quiet! The language of apes is difficult. Otherwise I can't understand it.

FIRST CHILD: But I thought apes didn't have any language.

VOICES OF THE OTHER CHILDREN: Quiet!

KASPER: Well, it's a remarkable story. See that big baboon sitting up there in the tree? Right now he's lecturing the younger apes, strictly warning them that they should always act silly when humans are around. He's saying: the dumber you seem, the better.

FIRST CHILD: But why?

KASPER: Well, that's what the younger apes are asking now. And you know what his answer is? If humans don't know how smart we are, and don't notice that we have a language of our own, then they won't force us to work.

FIRST CHILD: And now what are they saying?

KASPER: Now they're discussing the pros and cons of captivity. Most of them are pretty content, because they have food and playmates and a warm cage to protect them from the rain and cold.

The shrill cry of an ape.

FIRST CHILD: And the little one? What's he saying?

KASPER: He doesn't agree with the others. He says it would all be just fine, but he can find no comfort when here in the cage there are only apes, apes, and more apes, and an occasional human; he'd gladly give up all the apes and people for the sight of one parrot, or a giraffe, or even the tiniest butterfly.

Grunting noises.

KASPER: Did you kids hear the grunt from the orangutan over there? He's saying that it's a complete injustice that the butterflies have no cage in the zoo.

FIRST CHILD (*whispering*): You know something? I think he's lying.—Kasper, what are the elephants talking about over there?

KASPER: Ah, they're not happy because the sparrow hasn't shown up today, and every morning he brings them news of the other animals.

FIRST CHILD: Ask him how his baby is, Kasper.

Kasper growls something, and then:

KASPER: He says today the baby has already drunk ten bottles.

THE CHILDREN: But he doesn't have a baby. It isn't true.

FIRST CHILD: Kasper, what are the lions roaring about?

KASPER: They're trying to figure out what day it is.

FIRST CHILD: Ask them if they want some candies!

Kasper lets out a few screams, and then:

KASPER: Yes, very much so, they say.

THE CHILDREN: They don't eat candies. This is a hoax. (*Louder and louder.*) It's all a hoax! Shame on you, Kasper! Boo, Kasper! Get outta here!

Whistles and cries.

THE ZOOKEEPER: These kids are out of control again today. They're a menace, these brats.—Ah, life's tough.—I'm just pushing my meat cart around. But since my big lion Maholy died a few weeks ago, this whole feeding round just isn't the same. How I miss his deep and friendly roar when I would approach his cage with his evening meal! And how I miss that sparkle in his wild eyes, and the cloud of swirling sand that his tail would make as it lashed the ground of his cage. But my sorrow finds some consolation in the fact that the kind wardens have heeded my plea to have our good Maholy stuffed. At least now I'm spared the sight of his empty cage, because I can see just a little piece of his paw. We hid him way in the back there, behind the shed, so he wouldn't fade in the sun, and seeing just that little bit of his paw makes me feel so much better. But what am I standing around here for, blabbing away? My rounds aren't even half done.

Voices of the pursuers: Seal off the entire place! Kasper must be here in the zoo! Call the police! This time we'll get him for sure. Hey kids, where's Kasper?

KASPER: That awful Maulschmidt. He's back again with his posse, and quick. I haven't had a moment's peace since that business with the radio. What do I do now? Hang on! What's that there? The lion cage. Didn't Puschi say to me just yesterday that they've got a stuffed lion in there? Stuffed or alive, anything's better than having those louts on my heels. Be brave, Kasper, get in there and close the door behind you!

From an interior space:

KASPER: "Feeding and teasing prohibited."—I could feed him all I want, but if he's kicked the bucket, he won't taste much.

Voices of the pursuers, as above.

KASPER: That Herr Maulschmidt is still onto me. But this time I'll show him.

No longer from an interior space:

KASPER: Yes sir, gentlemen, come a little closer, please. All visitors are welcome. Entrance is free, ladies and gentlemen! And my friend here would be glad to say hello. Permit me to step on back and let him know you're here.

Again from the interior space: a ferocious roar.

HERR MAULSCHMIDT: Heaven forbid, the lion!

KASPER (*from the interior space*): And yes, my friend has agreed. Allow me to open the door for you and he'll come out and show you the way.

As soon as Kasper has finished speaking, he lets out a slowly escalating roar.

Voices of the pursuers: Heaven forbid! He's letting the lion out! Run for your lives! Help! Help!

The voices of the pursuers fade.

KASPER (*with a diabolical laugh*): Ladies and gentlemen, I think we've seen each other today for the last time.

Pause.

KASPER: Taxi!

Street noise.

Driver! Doohickey Alley 1–12, and fast!

Driver's voice: There must be a mistake, sir, there's only two houses on that street.

KASPER: On my street we count the windows, too. Now go!
Street noise. After a while, the sound of an explosion. Pause.
Bells tolling.

KASPER: I've been asleep. And those are the bells of Saint Catherine.
It's six in the evening and I'm still in bed?

FRAU PUSCHI: Not so loud, Kasper, you have to rest. Are you feeling any better?

KASPER: Back to being happy as a king.

FRAU PUSCHI: Oh, dear Kasper, when I think how they brought
you to me. Your leg bandaged, on a stretcher.

KASPER: I'll hear nothing of it. That's over now. It doesn't hurt at
all. Tell me, dear, what are these packages about?

FRAU PUSCHI: The children brought them for you, the ones you
were with at the zoo.

KASPER: Show me some, Puschi!
Amid the rustling of paper, Kasper and Puschi take turns calling out
the contents of the packages.

KASPER AND PUSCHI: A box of chocolate cigars.—A marzipan
revolver.—A praline doll.—A chocolate grandfather clock.—A
demon made of baked plums.—A festive bowl.—An edible
vase.—A gingerbread house.—A candied-sugar sword.

KASPER: Shall I eat the revolver first, or the sword?

FRAU PUSCHI: I want the revolver.

KASPER: You get the demon.

FRAU PUSCHI: No, the grandfather clock. I wanna eat it as a soup.

KASPER: We will begin with the vase, as an appetizer.

FRAU PUSCHI: That's not the way it works, Kasper. I'm the housewife, I make the menu.

KASPER: Right you are, and I have to make a plan.

FRAU PUSCHI: What sort of plan are you making?

KASPER: On account of Herr Maulschmidt.

FRAU PUSCHI: Why do you need a plan for him?

KASPER: I need to think about which of his bones to break first
when I see him again.

FRAU PUSCHI: But Kasper!

KASPER: Perhaps we'll begin with the collarbone. Yes, I think it's
nice to start with the collarbone. Then I imagine the shin would
come next. Now, if I only knew which, the right or the left. I
wouldn't like to break both. That would be mean.—After that, if
we continue on, the ribs would be up next. At this point one must
be very careful not to break the wrong rib. How many ribs does

Herr Maulschmidt have? What do you say, Puschi? He's so long, he must have at least twenty.

FRAU PUSCHI: But, Kasper, that's nonsense. Every person has only twelve ribs.

KASPER: A rib here, a rib there.—But say, Puschi, what was that whole thing with David and Goliath?

FRAU PUSCHI: But you learned all that at school, Kasper.

KASPER: I mean the guy who toppled over. Was that David?

FRAU PUSCHI: That was Goliath.

KASPER: Then my plan is done.—You just have to borrow a cart.

FRAU PUSCHI: But why do I need a cart?

KASPER: I'll tell you why.—When I break all of Herr Maulschmidt's ribs, he'll no longer be able to walk.

FRAU PUSCHI: He probably won't.

KASPER: So then! We'll just drive him around in the cart. And now I'll tell you where. We'll drive him to the market, right by the statue of Herr Kewlies, the guy who slayed the lions. We'll lean him up against it, and when enough people have gathered around, you'll walk around with a cup and I'll sing the whole story, just as it happened. Listen up, I've even written the song.

Half-sung, half-spoken in the style of street song:

> Because Puschi had commanded
> That he go and fetch a fish
> At the market Kasper landed
> A gloomy morning full of mist.

Knocking.

FRAU PUSCHI: Who is it?

HERR MAULSCHMIDT: I'm only here to give Kasper an envelope.

KASPER: Blast! Herr Maulschmidt again!

HERR MAULSCHMIDT: Good day, Kasper. I'm glad to see you're feeling better. I'm also glad to be able to deliver this.

KASPER: An envelope?

FRAU PUSCHI: An envelope?

HERR MAULSCHMIDT: And what's inside.

FRAU PUSCHI: A thousand marks?

HERR MAULSCHMIDT: Your fee from the radio station.

KASPER: The radio station?! The one that nearly had me killed?

HERR MAULSCHMIDT: Well, in doing so, we also got what we wanted.

KASPER: What's that supposed to mean?

HERR MAULSCHMIDT: It means that you spoke on the radio, even if you didn't know it.

KASPER: Well, that must have been in my sleep.

HERR MAULSCHMIDT: Not in your sleep, but in your bed.

FRAU PUSCHI: In bed?

HERR MAULSCHMIDT: He who laughs last, laughs loudest. We at the radio station are even cleverer than you. While you were out in the city perpetrating your scandalous deeds, we secretly installed a microphone in your room, under your bed, and now we have everything you said, on a record, and I just happened to bring one along for you. Listen to this:

The text above begins to play from the record, but in a somewhat distorted tone.

The record: . . . the guy who slayed the lions. We'll lean him up against it, and when enough people have gathered around, you'll walk around with a cup and I'll sing the whole story, just as it happened. Listen up, I've even written the song.

> Because Puschi had commanded
> That he go and fetch a fish
> At the market Kasper landed
> A gloomy morning full of mist.

KASPER: I've just heard for the first time what radio is.

FRAU PUSCHI: And I've seen for the first time what a thousand marks looks like.

KASPER AND FRAU PUSCHI: And we thank you very much, Herr Maulschmidt.

The ringing of bells, as above.

HERR MAULSCHMIDT: The honor is mine! And goodbye to you both! I must hurry as we're making a broadcast from Pumpernickel. This has been one unforgettable day.

"Radau um Kasperl," GS, 4.2, 674–95, with additional notes in GS, 7.2, 831–6. Translated by Jonathan Lutes.

Broadcast on Southwest German Radio, Frankfurt, on March 10, 1932, and on Western German Radio, Cologne, on September 9, 1932.

The Frankfurt broadcast was announced in the Südwestdeutsche Rundfunk-Zeitung *for March 10, 1932, from 7:45–8:45 pm; it was*

advertised as "Much Ado About Kasper, A Radio Play for Children by
Walter Benjamin." The listing notes that the broadcast would be directed
by Benjamin. It also makes a request: "As the title implies, Kasper's expe-
riences in this play are also connected with Radau [racket, row, hubbub,
din]. Children are asked to guess what the noises mean, and to share their
opinions with the radio station."[3]

The Cologne broadcast on September 9, 1932, from 4:20–5:00 pm,
was scheduled as part of the station's youth radio programming and was
directed by Carl Heil.

Much Ado About Kasper *is the only broadcast of Benjamin's for*
which an audio-recording exists, albeit a partial one. Benjamin's voice
cannot be heard. The audio fragment is most likely from the production in
Cologne.

In a letter to Scholem dated February 28, 1933, Benjamin gave Much
Ado About Kasper *an affirmative spin rare for his comments about his*
radio works. Speaking of his "works for radio" generally, he notes that
even he hasn't "been successful in collecting them all. I am speaking of the
radio plays, not the series of countless talks, which [will] now come to an
end, unfortunately, and are of no interest except in economic terms, but
that is now a thing of the past. Moreover, most of these radio plays were
written together with others. Notable from a technical point of view
perhaps is a piece for children, which was broadcast last year in Frankfurt
and Cologne; I may be able to secure you a copy at some point. It's called
'Radau um Kasperl.'"[4]

---

3   In addition to the typescript of the play, the Benjamin archive includes a text entitled
"Kasper and the Radio: A Story with Noise" [*Kasperl und der Rundfunk: Eine Geschichte mit*
Lärm], which the GS editors tentatively conclude was related to the Frankfurt broadcast and
the above request for the children to guess what the sounds were. The text of "Kasper and the
Radio" (reproduced in GS, 7.2, 832–6), is something like an outline or summary version of
Much Ado About Kasper. It describes the scenes of the play and the interrupting noises, and is
divided into divided into six "hubbubs" [*Radau*]. The text begins with an introduction: "The
following draft outlines a storyline containing a series of episodes in a fixed framework. The
basis of these episodes is a variety of characteristic types of sounds punctuated here and there
with hints and words. In a short introduction the speaker indicates the gist of the following
radio play to his listeners, placing before them the task of envisioning the episodes, which are
not fully fleshed out. The listeners are then asked to assess the respective sounds according to
their imagination and wishes, and to send their solutions to the radio station for a potential
prize" (GS, 7.2, 832–3). This short summary version, in other words, emphasizes the acoustic
elements and sound-play of the play.
4   Benjamin, *The Correspondence of Walter Benjamin*, 403–4.

CHAPTER 31

The Cold Heart

A Radio Play Adapted from
Wilhelm Hauff's Fairy Tale[1]

By Walter Benjamin and Ernst Schoen[2]

Dramatis personae
RADIO ANNOUNCER
COAL PETER
LITTLE GLASS MAN
DUTCH MICHAEL
EZEKIEL
SCHLURKER
DANCE HALL KING
LISBETH
BEGGAR
MILLER
MILLER'S WIFE
MILLER'S SON
A VOICE
POSTILION

---

1 Wilhelm Hauff (1802–1827), German writer best known for his fairy tales, including "The Cold Heart" (Das kalte Herz), first published in 1827. Throughout, Benjamin has incorporated characters and passages, many verbatim or nearly so, from Hauff's tale.

2 Ernst Schoen (1894–1960), a musician and composer, and a childhood friend of Benjamin's, was artistic director of the Frankfurt radio station. He is credited with helping Benjamin to obtain work on the radio. For Schoen's comments on this collaboration with Benjamin, and on the "dramatization of writings for children's radio or school radio" more broadly, see Schoen and Wilhelm Schüller, "Hörspiel im Schulfunk," in *Der Schulfunk* 10 (May 15, 1931), 323–5, cited in GS, 7.2, 651–2.

Prologue

RADIO ANNOUNCER: Dear Radio Listeners, welcome once again to the Youth Hour. Today I think I will read you another fairy tale. But which one shall I read? Let's have a look in our big dictionary, filled with the names of all of the writers of fairy tales, kind of like a telephone book. I should be able to pick one out from there. So, A as in abracadabra? That's not for us. Let's leaf through the book a little further. B as in Bechstein . . . that would be good, but we just had him recently.

A knock at the door.

C as in Celsius, as opposed to Réaumur. D, E, F, G.

Louder knocking at the door.

H as in Hauff, Wilhelm Hauff, yes, that's the one for us.

Even louder pounding at the door.

What is this devilish noise here at the radio station? Good heavens! How are we to get on with our Youth Hour! Very well, come on in! (*Whispering.*) They are ruining the whole Youth Hour—Well, what is it then? How strange you are! What do you want?

COAL PETER: We are the characters from "The Cold Heart," the fairy tale by Wilhelm Hauff.

ANNOUNCER: From "The Cold Heart" by Wilhelm Hauff? Well, you have come right on cue! But how did you get here? Don't you know this is a radio station? You can't just come barging in!

COAL PETER: Are you the Announcer?

ANNOUNCER: Indeed, I am.

COAL PETER: Well, then we are in the right place. Everybody, come on in and close the door. And perhaps now we should introduce ourselves.

ANNOUNCER: Yes, but—

The introduction of each character from the fairy tale is accompanied by a little melody played on a music box.[3]

COAL PETER: I am Peter Munk, born in the Black Forest. They call

---

3 The music for the Benjamin–Schoen production of *The Cold Heart* was written by Ernst Schoen. None of it is known to have survived. According to the *Südwestdeutsche Rundfunk-Zeitung,* the production strove to bring "live before the microphone the characters from [Hauff's] book, through the mediation of a radio announcer, who pops up in the middle of Hauff's story. The accompanying music, as much as possible written simply for two pianos, introduces the lead character by way of folk songs and children's songs in a thematic way and provides background atmosphere for various dramatic scenes" (cited in GS, 7.2, 652–3).

me Coal Peter, because along with my father's guild jacket with the silver buttons, and the red stockings for special occasions, I also inherited the trade of charcoal-burner.

LITTLE GLASS MAN: I am the Little Glass Man. I am only three and a half feet tall, but I have great power over the fates of human beings. If you were born lucky, Mr. Announcer, and some day you're taking a walk through the Black Forest, and you see a little man in front of you in a peaked hat with a broad brim, a doublet, pantaloons, and short red stockings, then make your wish quick, for then you have caught sight of me.

DUTCH MICHAEL: And I am Dutch Michael. My jacket is of dark linen, I wear my trousers of black leather with broad, green suspenders. And in my pocket I carry a ruler made of brass, and along with that I wear the boots of a raftsman, but all of it is so grossly oversized that for the boots alone a dozen calves were needed.

EZEKIEL: I am fat Ezekiel, so named because my girth is so colossal. And I can afford it. I am considered the richest man in the area, and rightly so. Twice a year I travel to Amsterdam to deliver lumber, and while all the others must return on foot, I can ride in a coach.

SCHLURKER: I am tall Schlurker, the tallest and thinnest man in the whole of the Black Forest. I am also the boldest; in an overcrowded pub, I always take up more room than four fat men together.

DANCE HALL KING (*coyly*): Allow me to introduce myself, Mr. Announcer. I am the Dance Hall King.

DUTCH MICHAEL (*interrupting him*): That'll do, Dance Hall King, no need to put on airs here. I know where your money comes from, and that you were once a lowly woodcutter.

LISBETH: I am Miss Lisbeth, the daughter of a poor lumberjack. I am, however, the most beautiful and virtuous woman in all the Black Forest and I am engaged to be married to Peter Munk.

BEGGAR: And I am the very last, for I am nothing but a poor beggar. Yet, I will have an important, if small, role to play.

ANNOUNCER: Well, I've heard so much about you, my head is spinning. But what brings you here to the radio station? Why are you disturbing me in my work?

COAL PETER: To tell you the truth, Mr. Announcer, we really wanted to visit Voice Land just once.

ANNOUNCER: Voice Land? Coal Peter, how am I supposed to understand that? You will have to explain in a little more detail.

COAL PETER: You see, Mr. Announcer, we've already been in Hauff's fairy-tale book for one hundred years now. Normally, we can only speak to one child at a time. But now it is supposedly the fashion for fairy-tale characters to step out of books and cross over into Voice Land, where they can introduce themselves to many thousands of children all at once. That's what we would like to do and we were told that you, Mr. Announcer, were just the man to help us.

ANNOUNCER (*flattered*): That may be true, if you mean the Radio Voice Land.

DUTCH MICHAEL (*rudely*): That's what we do mean! So, let us in, Mr. Announcer, there's no time to show us the fine print.

EZEKIEL (*rudely*): Stop your blabbing, Michael. Here in Voice Land one can't see anything at all!

COAL PETER: One certainly can see in Voice Land, but one cannot be seen. That's what's bothering you, I can tell. You are, of course, not happy when you can't get all rigged up in your chains and scarves and handkerchiefs. But consider what you get in return. Everyone can hear you, as far as the eye can see from the highest mountain in the Black Forest and beyond, and you don't even have to raise your voice.

DANCE HALL KING: Thinking about it, Coal Peter, I still can't agree. The Black Forest, well, that's a place I know my way around—but Voice Land, there I would get lost, I'm afraid, and every moment stumble over roots.

EZEKIEL: Roots! There aren't any roots in Voice Land!

COAL PETER: Don't let yourself be deceived, Dance Hall King. Of course there are roots. Just as on Earth, Voice Land has a Black Forest, and villages, cities, rivers, and clouds. But they can't be seen on Earth, only heard; on Earth, everything that goes on in Voice Land can be heard but not seen. But once you've entered, you'll quickly know your way around just as well as you do here.

ANNOUNCER: And if anything goes wrong—that's why I'm here: the Announcer. We at the radio station know our way around like the back of our own hands.

DUTCH MICHAEL (*rudely*): Well then, Mr. Announcer, let us in already.

ANNOUNCER: Not so fast, Dutch Michael, you brute! It's not that easy! You can come into Voice Land and speak to thousands of children, but I patrol the borders of this country and there's a condition you must first fulfill.

LISBETH: A condition?

ANNOUNCER: Yes, indeed, Miss Lisbeth, and one that will be especially difficult for you to fulfill.

LITTLE GLASS MAN: Well then, name your condition. I am certainly used to conditions, I often set them myself.

ANNOUNCER: Alright, listen closely, Little Glass Man, and you others too: whoever wishes to enter Voice Land must be very modest. He must surrender all finery and relinquish all external beauty, so that nothing is left but his voice. However, his voice will then be heard by thousands of children simultaneously.
Pause.

   Well, I'm afraid that is the condition from which I cannot stray. Think it over for a moment if you like.

COAL PETER (*whispering*): What do all of you think of that? Are you ready, Lisbeth, to give up your pretty Sunday dress?

LISBETH (*whispering*): Yes, of course, what is it to me! If we can really speak to thousands of children!

EZEKIEL (*whispering*): Hoho! That's not as easy as it sounds. (*Jingling his coins*) And what will become of these shiny ducats?

LITTLE GLASS MAN (*whispering*): Just be happy you're rid of them so easily, you scoundrel! (*Aloud*) Well, Mr. Announcer, we consent to your condition.

ANNOUNCER: Very good, Little Glass Man, in you come.

COAL PETER: We have but one request, however.

ANNOUNCER: And what would that be, Coal Peter?

COAL PETER: Well, you see Mr. Announcer, we have never actually been in Voice Land!

ANNOUNCER: Indeed, indeed! And so?

COAL PETER: Well, how will we find our way around?

ANNOUNCER: Good point, Coal Peter.

COAL PETER: I was thinking, since you're already the border patrol of Voice Land, couldn't you come with us as our guide?

DANCE HALL KING: As I always say, those who cling together swing together!

LISBETH: No one's going to swing, you dumb Dance Hall King! But please, if you would be so kind, Mr. Announcer—!

ANNOUNCER (*flattered*): Well then, I will guide you, only don't be upset if my papers occasionally rustle. (*Rustling paper*) Without my map, even I can't find my way around in Voice Land.
Pause.

   Well, if you've got nothing against it, I must ask you to go to the coat room! Miss Lisbeth, you must leave your Sunday bonnet here! Also the money belt—and the fancy buckled shoes—here, in exchange, is your voice robe. Mr. Peter Munk, the doublet with the silver buttons must go and the red stockings as well.

COAL PETER: Here they are.

ANNOUNCER: And you, Little Glass Man, must give up your hat, waistcoat, and bloomers.

LITTLE GLASS MAN: Already done.

ANNOUNCER: And how about you, Dutch Michael? No, no, no— no ruler, that has to stay here as well as your raftsman's boots.

DUTCH MICHAEL: If we must. Raise the devil!

ANNOUNCER: And Mr. Dance Hall King is ready, I see, and you, poor beggar, haven't much to leave behind! But what's that I see— fat Ezekiel has hung his ducat purse around his neck! No, my good friend, that won't do! Where we're going, your ducats will be of no use to you. All you need is a good, clear voice, one that hasn't been worn out in the tavern like yours has.

EZEKIEL (*ranting*): No, no, I won't go along with it! My good money is worth more than your entire Voice Land!

DUTCH MICHAEL: By Jove, I've got something to say to that! Hand over the money, you miserable wretch, or I'll smash you to pieces!

ANNOUNCER: Peace, my dear friends! Mr. Dutch Michael, control your temper, and you, Mr. Ezekiel, I can assure you that you will get your money back, down to the last penny, after your appearance in Voice Land.

EZEKIEL: Very well then, Mr. Announcer. Now, if I could get that in writing!

ANNOUNCER: Off to Voice Land!

Gong.[4]

Music: Peter.

ANNOUNCER: Hello, Coal Peter, hello!

Several voices: Hello!

COAL PETER: Can you see anything, Announcer? Who's that calling "hello"? Where are we?

ANNOUNCER: No, Coal Peter, in Voice Land there is nothing to be seen, only something to be heard.

Music: Mill.

MILLER'S SON: Can you see anything, father?

---

4 Benjamin's text does not indicate an end for the section introduced as "Prologue." Perhaps this moment of transition, where the characters from Hauff's story enter into Voice Land, can be read as its close. Still, it is not clear how, if at all, the distinction between the sections would have been rendered on air.

MILLER: There is so much fog that you can't see your hand in front of your face. I could trip over my own mill. What do you think, wife?

MILLER'S WIFE: Now I hear the voices coming closer.

Music.

COAL PETER: Announcer? There is a great whooshing sound here, as if there were a river. In all my days, I have never known even the tiniest brook here.

ANNOUNCER: You say here, Peter? As if you knew where you were? Now, don't be too shocked when I tell you, but we're lost.

COAL PETER: Lost? It can't be. I just heard voices.

ANNOUNCER: Strange voices.

Once again: Hello! Hello!

MILLER'S WIFE: Goodness me, where are you coming from so late at night?

ANNOUNCER: Hello, good woman, is it so late?

MILLER: Almost ten o'clock at night.

COAL PETER: Well, good evening, my good people. We've actually lost our way.

MILLER: You've been on your feet a long time.

COAL PETER: It didn't seem that long to us. But my bones are starting to ache.

ANNOUNCER: Mine too, Peter. But that doesn't help. I must go back and look for my other friends in Voice Land.

We hear: Good evening, Announcer. Be well. Good night. Bye!

MILLER'S WIFE: All right, come on in, Mr. Peter, for that must be your name. Be careful you don't get covered with dust. It's always dusty in a mill. Hurry, Hanni, bring the young man last night's potato fritters and a cherry brandy.

Pause. Sound of clattering plates.

MILLER'S SON (*whispering*): Mother, how strange Mr. Peter looks.

MILLER'S WIFE: What do you mean?

MILLER'S SON (*whispering*): As if something had spooked him.

MILLER'S WIFE: Silly boy, off to bed. And you, Mr. Peter, will not stay up much longer either. For as you know, at the mill, the racket starts early. It is no place for people who like to sleep in.

COAL PETER: Right, Mrs. Miller. But first you must allow me to thank you sincerely for the potato fritters.

MILLER'S WIFE: Don't mention it. But come along. I'll show you to your bed.

COAL PETER: I'm sure to sleep well here. So many pillows! They reach almost to the ceiling.

MILLER'S WIFE: Well you see, here in the Black Forest we don't have double windows. One must have thick comforters when the winter frost comes.

Again, voices: Have a good night's sleep! Good night! Don't forget to blow out the candles!

COAL PETER (*yawning*): Aah, how amazing that a person could be so tired. I believe that if the devil himself were to appear, I'd just lie here and turn the other way.

Brief pause. A knock.

COAL PETER: Was that a knock? It's not possible. They're all asleep.

Another knock.

COAL PETER: Someone must be at the door. Come in!

MILLER'S SON: Dear Mr. Peter, please, please, don't tell on me. Let me stay here with you for a little while. I am so afraid.

COAL PETER: Come now, what's wrong? Why are you so afraid?

MILLER'S SON: Mr. Peter, you'd be afraid too, if you had seen what I saw today.—Perhaps you did notice it when you came in—that book bound in red velvet lying on the table.

COAL PETER: Oh the album, yes, of course. With pictures inside, no?

MILLER'S SON: There are indeed pictures in it, Mr. Peter, and on one page there are three that I can't get out of my head; their eyes follow me everywhere. Fat Ezekiel and tall Schlurker and the Dance Hall King are their names, it says so underneath.

COAL PETER: What's that you say? Fat Ezekiel, tall Schlurker ... I've heard those names before. And the Dance Hall King? Isn't that the poor man who once was a servant to a lumber merchant and then became filthy rich all of a sudden? Some say he found a pot of gold under an old pine tree, while others insist that he speared a bundle of gold in the river Rhine, not far from Bingen, with a spear like those that raftsmen use to catch fish, and that the gold belonged to the great treasure of the Nibelungen that was buried there. In short, he had suddenly become rich, and young and old regarded him as a prince.

MILLER'S SON: But his eyes! You should have seen his eyes!

COAL PETER: Well, you know, it's quite possible. People who see something especially horrible can get a peculiar look in their eyes forever.

MILLER'S SON: But what do you think he might have seen that was so very horrible?

COAL PETER: Well, I'm not sure, but did you know that on the other side of the Black Forest, where the lumberjacks and raftsmen live, people say that something not quite right is going on?

MILLER'S SON: Oh, I know, you must be talking about Dutch Michael. My father has already told me about him. He's the giant of the forest, the coarse, broad-shouldered chap, and those who have seen him say they would not like to pay for the calves' hides it would take to make one pair of his boots.

COAL PETER: Yes, I was just thinking of him.

MILLER'S SON: So you do know something about him after all, Mr. Peter.

COAL PETER: Shame on you, child, for saying such a thing. How should I know anything about Dutch Michael? Sometimes when I hear what people are saying, I ask myself: Isn't it just envy? Aren't they simply envious of the lumberjacks who are always swaggering around like lords in their doublets with buttons, buckles, and chains, draped in half a hundredweight of silver? Anybody could get jealous, seeing that.

MILLER'S SON: Have you been envious of it too, Mr. Peter?

COAL PETER: Envious, good heavens no, I have no cause for that; I'm the last one to be envious.

MILLER'S SON: So that means then that you yourself are that rich, Mr. Peter? Or maybe even richer?

COAL PETER: Surely, my boy, you must have noticed that I am a poor wretch. I don't have an ounce of silver on me, here or at home. But I have something even better. Only I can't tell you what it is.

MILLER'S SON: Now you've made me curious. I won't leave your room until you've told me.

COAL PETER: Well, can you keep a secret?

MILLER'S SON: Of course, Mr. Peter, I promise you that no one will hear it from me.

COAL PETER: In that case, let me ask you something. Have you ever heard of the Little Glass Man? The Little Glass Man who never shows up without his peaked hat with a broad rim, a doublet, white trousers, and red stockings. The friend of glass makers and coal burners and all the other poor people who live on this side of the woods.

MILLER'S SON: The Little Glass Man? No, Mr. Peter, never heard of him.

COAL PETER: Then perhaps you've heard of Sunday's Child?

MILLER'S SON: Oh, yes, those who are born on Sunday at noon.

COAL PETER: Well, that's me. Do you understand?—but that's only half my secret. The other half is my rhyme.

MILLER'S SON: Now, I can't follow a word you are saying, Mr. Peter.

COAL PETER: The Little Glass Man, you see, he appears to Sunday's Children, but only under a pine hillock, where the trees are so dense and stand so tall that even in broad daylight it's almost night, and where one hears neither an ax nor even a bird, if one knows the right rhyme. And that my mother taught me.

MILLER'S SON: Surely, you are to be envied, Mr. Peter.

COAL PETER: Yes, one might envy me had I memorized the little rhyme, but when I stood there before the pine tree and wanted to recite it, I realized I had forgotten the last line. The Little Glass Man vanished as quickly as he had appeared. "Mr. Glass Man," I called, after some hesitation, "be so kind as not to make a fool of me. Mr. Glass Man, if you think I didn't see you, you are quite mistaken. I saw you peeking out from behind the tree." But there was no answer, and only at times did I hear a soft, rasping chuckle from behind the tree. Finally, I thought, with one leap, I could catch that little guy. When I sprang behind the pine tree, though, there was no Little Glass Man anywhere to be found; there was only a dainty little squirrel racing up the trunk.

MILLER'S SON: So, Mr. Peter, you've just come from the Little Glass Man?

COAL PETER: That's right.

MILLER'S SON: But now you must tell me your rhyme, as much as you remember of it.

COAL PETER: No, my boy. It's gotten late and we should get some sleep—and your three bad men, you will have forgotten them by tomorrow, and when we wake up, we'll all be cheerful.

MILLER'S SON: Well then, good night, Mr. Peter. But I'm not cheerful, because you didn't tell me the rhyme.

We hear the two saying goodnight.

COAL PETER: Now I'm alone and want to sleep. I don't want to recite the rhyme to anyone but the Little Glass Man, oh, if only I remembered it!

A little music. Peter sings along in a drowsy voice.

> Keeper of wealth in the forest of pine,
> Hundreds of years are surely thine:
> Thine is the tall pine's dwelling place—[5]

COAL PETER (*in a drowsy voice*): The tall pine's dwelling place, the tall pine's dwelling place—if I only knew the rest.
The music comes to an end. After a short pause, we hear six chimes.

ANNOUNCER: Here I am again, back in the Black Forest mill, together with Coal Peter. It's six o'clock. I bet Coal Peter slept the whole night in the back of a cart and it won't be so easy to wake him.
Coal Peter is snoring. Faint music grows slowly stronger. We hear one or two verses sung.

COAL PETER (*very drowsy*): Huh, a music box for an alarm clock. I would like to wake up to lovely music every morning, like a prince. But no, it's coming from outside: apprentice craftsmen! They're certainly up early.
We hear singing:

> I stood upon the brightest place,
> I gazed upon the plain,
> And then—oh then—I saw that face,
> I never saw again.[6]

COAL PETER: Hey, you there! Encore, encore! Sing it again!
The music fades away and the singing becomes fainter.
Well, they don't care much for me. And they're gone, beyond the hills.
(*More quietly and wistfully.*) How did it go again? (*Humming quietly to the same melody.*) Oh then—I saw that face, oh then—I saw that face—so then, "face," that's the rhyme. Face for place, now Little Glass Man, let's have our little chat again.
He whistles a little to himself.

ANNOUNCER: What's your hurry, Mr. Peter Munk? I had just been hopelessly wondering how to get you back on your feet and on

---

5 The translation of the rhyme is taken from Hauff's tale in English in *Tales from the German: Comprising Specimens from the most Celebrated Authors*, trans. John Oxenford and C. A. Feiling (London: Chapman and Hall, 1844), 54.

6 *Tales from the German*, 59.

your way home. And suddenly here you are, racing by in such haste.

COAL PETER (*in a hurry*): Let me go, Mr. Announcer, let me go. I just remembered my rhyme—

ANNOUNCER: Rhyme? What sort of rhyme?

COAL PETER: Shh, I'm on a mission. I can't say another word. You'll find out soon enough. Goodbye, Mr. Announcer!

ANNOUNCER: What an odd bird. (*Calling after him.*) Just steer clear of Dutch Michael! Bye, Peter!

COAL PETER: So, here's the tall pine. Now pay attention Peter, here we go:

> Keeper of wealth in the forest of pine,
> Hundreds of years are surely thine,
> Thine is the tall pine's dwelling place,
> Those born on Sunday see thy face.[7]

LITTLE GLASS MAN: You didn't get it quite right, but since it's you, Coal Peter, I'll let it slide. Did you run into that rascal, Dutch Michael?

COAL PETER: Indeed I did, Keeper of Wealth, and I was terribly scared. I've come to ask your advice. Things aren't going well for me, they're not easy. A coal burner won't get very far, and being young, I thought, perhaps I could make more of myself. I often look at others and think how far they've gotten in such a short time—I need only mention Ezekiel and the Dance Hall King, who are rolling in the dough.

LITTLE GLASS MAN: Don't talk to me about them, Peter! What good does it do them, if for a few years they appear to be happy yet afterwards are just as unhappy? Don't scorn your trade; your father and grandfather were honorable men, and they plied the same trade, Peter Munk! I do hope it's not laziness that brings you to me.

COAL PETER: No, not laziness. Mr. Keeper of Wealth in the Forest of Pine, I know very well that laziness is at the root of all vice; but you can't hold it against me if another rank pleases me more than my own. A coal burner is regarded as very lowly in this world, while the glass blowers and the raftsmen and the clockmakers are held in high esteem.

---

7 Ibid., 62.

LITTLE GLASS MAN: Pride goeth before a fall. You humans are a curious race! You're hardly ever satisfied with the condition into which you were born and raised. What's it all about? If you are a glassmaker, you would rather be a lumber merchant, and if you are a lumber merchant, you covet the forester's duties or the magistrate's residence. But so be it! If you promise to work hard, Peter, I will help you to attain something better. I grant three wishes to every Sunday's Child who knows how to find me. But be careful. With every wish I knock my glass pipe on this pine tree. The first two are free; the third I can refuse, if it's foolish. So wish for something now, Peter, but make it something good and useful.

COAL PETER: Hooray! You are a splendid Little Glass Man, and rightly do they call you the Keeper of Wealth; you do control a wealth of treasures. I shall wish what my heart desires. My first wish is that I be able to dance better than the Dance Hall King and always bring twice as much money to the tavern as he does. *Knocking of the pipe.*

LITTLE GLASS MAN: You fool! What a pathetic wish this is, to be able to dance well and have money for gambling! Aren't you ashamed, dumb Peter, to cheat yourself out of your own happiness like this? What good does it do you and your poor mother, if you dance well? What good is your money if it's squandered at the tavern, like that of the miserable Dance Hall King? Afterwards you'll have nothing left for the rest of the week and you'll suffer want just as before. I will give you one more wish freely; but be careful to make a more reasonable wish!

COAL PETER (*after some hesitation*): Well, then, I wish for the most beautiful and richest glass factory in the entire Black Forest with all its trappings and the money to run it.

LITTLE GLASS MAN: Nothing else, Peter? Nothing else?

COAL PETER: Well, you could add a horse and a small carriage.

LITTLE GLASS MAN: Oh, you stupid Coal Peter! (*The pipe shatters.*) Horse? Carriage? Brains, I tell you—it's brains, common sense and good judgment you should have wished for, not a horse and carriage. Now, don't be so sad, we will see to it that it doesn't cause you any harm; after all, the second wish wasn't entirely foolish. A good glass factory feeds its owner and workmen; if only you had added brains and good judgment to it, horses and carriages would have come into the bargain.

COAL PETER: But, Mr. Keeper of Wealth, I do have one wish left. I could wish for brains if you think I am in such need of them.

LITTLE GLASS MAN: No way! You will encounter many difficulties, and so, be glad you still have one wish left. Now go home! Here are two thousand guldens—and that's it—don't come back to ask me for more money; I'd hang you from the highest pine tree! That's how I've been handling things ever since I came to live in the forest. Three days ago, old Winkfritz died; he had that big glass factory in the lower forest. Go there early tomorrow morning and make a fair bid! Comport yourself well, be diligent, and I will come visit you now and again to advise and assist you, because you didn't ask for any brains. But, I say this to you in earnest, your first wish was evil. Beware of the taverns, Peter! They've never done anyone any good.

COAL PETER: He's gone? He can really smoke, that Keeper of Wealth. The smoke's so thick, I can hardly see him. (*He sniffs.*) I must say, though, it is a pleasant blend.
Gong.

ANNOUNCER: Yes, well then, where were we? You children have just listened in on the conversation between our good Peter Munk and our little Keeper of Wealth. You heard the foolish wishes Peter made, and how the Little Glass Man disappeared in a cloud of good Dutch tobacco smoke. Now let's see what comes next. (*He rustles some papers.*) Where is that next installment? (*Louder rustling.*)

LITTLE GLASS MAN (*whispering*): What's going on? Why aren't we continuing with the play?

ANNOUNCER (*whispering*): I have no idea what to do next, Mr. Keeper of Wealth. Fancy that! The forest wind must have blown away some of the pages; now we're in a jam. I have no idea how we will ever find our place again.

DANCE HALL KING (*whispering*): Disastrous, disastrous! What are we going to do?

DUTCH MICHAEL (*whispering*): As if you had any ideas, you dumb Dance Hall King. It's going to take something big. Let me think a minute!

DANCE HALL KING (*whispering*): That's a laugh: you, thinking! If only it were possible, Dutch Michael.

DUTCH MICHAEL (*whispering*): Save it, Dance Hall King. Go sing

"The Watch on the Rhine."[8] So, Coal Peter, now you have a huge amount of money from the Little Glass Man and you've got yourself a glass factory.

COAL PETER: That's right, that's right, Mr. Dutch Michael, I did indeed have a nice, big glass factory.

DANCE HALL KING: Yes, right, you *had* it, Coal Peter, but sure enough, you up and gambled it away with Fat Ezekiel at the tavern. Isn't that true, Fat Ezekiel?

EZEKIEL: Oh, give it a rest, Dance Hall King. I don't ever want to be reminded of that evening again.

ANNOUNCER: Yes, that's right, Coal Peter! I still remember that myself. You gambled away your glass factory. But you must ask yourself: wasn't that a colossal mistake on Coal Peter's part, wishing from the Keeper of Wealth that he would always have as much money in his pocket as Fat Ezekiel? It goes without saying that one evening you wouldn't have a single penny left and would have to sell your glass factory the very next day. Wait a minute: Had to sell—had to sell—? There it is on page sixteen! Thank God, I've found the thread again! Let's go, people, we can continue! While the bailiff and appraiser looked around the glass factory and checked and estimated the value of everything that was for sale, that's when Coal Peter thought: "It's not that far to the pine forest; if the little fellow couldn't help me, then I'm going to try it again with the big one." He ran to the pine forest as if the bailiffs were at his heels; as he ran past the place in the forest where he first spoke to the Little Glass Man, he felt as if an invisible hand were holding him back; but he tore himself away and kept running, all the way to the boundary he remembered from before. Well, Peter, now you're on your own; I certainly don't envy you for what happens next.

COAL PETER (*breathless*): Dutch Michael, Mr. Dutch Michael!

DUTCH MICHAEL (*laughing*): So you've come, Coal Peter. Did they fleece you and try to sell you off to your creditors? Well, keep calm, as I said before, all of your misery comes from the Little Glass Man, that separatist, that hypocrite! When one gives, one really has to give—not like that cheapskate! So come, come into my house; we'll see if we can make a deal.

COAL PETER: A deal, Dutch Michael? What is there to negotiate

---

8 "The Watch on the Rhine" [Die Wacht am Rhein], a nineteenth-century German patriotic anthem.

with you? Should I serve you somehow? What else do you want? And how will I make it over this great chasm?

DUTCH MICHAEL (*as if through a megaphone*): Just sit on my hand and hold on to my fingers. You won't fall.

Music with various rhythms that sound like ticking clocks; first softly, then louder.

So, here we are! Take a seat on the bench by the stove and let's drink a pint of wine together. Cheers, here's to your health, you poor fellow. Is it true that you've never left the gloomy Black Forest your whole life?

COAL PETER: Not yet, indeed, Dutch Michael, how would I?

DUTCH MICHAEL: In different company, of course! Every year I get to float down the Rhine to Holland atop a raft of timber. Not to mention the trips to foreign countries I allow myself in my free time.

COAL PETER: Oh, to do that just once!

DUTCH MICHAEL: It's up to you. Until now your heart has gotten in the way of everything.

COAL PETER: My heart?

DUTCH MICHAEL: When, in your whole body, you might have the courage and strength to do something, but a few beats of your stupid heart make you tremble, as do your misfortunes and insults to your honor—why should a smart fellow like you have to worry about such things? Was it your head that bothered you when they called you an impostor and a scoundrel? Did your stomach ache when the bailiff came to throw you out of your house? Tell me, please, what was paining you?

COAL PETER: My heart.

DUTCH MICHAEL: You have, and don't resent me for saying this, thrown away hundreds of guldens on vile panhandlers and other riff-raff; what good did it do you? They wished you good blessings and a healthy body; are you any healthier for it? For half that squandered money you could have gotten a doctor. Blessings—nice blessings those, when you are seized for debt and evicted! And what was it that drove you to reach in your pocket every time a beggar stretched out a tattered hat?—Your heart, once again, your heart, and not your eyes or tongue, arms or legs, but your heart; you took it, as they say, too much to heart.

COAL PETER: But what can be done to stop it? I try as hard as I can to stifle it, but nonetheless my heart beats, bringing me pain.

DUTCH MICHAEL (*with a sneering laugh*): You, poor rascal, can do nothing about it; but give me the palpitating thing and then you'll see how good you have it.

COAL PETER (*horrified*): Give you my heart? I would die on the spot! Never!

DUTCH MICHAEL: Well, if you had one of those honorable surgeons remove your heart from your body, you would surely die; but with me it's different; come into this room and see for yourself!

Music: Fugue of the Pounding Heart.

COAL PETER: For God's sake! What is that?

DUTCH MICHAEL: Yes, take a good look at what's in those spirit glasses! They cost me a wad of dough! Take a closer look and read the names on the labels.

After reading each name aloud, corresponding music.

Here we have the bailiff and here Fat Ezekiel. This is the heart of the Dance Hall King and that of the Head Forester. And here we have a whole collection of racketeers and recruiting officers. Look, all of them got rid of a life of fear and worry; none of these hearts beats with worry and fear anymore, and their former owners feel they've gotten an unruly guest out of the house.

COAL PETER (*fearfully*): But what do they carry in their chests now?

DUTCH MICHAEL: A meticulously manufactured stone heart like this one here.

COAL PETER (*shuddering*): Really? A heart of marble? Listen here, Mr. Dutch Michael, that must feel awfully cold in one's chest.

DUTCH MICHAEL: Well, yes, but quite pleasantly cool. Why should a heart be warm? In the winter that warmth is of no use to you at all—a good cherry brandy is of greater help than a warm heart. And during the summer, when it's hot and humid, you wouldn't believe how such a heart can cool you down. And as I said, neither fear nor dread, nor foolish compassion nor any other misery throbs in such a heart.

COAL PETER (*annoyed*): And that's all you have to offer? I was thinking of money, and you offer me a stone!

DUTCH MICHAEL: Well, I think, 100,000 guldens should be enough for you as a start. If you manage it shrewdly, you will soon be a millionaire.

COAL PETER (*happy*): Hey you, don't beat so fiercely in my chest! We will soon be done with one another. Very well, Michael, give me the stone and the money, and remove the worry from its dwelling place!

DUTCH MICHAEL (*happy*): I knew you were a sensible fellow. Come, let's have a drink, and then I'll fork over the money.

The heart music fades into a Post Horn Fugue.

COAL PETER (*wakes up and stretches*): Aah! I slept a long time. Was that a post horn that just woke me? Am I awake, or am I still dreaming? It seems to me that I am riding somewhere, and there is a postilion and horses up ahead. I am, in fact, sitting in a stagecoach. And the mountains, back there in the distance, that's the Black Forest. And even my clothes have changed. Why am I not even a little melancholy that I am leaving, for the first time, the forests where I lived for so long? What is my mother doing? How strange, she's probably sitting there, helpless and in despair, and yet this thought cannot draw a single tear from my eye. I am indifferent to it all. Why? Oh, that's right, tears and sighs, homesickness and melancholy come from the heart and, thanks to Dutch Michael, mine is cold and made of stone. If he kept his word about the hundred thousand, as he did with my heart, then I should be happy. Sure enough, here is a purse with thousands of coins and bills from the commercial houses of all the big cities.

Post horn melody.

JUMBLE OF VOICES: Frankfurt am Main! Frankfurter sausages! Goethe House! Frankfurt Radio! Apple wine! *The Frankfurt Times*! Marzipan cookies! Frankfurt is teeming with curiosities!

COAL PETER: What's there to eat and drink? Wrap up a couple dozen sausages for me, a couple jugs of apple wine, and a couple pounds of marzipan cookies.

Post horn melody.

JUMBLE OF VOICES: Paris! *Le Matin*! *Paris–Midi*! *Paris–Soir*! Cacahouètes, cacahouètes, and cacahouètes! The Louvre! The Eiffel Tower! Eskimo pops, goody bags! Surprises!

COAL PETER (*sleepy*): Where are we now? Oh, in Paris! Then pack up some champagne, lobsters, and oysters, so I don't die of hunger and thirst!

A VOICE: Mr. Postilion, who is that sleepy gentleman?

POSTILION: Oh, that's Mr. Coal Peter from the Black Forest, who ate and drank so much in Frankfurt that he can hardly move.

Post horn melody.

JUMBLE OF VOICES: London! Britannia rules the waves! Ginger ale! Scotch Whisky! Toffees! Muffins! *The Morning Post*! *The*

Daily News! *The Times*! Turkey and plumcake!
Coal Peter snores.

A VOICE: Mr. Postilion, who is that snoring gentleman over there?

POSTILION: That's Mr. Coal Peter from the Black Forest, who ate and drank so much in Paris that he can hardly keep his eyes open.
Post horn melody.

JUMBLE OF VOICES: Constantinople! Visit the Bosphorus and the Golden Horn! Carpets! A hookah perhaps? Bagpipes made in Constantinople! Rahat lokum! Visit the whirling dervishes in Gallipoli and the minarets of the Hagia Sophia!
Coal Peter snores.

A VOICE: Mr. Postilion, who is that snoring gentleman over there?

POSTILION: That's Mr. Coal Peter from the Black Forest who has already eaten and drunk so much at the previous stops that he can't keep his eyes open at all.
Post horn melody.

JUMBLE OF VOICES: Roma! *La Stampa di Roma*! *Il Corriere della Sera*! Il Foro Romano! The Coliseum! Giovinezza! Vino bianco e vino rosso! Spaghetti! Polenta! Risotto! Frutti di mare! Antiquities! Visit the Pope and Il Duce!
Coal Peter snores.

A VOICE: Mr. Postilion, who is that snoring gentleman over there?

POSTILION: That's Mr. Coal Peter from the Black Forest who has already eaten and drunk so much at the previous stops that he can't even open his eyes.
Post horn melody.

POSTILION: A town in the Black Forest! Everybody off!
Gong.

ANNOUNCER: Now we have Coal Peter, back at home. You heard the post horn with which the Postilion announced his arrival. Hopefully, you understood all of the other stops the Postilion announced, but you didn't understand that last one. That is no accident. We don't know the name of the place Coal Peter calls home. It's not named in the book from which you, Coal Peter, and you, Fat Ezekiel, and you, Tall Schlurker, and you, Dutch Michael, and you, Little Glass Man, have emerged. And we don't want to pry. It's enough that he's here, back at home, in the Schwabian Black Forest. He knows this, but only in his head, not his heart. He recognizes that he is back home but he doesn't feel it. What should he do? His charcoal kiln no longer burns, he sold his glass factory, he has so much money that working would seem stupid to him. Therefore, to pass the time, he looks for a wife. He is still a handsome fellow. One cannot see from the outside that he has a heart of stone. Before, when he had his real heart, everyone liked him very much and they all remember this now, especially Lisbeth, the poor lumberjack's daughter. She lived quietly and in solitude, diligently taking care of her father's house. She was never seen on the dance floor, not even on Pentecost or at the fair. When Peter heard of this marvel in the Black Forest, he rode to her cottage, which had been pointed out to him, and sought her hand in marriage. The father of beautiful Lisbeth was surprised to see such a distinguished gentleman and was even more astonished when he heard that it was the rich Mr. Peter who wanted to become his son-in-law. He didn't reflect for long; he thought that all his worries and poverty would come to an end and so he accepted. And Lisbeth, being a good child, was so obedient that she became Mrs. Peter Munk without protest. Lisbeth had no money, but she brought a wonderful dowry to Peter's house: a cuckoo clock that had been in her family for generations. This clock was quite peculiar; it was not without reason that people said the Keeper of Wealth had given it long ago to someone very dear to him. What was important about the clock was this: it worked like a true Black Forest cuckoo clock, and chimed on the hour. At noon it chimed twelve times, but only if there were no evil person in the room where it was hanging. If there were an evil person in the room, it chimed exactly thirteen times. We are now in the very room where the cuckoo clock hangs. Coal Peter sits at the table with Lisbeth.

The cuckoo clock chimes eleven times.

LISBETH: Eleven o'clock? I must hurry and put the carrots on the stove.

PETER: Carrots again, ugh, disgusting.

LISBETH: But it's your favorite dish, Peter.

PETER: Favorite dish! Favorite dish, none of this grub pleases me. Now, if you were to bring me a big glass of brandy ...

LISBETH: Don't you remember what the minister said last Sunday, when he spoke of drinking?

PETER (*stomping his foot*): So, what about it? Are you going to pour me a glass or not? (*Threateningly.*) Well?

LISBETH (*we hear her whimpering*): Here, have your way. But it won't end well.

PETER: As long as it starts well. Life is already sad enough for me.

But it really gets annoying when people go on and on about Sunday or good weather or spring. It all seems quite foolish, to my mind.

LISBETH: Are you in pain?

PETER: No, that's just it, I feel neither pain nor happiness. Recently I cut my finger and hardly felt it. Remember? When I was chopping up the old chest that you received from your grandmother as a christening present?

A knock at the door.

PETER: Whatever you do, don't answer it.

A second knock at the door.

PETER: He won't dare enter before I say "come in." And I won't say "Come in."

LISBETH: Why? You can't possibly know who it is.

PETER: It's certainly not the postman delivering a money order. Miserable beggars, no doubt.

A knock at the door.

LISBETH: Come in!

PETER: So there, you impudent fool. Of course it's a beggar.

BEGGAR: Could you spare a little something?

PETER: You should be asking the devil, and he can have you.

BEGGAR: Have mercy, good woman, and give me a drink of water.

PETER: I'd rather pour a whole bottle of brandy over his head than give him a glass of water.

LISBETH: Leave me alone. I want to give him a drink of wine, a loaf of bread, and a dime to take on his way.

PETER: That's the way you see things. It's so typical of you, you idiot. Why can't you just accept your husband's wise judgment? Maybe you think I am cruel and hard-hearted. Do you not understand that I have weighed everything carefully? Do you not know what happens once you let such people across the threshold? They are beggars. One tells the next. They leave a secret mark on the door. Their trickster's code. They spy out every opportunity, which means they take everything that's not nailed down. Once you have hosted two or three of these wretches, within a year your home will be stripped bare.

BEGGAR: Oh, people as rich as you are, you don't know how it hurts to be poor, and how much good a cold drink does in such heat.

PETER: Time drags on in the midst of such chatter.

The cuckoo clock begins to chime.

LISBETH: Heaven help me, I have forgotten the carrots, and you, good man, take everything I have and be on your way.

The chiming of the clock must be loud and one chime should follow slowly after another, so that the preceding words of the wife can be heard between the first and second chimes.

PETER (*counts along with clock, in a monotonous voice, as if lost in thought*): One, two, three, four, five, six, seven, eight, nine, ten, eleven, twelve.

Utter silence. The clock strikes for the thirteenth time. We hear a thud.

LISBETH: My God, Peter has lost consciousness. Peter, Peter, what's wrong with you? Wake up!

Moaning, sighs, and tears.

Gong.

ANNOUNCER: Peter has not only lost consciousness. He has almost lost his life to arrogance and godlessness. Now, as the clock strikes thirteen, he comes to, reflects, and decides, for his third and final wish from the Keeper of Wealth, to ask for his heart back. Let's see what happens!

Gong.

PETER:

> Keeper of wealth in the forest of pine,
> Hundreds of years are surely thine:
> Thine is the tall pine's dwelling place—
> Those born on Sunday see thy face.[9]

LITTLE GLASS MAN (*in a hollow voice*): What do you want, Peter Munk?

PETER: I still have one wish, Mr. Keeper of Wealth.

LITTLE GLASS MAN: Can hearts of stone still wish? You have everything you need for your rotten mind, and I am not inclined to fulfill your wish.

PETER: But you promised me three wishes; I still have one left.

LITTLE GLASS MAN: If it is foolish, I can refuse to grant it. But go ahead, let's hear your wish.

PETER: Take this dead stone out of me and give me back my living heart.

LITTLE GLASS MAN: Did I make that trade with you? Am I Dutch Michael, who bestows fortunes and cold hearts? You will have to seek your heart from him.

---

9 *Tales from the German*, 77.

PETER: Oh no, he will never give it back to me.

LITTLE GLASS MAN (*after a pause*): I pity you, even as bad as you are. But because your wish is not foolish, I cannot deny you my help. Can you remember a verse?

PETER: I think so, even though I once forgot yours, Mr. Keeper of Wealth.

LITTLE GLASS MAN: Then repeat after me. If you forget it, all is lost: "You were not sent here from Holland . . ." Repeat.

PETER: "You were not sent here from Holland . . ."

LITTLE GLASS MAN: "Mr. Michael, but from hell-land." Repeat.

PETER: "Mr. Michael, but from hell-land." Oh, now I have it, Mr. Keeper of Wealth, that's great. Surely it's a magic spell, and when Dutch Michael hears it, he will be powerless to harm me.

LITTLE GLASS MAN: That's right, but what else?

PETER: What else? Nothing else. I go to him and say:

> You were not sent here from Holland,
> Mr. Michael, but from hell-land.

With that he will be powerless to harm me.

LITTLE GLASS MAN: That's one way of seeing it. Although he can no longer do anything to you, as soon as you have spoken these words, Dutch Michael will have disappeared. And the devil knows where. You, however, will stand in front of all those hearts and be unable to find your own.

PETER: O God, how will I manage it?

LITTLE GLASS MAN: That I cannot tell you. So far, you have reflected little in your life. It's high time you started. And now I have to tend to the woodpeckers on my pines, which don't cause me as much grief as Sunday's Children do.

Gong.

ANNOUNCER: Now I have to tell you something: Wait—and if I must wait, I prefer to wait in Human Land than in Voice Land. Here everything seems to be in a dense fog. One can't see a thing. One can only prick up one's ears, and I've been doing that for hours now. But in the forest, where the Keeper of Wealth lives, not a single branch stirs, no woodpecker pecks. Nor is there a chirrup from a nest. Fine by me, but what kind of stories are these, anyway, that I resort to poetry out of sheer boredom? But I hear some crackling, or is it a whisper? Is that the voice of the Keeper of Wealth, or Coal Peter's voice?

COAL PETER (*very hollow and sad*): Coal Peter.

ANNOUNCER: He doesn't sound so good.

COAL PETER (*very hollow and sad*): Is there an echo in these woods?

COAL PETER (*very hollow and sad*): Oh!

ANNOUNCER: You are not very good company in these woods. And what is that I hear ringing from afar? That sounds just like Dutch Michael's haunting glass music. Well, say something! Why are you so silent?

COAL PETER (*as above*): Hmm!

ANNOUNCER: Now that's a bit much. Too mysterious and uncertain. No hard feelings, Mr. Coal Peter, but I'm going to look for a new route.

COAL PETER (*as above*): Farewell! (*He knocks and calls out.*) Dutch Michael!

Repeats three times.

DUTCH MICHAEL: Good that you have come. I couldn't have stood it either, living with Lisbeth, that clumsy, complaining wench who throws money away to beggars. You know what? If I were you, I'd go traveling again. Stay away for a few years. Who knows, when you come home, Lisbeth might be long dead.

COAL PETER: You guessed it, Dutch Michael, I want to go to America. But I do need money for that; it's rather far away.

DUTCH MICHAEL: And you shall have it, my little Peter, you shall have it. (*We hear jingling and counting.*) One hundred, two hundred, five hundred, eight hundred, a thousand, twelve hundred. Not marks, dear Peter, all thalers.

COAL PETER: Michael, you're one in a million but you're a real crook. You lied to me, saying I had a stone in my chest, and that you had my heart.

DUTCH MICHAEL: Isn't it true? Can you feel your heart? Isn't it as cold as ice? Are you afraid or grieving? Are you capable of regret?

COAL PETER: You merely stopped my heart, but I still have it, just as always, in my breast, and the same with Ezekiel. He told me that you lied to us; you cannot tear the heart out of a man's chest, neatly and unseen; for that you would have to work magic.

DUTCH MICHAEL: But I assure you, you and Ezekiel and all the other rich people who sought me out have cold hearts just like yours, and I have their real hearts in my cabinet.

COAL PETER: Eh, how easily lies flow from your tongue! Find someone else to believe that! Do you really think I haven't seen such stunts a dozen times in my travels? Those hearts in the cabinet are made of wax. You're a rich guy, I grant you, but you can't work magic.

DUTCH MICHAEL: Come on in and read all the labels. That one there, look, that's Peter Munk's heart. See how it quivers? Could anyone make that out of wax?

COAL PETER: And yet, it is made of wax; that's not how a real heart beats. Mine is still in my chest. No, you can't do magic.

DUTCH MICHAEL: I will prove it to you! You shall experience it yourself—this is your heart. Here, I'll put your heart back into you! How do you feel now?

COAL PETER: Sure enough, you were right. I just didn't believe such things were possible!

DUTCH MICHAEL: You see? I can do magic. Now, come here; I want to put the stone back.

COAL PETER: Slow down, Mr. Michael! You can catch mice with bacon, but this time you're the one who's been tricked. Listen to this:

He stutters at first and then calls out ever more bravely, louder and faster, repeating his incantation several times:

> You were not sent here from Holland,
> Mr. Michael, but from hell-land.

The hearts beat loudly. Dutch Michael groans. Thunder.

COAL PETER: See how he writhes, the evil Dutch Michael. But what terrible thunder. I'm afraid. Quick, back home now, to my Lisbeth.

Gong.

ANNOUNCER: Finding anything here in Voice Land is like playing a game of blind man's bluff. Ah, that must be Coal Peter's glass factory. As for his wife, she can't be far away either, for whose voice could that be but dear Lisbeth's!

LISBETH (*singing*):

> Tiny glasses, hollow blown,
> Why must I be so alone?
> My dearest Peter sneaking by
> Like a scoundrel prone to lie.
> I know already what to do:
> Little diapers, little shoe

> I weave and knit for Peter's son,
> Time passes by, it's nearly done.
> Hollow glasses, tiny all,
> Bodice, stockings sewn so small;
> Into the world, a baby dear,
> All is ready, I am here.

ANNOUNCER: It appears Peter will have a son. That makes it twice as unfair that he prowls around away from home. But it's a good opportunity for me. I've been waiting to speak with Lisbeth for a long time now. Why should I speak only with Peter in Voice Land? So, what shall I do to make her notice me? I can't just cry out; my deep voice would only frighten her, while she still hears her own, which sounds so sweet.
Brief pause.
I know what I'll do. I'll just rap against these glasses.
A snatch of glass music.

COAL PETER: Here I am!
LISBETH AND ANNOUNCER: Who is it?
COAL PETER: I have my heart back.
LISBETH: Mine has always been yours.
ANNOUNCER: Now I take my leave, but first you must promise me one thing: when little Coal Peter is born, choose the Keeper of Wealth to be his godfather.
Brief pause. The names of the months are read aloud.
ANNOUNCER: How quickly a year passes here in Voice Land! There stands Coal Peter in the pine forest, reciting his little rhyme.
Gong.
COAL PETER:

> Keeper of Wealth in the forest of pine,
> Hundreds of years are surely thine:
> Thine is the tall pine's dwelling place—
> Those born on Sunday see thy face.[10]

Mr. Keeper of Wealth, just hear me out; I want nothing more than to ask you to be godfather to my little son!
Wind.

---

10   Ibid.

Then I will take these pine cones to him as a souvenir, as you prefer not to be seen.

ANNOUNCER: Children! Can you imagine what these pine cones turned into? Brand new Schwabian thalers, and not a counterfeit among them. That's what Baby Peter received as a christening gift from the little man in the pine forest.

—And now, do be kind and give me your thanks. I don't mean the children who have been listening to us, but Coal Peter and Mr. Keeper of Wealth and Dutch Michael and the whole bunch from Hauff, whom I brought to Voice Land as they wished and whom I will now leave safe and sound at the border.

EZEKIEL: Safe and sound? You talk a good game. I won't speak of being safe or sound until I have my money back.

LISBETH: Pah, Fat Ezekiel, you'll never change. And I, Lisbeth, stand by it.

ANNOUNCER: Let him be, Madam. He'll get his money back, down to the last cent.

LISBETH: Yes, Mr. Announcer, and a special thanks to you for bringing me such joy with your glass music; for it was you, wasn't it, who played the bottles so delightfully.

ANNOUNCER (*in a gruff voice*): Yes, yes.

LISBETH: I was a bit worried after everything suddenly came to a stop and you lost your way in Voice Land.

ANNOUNCER: Yes, but do come closer, Mrs. Lisbeth. Look here, on this page ... Here, Hauff himself calls for a long pause. And just by chance, imagine, our pause fell on just the same passage.

DUTCH MICHAEL: Well, I call that a blessing in disguise.

ANNOUNCER: Indeed, the writer himself created the pause. And why? This story is like a mountain, like the Black Forest range itself, and its climax is like a peak from which one can look down to either side: to the bad outcome or the good.

A MURMUR OF VOICES: Goodbye, Mr. Keeper of Wealth, Madam, Mr. Peter, *etc.*

DUTCH MICHAEL: Hello, Hello. Now wait a minute, Ladies and Gentlemen, why are you in such a hurry? I am not very happy with the villainous part I've played here. I wanted to let you know that in Hauff's stories there are all kinds of scoundrels. Read, for example, "The Ghost Ship," "The Tale of the Severed Hand," and many other stories by Hauff where even worse rascals than I play their part in the happy ending. But no hard feelings. I see that the others have already left. Goodbye, then!

ANNOUNCER: Goodbye, Dutch Michael. Nice people. But now I am thrilled to be once again alone in my office. Well, I wanted to do a Youth Hour. Was that a Youth Hour?

Gong.

"Das kalte Herz," GS, 7.1, 316–46. Translated by Diana K. Reese.

Broadcast on Southwest German Radio, Frankfurt, May 16, 1932, with music by Ernst Schoen. "'The Cold Heart: A Radio Play based on Hauff's Fairy Tale,' by Walter Benjamin and Ernst Schoen, with Music by Ernst Schoen," was announced in the Südwestdeutsche Rundfunk-Zeitung *for May 16, 1932, from 7:00–8:00 pm.*

Radio Talks, Plays, Dialogues, and Listening Models

The following texts, ordered chronologically according to date of broadcast (or, in the case of *Lichtenberg*, which was never broadcast, of commission and completion), are among the surviving manuscripts of Benjamin's radio works not produced specifically "for children."

The materials include a variety of programming-types: the radio lecture or talk ("Children's Literature," "Sketched in Mobile Dust," "E. T. A. Hoffmann and Oskar Panizza," "Carousel of Jobs"); the radio conversation or dialogue ("Prescriptions for Comedy Writers," with Wilhelm Speyer); the *Hörmodell* or listening model ("A Pay Raise?! Whatever Gave You That Idea!" with Wolf Zucker); and the radio play (*What the Germans Were Reading While Their Classical Authors Were Writing* and *Lichtenberg*).[1]

---

1 While we have included all of the extant texts of Benjamin's dialogues, listening models, and radio plays, we were unable to include all of the surviving materials from Benjamin's contributions to the first category, that of the radio lecture or talk. For additional titles, dates, and surviving materials related to the "literary radio talks," see GS, 7.2, 608–9. For additional texts that fall under the broad category of the talk or lecture, see the Appendix.

CHAPTER 32

Children's Literature

Dear invisible ones!

Surely you have often heard it said: "God! We didn't have it this good when I was young. We were still terrified about our grades then; we weren't yet allowed to walk barefoot on the beach." But have you ever heard someone say: God! We didn't play this nicely, either, when I was young. Or: When I was little there weren't such beautiful storybooks. No. Whatever one reads or plays during one's childhood is remembered not only as the most beautiful and the best, but often, and quite incorrectly, as unique. And it is completely commonplace to hear adults bemoan the vanishing of toys that they could actually buy in the nearest store. In thinking about *these* objects, everyone becomes a *laudator temporis acti*, a reactionary. That's why they must have a special significance. Although we won't speak about that for the moment, we do not want to forget during the following that children may find, as they do in all things, something very different in books than an adult does.

There is a great deal—to begin with the primer—that one could draw out of the relationship of the child to the alphabet. From the earliest stages, when every character in the alphabet is a yoke through which hand and tongue have to slip, humiliated, on through the later stages, when the child handles the sounds playfully and founds his first secret society deep in the thicket of the "Robber" and "Peas" languages.[1] Surely no story of seafarers or ghosts gets as deep under a growing boy's skin as the primer did when he was little. The first German primers still approached children with naïve pedagogical skill. These "little voice books" were set up

---

1 The "Robber" and "Peas" languages are something like pig Latin, additional syllables put into words to create a language that is impossible for the uninitiated, particularly adults, to decipher. [Trans.]

onomatopoetically. The "O" rings out from the mouth of a wagoner who is driving his horses in the picture, the "Sh" comes from a woman who is shooing hens on another page, the "R" is the growling of a dog, and the "S" is put into the hissing throat of a snake. But soon this auditory emphasis receded, and ever since the Counter-Reformation we have had primers in which the grandeur of the characters appear to the startled child's eye in clouds of flowery phrases and flourishes. That was followed by the compartments and boxes system of the eighteenth century, in which the little reading words were pressed into military cadres that stood joylessly close together, and the letters were the drill sergeants who, as capital letters, gave orders to their nouns. Some primers that date from this time have title pages that promise the abecedarian 248 illustrations. On closer inspection, the whole thing is eight pages long and the illustrations are placed one next to the other in tiny frames. Admittedly, no primer can be so eccentric that the child doesn't take from it what he or she needs in the end, as Jean Paul shows so beautifully in his description of the one by Schoolmaster Wuz: "Cheerfully and undisturbed, he copied the ABC in beautiful official handwriting. Between all the black letters, he stuck in red ones to grab everyone's attention; thus most children in Germany remember the pleasure with which they fished out the boiled red ones from the black ones and enjoyed them like cooked crabs."[2]

The schoolmasters, of course, quickly found out that not only does the child have the most difficulty with the primer, but, of all books, the primer has the most difficulty with the child. The most obvious thing to do was to emancipate the visualization as much as possible from the word, not to mention the letter. The first attempt along these lines was the *Orbis pictus* by Amos Comenius, printed in 1658.[3] It depicts the objects of daily life, as well as of supersensory life, in simple, crude representations shown on several hundred tables the size of map sheets. The text was limited to a German–Latin table of contents. This work was one of the great and rare successes in the realm of pedagogical

---

2 Jean Paul Richter's "Leben des vergnügten Schulmeisterlein Maria Wutz in Auenthal: Eine Art Idylle" [Life of the Cheerful Little Schoolmistress Maria Wutz in Auenthal: A Kind of Idyll] appeared in 1793. For the passage quoted by Benjamin above, see Jean Paul's *Leben Fibels, Werke*, vol. 6, ed. Norbert Miller (Munich: Hanser, 1975), 428. Benjamin appears to have quoted the slightly modified passage from Karl Hobrecker's *Alte vergessene Kinderbücher* [Old Forgotten Children's Books] (Berlin, 1824), 14.

3 Johann Amos Comenius, *Orbis Sensualium Pictus*, often referred to as the first picture book for children.

children's books, and if one really thinks about it, it appears to be the beginning of a very momentous development, which has, even today after two and a half centuries, still not come to a close. Yes—today less than ever. The extraordinary timeliness that all attempts to develop instruction based on visualization possess stems from the fact that a new, standardized, and wordless system of symbols seems to be arising in very different areas of life—in traffic, art, statistics. Here, a pedagogical problem touches upon a wide-sweeping cultural one, which could be expressed with the slogan: For the symbol, against the word! Perhaps there will soon be instructive picture books that introduce the child to the new language of symbols for traffic or even statistics.

As far as the old picture books are concerned, the milestones in their development are marked by Comenius's *Orbis pictus,* Basedow's *Elementary Work,* and finally Bertuch's *Picture Book for Children.*[4] This last is composed of twelve volumes, each with one hundred colored copperplates, and was published in Weimar between 1792 and 1847 under Bertuch's direction. Its careful execution exhibits the great dedication with which work for children was done at the time.[5] To infuse the instructive picture book with text—to structure the text in an elementary way without allowing it to become a primer—that is admittedly a difficult, almost insoluble task. It has rarely been achieved. Thus Wich's ingenious, instructive book *Hobby Horse and Doll,* published in Nördlingen in 1843, seems all the more remarkable. The following verse is taken from it:

> In front of the little city sits a little dwarf,
> Behind the little dwarf is a little mountain,
> Out of the little mountain flows a little brook,
> On the little brook swims a little roof,
> Under the little roof is a little room,
> In the little room sits a little boy,
> Behind the little boy stands a little bench,
> On the little bench rests a little cupboard

---

4 See Johann Bernard Basedow, *Elementarwerk,* illustrated by Daniel Chodowiecki (1774), and Friedrich Justin Bertuch, *Bilderbuch für Kinder,* 12 vols. (1792–1830).

5 For a similar comment on these texts by Comenius, Basedow, and Bertuch, see Benjamin's discussion of Hobrecker (above) in "Old Forgotten Children's Books," in SW, 1, 408 ("Alte vergessene Kinderbücher," GS, 3, 16).

> In the little cupboard is a little chest,
> In the little chest is a little nest,
> In front of the little nest sits a little cat,
> I want to remember that little place.[6]

If there is any field in the world where specialization must invariably fail, it is in the creation of works for children. And the beginning of the misery in children's literature can be described with one word: it happened at the moment when it fell into the hands of specialists. The misery of children's *literature* is admittedly not at all the misery of the children's *book*. Because it was great good fortune that for a long time pedagogues paid little attention to the illustrated part of the books, or at least could not grab a hold of it with their standards. And so something was preserved here that became increasingly rare in the literature: the pure seriousness of mastery and the dilettante's pure playful joy, both of which create for children *without knowing it*. Rochow's *Kinderfreund* [The Child's Friend] from 1772, the first reader, is also the beginning of actual "youth literature."[7] One has to distinguish between two epochs here: the moral, edifying epoch of the Enlightenment, which met the child head-on, and the sentimental epoch of the last century, which insinuated itself into him. The first was certainly not always as boring and the second not always as dishonest as today's parvenu pedagogics would like to believe, but both are characterized by an average of wretched mediocrity. A beautiful and above all linguistically highly unsuccessful example, on the watershed between these two genres, follows here:

> After she returned home, *Emma* got right back to work, because she had promised *Auguste* she would embroider the letters A. v. T. on six handkerchiefs ... *Auguste* and *Wilhelmine* sat down on either side of her; *Charlotte* and *Sophie*, who had brought their work with them, sat down, too. It was a pleasant sight to see the four young girls occupied so industriously, each eager to outdo the others.

---

6 Johann Paul Wich, "Wie das Kind ein Plätzlein sich merkt," *Steckenpferd und Puppe* (Nördlingen, 1843), 57. See also Benjamin's "A Glimpse into the World of Children's Books," SW, 1, 436 ("Aussicht ins Kinderbuch" [1926], GS, 4, 610) where Benjamin cites the same verse.

7 See Friedrich Eberhard von Rochow, *Der Kinderfreund. Ein Lesebuch zum Gebrauch in Landschulen* (Frankfurt, 1776); see also Rochow's *Versuch eines Schulbuches für Kinder der Landleute* (Berlin, 1772).

While they were working, *Auguste* wanted to use the time for additional instruction. So she asked *Emma*:

"What day is it today?"

"I think it is Tuesday."

"You are wrong, child! Yesterday was Sunday."

"Then today is Monday."

"Right, Monday. How many days are there in a week?"

"Seven."

"But how many in a month?—Do you know?"

"How many?—I seem to recall you told me numerous times already that in regard to the days the months are not all the same."

"I did tell you that. Four months have thirty days, seven thirty-one, and one alone has twenty-eight and sometimes twenty-nine."

"Thirty days. That's very long."

"Can you count that far?"

"No!"

"How many fingers do you have?"

"Ten."

"Count those fingers three times and then you will have thirty, the same amount as four months of the year have days."

"That is a saeculum."

"A saeculum?—Where did you pick that word up.—Do you know what a saeculum is?"

"No, I don't."

"And you use a word that you don't understand?—That smacks of showing off! You want to be thought smarter than you are. A saeculum consists of one hundred years, a year of twelve months, a month consists, as I've already told you, of sometimes thirty, sometimes thirty-one days, with the exception of one every year. A day consists of twenty-four hours. The hours are divided into minutes and these again into seconds. The number of the latter amount to sixty in an hour."

"It's true, isn't it? A second is something very negligible?"

"A second flies away like lightning, it's a blink of an eye."

"So a person's life consists of an endless number of seconds?"

"And still it races away very quickly. In its fleetingness, we should never forget the passage to another world, which is to say we should never forget to try to fulfill our duties to God, to our fellow human beings, and to ourselves so that when the Creator and Ruler of the Universe decides in his all-knowing wisdom to call us we will be deemed worthy to enter Heaven, where our reward is awaiting us if we have behaved devoutly and honestly on Earth."

"But what will happen to the little girls who behave badly?"

"They go to hell."

"Are they unhappy there?"

"Oh, certainly! They feel the agonies of remorse for their offenses for all eternity."

"For all eternity?—Oh, I will take great care never to behave badly."

Auguste saw that *Emma* could not understand this as clearly as she could, as she had read about it in her catechism and had it thoroughly explained to her. She would have acted more wisely if she had frightened her little pupil not with hell but with the cane or Knecht Ruprecht.[8]

There can hardly be anything more bizarre than this, but there is better. Despite Johanna Spyri's beautiful, justly famous *Stories for Children and Those Who Love Children*,[9] it is characteristic that the later direction of children's literature produced no masterwork. But we do possess a masterpiece from the moral-edifying literature that is also a masterpiece of the German language: Hebel's *The Treasure Chest*.[10] It is not, as we know, writing for young people in the strictest sense. After all, it emerged wholly from the philanthropic interest in the broad mass of readers, particularly rural readers.[11] If one is even permitted to attempt to describe this incomparable prose writer, in whom the wide range of the epic poet merged with the

---

8 See *Wie Auguste und Wilhelmine ihre Puppe erzogen: Von einer Kinderfreundin* (Berlin, 1837), 81–5; the passage was expanded by the editors of the GS based on Benjamin's notations.

In German folklore, Knecht Ruprecht is the companion of Saint Nikolaus, who children are told comes to the house on December 6 leaving sweets, nuts, and small gifts for good children. Knecht Ruprecht is Saint Nikolaus's alter-ego, usually depicted wearing dark fur or straw on a brown, hooded cloak and carrying a switch and a sack, sometimes filled with coal or ash, sometimes to pop an errant child into it. While Saint Nikolaus consults a book in which the good and bad deeds of a child are listed, Knecht Ruprecht waits to hear of bad deeds and draws closer to a child every time one is mentioned. Knecht Ruprecht still appears in processions, particularly in Southern Germany. In his *German Mythology*, Jacob Grimm associated Knecht Ruprecht with pre-Christian house spirits. [Trans.]

9 See Johanna Spyri, *Geschichten für Kinder und solche die Kinder liebhaben*, 16 vols. (Gotha: F. A. Perthes, 1879–1895).

10 Johann Peter Hebel, *Schatzkästlein des rheinischen Hausfreundes* (Tübingen: Cotta, 1811).

11 In the 1770s, German educational reformers began the "philanthropist" movement, which sought to replace rote, Latin-based education with a more practical, experience-based curriculum. In 1774, Johann Basedow, mentioned by Benjamin above, established the *Philanthropinum* school in Dessau, which became the model for similar educational institutions of the period.

conciseness of the lawmaker to form an almost unfathomable whole, then it is imperative to recognize how the Enlightenment's abstract morals are overcome with the political-theological in Hebel. Just as in Hebel, this never proceeds in any other manner than the casuistic, from one case to the next, so it is also hardly possible to present a concept of it in any way other than very concretely. In an image. When he tells his stories, it is as if a watchmaker were showing us a clockwork and explaining and elucidating each of the springs and little gears. Suddenly (his moral is always sudden) he turns it around, and we see how late it is. And in this, too, these stories are like a clock in that they awaken in us our earliest, childlike amazement and do not stop accompanying us all our lives.

A few years ago, as tends to happen from time to time, a literary magazine had the idea to ask a number of well-known people about their favorite childhood book. There were certainly some books written for children among the responses. But it was curious that the great majority named works such as *The Leatherstocking Tales, Gulliver, Treasure Island, The Adventures of Baron Münchausen*, the *1001 Nights*, Andersen, Grimm, Karl May, Wörishöffer; and some works that were long forgotten and whose author they could no longer name. If one tries to bring some order to the multifarious responses, then the following is revealed: almost never mentioned are books that were written for children or young people. Again and again it is the great works of world literature, books of colportage, fairy tales that are mentioned. Among those who responded to this survey is Charlie Chaplin, with *David Copperfield*.[12] And here is a great case from which we can study what a children's book can mean, that is to say, a book that a child resolves to read. *David Copperfield* prepared the space for this man's great intuition. A French critic drew a parallel, with great insight, between the art of Dickens and that of Chaplin. And Chaplin "himself has said how he first had the idea to set the character of the man with the bowler hat, the little, choppy steps, the small, closely cropped mustache, and the bamboo cane out into the world when he saw the lesser employees of the London Strand district." But how close the other characters in his films are to the dark London of Oliver Twist or David Copperfield: "the young, shy, winning girl, the burly lout, who is always just on the verge of

---

12 See "Der größte Eindruck meiner Kindheit," in *Die literarische Welt* (December 3, 1926), 2.

lashing out with his fists and who flees when he sees that one is not afraid of him, and the pretentious gentleman, recognizable by his top hat."[13]

However, one should not think that an adolescent can only receive substantial, hearty nourishment from the masterpieces of Cervantes or Dickens, Swift or Defoe. It can be found just as well in certain—admittedly not all—works of colportage or pulp fiction, which appeared simultaneously with the upswing in technical civilization and that leveling out of culture, which was not without a connection to it. The dismantling of the old, spherically tiered order of life had been completed by that time. In the process some of the finest, noblest substances often ended up at the bottom. Thus, the person who sees more deeply will find the elements he is searching for precisely in the depths of written and illustrated works instead of in the acknowledged cultural documents, where he has searched for them in vain. With thoughts such as these, Ernst Bloch attempted to rescue the panned Karl May in a beautiful essay written recently.[14] And one could name so many books here, books one borrowed from the school library on library day or even books one dared to ask for in a newspaper store with quiet shame: *The Regulators in Arkansas, Beneath the Equator, Nena Sahib.*[15] And if it was precisely these books that reached beyond the horizon of their young readers in some spots, then that only made them more impressive and full of life. For with their expressions and concepts they seemed to hold the talisman that would guide one over the threshold of youth into the promised land of manhood. And that is why they have been devoured ever since.

To devour books. A strange metaphor. It makes one think. Indeed, no other artistic form is carried away, broken apart, and destroyed as it is being enjoyed to the extent that narrative prose is. Perhaps one really can compare reading and consumption. When thinking about it, one must above all bear in mind that the reasons why we need to

---

13 See Philippe Soupault, "Charlie Chaplin," in *Europe*, vol. 18 (November 1938), 395; for this passage, see also Benjamin's 1929 review, "Rückblick auf Chaplin," GS, 2, 158–9 ("Chaplin in Retrospect," SW, 2, 223).

14 See Ernst Bloch, "Rettung Wagners durch Karl May" [Rescuing Wagner through Karl May] in *Anbruch* 11 (January 1929), 4–10, and Bloch, *Heritage of Our Times*, trans. Neville and Susan Plaice (Berkeley: University of California Press, 1991).

15 *Die Regulatoren in Arkansas* [The Regulators in Arkansas] (Leipzig: O. Wigand, 1846) and *Unter dem Äquator* [Beneath the Equator] (Leipzig, 1861) were both written by the German traveler and adventure novelist Friedrich Gerstäcker. *Nena Sahib oder Die Empörung in Indien: Historisch-politischer Roman aus der Gegenwart* [Nena Sahib or The Outrage in India: Historical-political Novel of the Present], 3 vols. (Berlin, 1858/59), was written by Sir John Retcliffe, pseudonym of Hermann Ottomar Friedrich Goedsche.

nourish ourselves and why we eat are not exactly identical. Thus, the older theory of nourishment is so instructive because it derives from eating. It says: we nourish ourselves through the incorporation of the spirits of things eaten. Now we don't nourish ourselves this way, but we eat for the sake of an incorporation that is more than a need for the bare necessities of life. And we read because of such an incorporation. Not to further our knowledge, the treasuries of our memory and our experience. Such psychological substitution theories are the theories of nourishment that assert that our blood comes from the blood that we consume, animal bones become our bones, and so on. It's not that simple. We read to augment not our experiences but ourselves. But it is especially and always children who read in this way: incorporating, not feeling their way in. Their reading has an intimate relationship, much less to their education and knowledge of the world, than to their growth and their power. That is why it is something as great as any genius that is contained in the books they resolve to read. And that is the special significance of the children's book.

"Kinderliteratur," GS, 7.1, 250–7. Translated by Lisa Harries Schumann.

Broadcast on Southwest German Radio, Frankfurt, August 15, 1929. The broadcast was announced in the Südwestdeutsche Rundfunk-Zeitung *for August 15, 1929, from 7:05–7:25 pm, as "'Children's Literature,' Talk by Dr. Walter Benjamin."*

CHAPTER 33

"Sketched in Mobile Dust"

A Novella[1]

There he sat. He always sat there in those days, but not like this. Normally he would sit with his gaze fixed on something afar, but today the motionless man just glanced idly around. And yet it appeared to be in vain; he was looking but he did not see. The mahogany cane with the silver grip lay not beside him, leaning on the edge of the bench as was usually the case; he was holding it, steering it. It glided over the sand; *O*, and I thought of fruit; *L*, I hesitated; *Y*, and I was embarrassed, as if I were caught spying. For I saw that he was writing the thing like someone who doesn't want to be read: each character looped into the next, as if each wanted to merge with the other; in almost the same spot followed *M P I A*, the first letter already beginning to vanish as the most recent ones emerged. I approached. Even that didn't make him look up—or shall I say wake?—so familiar to him was my presence. "Reckoning again, are you?" I asked, not letting on that I had seen. I knew that his musings were focused wholly on the imaginary expenses of distant journeys, to Samarkand, or to Iceland, voyages that he would never take. Has he ever left the country? Except for this secret journey, of course, the one he made to flee the memory of a wild and, as they always say, worthless and shameful young love: Olympia, whose name he had just now absentmindedly conjured before him.

"I'm thinking of my street. Or of you, rather; they're one and the same. The street where a word from you became so alive, like none

---

1 Benjamin borrows the title from Goethe's poem, "Nicht mehr auf Seidenblatt" [No longer on a leaf of silk], a verse posthumously added to the *West–östlicher Divan (West-Eastern Divan),* "Book of Suleika." Benjamin refers to this verse in "Goethe's Elective Affinities," where he calls it "perhaps the most powerful poem in the *Divan"* (SW, 1, 329; GS, 1.1, 167).

I had heard before or since. It's what you once told me in Travemünde: in the end, every adventure worth telling is wound around a woman, or at least a woman's name. For you said it provides the grip on the thread necessary for a story to be passed from one teller to the next. You were right, but when I ascended that hot street, I could not yet fathom how strange it was, and why, that for a few seconds my own steps in the deserted, reverberating alley seemed to me to be calling out as if with a voice. The houses around me had little in common with those for which this little southern Italian town was famous. Not old enough to be weathered and not new enough to be inviting, it was a gathering of whims from the limbo of architecture. Closed shutters underscored the obduracy of the gray facades and the glory of the South seemed to have withdrawn into the shadows, which became more frequent among the earthquake supports and arches of side streets. Every step I took carried me farther from everything for which I had come; pinacoteca and cathedral remained behind, and I would hardly have found the power to change direction, even if the sight of red wooden arms, candlesticks of a sort, had not instilled in me new material for reverie. It occurred to me only now that these grew in regular intervals from the walls on both sides of the street. Reverie, I say, precisely because I could not fathom, and did not even attempt to explain, how the remains of such archaic forms of lighting in the poor but nevertheless irrigated and electrified mountain village had managed to survive. So it seemed to me perfectly reasonable, a few steps farther, to come across shawls, curtains, scarves, and floor mats that people here seemed just to have washed. A few crumpled paper lanterns in front of the murky window panes completed the picture of pathetic and shabby house-keeping. I would have liked to ask one of the residents how I might get back to town by a different route. I had had enough of the street, not least because it was so devoid of people, which is why I had to abandon my purpose and, nearly humbled, almost tamed, walked back the way I had come. Determined to make up for lost time, and to atone for what seemed to me as a defeat, I forewent lunch and, even more bitterly, my noonday rest, and after a short climb up the steep stairs, I was standing on Cathedral Square.

"If before the oppressive dearth of people had seemed confining, now it was liberating solitude. My mood thus changed in an instant. Nothing would have pleased me less than to be spoken to, or even observed. All at once I was returned to the destiny of my voyage, my solitary adventure, and again the moment arrived as when, while riven with pain, it first came to me above Marina Grande, not far from Ravello. Again I was surrounded by mountains, but instead of the stony cliffs with which Ravello descends to the sea, it was the marble flanks of the cathedral, and over its snowy slope, countless stone saints seemed to be descending in pilgrimage to us humans. As I followed the procession with my gaze, a deep fissure became apparent in the building's foundation: a passageway had been excavated, which, after several sharp, even steps into the earth, led to a bronze door that was slightly ajar. I don't know why I crept through this secluded underground entrance; perhaps it was only the fear that often engulfs us when we ourselves enter a place we've heard described thousands of times before, a fear that had dictated my roundabout route. But if I had believed that I would be entering the darkness of a crypt, I was duly punished for my snobbery. Not only was this room the vestry, whitewashed and bathed in bright light from its upper windows, but it was also filled with a tourist group, before which the sexton was about to share, for the hundredth or thousandth time, one of those stories in which the words echo the ringing of the copper coins he raked in each of the hundred or thousand times he told it. There he stood, pompous and corpulent, beside the pedestal upon which the attention of his listeners was fixed. Attached to it with iron clamps was an early Gothic capital, by all appearances ancient yet extraordinarily well preserved. In his hands the speaker held a handkerchief. One would have thought that it was because of the heat; indeed, sweat was streaming from his forehead. But far from using it to dry himself, he only absentmindedly dabbed it on the stone block from time to time, like a maid who, trapped in an embarrassing conversation with her master, occasionally glides her duster over shelves and tables out of habit. My inclination toward self-torment, which anyone who travels alone has surely experienced, again gained the upper hand and I let his declarations rattle my ears.

"'Two years ago'—this was the content, if not the wording of his dragging speech—'we still had a man here among the townspeople who, through the most ridiculous fit of blasphemy and crazed love, made this town the topic of everyone's conversation for quite some time, only to try for the rest of his life to make amends for his false step, and even to atone for it, well after the offended party himself, God, had probably already forgiven him. He was a stonemason. After spending ten years as part of a team restoring the cathedral, through his abilities he rose to become head of the entire restoration. He was a man in the prime of his life, a domineering sort, with no family or attachments, when he fell into the web of the most beautiful and shameless cocotte ever seen in the demimonde of the neighboring seaside resort. She was taken with the gentle and stubborn nature of this man; no one suspected that her affection lay with someone else. Yet no one could have guessed at what price. And it would have never come to light, if the structural inspection team had not come from Rome for a closer look at the renowned renovation. Among the group was a young, impertinent yet knowledgeable archaeologist, who specialized in the study of Trecento capitals. He was in the process of improving his forthcoming, monumental publication by adding a treatise entitled "A Pulpit Capital in the Cathedral of V . . ." and had announced his visit to the director of the Opera del Duomo, who, more than ten years past his prime, was living in seclusion; his time to shine and be bold had come and gone.

"'What the young scholar took home from this meeting was anything but instruction in art history. It was a conspiracy, which did not remain private and ultimately resulted in the following being reported to the authorities: the love that the cocotte had yielded to her suitor had proved no obstacle to her, but rather an impetus to charge a satanic price for her affections. She wanted to see her nom de guerre—the kind of name that women of her trade have traditionally assumed—chiseled in stone in the cathedral, as close as possible to where the Blessed Sacrament is delivered. Her lover resisted, but his power had limits and one day, in the presence of the whore herself, he began work on this early Gothic capital, which he disguised as older and more weathered, and deliberately misrepresented until it landed as corpus delicti on the desk of the ecclesiastical judges. Several years passed until all the formalities had been acquitted and all the documents were in place, at which point it proved to be too late. A broken, feebleminded old man stood before his work; no one suspected foul play when his once-imposing head, with furrowed brow, craned over the chaos of arabesques and tried in vain to read the name he had hidden there countless years before.'

"I was surprised to notice that I—why I don't know—had been creeping closer; but before being near enough to touch the stone, I felt the hand of the sexton on my shoulder. Well-meaning but puzzled, he tried to ascertain the reason for my interest. In my insecurity and fatigue, I stammered the most senseless thing possible: 'Collector,' and promptly headed home.

"If sleep, as many maintain, is not only a physical need of the organism, but also a compulsion from the unconscious that acts on consciousness—causing it to leave the scene to make room for drives and images—then perhaps the weariness that overtook me had more to say than it normally would in a southern Italian mountain town at noon. Be that as it may, I dreamt, I know I dreamt the name. But not as it had stood before me yesterday, undiscovered in the stone; it had been abducted into a different realm—elevated, disenchanted, and elucidated all at once—and amid the intertwining grasses, foliage, and flowers, the letters, which in those days made my heart beat most painfully, swayed and quivered their way over to me. When I awoke it was after eight. It was time to eat dinner and broach the question of how the rest of the evening should be spent. My hours of napping forbade me from finishing the day early, and a lack of money and inclination prohibited me from seeking out adventures. After a few hundred indecisive steps, I came upon an open piazza, the Campo. It was getting dark. Children were still playing around the fountains. This piazza, forbidden to vehicles, was no longer a meeting place, only a marketplace; it had found its purpose as the great stone bathing area and playground for children. Which is why it was also a favorite location for carts selling sweets, peanuts, and melon, two or three of which were still gathered on the piazza and starting to light their torches. A blinking light escaped from the circle of idlers and children who had gathered around the one nearest me. Upon approach, I could make out brass instruments. I am an observant stroller. What will or what hidden wish had forbidden me to notice what could not have eluded the attention of even the most distracted? In this street, at whose entrance I now found myself again, without having expected it, something was afoot. The silk mats hanging from the windows were not drying laundry, after all, and how could I have thought that the old style of lighting would survive here and yet nowhere else in the country? The music got under way, penetrating into the street, which quickly filled with people. It now became apparent that wealth, where it brushes up against the poor, makes it even more difficult for them to enjoy what is theirs: the torches and candlelight clashed with the yellow circles of light cast by the arc lamps across the pavement and exterior walls of the houses. I was the last to join the throng. All these preparations had been made to receive the procession before a church. Paper lanterns and light bulbs stood intimately side by side, and the dense band of the faithful detached from the celebrating masses in their wake, disappearing through the curtain folds that shrouded the open portal.

"I had paused a distance from the heart of this red and green glow. The people now packing the streets were hardly a colorless mass. It was the clearly defined, closely related population of the local neighborhood; because it was a petit-bourgeois community, there was no one from the upper classes present, let alone any foreigners. As I stood by the wall, I should surely have been conspicuous due to my clothing and general appearance. But strangely, no one paid me any heed. Did no one notice me, or did the man who was lost within this scorching and singing street, the man I more and more became, appear to them as one of their own? This thought filled me with pride; I was overcome with delight. I didn't enter the church; content merely to enjoy the profane part of the festivities, I was heading back with the first satiated partici- pants, long before the overtired children would do the same, when I caught sight of some marble plaques, the kind with which the poor towns of this region put the rest of the world's street signs to shame. They were drenched in torchlight, appearing to be on fire themselves. However, crisp and glowing letters emanated from their centers, newly forming the name, which, mutating from stone into flowers, from flowers into fire, grabbed at me with increasing, all-consuming intensity. Firmly determined to get home, I set forth and was happy to find a little alley that promised to shorten my route considerably. Signs of life had already subsided. The main street, where my hotel was located and which was still so lively just a short while before, seemed not only quieter, but narrower as well. While I was still musing on the laws that dictate such couplings of phonetic and optical images, a distant and powerful music struck my ears. Upon hearing the first notes, suddenly I was struck: here it comes! That is why so few people, so few of the bourgeoisie, were in the street. This is the great evening concert of V . . . , for which the local residents gather every Saturday. All at once, a new expanded city, indeed a richer and more animated city history, stood before my eyes. I quickened my pace, turned a corner and stopped, para- lyzed with astonishment. Once again I stood in that street that had snatched me up as if with a lasso. It was already pitch dark, and the music band was offering its last forgotten melody to this tardy and solitary listener."

Here my friend broke off. His story seemed suddenly to desert him. His lips alone, which had just now spoken, offered a long smile in farewell. I looked reflectively upon the signs blurred in the dust at our feet. And the imperishable verse marched through the arch of this story as if through a gate.

"Dem Staub, dem beweglichen, eingezeichnet, Novelle," GS, 4.2, 780–7. Translated by Jonathan Lutes.

Broadcast on Southwest German Radio, Frankfurt, December 16, 1929. The broadcast was announced in the Südwestdeutsche Rundfunk-Zeitung *for December 16, 1929, from 6:35–7:00 pm.*

CHAPTER 34

E. T. A. Hoffmann and Oskar Panizza

I would be delighted if the series "Parallels," whose announcement you will have read and which I am hereby inaugurating, has aroused suspicion in a few of you.[1] It is precisely because of this suspicion, I would like to suppose, that I have a chance of being understood in my attempt to keep this endeavor free of misinterpretation. You all know of the suspect eagerness with which an earlier contemplation of literature often concealed its bafflement at certain works, its inability to penetrate their structure and their meaning, how it hid behind research into so-called influences, into parallels between subject matter or form. Nothing of the sort will be dealt with here. Yet a pointless hunt for analogies would be even worse. To point out some affinities between the creations of various writers, from various epochs, may at most satisfy a pedantic anxiety to improve one's mind, but it leads nowhere and would not be sufficiently accredited—even if in such instances now and then a younger, misjudged writer is rehabilitated by the name of a great and intellectually compatible predecessor. We do not wish to deny that such a rehabilitation of Oskar Panizza, as unknown as he is discredited, is a secondary aim of these observations. But here, at the beginning not only of these observations but of an entire series, we shall deal primarily with identifying its main intention, and to this end we must allow ourselves a little digression.

One likes to speak of the eternity of works of art; one strives to grant the greatest among them endurance and authority for centuries, without realizing how one thus runs the risk of letting them ossify into museum-like copies of themselves. Because, to say it in a word, the so-called eternity of works of art is by no means identical

---

1 For Wednesday, March 26, 1930, the *Südwestdeutsche Rundfunk-Zeitung* announced the opening of a series entitled "Parallels" with the listing, "Parallels I: E. Th. Hoffmann and Oskar Panizza. Lecture by Dr. Walter Benjamin."

to their vital endurance. And what reason there truthfully is for this endurance is most prominently to be seen in their confrontation with similar creations from our own epoch. Then it becomes clear that only certain unformed tendencies or vague dispositions can be called eternal, and that the work that has a fully-formed, vital endurance, is instead the product of that tenacious, sly force with which not only the eternal moments assert themselves into the current moments, but the current ones assert themselves in the eternal. Yes, the work of art is much less the product than the setting of such a movement. And while its so-called eternity is at best a rigid, exterior continuation, its endurance is a vital, interior process. That is why, as we look at these parallels, we are dealing not with analogies, nor dependencies of individual works on one another, nor studies of the writers, but rather with the primal tendencies of literature itself, and how they assert themselves from epoch to epoch in an inwardly transformed sense.

The fantastic tale, which we want to discuss today, is one of those primal tendencies. It is as old as the epic itself. It would be a mistake to think that the magical tales, the fables, the transformations, and ghostly deeds contained in humanity's oldest stories are nothing more than traces left by the oldest religious ideas. Certainly the *Odyssey* and the *Iliad* and the *1001 Nights* are material that was merely told; but it is equally true to say that the material of this *Iliad*, this *Odyssey*, this *1001 Nights* was only woven together in the telling. The tale took no more from humanity's oldest legends than it gave back. To tell a story using other words—with the fabulation and playfulness, the fantastical, all unfettered by responsibility—is, however, never merely invention but a transmitted, modifiable conservation within the medium of fantasy. This medium of fantasy is certainly of a very different concentration during, on the one hand, the first bloom of Homeric or of Oriental epic and, on the other, during the latest flowering of European Romanticism. But true storytelling always retained its conservative character, in the best sense of the word, and we cannot imagine any of the great storytellers as detached from humanity's oldest body of thought.

The reason for the seemingly arbitrary permeation of eternal and current moments in a story emerges perhaps all the more sharply the more fantastic it is. This is palpable in Hoffmann as well as in Panizza. Palpable, too, is the tension between the two writers, stretched over the arc between the beginning and the end of the Romantic intellectual movement in Germany during the past century. The inexpressibly convoluted fates in which E. T. A. Hoffmann mires his characters—Kreisler in *Tomcat Murr*, Anselmus from *The Golden Pot*, *Princess Brambilla*, much maligned in Germany, much loved in France, and finally *Master Flea*²—these fates are not only directed or influenced by supernatural powers, they have been created primarily in order to preserve the figures, arabesques, and ornaments in which the old spirits and natural demons seek to cast their endeavors in the bright daylight of the new century as inconspicuously as possible. Hoffmann believed in effective connections to the most distant, primal times, and as his favorite characters' figures of fate are basically musical, he particularly established this connection through the aural: the fine singing of the little snakes who appear to Anselmus, the heartbreaking songs of Antonie the daughter of Krespel, the legendary tones he thought he heard on the Courland Spit, the devil's voice on Ceylon, and the like. Music was to him the canon through which the spirit world manifested itself in daily life. At least insofar as we are dealing with the manifestations of benevolent spirits.

The greatest magic of the people Hoffmann described, however, rests precisely in the way that in even the most noble and exalted characters, with the exception of some of his girl figures, there is something satanic going on. This storyteller insists with a certain obstinacy that all the reputable archivists, medical officers, students, apple-wives, musicians, and upper-class daughters are much more than they appear to be, just as Hoffmann himself was more than just a pedantic and exacting court of appeals judge, which is how he made his living.³ Hoffmann's uncommon observational ability, coupled with his character's satanic elements, enabled something like a short circuit between moral judgment and physiognomic views to emerge. The ordinary person, who had always been the object of his entire hatred, seemed to him more and more to be, in his virtues as well as in his beauties, the product of a heinous artificial mechanism, whose innermost parts are ruled by Satan. He equates the satanic with the automatic, and this ingenious schema, which underlies his tales,

---

2   See Hoffmann, *Lebens-Ansichten des Katers Murr nebst fragmentarischer Biographie des Kapellmeisters Johannes Kreisler in zufälligen Makulaturblättern* [The Life and Opinions of Tomcat Murr] (Berlin: F. Dümmler, 1820–1822); *Der goldne Topf: Ein Märchen aus der neuen Zeit* [The Golden Pot: A Modern Fairy Tale] (Bamberg: Kunz, 1814); *Prinzessin Brambilla: Ein Capriccio nach Jakob Callot* [Princess Brambilla: A Capriccio after Jacques Caillot] (Breslau: Max, 1821); *Meister Floh: Ein Märchen in sieben Abentheuern zweier Freunde* [Master Flea: A Fairy-Tale in Seven Adventures of Two Friends] (Frankfurt: F. Wilmans, 1822).

3   For this description, see also "Demonic Berlin" (26).

allows him to claim life entirely for the pure and genuine side of the spirits so as to glorify it in figures such as Julia, Serpentina, and Antonie. With this moral conflict between life and appearance, Hoffmann has articulated, unless I am very much mistaken, the primal motif of the fantastic story. Whether we speak of Hoffmann, Poe, Kubin, or Panizza, to name only the greatest, the work is always based on the most definitive religious dualism; one might call it Manichean. And for Hoffmann this duality did not stop at what he considered most holy; it did not stop at music. Could one not produce the primal tones of which we spoke, this last and most certain message from the spirit world, by mechanical means? Were not the Aeolian harp and the clavichord successful first steps on this path? It was then that it became possible to ape our deepest, holiest yearning with mechanical art works; it was then that every love that spoke to us in tones from home became a phantom. These questions constantly move Hoffmann's writing. And we will find them again, unchanged, although in a thoroughly transformed, thoroughly alienating atmosphere, when we now turn to Panizza.

At the present time, Panizza's name and work are in exactly the same state as were Hoffmann's from the middle of the last century through the turn of this one. He is as unknown as he is discredited. But although the memory of Hoffmann, extinguished in Germany, had never ceased to be celebrated in France, it is not to be expected that similar amends will be made to Panizza. There are unimaginable obstacles in Germany today to compiling his writings with anything approaching completeness. Although a Panizza Society was established last year, it has not yet found the ways and means to reprint his most important works. There are many reasons for this, but perhaps the most important is that one of these writings would today be forfeited to the district attorney, just as it was thirty-five years ago. In fact, Panizza's brief fame can be tied to a few scandalous trials. In 1893, on the occasion of the fiftieth anniversary of Pope Leo XIII's appointment as a bishop, his *The Immaculate Conception of the Popes* appeared, with the apocryphal comment: "Translated from the Spanish by Oskar Panizza."[4] Two years later, it was followed by *The Love Council: A Heavenly Tragedy in Five Acts*, for the publication of which he spent a year in the

---

4 In 1893, Panizza published his controversial parody of the doctrine of Immaculate Conception, *Die unbefleckte Empfängnis der Päpste: Von Bruder Martin O.S.B; Aus dem Spanischen von Oskar Panizza* [The Immaculate Conception of the Popes: By Brother Martin O.S.B; Translated from the Spanish by Oskar Panizza] (Zurich: J. Schabelitz, 1893).

Amberg prison.[5] After serving his sentence, he left Germany, and when, forced by the confiscation of his property, he returned in 1901, he spent six weeks in investigative custody in a psychiatric clinic, after which he was declared certifiably insane and released. The cause of this last custody was *Parisjana, German Verses from Paris*, pervaded by fierce attacks against Emperor Wilhelm II.[6] Besides these reasons for the condemnation of his name and the disappearance of his writings, every feature of a certain characteristic, more closely examined, will add a few more. For this characteristic we can discard mental illness, to which one might be tempted to make a connection. There is no doubt of its reality: it was paranoia. If, however, the paranoid systems already exhibit theological tendencies, then one can say that this illness, insofar as it had any influence on his creative work other than to impede it, in no way contradicted the fundamental nature of the man. Panizza was—and here his radical attacks against the Church and the papacy cannot deceive us—a theologian. Admittedly, a theologian who stood in irreconcilable opposition to professional theologians, just as E. T. A. Hoffmann stood, as an artist, in opposition to the art-loving circles of Berlin society, upon which he heaped all his scorn and ire. Panizza was a theologian, and, from his own point of view, Otto Julius Bierbaum saw quite rightly when he wrote after the publication of *The Love Council*, which in its devastating sarcasm left all other anticlerical writings far behind, that the author had not seen far enough. "What is rebelling," says Bierbaum, "is actually the Lutheran in him, not the whole, free person."[7] And it certainly is also a paradox—although a paradox of righteousness—that one of Panizza's most loyal friends, the man who stayed close to him throughout his long illness and who saw to his estate, admittedly not without incident, was a Jesuit, the now eighty-six-year-old Deacon Lippert.[8]

So, Panizza was a theologian. But he was one in the same sense in that E. T. A. Hoffmann was a musician. Hoffmann understood music no less than Panizza did theology. But what remains from

---

5 See Panizza's *Das Liebeskonzil: eine Himmels-Tragödie in fünf Aufzügen* (Zurich: J. Schabelitz, 1895), for which he was charged and convicted of blasphemy.

6 Panizza, *Parisjana, deutsche Verse aus Paris* (Zurich: Zürcher Diskußionen, 1899).

7 Panizza, *Visonen der Dämmerung* [Visions of Gloaming] (Munich: G. Müller, 1914), xiii.

8 See the account of Panizza's life by Deacon Friedrich Lippert, *In memoriam Oskar Panizza* (Munich: Horst Stobbe, 1926).

him are not musical compositions, but the literary work in which he plays with music as the spirit home of mankind. And it is precisely this spirit home of mankind that is dogma for Panizza. The transformation from the beginning to the end of German Romanticism is reflected in this relationship. Panizza was no longer, as Hoffmann was, carried on that broad wave of enthusiasm for primal times, for poetry, folk traditions, and the Middle Ages; his intellectual affinities are with the European decadents. And among those, the closest to him was Huysmans, whose novels so unwaveringly play on medieval Catholicism and especially its complement, the black masses, the beings of witches and devils. But that is why it would be so wrong to imagine Panizza as an "artist," a man of *l'art pour l'art*, as Huysmans was. To first state the negative: there is no one who writes worse. His German is dissolute in a way that is unprecedented. When he begins some of his tales, almost all told in the first person, with a description of his state, how he marches along some icy rural road in Lower Franconia as a tired, ragged journeyman—everything that follows could truly be taken for the notes of a traveling journeyman, due to the sloppy language in which it is written. Admittedly, there is no contradiction here: despite everything, and at all costs, it must be taken for that of a great storyteller. The storyteller is less a writer than a weaver. Storytelling—and here we refer back to our opening remarks—is, in contrast to novel writing, for example, not a matter of education but of the folk. And Oskar Panizza's art is rooted in folk. One should read his genial *Church of Zinsblech* or *The Inn of the Trinity* to understand what a rooted-in-the-soil decadent is.[9]

Let us stay for a moment with this last novella—even if only to get to know one aspect of Panizza, who appears like a student, or perhaps one should say trustee, of E. T. A. Hoffmann in Christian dogma, through his cast of characters. The tired wanderer Panizza finally stops at an inn, slightly off the road and not marked on any map, where he soon abandons the attempt to explain the place's strange inhabitants. It is enough to mention here that an old, irascible Jew and his unworldly, hectic son, immersed in his theological studies, are housed there together with a Jewess, Maria, who is described as the boy's mother. The narrator partakes of a gloomy, silent evening meal among this disconcerting group, then goes to

---

9   See "Die Kirche von Zinsblech" [The Church of Zinsblech] and "Das Wirtshaus zur Dreifaltigkeit" [The Inn of the Trinity] in Panizza, *Visionen: Skizzen und Erzählungen* (Leipzig: W. Friedrich, 1893).

his room on the second floor and sneaks back down at night in order to peek into the forbidden chamber, which he had passed in the evening but was not allowed to enter. He opens the door, the moon fills it, and between the half-opened shutters he sees how a dove, fearfully beating its wings, is trying to escape into the open. And now comes the actual Hoffmannian inspiration in all of this. In a shed adjoining the house, a creature is kept, a person with horse's hooves, who continually bangs against his enclosure with an iron force, making the walls tremble, and now and again, at certain turns, as if on cue, bursts into repellent laughter.

Here is the dualist metaphysics that Panizza so completely shares with Hoffmann and that, following the inner necessity of which we have spoken, takes the form of a contrast between life and automaton. It has given him the story of the "People Factory," where people are manufactured with clothes already grown on.[10] It takes a still unmistakably theological turn in the following passage of *The Immaculate Conception of the Popes*: "The pope pulled . . . a glass-like, idiotic-looking doll out of the mouth of every person as soon as he died. The doll was transparent, and a balance sheet of all the deeds— both good and evil—of the person in question were contained in it. This doll, which was a small person, had two wings of starched fabric glued to its back and was let walk or fly. It was directed by that new realm created by the pope outside the world. There, the doll would be immediately received and laid in a big, shiny, clean brass scale, which had two equal scale pans. The doll's good deeds weighed heavily, the bad ones lightly. On the other scale pan sat an equal-sized normal doll, in whom good and bad deeds were exactly equally balanced. If the new arrival was only one grain lighter than the normal doll on the other side, it meant that the bad deeds outweighed the good." It was sent to hell. However, "The dolls who were heavy enough were mercifully allowed to climb down from the scale and run into heaven, coelum, about which more anon."[11]

This art would be an anachronism if, as many assumed, it only amounted to invectives against the papacy. But it is anachronistic in no different a sense than the Bavarian painters around Murnau and Kochelsee, who, up until a few years ago, painted their holy images on mirrors. A heretical painter of holy images: that is the shortest formula for Oskar Panizza. His image-fanaticism was not even

---

10 Panizza, "Menschenfabrik" [The People Factory], in *Dämmrungsstücke: Vier Erzählungen* (Leipzig: W. Friedrich, 1890).

11 Panizza, *Die unbefleckte Empfängnis der Päpste*, 7ff.

extinguished at the heights of theological speculation. And it was combined with a keen, satirical insight, just as Hoffmann practiced it on the holy canon of the philistines. Both heresies are related. In both of them, however, satire is only a reflex of poetic fantasy, which safeguards its ancient rights.

"E. T. A. Hoffmann und Oskar Panizza," GS, 2.2, 641–8. Translated by Lisa Harries Schumann.

Broadcast on Southwest German Radio, Frankfurt, on March 26, 1930. Benjamin dated the typescript "Frankfurt Radio, 26 March 1930," and for this date the Südwestdeutsche Rundfunk-Zeitung *listed, from 6:05–6:35 pm, "Parallels I: E.Th. Hoffmann and Oskar Panizza. Lecture by Dr. Walter Benjamin," as the first in a series called "Parallels."*

CHAPTER 35

Prescriptions for Comedy Writers

A Conversation between Wilhelm Speyer and Walter Benjamin[1]

BENJAMIN: Did you hear, Stefan Großmann is suing Fehling!

SPEYER: You could at least say "Good day."

BENJAMIN: Good day.

SPEYER: Good day. Now why is he suing?

BENJAMIN: You must know that Fehling staged Großmann's play *Apollo, Brunnenstraße* in Berlin.[2] If I'm not mistaken, you were even at the premiere. The long and short of it is, he's suing him because he feels artistically compromised by their collaboration.

SPEYER: I'm very sympathetic to Großmann's cause, suing his colleague. You see, we too have joined forces for some collaborative work. You, the critic, and I, the playwright. It was probably a mistake. Earlier on, at least, I was always of the opinion: massacre the critics. But now you've got me saying "good day" to you, shaking your hand, and allowing you to jam my signals with every one of your critical aperçus as I write.

BENJAMIN: I'm deeply saddened, dear Speyer, to see that you have

---

1 Wilhelm Speyer (1887–1952) was a writer, former classmate, and friend of Benjamin's with whom he collaborated on several projects. In addition to "Prescriptions for Comedy Writers," Benjamin consulted on Speyer's novel *Gaby, weshalb denn nicht?* [Gaby, Why Not?] (Berlin, 1930), and his plays *Jeder einmal in Berlin* [When in Berlin] (Berlin, 1930), *Es geht. Aber es ist auch danach* [It Works. And How!] (Munich, 1929), and *Der große Advokat* [The Great Advocate] (1932). According to a written agreement between them, Speyer promised to pay Benjamin "'10% (ten)' of the 'box-office takings' or max. RM. 5,000 (five thousand) as payment for his advice" (quoted in Momme Brodersen, *Walter Benjamin: A Biography*, trans. Malcolm R. Green and Ingrida Ligers, ed. Martina Derviş [London: Verso, 1996], 198, 298 n.84; on their collaborations and the remuneration Benjamin received, see also GS, 6, 794, and GS, 7.2, 609).

2 Stefan Großmann's play, *Apollo, Brunnenstraße*, written with Franz Hessel, debuted on January 9, 1930 at Berlin's Volksbühne, directed by Jürgen Fehling.

once again reverted to erroneous thinking. So we've met here today by coincidence, just like that? What's the matter all of a sudden?

SPEYER: I have a little problem, my dear critic. In the third act.

BENJAMIN: And in just such a situation you want to chase away so useful a demon as the critic? Did the critic not speculate with you in great detail about the world and people and especially about the state of social drama today, before one day deciding to put these musings to the test? Let me remind you that at that time we were in agreement on the main point: that the writer, especially the playwright, and particularly the author of social comedies, is currently in a very exposed position. Because what does today's society give him? Does it give him a firm measure of the important questions in life—that is, in terms of marriage or fortune or status—or a clear notion of state or civic virtue or the like? Not a chance! Sometimes society swears by the itinerant preacher, other times by the snob, and each week it's something new. So, that's what it gives the playwright: nothing. And what does it demand from the playwright? Everything! When society doesn't know where to turn, he is expected to furnish the answer. When standards are lacking, he is expected to provide them. When it is deluding itself, he is to point the way, and because he is a comedy writer, everything has to be enjoyable, delivered gently and cajolingly. In short, everything should serve to entertain.

SPEYER: I have the feeling that lurking in what you just said is a small attack on the writer. Of course, you are yet again of the opinion that the critic can intervene with a healing effect on the comedy writer's difficult situation ... Once again you fancy yourself the doctor of poetry, like most of your colleagues.

BENJAMIN: Doctor is a well-chosen word. For a doctor has other tasks besides curing an illness, namely, diagnosing it.

SPEYER: I would be grateful if you could provide a good diagnosis of the ailments currently besetting me, which cause me to be apprehensive and, thankfully, allow me to see the value in collaboration, which—if I may speak earnestly—I have often tried in the past. At the moment, perhaps the most appropriate thing is to abide by the words of Nietzsche: "Go not to the people, stay in the desert." In other words: a friend of mine has a cabin in the mountains of Upper Bavaria. I will go there to reflect on the problem in my third act.

BENJAMIN: As always, your escape plans will end, as far as I can tell, in a shared car ride, and I am hereby ready to take part.

SPEYER: I would like to remind you that your dramaturgical theories are the most expensive ones around. The last time you shared your constructive ideas about our social comedy, during a particularly riveting aperçu I drove straight into the guardrail on the road from St. Moritz to Tarasp. This aperçu cost my car insurance company three hundred marks.

BENJAMIN: Of course, you say nothing of what it earned you.

SPEYER: A play that lacks a final act, dear Dr. Benjamin, earns absolutely nothing. I have no intention of giving German literature a new Robert Guiscard. So let's try to cure the disease! Are you honestly of the opinion that I should not go to my cabin?

BENJAMIN: I'm happy to share my thoughts on your literary housing schemes. For one thing: enough of this going-it-alone business! For the writer of dramas of any kind, collaboration is practically the rule. If not in his study, then later in stage rehearsals.

SPEYER: But there is a fundamental difference between those two things.

BENJAMIN: I grant you. That's what I was getting at. But let's first agree on one thing: the drama is a collaboration to a much higher degree than any other literary work.

SPEYER: But is collaboration today anything like it was fifty years ago, with Sardou and Scribe?[3]

BENJAMIN: Not in the least. You have to adhere to the most modern tendencies of the theater, where the collective itself writes the plays.

SPEYER: This does seem to be your inclination.

BENJAMIN: Indeed! But I'm not interested in what has come from these experiments that, for the most part, remain wholly unsatisfactory. Here's what does interest me: how do such efforts come about? It's very simple: precisely because our concept of society is shattered and in flux, the theater, and the playwright, need correctives and control measures so as not to lose the ground under their feet. Fifty years ago it was very different; collaboration could be a mere act of improvisation, of whim, of mutual enjoyment. Hopefully this is also true for us from time to time. But behind it lies an imperative about which, I believe, we both are clear.

SPEYER: But in using such methods there's always the risk of the

---

3 Victorien Sardou (1831–1908), and Eugène Scribe (1791–1861), French dramatists best known for their pursuit of the "well-made play," a term associated with formulaic, commercially motivated theater.

central literary idea getting completely lost. Everything becomes just a montage.

BENJAMIN: But that's just it: the central idea should not be sheltered, so to speak, in a literary finishing school, protected from the harsh winds of reality. It should develop in this harsh reality amid the objections of the critic, the dramaturge, etc., etc.

SPEYER: I relinquish my literary solitude to you, because something has become very clear to me in the last few days: I need to be challenged by you, my dear Dr. Benjamin, to take a stand.

BENJAMIN: What do you mean, "take a stand"?

SPEYER: I'll explain in a moment, and in so doing, we will have arrived at the difficulties concerning my third act. Writing my last act is not so much a technical problem as a moral one.

BENJAMIN: You'll have to address this moral problem in dialogue on stage. As in life, a problem is best conceptualized through conversation, for which I stand at the ready.

SPEYER: Once again I've seen that nothing is easier than writing the opening acts. The hand just flies over the paper, as it's all about creating expectations. And creating expectations that you cannot later fulfill? That has a name: literary swindle. You know, the whole problem with drama comes down to an issue of credit. In the first two acts you can write out an almost unlimited number of promissory notes.

BENJAMIN: Until, in the third act, the audience comes to cash them in.

SPEYER: Mark Twain illustrated this very nicely. He began one of his stories with the most outrageous characters and events. At breakneck speed, twists are piled on twists, leaving the impression that the author cannot possibly extricate himself from his own ideas. The reader's heart races in anticipation of how all these tensions will be resolved, how this tangled web will ever be unraveled. But then, right in the thick of it, Mark Twain suddenly breaks off: "I've lost my way in this story of mine," and leaves the reader adrift with the characters.

BENJAMIN: Hmm. That's an example and at the same time no example at all. For the imbroglio in the last act is perhaps not so much about resolving the plot as, in doing so, showing the author's true colors. With a writer of tragedy, after a few scenes it will usually be clear what he thinks of his hero and the other characters. For the author of today's social comedies, it's an altogether different matter. He can, and perhaps must, maintain a certain air of neutrality. He should not throw himself at his heroes. He should let them quietly be. But at the end the audience will certainly demand that the man—that is, the author—make his own opinion known while refraining, as far as possible, from putting the words directly in the mouth of one of his characters.

SPEYER: This is precisely my difficulty. You get the picture. We have a man and two women, the famous triangle in the social comedy. This man marries the girl he loves. But he can't break away from his previous lover: whether due to sensual attachment, sympathy, or human solidarity. His wife accepts this lover as part and parcel of the marriage, as she believes that there can be no moral obstacle for three people if the people involved are of strictly noble convictions, and we are certainly dealing here with three fair and levelheaded people.

BENJAMIN: But that is precisely the crux of your social comedy, to see how far modern people get with their vaunted sporting fairness.

SPEYER: Of course. We have two ladies and one gentleman, in the best sense of these words. But it emerges: in such a situation ordinary people would say, "My dear man, you have just married; you must give up the lover from your bachelor years." But that's not brave enough or fair enough for our people. It turns out, of course, that marriage is not a sport and that fairness has no place in the human proto-relationship. In fact, instead of simplifying things, it complicates them to a degree that was previously unimaginable for our three people. As time goes on, one of the women obviously has to go. The casualty is of course the lover.

BENJAMIN: That would still be much too easy. Now, to show myself as a critic of a somewhat more pleasant nature, I would like to draw your attention to something beautiful and important in your play, something that is worth considering: you say that the man married the woman he loves. As is proper. But the reason he hangs onto the other woman, with whom he had been together for years, has absolutely nothing to do with devotion. He loves this other one too. Only he loves her with a vague and somewhat extravagant love that conforms to his concepts of chivalry and fairness. Our hero is actually a man living in two eras: sometimes as troubadour and knight, and other times as a citizen of today's Berlin.

SPEYER: Now we're left to come to the right decision for the last act: how to proceed with the third woman. There are many possible resolutions. Even Goethe once allowed himself to coolly juxtapose two final scenarios in examining a very similar subject, with his *Stella*.[4] In the first and lovelier version the hero pulls to his chest both his beloveds: his spouse and his mistress.

STELLA (*embracing him*): May I?—
CECELIA: Are you grateful that I kept you from fleeing?
STELLA (*embracing her*): Oh you!—
FERNANDO (*embracing both*): Mine! Mine!
STELLA (*seizing his hand, hanging on him*): I am yours!
CECELIA (*seizing his hand, embracing him*): We are yours!

In the second version, Fernando shoots himself and Stella takes poison.

BENJAMIN: And you've managed to squeeze as many as three different resolutions out of me:

The elegiac, in which Marie—our Stella is called Marie—departs, waving;

The cynical, as in "Let's try it all again and somehow it will work";

The heroic, as in the first Stella version.

SPEYER: You don't yet know my fourth, which I came up with last night. I'm a little anxious about what you'll say, because in this case I've disregarded our underlying plan. You were never in agreement that we should simply find a second man for our poor Marie to fall in love with.

BENJAMIN: That doesn't worry me too much. The underlying plan is there so that it can be breached at times.

SPEYER: But I didn't go about it so lightly. As a matter of fact, last night I made a peculiar discovery. I'd like to apply to poetry Bismarck's principle of occasional candor in diplomacy. You know of the immense impact Bismarck sometimes achieved in ruthlessly deploying Machiavellian plans when his interests required it. In my case, the spectators have gone into the intermission after

---

4 In the first version of Goethe's play *Stella* (1776), the play ends with the three protagonists vowing to live together under the motto, "One apartment, one bed, one grave." In the second version (1806), Fernando and his lover Stella commit suicide, he by pistol and she by poison, while the wife, Cecilia, lives on. For the quotation that follows, see Goethe, *Stella: Ein Schauspiel für Liebende in fünf Akten* [Stella: A Play for Lovers in Five Acts] (Berlin: August Mylius, 1776), 115.

the second act thinking: "How will the author get himself out of these difficulties?" So I will show them. I will transpose the difficulties, which plague me in my work, into my work itself.

BENJAMIN: So your heroes are to become drama writers of a sort?

SPEYER: That's right. I'm making them into colleagues, as I can't seem to manage with just you.

BENJAMIN: I will most likely find these colleagues more pleasant than my previous one.

SPEYER: I hope I have done all I could to make them pleasing to you. Here's my draft from last night:

Sitting together we have our two women, Luisa and Marie, along with their man, Golo, who is loved by them both, and finally the new man, the fourth, whom you will meet here for the first time, a man by the name of Walter. Marie says: . . .

[Here, the manuscript breaks off.][5]

BENJAMIN: So, you have made a moral decision, but I don't know whether you will be satisfied with my interpretation. Do you know why you were able to bring in a new man in the last act?

SPEYER: Hmm.

BENJAMIN: If it were an important character, this fourth one, it would be a flagrant technical violation to introduce him at the last minute. But do you want to hear what he actually is? He's nothing at all. He's the first available man. And perhaps that will be your moral position, that our friend Marie consoles herself with the first available man. That marriage today is frequently not all that important, at least relatively speaking; but that the things that tend to rattle, complicate, or call it into question are not more important than the marriage itself.

SPEYER: I have nothing against the interpretation, for it reflects the Berlin of a certain social class today. You know, it's not so easy for me to show how these three people of noble convictions carry their death sentence around in their pockets, the man in the pocket of his dinner jacket and the two women in their evening bags.

BENJAMIN: Or better yet: each the death sentence of the other.

SPEYER: It's not so easy to be in love with a certain social class, as I am, and to point the finger at it, saying: you are despicable, you

---

5 In place of the implied line by Marie, Benjamin's typescript provides a reference: "see pp. 68–69 of the manuscript . . . *Welt* [world]." The manuscript of Speyer's play containing this quotation was not available to the editors of the GS, who indicate that the published edition (Wilhelm Speyer, *Es geht. Aber es ist auch danach!* [Munich and Berlin: Drei Masken, 1929]) contains a significantly different version, in which the character of Walter does not appear.

are lost. And how difficult these occasional hints are in comedies when one tries to avoid the perils of becoming obtrusive.

BENJAMIN: But do you not experience the consolation, the great consolation of the comedy writer: that the audience takes its castigation as entertainment?

SPEYER: Of course! And the comedy of today, in contrast to the relentless and cruel comedies of Molière—think of *Georges Dandin*—is a mirror, but in a silver frame. No matter how much it reflects the misshapen and murky nature of today's society, it's still enclosed in a finely wrought metal, and he whose gaze falls upon it takes it not as a mirror, but as a painting.

BENJAMIN: Right you are. But it's a good thing no one heard us.

"Rezepte für Komödienschreiber, Gespräch zwischen Wilhelm Speyer und Walter Benjamin," GS, 7.2, 610–16. Translated by Jonathan Lutes.

Broadcast on Southwest German Radio, Frankfurt on May 9, 1930. The Südwestdeutsche Rundfunk-Zeitung *announced the broadcast for this date from 6:05–6:35 pm.*

CHAPTER 36

Carousel of Jobs

Put yourselves, ladies and gentlemen, in the position of a fourteen-year-old who has just left primary school and is now faced with choosing a job. Think about the largely vague, sketchy images of jobs that float in his mind, about how impossible it is to attain a more exact insight into them without paying for a costly experience, about the many considerations that must influence a well-deliberated decision and of which he can only act upon a few: the economic situation of each line of business, the demands on or dangers to one's health, the special nature of professional colleagues, the possibilities for advancement, etc. Does not the image of a carousel seem particularly apt—a carousel of jobs that whirls at such a speed past the candidate, who stands there ready to leap on, that it is impossible for him to study the individual spots that it offers? And, furthermore, you know how grave and oppressive all questions of career choice have recently become, because of unemployment in Europe. Where previously the question of aptitude—the expectation of producing one's top performance in this or that profession—could direct a young person, now what predominates is the task of snatching a spot where the risk of slipping back down— the danger of being driven out of the production process, never perhaps to gain access to it again—seems as low as possible. The simple slogan "The right man in the right place"[1]—still often heard these days—actually comes from a more idyllic era of professional life; in fact, it comes, at least in its official recognition, from the time of demobilization. At that point, it was about directing the fifteen- to seventeen-year-old apprentices who had earned eighty to ninety marks a week in the munitions factories toward a regular job. For this reason, the commissioner for demobilization promoted career

---

1 In English in the original. [Trans.]

counseling. But the slogan that circulated then has a very different meaning today. Today, the right place is the place where there's a chance of holding on.

In this sense, the position of the skilled worker has also changed. In very many cases, he can no longer count on keeping his job. But the prospects of quickly adapting to a new job are much greater for him than for an unskilled worker. We have just mentioned the term "career counseling." Qualified authorities, so I hear, have just informed you about this topic in numerous reports on Southwest German Radio. Many of you will have gained insight into the great system of tests and manifold methods of evaluation, into the powerful laboratory that has so rapidly generated a new science, the science of work, particularly in Germany. However, today we will scarcely touch upon the concept that will be most familiar to you: the concept of the performance test. Just as we will merely glance at career counseling. The science of work has two sides: on the one hand, it studies the individual, to determine for which job he is particularly suited; on the other, it approaches the job itself and enquires: What hidden, and therefore strongest, drives in a person are best suited to individual jobs? Above all: how does the job develop and change—not just the task itself, but the milieu in which it occurs, the transference of job habits to life at home, and the character of colleagues—and how does that all change and develop a person?

How does the job impact the individual, and through what? This is the question to which I would not only like to call your attention today, but for which I would also like to ask for your assistance. Hopefully, the following explanations will make the purpose of our request, which the radio station has asked me to direct to you, completely clear. The request: to send to the station communications of any kind in which you describe the influence of your own job on your mood, your views, your relationship to your colleagues, what strikes you when you think about the person you were when you took the job compared to the person you became in the job. It is possible that you would rather, or more easily, make these observations about colleagues than about yourself. Such communications are equally welcome. The material you provide will be reviewed in a second report, and presented along with the conclusions that can be drawn.[2]

---

2 About this request to the audience for their participation and input, Schiller-Lerg

How does the job impact the individual, and through what? You know, this question was effectively resolved at one time, centuries ago. It happened in the guilds; their members' entire lives, down to the most private matters, were consciously subordinated to the necessities and forms of the work process. Since the last remnants of the guild system disappeared in the nineteenth century, these questions, which are of such importance to the life of every individual, were disregarded for a long time. Lately that has changed, because of the decisive advances made in the science of work, newly subjecting the unilluminated, unscrutinized course of everyday work life to the control of human cultural will. There have been three advancements in the science of work: the first in sociology, in the form of research into the social structure of the professions; the second in psychology, in the form of research into the so-called work environment; and finally, the new American movement of behaviorism. This last, disconcerting concept demands explanation. "To behave"[3] means *sich verhalten*. The foremost proponent of this new science of *Sichverhalten*,[4] Watson—some of whose works have been translated and published by Deutscher Verlagsanstalt, Stuttgart—declares that people's habitual behavior is the foundation upon which all of anthropology rests.[5] It is clear why this approach places the science of work and jobs on a new, much broader basis. In what other environment are habits formed more easily, where else are they more ingrained, where do they include whole groups more intensely, than in the workplace? This behaviorism inherently contrasts with the psychology of the individual, which attempts to understand the behavior of the individual essentially through his nature. To the contrary, nature is important to behaviorism only in its malleability. Behaviorism is interested in the profoundly transformative, profoundly invasive effects of the work process on character.

We have just received a book that is a significant and gratifying indication that the science of business is recognized everywhere. It is *German Occupational Studies*, published by the Bibliographic

---

notes that no further information or related materials have been found (see *Walter Benjamin und der Rundfunk*, 333–4).

3 "To behave" is in English in the original. [Trans.]

4 *Sichverhalten*: Benjamin creates a compound word. [Trans.]

5 John Broadus Watson (1878–1958) was an American psychologist known for his contributions to behaviorism.

Institute in Leipzig.[6] You can get an idea of the scope of the work, on which a number of specialists collaborated, when you consider that it surveys all German jobs in their incalculable specializations. Its vibrancy can best be illustrated with an example. I will not pick one out at random. What the newest efforts in this field have in common is that they capture the attitude represented in each job in terms of gesture, affinity, and ability, independent of and detached from the material of work. Thus, in a way, they put the example to the test by describing personality types, for which certain jobs would have to be invented if they did not yet exist. Thus I present to you, from *German Occupational Studies,* the description of a cobbler who is actually a journalist type. The author of the following pages is Peter Suhrkamp.

The particular nature of the journalistic person can be discovered in places where this person can still live without contact with newspapers. One can still find such people today in villages where no newspapers are published. In my hometown there was *a shoemaker*; but the last thing one could ask from him was that he make shoes. He could not stay in his workshop. Instead, he was on the go and worked wherever an opportunity beckoned, whatever it might be. He cleaned and repaired clocks. And when one of the cattle or a child was sick on a farm, he turned up. If a threshing machine was out of order at a farm, there he was. You didn't go fetch him (because no one counted on him) but he was everywhere where anything happened, where "something was going on," as if he could sense it. He came as if by coincidence, stood around for a while and chatted, and then he got to work. And if help was needed with anything, there was nothing that he could not fix. Things he could have no knowledge of—the mowing machines, for example, were then completely new—he adjusted; after a short time looking at a machine, he would have a better understanding of it than the blacksmith. When I saw him for the last time, just before the war, an airplane flew over the village. He shook his head and said, "That thing is not right. Something's not right with the motor, anyone can see that." He tried to explain to me then that there are birds that can't fly, that fly wrong, sparrows, for example. In the village he was considered a drinker, although he was never drunk,

---

6 *Deutsche Berufskunde: Ein Querschnitt durch die Berufe und Arbeitskreise der Gegenwart* [German Occupational Studies: A Cross-Section of Contemporary Professions and Working Circles], eds. Ottoheinz von der Galblentz, Carl Mennicke (Leipzig: Bibliographisches Institut, 1930).

because one could meet him in any one of the village's three pubs; one could find him there late at night disputing with the teacher or with a traveler. I will never forget one rainy day when we waited together, pressed into a haystack, for the weather to clear up, and he developed for me, the young boy, his theory of starry space; it was as beautiful as a fairy tale.

It was said that he visited the pastor and argued with him. His reputation was not good. He had his celebratory days, certainly! If he was successful at doing something the experts had failed to do (and, by the way, he never accepted payment for his work, and so lived, as one can imagine, in poverty), then he made a celebration of it and as many people as possible had to participate; he sat in a circle then and told stories tirelessly. But in general he was not respected. He was described to us children as a wastrel. (Our parents were people with Bismarck's morals.) But when the cobbler came, people were friendly; they were afraid of him because of his witty, barbed remarks and because of the little ditties he made up about the villagers, which persisted among the people as if they were carved in stone. On the evening of an election day, he surprised the village with a caricature of Friedrich Naumann; it was stretched over a wooden box, and in the box a carbide lamp burned.[7] This poster was the first illuminated advertisement to appear in a village (it was not long after 1900).

This cobbler was the finest person and the cleverest mind in the village—although he would never be influential, as he could never fill a certain spot in the village—and he was the poorest and therefore weakest man in the village. But that was all due to himself. When he was alone, he did not live. Inside, in his workshop, he was full of agitation and quite incapable; one had to stay with him so that he would finish anything at all. Shoes! Were shoes anything worthy of work! And did objects even deserve the labor of making them! He had to be where things were happening, even if the events were negligible! He had to have faces and conversations around him! If he ever wrote anything down, then it was surely not a chronicle of the place but rather his views on machines and people, preferably observations about the great events of the time—which for the most part only penetrated the village as rumors—stories, anecdotes, and projects (such as how the meadows in the Hunte valley should be irrigated). He was a journalist without a newspaper. All that was missing were newspapers: and then this person would have begun to write and

---

7   Friedrich Naumann (1860–1919), German liberal politician.

become great. And all that was missing was a certain tendency toward the practical in order for the newspaper to have emerged.[8]

This description epitomizes the modern attempts to illustrate the attitude, the language of gestures, the lifestyle, the views of a professional class in depth, and not merely on the surface by describing the object; rather it is done, either, as with this cobbler-journalist, without connection to the actual object (in this case the newspaper), or—and this will be the rule here—by presenting a very precise examination of all the elements that make up daily professional life. In Suhrkamp's characterization of a journalist, one can observe exactly how he starts from an assumption at one point about the material of work—that is, the word—and at another point about the "feeling for work"—namely the will to get published—then again about the workplace—namely the editorial office or the hustle and bustle of an external news agency—or about the perception of one's standing in society—the journalist as the expression of public opinion. Again and again it all depends on describing the constitutive, formative, restructuring influence of these external circumstances on the existence of the members of a profession, and with such clarity that what we previously described as the paramount task of career counseling is achieved: for the biologically meaningful unity of the private person with the professional person to emerge in the member of or aspirant to a profession.

Now, one might think that it would be an easy matter to prove such things as they apply to members of the so-called intellectual professions; but that all these behaviorist attempts to describe habit, the everyday, as decisive not only for the job as means of life but also for the job as purpose of life must find their limits when applied to the common, as one says, the uncomplicated jobs. There is no better way to counter this opinion than to single out a job that is counted among the most primitive, not to say most brutal, which would seem at first glance unlikely to exert a formative or even positive influence on its practictioners. We are speaking of the job of slaughterer. Such an analysis, however, cannot be made in the abstract; in order for us to be truly introduced to the essence of such a job, a

---

8 Peter Suhrkamp, "Der Journalist," in *Deutsche Berufskunde*, 382–3. The passage was provided by the editors of the GS based on their reading of notes in Benjamin's typescript. For their comments on the challenges of editing this manuscript, and the appearance of this passage in particular, see GS, 2.3, 1457–8. Peter Suhrkamp would later found the publishing house Suhrkamp Verlag, which became the major publisher of Benjamin's works.

variety of circumstances must come together in a stroke of fortune. We have just such a fortunate case here.

I mentioned previously that the "Basic Principles of the Career Counselor" were written by Hellmuth Bogen, head of the Berlin Office for Professional Aptitude Tests, and I was able to discuss with him at some length the matters I am reporting to you today.[9] This highly unusual man was born into a poor background in Berlin, and as an eleven-year-old he was already earning pocket money behind his parents' backs by driving the animals intended for slaughter at the central abattoir. He naturally gained, therefore, detailed knowledge of the professional classes that earn their living there, especially cattle traders and slaughterers, and could later combine that with very unusual knowledge of the various professional atmospheres, social relations, class concepts, and so forth. Before I begin to tell you about this truly classic representation—because why should there only be classic representations of individual life stories, and not whole professional classes—before I begin to tell you about it, I would stress that such a diffusion of practical and theoretical experience, knowledge such as is evident here, is the alpha and omega of the science of work. Thus in Russia, for example, career counseling specialists must be active for a certain period of time each year in the practice of those jobs for which they head a department at the counseling office. Among the career counselors there are miners as well as mechanics, locomotive engineers, bakers, etc. The interest in this new science is especially lively in Russia. Gastajeff opened the first Institute for the science of work in 1919, and in 1933 the Sixth International Conference on Psychotechnics will take place in Moscow.[10]

---

9 Hellmuth Bogen was the author of numerous books on career counseling and psychology, including *Psychologische Grundlegung der praktischen Berufsberatung: ein Lehr- und Handbuch* [The Psychological Foundation of Practical Career Counseling: A Textbook/ Handbook] (Langensalza: J. Beltz, 1927). Bogen was head of vocational psychology at the regional employment office in Berlin. The title Benjamin gives, "Leitsätze des Berufsberaters," has not been found.

10 The Sixth International Conference on Psychotechnics took place in Barcelona in 1930. The Seventh International Conference would take place in Moscow in September 1931. "Psychotechnics," a term coined by the German psychologist William Stern, broadly designated a branch of applied psychology focused on creating a scientific study of labor management, i.e., the testing and reengineering of human labor to increase productivity, improve working conditions, overcome postwar labor shortages, optimize specialization, etc. The discipline spawned debates over the politics, ethics, and limits of such interventions and their relationship to capital and other interests. (For instance, at the Seventh Conference, the Soviet delegation attacked bourgeois industrial psychology.) Benjamin's reference to Gastajeff suggests Aleksei Gastev, director of Moscow's Central Institute of Labor, known for its dedication to Taylorism.

We do not want to lose sight of the following: that the short extract I will now convey to you from this masterly characterization of the slaughterer's job should be understood, not as a description of special dispositions or tendencies that the slaughterer carries with him from the outset, but as a formative power that is inherent in his job.

> The main feature of his being is the awareness of bodily power and vitality with which he overcomes the resistance to work in his job, and which also endow him with the necessary resistance to adverse temperatures, the influences of dampness, and the occasionally irregular shifts. From his contacts with animals, he accrues a quietness and certainty of movement; from the type of work operations, his movements gain their heavy stolidity, often amplified by corpulence. The cleanliness that is developed in respect to the work product is also pronounced in personal life. Although they very often have to engage in dirtying work, dirty slaughterers are rare. Slaughterhouse, apartment, clothing, all display the same character of cleanliness. The slaughterers are business people with an artisan's tendency to produce exceptional quality ... Advantageous financial rewards lend them a satisfaction with their lives that they are glad to share with others. All of this results in a sense of self that allows the slaughterer to observe his fellow man without envy, with respect, and, if he steps against him as an opponent, to quickly and roughly hold him at arm's length. Good-naturedness, joviality, and robustness are thus allied. Out of the entire situation and the awareness of the job's meaning, a healthy pride grows that finds it unnecessary to assert itself in any way on the outside.[11]

You all know of graphologists, palmists, phrenologists, and the like who claim to glean deep insights into people from particulars of physique, posture, etc. Regardless of how one mistrusts them, there remains much that is interesting and true in their observations. They assume that there is an indissoluble correlation between the inner and the outer. In their opinion, size, physique, and genetic material determine fate, just as fate, in their opinion, effects changes to the lines of the hand, the gaze, the facial features, etc. But what fate

---

11 See Fritz Giese, *Psychotechnik der Organisation in Fertigung: (Büro-)Verwaltung, Werbung. Handbuch der Arbeitswissenschaft* [Psychotechnics in the Organization of Manufacturing: (Office) Administration and Recruitment. Handbook of Occupational Science] (Halle: Carl Marhold, 1928), 92.

would more consistently call forth such effects, both inner and outer, than the job? And where would such determinations be easier to make than at the job, where thousands of people are subjected to the same fate day in and day out? The question—which we previously urged you to assist us with, and in closing will urge you again to assist by sending us communications—is not only a question of the science of work and jobs, it is a question of the knowledge of human nature and the gift of observation, and that can leave no one who has ever considered it uninterested. To prompt you—many more of you—to consider it was the purpose of these words.

"Karussell der Berufe," GS, 2.2, 667–76. Translated by Lisa Harries Schumann.

Broadcast on December 29, 1930, on Southwest German Radio, Frankfurt. The talk was broadcast from 6:05–6:30 pm. It was part of a series on the theme, "Young People in Crisis" [Jugend in Not] (see Schiller-Lerg, Walter Benjamin und der Rundfunk, 332–4).

CHAPTER 37

"A Pay Raise?! Whatever Gave You That Idea!"

By Walter Benjamin and Wolf Zucker[1]

THE SPEAKER: Ladies and gentlemen, we'd like to call your attention to one of your colleagues, Herr Max Frisch. If you work in an
office, a shop or a business, you're sure to know him. He's the one
who's invariably on top, always a big success. He knows just how
to assert himself and he gets exactly what he wants. We have
invited Herr Frisch here today to let us in on his secrets, to explain
to us just how he manages to remain on everyone's good side and
still make a living in times like these. How does he keep his cool?
What makes him so pleasant to work with? If you want to learn
how he does it, just listen up! Herr Frisch is one of you, he's someone who shares your hardships and your sorrows. Very often,
however, he knows how to deal with them better than you do.
Still, we would not have you think that Herr Frisch is just an
exception, a darling of fortune! Herr Frisch is not here to arouse
your envy; he's here to tell you how he manages to be so lucky.
THE SKEPTIC: Please forgive the interruption, but are you suggesting that a single, lousy individual has the power, all on his own, to
transform his life into a better one? Do you really believe that?
THE SPEAKER: Yes, nearly one hundred percent, absolutely.

---

1 Wolfgang M. Zucker (1905–?), Benjamin's collaborator on the *Hörmodelle*, or
listening models, was a critic who wrote for periodicals including *Die Weltbühne*, where he
reviewed Benjamin and Franz Hessel's translation of Proust (*Die Weltbühne* 14 [April 5,
1927], 556–8). After emigrating to the US, he became a professor of Philosophy at Upsala
College. He discusses his radio collaborations with Benjamin in Wolfgang M. Zucker, "So
entstanden die Hörmodelle" [Creating the Listening Models], *Die Zeit* 47 (Nov. 24, 1972).
According to Zucker's recollections, he and Benjamin wrote "five or six" listening models
together, the first of which was "A Pay Raise?!"

THE SKEPTIC: But what if he has no money? What if he's had to make do for years on a small salary that's never really enough? What then?

THE SPEAKER: Perhaps he should ask his boss for a pay raise?

THE SKEPTIC (*sarcastic laughter*): Well, I guess you aren't all that familiar with bosses. A pay raise in times like these? You must be joking!

THE SPEAKER: Certainly not. And Herr Frisch is here to show you how. He wants to tell you what to do from a practical standpoint.

THE SKEPTIC: Your Herr Frisch can tell us all he wants. I've been in the business world for years and I know what happens nowadays when a fellow wants a raise. He'll be glad if he keeps his old salary and doesn't get himself fired.

THE SPEAKER: Then he's not so clever, it would seem to me.

THE SKEPTIC: It doesn't matter how clever you are. Just come by my office sometime and I'll show you how things play out.

THE SPEAKER: Sounds good to me. Perhaps we'll even get to the real reason most people have no luck.

THE SKEPTIC: Allow me then. I introduce to you one Herr Zauderer.[2] Herr Zauderer is in exactly the situation we want to illustrate. For several years now he's had a salary of 250 marks. In order to get by, he has to earn at least fifty marks more. If he goes to his boss now, I bet he gets nothing.

THE SPEAKER: Sure, it's possible. Or maybe he has only himself to blame. Could it not be his own fault?

THE SKEPTIC: Fault? Nonsense. The boss won't budge. End of story.

THE SPEAKER: Let's have a listen. Maybe we'll uncover his mistake! *A faint knock.*

THE BOSS (*grumpy*): Come in! *More knocking.*

THE BOSS (*grumpy*): I said come in! How many more times do I have to shout?

ZAUDERER (*rushed and nervous*): Oh, excuse me, Director, Sir, I didn't mean to disturb you ... if you have a second ...

THE BOSS: It's good that you're here. I've been wanting to talk to you. I can't go on like this. My entire desk is covered with complaints, some from Leipzig, some from Erlangen, and these

2 We have chosen to leave "Zauderer," a common enough surname, untranslated. It could be rendered as something like Waverer or Procrastinator. Similarly, the name "Frisch" given to the smarter employee might be translated as Cool, Hip, or the more literal Fresh.

from Elburg. And even some from Magdeburg, our best customer. I can't go on like this. All day long, nothing but headaches and complaints. To one customer you send too much, to another you send too little, and Magdeburg gets invoiced for a shipment they paid for three months ago. So, what do you say to that, Zauderer?

ZAUDERER (*more and more confused*): Um, well, I don't know, I did see a few things in the mail a while back. But I couldn't explain what the problem is.

THE BOSS: I'm sorry, but that doesn't cut it. What good are you to me if things don't run smoothly?

ZAUDERER: Um, well, I don't know, Herr Director. The new bookkeeper makes one mistake after another. You know I sit here entire nights working on the receipts. You can't accuse me of not caring.

THE BOSS (*annoyed but not impatient*): My dear Herr Zauderer, let me tell you something. Have a seat. Look, I know you're a reasonable person, and I also know that you aren't cheating me. This is why I've kept you around so long at the firm. But do try to put yourself in my place for once: all day long, whenever the mail arrives, I get nothing but trouble. And what do you have to say for yourself? It's not your fault, the bookkeeper makes mistakes, you don't know what's going on. And I'm supposed to be satisfied with that? You tell me.

ZAUDERER: Okay, so I don't have an answer. But I'm doing my best to improve. A person can't ask for more!

THE BOSS: I'm not so sure about that. In any case, it's up to you. For all I care, you can come for two hours a day. But things have to work. You have to realize that!

ZAUDERER: Yes sir.—But,—but—(*He hesitates.*) I wanted to . . .

THE BOSS (*somewhat astounded*): Yes? You've something to add?

ZAUDERER: Not to that, Herr Director. But . . .

THE BOSS: Well, that's the most important thing to me. Nothing else matters.

ZAUDERER: I wanted . . . I wanted to ask for a raise!

THE BOSS: What?! After all that? Now I've heard it all. I've had to be on your case for weeks now, and you want a raise?

ZAUDERER: Yes, Herr Director. I really didn't want to bother you, sir, but I can't get by on my salary. I was just trying to ask for more money.

THE BOSS: It confounds me how you could have imagined any

such thing. A raise? Now? In these times? And you of all people! Incomprehensible!

ZAUDERER: Herr Director, I thought . . . well . . . I just wanted to ask whether, perhaps . . . but please try to understand that on this salary I can't make ends meet.

THE BOSS: My dear Herr Zauderer, let me tell you something: a pay raise is completely out of the question. First of all, now is simply not the time; secondly, I'm thoroughly unsatisfied with your performance of late; and thirdly, I should tell you that it is only out of special consideration for you that I have refrained from letting you go.

ZAUDERER (*slightly insulted*): Well, then I should probably move on. I had hoped that you, Herr Director, would understand me a bit better. If how hard I work is not good enough for you, I guess I'll just have to give up my post here at your company.

THE BOSS (*placatingly*): Don't talk nonsense, Zauderer. I told you I have nothing against you personally. But don't be foolish, why would you not want to stay here with me? You're certainly not going to find a job anywhere else these days.

ZAUDERER (*plaintively*): Yes, Herr Director, please forgive me, but since I've been here I've been treated unjustly. Herr Meier, who joined the firm at the same time I did, already earns seventy marks more.

THE BOSS: And so? Salary adjustments are my concern. My dear fellow, a word of advice. Do your job with Herr Meier's accuracy and reliability, and you won't feel like you are being treated unjustly.

ZAUDERER: Yes, but I do . . .

THE BOSS (*interrupting*): On that note, I think we can bring an end to this conversation. Good morning!

ZAUDERER (*deflated*): Good morning.

A door slams.

THE SKEPTIC (*sarcastic laughter*): Well, what did I tell you? That's the way it goes when you ask for a raise these days. Has this scene sufficiently convinced you, sir?

THE SPEAKER: No. We've just heard a textbook case of virtually all the mistakes an employee can make in a conversation with his boss.

THE SKEPTIC: What mistakes? The boss refused and that was the end of it.

THE SPEAKER: No. The conversation lasted four minutes. Do you know how many mistakes Herr Zauderer made? At least seven!

THE SKEPTIC: Such as?

THE SPEAKER: First off, the dumbest thing you can do is to ask for something when the boss already has reason to be miffed. Second, if you notice that the boss is in a bad mood, don't keep harping on the salary issue. Third, when speaking with the boss, you can't be perpetually shy, fearful, and submissive. Never be impolite or arrogant. One must maintain one's dignity. But stay on point and speak your mind. Fourth: Herr Zauderer responded to the criticism from his boss by passing the blame onto a colleague. This is unfair and makes a poor impression. Fifth: Herr Zauderer addresses the question of the pay raise in terms of his needs alone. The boss is interested in his business, not in the private life of his employees. Sixth: a very stupid maneuver: Herr Zauderer threatens to quit when he sees he's lost the cause. The boss knows, of course, that there is no chance Herr Zauderer can seriously consider walking away. It is most inept of Herr Zauderer to insist on playing the injured party. It never works. And finally, seventh: the word *unjust* is never appropriate. A boss does not let himself be told to which employee he will give more or less pay. That is his concern. It is inappropriate for Herr Zauderer to speak to him about other employees' salaries. So, that's what I would say about the scene you have just shown me.

THE SKEPTIC (*a bit unsettled*): Very well, I'm willing to admit that Herr Zauderer did not conduct himself with much finesse. But how could it be done any better?

THE SPEAKER: Perhaps Herr Frisch can show us. He is, after all, the man who accomplishes everything he sets out to do. He'll look for ways to avoid mistakes and maybe he'll even play a few aces, those special trump cards every employee holds in his deck. Let's visit him in his office. Could this be Herr Frisch? Good day, Herr Frisch.

FRISCH: Good day.

THE SPEAKER: Would you like to show us, Herr Frisch, how you would go about getting a raise?

FRISCH: I'll give it a shot. Whether it'll work out or not, who knows. But there's no harm in trying.

THE SKEPTIC: Now I'm curious. How much do you earn, Herr Frisch?

FRISCH: Three hundred and fifty marks, forty of which go to taxes and insurance.

THE SKEPTIC: And you think you can get even more? What do you do for a living?

FRISCH: Head of accounting at a wholesale knitwear company.

THE SKEPTIC: And what is the salary you want to make?

FRISCH: Four hundred and fifty marks, which would mean I'd net around 400.

THE SKEPTIC: So that's a thirty percent raise!

FRISCH: That's right. No harm in trying. Quiet now, I'm going in to see the boss.

A knock.

THE BOSS: Come in.

FRISCH: Good morning, Herr Director.

THE BOSS: Morning. What's the good word, my dear Frisch?

FRISCH: May I trouble you for a moment?

THE BOSS: What is it then, nothing unpleasant I hope? Have you uncovered more irregularities?

FRISCH: May I be seated? Thank you.—No, the new account entries have gone through without a hitch. Every order from the warehouse now gets its own entry and must be signed by the manager. No shipment is authorized unless I have a copy.

THE BOSS: So, you think this will prevent us from being cheated again?

FRISCH: Absolutely. The entire bookkeeping department would have to be made up of swindlers.

THE BOSS (*with satisfaction*): Well, we certainly don't need to worry about that, thank goodness.

FRISCH: Indeed we don't.

THE BOSS: But doesn't the new bookkeeping system entail increased delays? You know, it's even more important now that our deliveries move as fast as possible.

FRISCH: Quite the opposite, Herr Director. I've just spoken with shipping. It's now going faster than before. With my method, confirmations are no longer necessary.

THE BOSS: Let's hope so. In any case it was very sensible of you to take care of the shipping.

FRISCH: Yes, and I'll continue to.

THE BOSS: Excellent. Is that all that you wanted to tell me?

FRISCH: No, if you wouldn't mind, there's a personal matter I'd like to discuss.

THE BOSS: What? Does it have to be now? As you can see, my desk is covered with mail. I still haven't had a chance to open it.

FRISCH: I'm sorry about that. I won't keep you. Anyway, the men from the new factory in Zwickau are coming soon and there isn't time. We'll have to do some in-depth negotiating with them so I've left my evening free.

THE BOSS: Yes indeed, very important. I've got a lot riding on this deal. We must get it done.

FRISCH: You can count on me, Herr Director.

THE BOSS: Great, so what's on your mind?

FRISCH: Right. I'd like to ask for a raise.

THE BOSS: Well, excuse me, *now* you're bringing this up? How very curious.

FRISCH: I'm sorry to surprise you, but I think my work is worth more than you've been paying me.

THE BOSS: I don't get you. You know very well that we are constantly letting people go, that we employ twenty-five percent more personnel that we can actually afford, and now you're telling me you want a raise?

FRISCH: Herr Director, there's no reason we can't discuss this calmly. Let me tell you why I need more money, and why I believe the firm can pay it. If you disagree, I only ask that you try to explain your reasons.

THE BOSS: Reasons, oh, please. The money I pay my employees is my concern. You know I have a perfectly good sense of what my people want, so don't annoy me with that.

FRISCH: But why, Herr Director? You have always trusted me, and we did handle the last round of negotiations together. All I want is for you to allow *me* to trust *you* enough to talk about my concerns. Is that unreasonable?

THE BOSS: Alright then, fine, go ahead. I can hardly blame you. I too would like very much to make more money. Who wouldn't? Everyone does.

FRISCH: Yes sir, I couldn't agree more. For starters, I need to make more than I do now.

THE BOSS: How much do you make?

FRISCH: 350 pre-tax.

THE BOSS: Well, that's a big chunk of money!

FRISCH: I don't think it's enough for the head bookkeeper in a firm like ours to keep up appearances.

THE BOSS: Why? Who cares how you look?

FRISCH: Don't say that. If the people from Zwickau come today, they'll have a very good look at every one of us. They notice everything: this is an employee the firm respects, who earns enough not to worry about every single penny, who dresses well, eats enough—you understand what I mean.

THE BOSS: To hear you talk, one would think I ran a fashion house and you were my model.

FRISCH (*laughing*): Herr Director, you're not entirely wrong. All of your employees are models of a sort—models for the firm. It is based on them that people draw their conclusions about the productivity, reliability, and security of our whole operation. Believe me, every well-dressed, well-groomed employee is good promotion for the company at large. So then, about this raise you want to grant me, what do you say we put it on the books as a general advertising expense? Sound good?

THE BOSS: Hold on! Hold on! We're not there yet, my dear Frisch! What you're saying sounds well and good, but what am I supposed to do when our current business plan effectively allows no new costs whatsoever! As head bookkeeper, you of all people should know this.

FRISCH: Sure enough, Herr Director, I do know our present situation better than anyone, but I would like to draw your attention to something else. You know that last year we celebrated our fiftieth anniversary, and every one of us employees received, along with a special bonus, an anniversary publication written personally by you. I read through this booklet with much interest.

THE BOSS: What does that have to do with your raise?

FRISCH: Just a second, now. What you write there is very interesting: about how, in the chaos that ensued after the Founding Years,[3] your esteemed father had the pluck to build up his new business and to position it on a solid footing; about how he spared no sacrifice to produce only first-class goods; about how he spent great sums on new mechanical equipment because he trusted that the investment would pay off; about how he paid his employees more than the competition did because he wanted them to be committed to his firm. Is it not true, Herr Director? Do you see what I mean?

THE BOSS (*sympathetically*): Well now, you really studied that little booklet. But these are different times, my good fellow. Oh Lord, how simple things were back then!

FRISCH (*firmly*): Yes, perhaps these are different times, but our

---

3 The Founding Years refers to the period just after the unification of Germany in 1871, used here to refer to the economic boom period from 1871–1873, which was followed by a crash.

firm has, I think, remained very much the same. You have continued to operate in the same spirit as your dear father. And do you
not believe that in these difficult times it is all the more important
to enlist help that is totally reliable, people to whom you can
entrust the firm? I believe it's even more critical today than it was
back then.

THE BOSS (*somewhat moved*): Well, well, I suppose you're right, my
good fellow. So, now tell me: what is it you want exactly?

FRISCH (*after a brief pause*): Five hundred.

THE BOSS: I beg your pardon?

FRISCH (*decisively*): Five hundred marks.

THE BOSS: I keep hearing 500 marks.

FRISCH: Sure, that's what I *said* as well.

THE BOSS: Well, banish the thought, my dear friend. I'm no
millionaire, after all.

FRISCH: Hmm. I'm no millionaire either if I earn 500 marks. And
I believe, Herr Director, without wanting to sound presumptuous,
that my expertise saves your company more money in one week
than the extra pay I'm asking for each month.

THE BOSS: Oh no, I seriously doubt that.

FRISCH: Yes, really! If you calculate the losses due to theft, and so
forth, in the most recent closing, you'll see I'm right.

THE BOSS: I don't want to argue with you. But please, you must
consider our current circumstances. We're not going to make even
sixty percent of what we made last year.

FRISCH: Yes, yes, we must keep at it. We've got to make an effort,
and I for one shall do my part to get revenue back up again.

THE BOSS: That's what I would expect from you. So let's talk this
over sensibly. Are you satisfied with 400 marks?

FRISCH: No. That's only fifty more than I earned before. Please
don't be offended, Herr Director, but I was expecting more.

THE BOSS: Very well. I appreciate your value to the company. I
would not have you think me petty. Let's agree on 450.

FRISCH (*after a pause*): Alright then, considering our current
circumstances, 450 marks. I will do my utmost to ensure that the
next time I ask for a raise, you will no longer have this excuse as a
reason to object.

THE BOSS (*laughing*): That's just fine by me. If our revenue goes
up, you won't be the last to benefit.—But you know, you really are
quite an odd fellow. And come to think of it, sometimes it seems
to me that you're the boss and I'm the employee. It's very strange.

FRISCH (*earnestly*): Yes, of course! If I may, allow me to explain: at your firm, I don't feel like an employee who does his duty for eight hours and then goes home. If you'll forgive my saying so, sometimes I actually feel like I am the boss, at least as far the headaches are concerned.

THE BOSS: That truly gives me pleasure. As you well know, I only team up with independent, responsible people.

FRISCH (*with a touch of irony*): Well, perhaps this, too, will be reflected come payday.

THE BOSS (*laughing*): Are you on with that again? Enough is enough. I think you can be quite satisfied for today.

FRISCH: That I am—for today. And I thank you very much.

THE BOSS: Alright—but please get busy on this Zwickau matter right away.

FRISCH: Consider it done. Good morning.

THE BOSS: Good morning. (*To himself.*) Crafty fellow, that Frisch. *A door closes.*

THE SPEAKER: Now, there you are. Herr Frisch got exactly what he wanted. A pay raise of 100 marks. And did he not go about it most sensibly?

THE SKEPTIC: Hmm. I can't deny you that. Your Herr Frisch is indeed a master of subtlety.

THE SPEAKER: Quite so. And I dare say the boss had the same idea. He was thinking: if Frisch was so clever at roping me in, imagine what he could do when negotiating with our clients! I need a man like that. I can't let that kind of talent go.

THE SKEPTIC: Yep, I'll grant you that. Still, your Herr Frisch is just an isolated case.

THE SPEAKER: Of course he's an isolated case. Every person is an isolated case. Nevertheless, there will always be certain situations in which the same rules apply to everyone.

THE SKEPTIC: True. And your Herr Frisch was a smooth operator. He avoided precisely those mistakes Herr Zauderer made only a moment ago. But isn't there more to success than avoiding mistakes?

THE SPEAKER: Yes, you're absolutely right. I agree. Something else is necessary.

THE SKEPTIC: And what would that be?

THE SPEAKER: A fundamental attitude, a state of mind.

THE SKEPTIC: Meaning?

THE SPEAKER: Meaning an inner bearing, the basic values Herr

Frisch displays at work, with the boss, and in his entire life. He is clear, determined, and courageous. He knows what he wants and therefore he can remain both calm and polite at all times. He understands how to attune himself to his opponent's state of mind without sacrificing his dignity in the slightest.

THE SKEPTIC: Well then, how very fortunate for him. To be blessed with such a fine disposition is lucky indeed. But what if everything hadn't gone his way? If for some reason the boss had not been persuaded?

THE SPEAKER: Herr Frisch anticipates such an eventuality. Herr Frisch is always prepared. Even in failure, he is composed. He is not easily discouraged. Herr Frisch considers his struggles to be a kind of sport, and he approaches them as he would a game. He contends with life's difficulties in a relaxed and pleasant manner. He keeps a clear head even when things go wrong. And please believe me when I tell you: successful people are never sore losers; they're the ones who don't whine and give up after every failure. Indeed, they are the ones who keep their chins up, weather life's misfortunes, and live to fight another day. Who will be first to fail the test? The timid and the faint of heart. The whingers, the complainers. He who goes to the exam cool and calm is already halfway there. Such people are in great demand today. That is, I believe, the secret of success.

"'Gehaltserhöhung?! Wo denken Sie hin!'" GS, 4.2, 629–40. Translated by Jonathan Lutes.

*Listening model (*Hörmodell*) broadcast on Radio Berlin, February 8, 1931, under the title, "How Do I Deal with My Boss?" ("Wie nehme ich meinen Chef?"), and on Southwest German Radio, Frankfurt, on March 26, 1931 as "A Pay Raise?! Whatever Gave You That Idea!" ("Gehaltserhöhung?! Wo denken Sie hin!").*

As early as 1929, Benjamin had outlined a series of such listening models. See "Listening Models" (373). See also Benjamin's 1929 essay, "Conversation with Ernst Schoen," in which Benjamin discusses Schoen's plans for Radio Frankfurt to "develop a series of models and countermodels of techniques of negotiation—'How do I deal with my boss?' and the like."[4] According to his collaborator Wolf Zucker, Benjamin saw these

---

4 Benjamin, "Conversation with Ernst Schoen," trans. Thomas Y. Levin, in *The Work of*

listening models as a way to "use the new medium of radio to teach the listener certain practical techniques for typical conflict situations of modern life." The possible superficiality and problematic simplicity of giving such advice was, of course, hardly lost on Benjamin, who, Zucker writes, "warned [Zucker] not to think that his ideas had anything to do with real solutions to real problems. Rather, the listening models should be like the example of Emily Post [Freiherr von Knigge], instructions for dealing with people, i.e. instructions for the operation of a very complex system, whose internal structure the user does not in the least understand."[5]

The Berlin broadcast, directed by Edlef Koeppen, aired on the morning of Sunday, February 8, 1931, from 11:20–12 noon, as part of the station's experimental series "Studio." Directed by Ernst Schoen, the Frankfurt broadcast on March 26, 1931, aired during the evening, from 8:30–10:00 pm, and featured a discussion following the play. It was listed in the Südwestdeutsche Rundfunk-Zeitung *as: "Listening Model I: A Pay Raise?! Whatever Gave You That Idea! By Walter Benjamin and Wolf Zucker. Performance followed by discussion." The* Südwestdeutsche Rundfunk-Zeitung's *"Weekly Program" added that during the discussion, "Labor representatives will voice their opinions of the listening models. Coauthor Dr. Benjamin will also take part in the discussion."*[6]

Art in the Age of its Technological Reproducibility and Other Writings on Media (Cambridge, MA: Harvard University Press, 2008), 398.

5   Zucker, "So entstanden die Hörmodelle." Friedherr von Knigge was the author of *Über den Umgang mit Menschen* [On Human Relations] (1788), a practical guide to decorum.

6   Schiller-Lerg, *Walter Benjamin und der Rundfunk*, 196, 208–13.

CHAPTER 38

What the Germans Were Reading While Their Classical Authors Were Writing

Dramatis Personae

THE ANNOUNCER

THE VOICE OF THE ENLIGHTENMENT

THE VOICE OF ROMANTICISM

THE VOICE OF THE NINETEENTH CENTURY

THE PUBLISHER JOHANN FRIEDRICH UNGER

THE AUTHOR KARL PHILIPP MORITZ

THE ACTOR IFFLAND

FIRST MAN OF LETTERS (*identical with the Voice of the Enlightenment*)

SECOND MAN OF LETTERS (*identical with the Voice of Romanticism*)

PASTOR GRUNELIUS

BOOKSELLER HEINZMANN

WAITER, AUCTIONEER, CRIER, DIRECTOR, TWO ACTORS

Director's Address

Ladies and Gentlemen,

Ordinarily it is the task of the Announcer to make the kind of introductory remarks I will now deliver. You will soon recognize, however, that the Announcer is, on this occasion, entangled in such a peculiar form of conversation with spirits that we must release him from so profane a task as a mere announcement. You will also soon have detected from his conversation that perhaps he lacks the necessary calm and objectivity of an announcer. It is a somewhat irritable, agitated tone that you will notice in him. The Enlightenment, with whom he deals first, doesn't seem to sit well with him. Romanticism, who will interrupt him during his second outburst, has absolutely no credit with him, and the nineteenth century, whom he runs up against at the end, is forced to flee from his critical objections to the sheltering protection of Goethe.

Aside from this, you will not have to endure the society of this rather unpleasant person for too long. He will only appear at the thresholds of our play. That is to say: at the beginning, the end and the middle when, during his dispute with Romanticism, we make our way from a Berlin coffee house—into which we are first led—to the basement of the Leipzig bookseller, Breitkopf, where we listen to several people who have gathered for the book fair.[1] It will do no harm if, at the same time, you think of this trip between Berlin and Leipzig as a trip through a lustrum—a span of five years. In any case, we will remain in both locations in the decade between 1790 and 1800. Our guide will be the publisher, Johann Friedrich Unger, just as he played guide to no small number of writers at the time.[2] We find at his side two nameless, stereotypical figures, two men of letters, the first of whom has assumed the Voice of the Enlightenment, and the second that of Romanticism. Other historical figures besides Unger are the author Karl Philipp Moritz and the actor and playwright, Iffland, figures who have, after all, stood sufficiently in the shadows of greater men as to be included in this little literature play without any injury to their rank.[3] Finally, we will mention, from the first tableau, the Pastor Grunelius, whom we have invented, and from the second, the bookseller Heinzmann from Bern.[4]

THE VOICE OF THE ENLIGHTENMENT: You're taking too long, sir. Voices are not used to waiting in the lobby.

DIRECTOR: And I am not here for the purpose of talking with voices. That is the business of the Announcer.

THE ANNOUNCER: Of the Announcer. Just as you say. Who, in turn, is not used to inconveniencing himself with voices.

---

1 Benjamin refers here to the Leipzig publishing house of Breitkopf, renowned for music and scholarly works on music, founded in 1719 by Bernhard Christoph Breitkopf. The Leipzig Book Fair rose to prominence in the eighteenth century to become Germany's leading venue for the national and international book trade.

2 Johann Friedrich Unger (1753–1804), German printer, bookseller, and publisher of authors including Goethe, Schiller, and the Schlegel brothers.

3 Karl Philipp Moritz (1756–1793), German author of works including *Versuch einer kleinen praktischen Kinderlogik* [Logic for Children] (1786) and *Anton Reiser* (1785–1790); and August Wilhelm Iffland (1759–1814), German actor and dramatist.

4 Johann Georg Heinzmann (1757–1802), conservative Swiss bookseller, publisher, and author of *Appell an meine Nation: Über die Pest der deutschen Literatur* [Appeal to my Nation: Concerning the Pestilence of German Literature] (Bern, 1795).

THE VOICE OF THE ENLIGHTENMENT: The Enlightenment is not so touchy.

THE ANNOUNCER: Then may I be quite direct? I heard that you wished to set up your headquarters for today in a coffeehouse.

THE VOICE OF THE ENLIGHTENMENT: At Zimmermann's on Königstraße.

THE ANNOUNCER: Your enemies—and you are aware you still have some today—will assume that you also originated in a Berlin coffeehouse.

THE VOICE OF THE ENLIGHTENMENT: The enemies of Enlightenment must just be ill-informed. I originated in the Bastille, when it was stormed in '89.

THE ANNOUNCER: And what did you bring to the people?

THE VOICE OF THE ENLIGHTENMENT: Justice and a good bargain.

THE ANNOUNCER: A bargain? You must mean that figuratively.

THE VOICE OF THE ENLIGHTENMENT: What do you mean?

THE ANNOUNCER: That your friends' books are plenty expensive. Schiller's *History of the Thirty Years' War*, as I saw in one of Göschen's catalogs, costs eighteen marks. For *Benvenuto Cellini* they're asking twenty-four marks. And the 1790 edition of Goethe's complete works is listed at fifty-seven marks in the catalogs.[5]

THE VOICE OF THE ENLIGHTENMENT: I regret that. But it proves not only that reading classical writers was difficult to afford, but also how much people were prepared to sacrifice for it. A classical edition was an acquisition for a lifetime—indeed a bequest to son and grandson.

THE ANNOUNCER: They sat on the shelves, but were they read? At the end of his life, Goethe, who must have known, said: The larger public has as little judgment as taste. It shows the same interest in the common as in the sublime.[6]

THE VOICE OF THE ENLIGHTENMENT: I am not only concerned with the greater public nor only with taste, I am just as concerned with the people and basic knowledge. With the "Advice Manual

5   Friedrich Schiller, *Geschichte des Dreißigjährigen Krieges* (1791–1793); Goethe, *Leben des Benvenuto Cellini*, (1803). The Göschen publishing house was a leading Leipzig printer and publisher, led by Georg Joachim Göschen, known for having published the first collection of Goethe's writings.

6   See Johann Peter Eckermann, *Gespräch mit Eckermann in den letzten Jahren seines Lebens*, ed. H. H. Houben (Leipzig: Brockhaus, 1910), 683.

for Peasants," which, when it was published in 1788, sold 30,000 copies.[7] With Pestalozzi's chapbooks,[8] Eberhard von Rochow's works for children, in short, books for children and farmers.[9] I also wish to discuss *this* with my friends.

THE ANNOUNCER: So you're going to the smoking room to meet your friends.

THE VOICE OF THE ENLIGHTENMENT: As well as my opponents. There will be a pastor there who does not wish me well.

THE ANNOUNCER: But also your friends; and who might they be?

THE VOICE OF THE ENLIGHTENMENT: The Berlin bookseller, Johann Friedrich Unger, the publisher of *Wilhelm Meister* and of the new writings of Goethe, of *The Maid of Orleans* and Schlegel's *Alarcos*, not to forget the theology of Karl Philipp Moritz, whom I will also be meeting there.

THE ANNOUNCER: And in what guise, may I ask?

THE VOICE OF THE ENLIGHTENMENT: In one of a hundred. My voice is the voice of the great philosopher Immanuel Kant or of the scribbler Merckel, the voice of the Jewish doctor, Markus Herz, or that of the platitudinous and blustering Nicolai.[10] Soon you'll hear it afresh, for it is the voice of someone with a brand-new master's degree.

We hear the prelude to the hymn that follows.

THE VOICE OF THE ENLIGHTENMENT: Shhhh! Stop talking! Listen!

We hear a hymn (possibly in several voices):

> From Heaven above to earth I come,
> To bear good news to every home;
> Glad tidings of great joy I bring
> Whereof I now will say and sing.

---

7 Rudolf Zacharias Becker, *Noth- und Hülfsbüchlein für Bauersleute* (Gotha, 1788). Becker (1751–1822) was a proponent of the "popular Enlightenment" (*Volksaufklärung*), which advocated social stability through the extension of liberal Enlightenment ideals and benefits to the peasants and lower classes. His advice book was one of the great commercial successes of his time.

8 Johann Heinrich Pestalozzi (1746–1827), Swiss educational reformer.

9 Friedrich Eberhard von Rochow, author of *Der Kinderfreund* (Frankfurt, 1776).

10 Possibly Garlieb Helwig Merkel (1769–1850), Baltic German writer; Markus Herz (1747–1803), German Jewish physician, philosopher, student and correspondent of Kant, friend of Mendelssohn; and Friedrich Nicolai (1733–1811), polemical German writer, critic, bookseller, and publisher.

> To you, this night, is born a Child
> Of Mary, chosen mother mild;
> This tender Child of lowly birth,
> Shall be the joy of all your earth.
>
> 'Tis Christ our God, who far on high
> Had heard your sad and bitter cry;
> Himself will your salvation be,
> Himself from sin will make you free.
>
> He brings those blessings long ago
> Prepared by God for all below;
> That in His heavenly kingdom blest
> You may with us forever rest.
>
> Glory to God in highest Heaven,
> Who unto man His Son hath given,
> While angels sing, with pious mirth,
> A glad New Year to all the earth.[11]

PASTOR GRUNELIUS: Yes, my dears, these children need only be heard and they immediately impart the Christmas spirit even to so worldly a place as this, into which today—as an exception, as you well know—I have set foot . . . Well, you can hardly take your eyes off the window, Deputy Headmaster.[12]

FIRST MAN OF LETTERS (*in a low voice*): I think, Pastor, we'll leave him alone for now. I have the impression he wants to be alone . . . (*More loudly.*) Here, then, I can tell you. I know why the Deputy Headmaster remains standing by the window.

PASTOR GRUNELIUS: I don't understand your tone. What are you saying?

FIRST MAN OF LETTERS: That concerning these itinerant schoolboys' choirs there are differing opinions, as you surely know. I can only tell you that I recently saw an educational authority expressing his views concerning these poor

---

11 From the Christmas hymn for children by Martin Luther, "Vom Himmel hoch," translated by Catherine Winkworth, in *Lyra Germanica: Hymns for the Sundays and Chief Festivals of the Christian Year* (London: Longman, 1856), 12–14.

12 The "Deputy Headmaster" is Karl Philipp Moritz, who worked for a time as an educator and schoolmaster in Berlin.

schoolboys' choirs in Campe's *Braunschweig Journal*.[13] The man urges the abolition of these choirs, and I am convinced he is right. The paltry gains for such children from this free education hardly compensates, he contends, for the moral corruption and running wild that unavoidably results from being dragged to and fro around the courtyards and streets. The charities that have been created for this should simply, he proposes, be used to provide clothes and free education for poor boys. Moreover, there can be no thought of a proper education for poor schoolboys when they spend all the time they should be in school caterwauling in the street.

PASTOR GRUNELIUS: These are matters, venerable sir, concerning which we shall indeed not agree. Furthermore, I will tell you quite openly that it is not at all clear to me what this has to do with Herr Moritz.

FIRST MAN OF LETTERS: But surely you are acquainted with *Anton Reiser*?

PASTOR GRUNELIUS: Herr Moritz's novel? To be quite honest, no. It must be a very sad book.

FIRST MAN OF LETTERS: Sad, certainly. In that it relates the story of our beloved Moritz's childhood.

PASTOR GRUNELIUS: What, this Reiser is he? In that case, I can make sense of a few things.

FIRST MAN OF LETTERS: And, above all, you now understand why he is standing there like that. He was once one of these choirboys.[14] The last time we sat together in Kameke's garden, he described it to me for hours on end, how in snow and rain they waited, crammed close together on the street, until a messenger brought word that in some house or another singing was required. How they then all crowded into the room and, perched one on top of the other, sang an aria or motet and expressed their happiness when someone offered them a glass of wine or coffee and cake.

Din of falling chairs, disgruntled shouting:

I beg your pardon, but the impertinence, my good man!

---

13 Joachim Heinrich Campe (1746–1818) was a prominent pedagogue and one the editors of the *Braunschweig Journal*, which focused on issues related to education, individual and societal enlightenment, and reform. He was author of *Robinson der Jüngere* [Robinson the Younger, or the New Crusoe] (1779).

14 Moritz describes the experience of participating in a poor schoolboys' choir in *Anton Reiser*.

PASTOR GRUNELIUS: Distinguished Scholar, you don't seem very steady on your feet today.

FIRST MAN OF LETTERS: Maybe he's had one too many.

SECOND MAN OF LETTERS: Keep your insinuations to yourself, esteemed colleague. The ascent to our local river Spree Olympus is icy, as you no doubt have noticed.

MORITZ: If you mean by that that the steps to the Café Kranzler are a little slippery, then you're right. But your speech is sufficiently florid.

SECOND MAN OF LETTERS: My speech is nothing in comparison with the blooming flower I bear.

PASTOR GRUNELIUS (*in a low voice*): I can't find much on him that's blossoming besides his nose.

SECOND MAN OF LETTERS: So then guess, gentlemen, how many books I have with me.

FIRST MAN OF LETTERS: Your collected poems, I suspect—I have yet to see you without them.

PASTOR GRUNELIUS: That would not yet even make one.

SECOND MAN OF LETTERS: Thirty-eight books, venerable sirs.

PASTOR GRUNELIUS: You are not to be taken seriously.

SECOND MAN OF LETTERS: Wager? For a bottle of champagne?

FIRST MAN OF LETTERS: Stop talking nonsense.

SECOND MAN OF LETTERS: Then, please, see for yourself.

> *We hear a progressively louder "Ah, ah, ah" from all parties. The titles can be altered at will and should be divided among the various speakers in turn:*
>
> *Almanac of German Muses, Almanac for Noble Souls, Calendar of the Muses and the Graces, Genealogy of the Braunschweig-Lüneburg Electorate, Almanac for Health Fanatics, Church and Heresies Almanac, Handbook of Social Amusements, Almanac for Children and Youth, Almanac for the Promotion of Domestic Happiness.*

PASTOR GRUNELIUS: *Almanac for the Promotion of Domestic Happiness.* Yes, we were lacking that. Since nine tenths of all domestic distress derives from just this damned reading of Almanacs—by way of which every wench fancies herself a Chloe or even an Aspasia.

MORITZ: Yes, that is an accursed collection you have put together. And a poor schoolteacher such as myself wonders how he could rival so much erudition.—I reproach these calendars with their rhymes, anecdotes, songs, excursions, and dances, little essays and notices, geographical maps and small copperplate engravings and costumes for diverting even the educated public from serious works.

PASTOR GRUNELIUS: That's exactly it, Deputy Headmaster. Everything is fragment, shadow, and sampler. I can see the day coming when they will even trivialize the Holy Scriptures, and fill the Old Testament with cartoons of the Patriarchs.

MORITZ: We are caught in the middle. The better public are devoted to dalliances, amorous verses, maudlin novels; and the simpler folk—insofar as they read—are in the clutches of the colporteurs who bring robber and ghost stories directly to their house by the sheet. In this you have it better, Pastor: Heaven and Hell have something to say to every class of society.

PASTOR GRUNELIUS: If you think that my sermons are a match for those fashionable new tales of chivalry, then you are mistaken. One would have to be an Abraham a Santa Clara to hold people's attention.[15] And it just gets worse from one Mass to the next.

SECOND MAN OF LETTERS: One moment, gentlemen. That must be Unger there, sitting right behind you. He surely has the most recent catalog for the book fair, so we'll see right away.—One moment, please, my esteemed Unger.

UNGER: Oh, it's you, my dear man. To be honest, had I known, I would have had my coffee elsewhere. You are right to remind me. But ask all of my authors, ask Moritz, I can't print anything until I resolve the question of the new typeset with my colleague Didot in Paris.[16]

SECOND MAN OF LETTERS: But I beg of you, I will not press you. It's not at all about that. Set aside your *Berlin Monthly*[17] for a moment, reach in your pocket and pull out the new book fair catalog.—You see, my gentlemen, we've already got it.

PASTOR GRUNELIUS: Gentlemen, one moment's peace! Listen to this! You will blush for shame. Have you ever heard of the

---

15 Abraham a Santa Clara (1644–1709), ecclesiastical name of Johann Ulrich Megerle, Augustinian friar known for the popularity of his sermons.

16 François Ambroise Didot, along with his two sons Pierre and Firmin, led a French typography and printing company after whom the font is named. In addition to being a publisher, Unger was, along with the Didots, a typographer interested in the production of new, hybrid, and more modern typefaces. After publishing *Probe einer neuen Art deutscher Lettern, erfunden und in Stahl geschritten von JF Unger* (1793), on reforming the typeface Fraktur, he created the new typeface Unger-Fraktur.

17 The *Berlinische Monatsscrift* [Berlin Monthly], a journal known for featuring major debates of the German Enlightenment. It was published from 1783 to 1796 by Haude and Spener. Some editions of its first volume (January–June, 1783) list Unger as the publisher.

Widtmann Press in Prague? Neither have I. And wrongly so, gentlemen, wrongly so. To this publishing house we will soon owe the masterpiece of the following title: "The Little Jewish Grandmother, or, The Terrifying Specter of the Woman in the Black Robe."[18] But Mr. Widtmann has competition in Prague. What do you say to: "The Night Watchman, or, the Ghost Encampment at Saaz in Bohemia. A Horrifying Tale from the Age of Gruesome Sorcery."[19]—Or listen to this—no, you won't believe it possible, my esteemed Deputy Headmaster. Step over here and take a look: *Adelmar von Perlstein, the Knight of the Golden Key; or, The Twelve Sleeping Maidens, Protectors of the Enchanting Young Man. Knight's Tales and Ghost Stories from the Middle Ages as Companion to Knight Edulf von Quarzfeld.*[20]

FIRST MAN OF LETTERS: Clearly, Mr. Waldner, who wrote that, need not fear any competition from our good Mr. Vulpius.

SECOND MAN OF LETTERS: And what dross is he coming out with this time? He will certainly not fail to weigh in.

PASTOR GRUNELIUS: But, of course. Here it is: "Rinaldo Rinaldini, Robber Captain."[21] By the way, this Vulpius . . .

MORITZ: Just don't tell me that he is the future brother-in-law of Mr. von Goethe. First of all, we're not that far along. Second, I hold the composition of robber stories to be a thoroughly honest profession. Yes, Pastor, you will contradict me. But I must tell you, these are all completely harmless things in comparison to that worthless trash put out by this Mr. Spieß, for example, who decks his miserable products in all manner of prettifying or cloying trappings.[22]

UNGER: Yes, our Spieß is edifying: in him you lost a colleague,

---

18 *Das jüdische Großmütterchen oder Der schreckbare Geist der Frau im schwarzen Gewande* (Prague: Widtmann, 1798).

19 Franz Antonin Pabst, *Der Nachtwächter oder Das Nachtlager der Geister bei Saatz in Böheim: Eine fürchterliche Sage aus den Zeiten des grauen Zaubralters* (Prague, 1798).

20 *Adelmar von Perlstein, der Ritter vom geldenen Schlüssel oder Die zwölf schlafenden Jungfrauen, die Beschützerinnen des bezaubernden Jünglings: Ritter- und Geistergeschichte aus dem Mittelalter als Seitenstück zu Ritter Edulf von Quarzfeld.* For an illustration from this title, see Benjamin, "Dienstmädchenromane des Vorigen Jahrhunderts" and Figure 17, GS, 4.2, 620–2 ("Chambermaids' Romances of the Past Century," SW, 2, 226).

21 Christian August Vulpius, *Rinaldo Rinaldini der Räuberhauptmann* (Leipzig: Wienbrack, 1798). Vulpius's sister Christiane was married to Goethe.

22 Christian Heinrich Spieß (1755–1799), popular writer primarily known for his romances, ghost stories, and robber fiction.

Though Spieß is an historical figure, his name also connotes "one who is narrow-minded, pigheaded, petit-bourgeois," and this sense plays throughout the ensuing dialogue. [Trans.]

Pastor. Sometimes one would really sooner believe one was reading a high-minded book of meditations from 1650. But in the
end there's really only one of these tearful domestic stories behind
it all. I haven't actually read any of them. The title of his last was
enough for me . . . What was that thing called again?

SECOND MAN OF LETTERS: *The Injustice of Humankind*, if I'm not
mistaken. *The Injustice of Humankind or the Journey through Dens of
Woe and Chambers of Misery.*[23] In truth, a disgusting mess.

MORITZ: Allow me to return to this once more, gentlemen. What
strikes me as reprehensible is the hypocrisy with which such
scribblers, with their comfortable earnings, behave as though
their sole concern were the enlightenment of the human race,
civic-mindedness, and the promotion of propriety. Of course,
these things have already penetrated into the schools. Look here,
please! Less than three hours ago, during a Greek lesson, I caught
a rascal with this book under the bench.

UNGER: No, really, Deputy Headmaster, let me see! I've never read
a word of this Spieß.—*Biographies*—No, listen to this: *Biographies
of the Insane.*[24]

PASTOR GRUNELIUS: And what if I were to tell you that the man
has already completed four volumes, and I believe the thing has
not yet run its course.

UNGER: No, Pastor, give me that! In the debate between Mr. Moritz
and his student, I would at least like to be the *tertius gaudens* and
actually look at something the man wrote.

SECOND MAN OF LETTERS: Read aloud, Mr. Unger! Our society
is really far too refined. None of us has ever seen anything by
Spieß.

UNGER: As you wish, my gentlemen, as you wish. But I think we'll
limit ourselves to the Preface.

PASTOR GRUNELIUS: Let's say, a small section of it. That should
suffice.

UNGER: "Can I expect thanks," writes this Spieß:

> Can I expect thanks, if I warn those who stray away from the abyss; is
> it my duty to caution the parched wanderer against taking a precipi-
> tous draught from that cool well through which he will meet his

---

23 See Christian Heinrich Spieß, *Meine Reisen durch die Höhlen des Unglücks und
Gemächer des Jammers* (Frankfurt and Leipzig, 1797).
24 See Christian Heinrich Spieß, *Biographien der Wahnsinnigen* (Leipzig: Voss, 1795–
1796), 4 vols.

death? If so, then I have fulfilled it, and can ask you, dear Reader, to take the content of this little book to heart. Insanity is terrifying, but more terrifying still is how easily a man can fall prey to it. Overwrought, violent passion, deluded hope, lost perspective, and often merely fancied dangers can rob us of that precious gift of our Creator, our understanding—and what mortal can boast that he was never himself in a similar position, and, it follows, in the same danger? When I relate to you the biographies of these unfortunates, I wish not only to awaken your compassion, but also to offer you excellent proof that each was the author of his own misfortune, and that accordingly it remains in our power to avert similar misfortunes. Admittedly, I cannot hold out against the torrential current if I dare recklessly to venture into its depths, but he who convinces me of its depths through examples and warns me of the imminent danger before I have stepped from the bank deserves my thanks and praise. How richly, how sublimely, would I think myself rewarded were my stories to restrain the gullible maiden, the careless young man, from the execution of a bold plan that could someday rob them of their understanding.[25]

MORITZ: Indeed, perfidious enough. No wonder that made it into the best houses.

FIRST MAN OF LETTERS: Yes, Deputy Headmaster, there you have the greatest failing of our entire current educational system. We enlighten man as to his natural virtue and original disposition, and then come these enthusiasts, pietists, genius-worshippers, *Sturm und Drang*-ers, to make fog and renewed agitation out of everything again.

PASTOR GRUNELIUS: Look here, my dear man. That should give you cause to reflect. I mean, you and your colleagues should ask yourselves why your Apostle, Jean-Jacques Rousseau, the preacher of nature and virtue, was such an unnatural and unvirtuous man. In short: to a positive theologian, your entire Enlightenment can't seem much more than a man who needs a candle lit in front of his nose on a sunny day.

SECOND MAN OF LETTERS: No, Pastor, we don't wish to argue in this way. It is not the right tone. I believe the Deputy Headmaster would call something of that kind *argumentatio ad hominem*, which is unworthy of a citizen of the academy. Come at me with Rousseau in this way, and I could come at you with Lavater, who

---

25 See Spieß, Preface to *Biographien der Wahnsinnigen*, vol. 1, 3–4.

so well understood how to connect positive religion to a hodge-podge of mysticism, genius, and enthusiasm, that over time, as you know, all serious readers were frightened off.[26]

MORITZ: Worst of all, however, is that such people then believe they must follow a career educating children. I recently ran across the *Ethical Primer for Country Children*.[27] And I must confess that I believe—of course, one shouldn't say this—but I believe none-theless, I did it better in my *Logic for Children*.[28]

WAITER: If the honorable sir would forgive me a thousand times, but if the gentleman would step to one side, because I would like to light the lamps in the store window—and then, no offense, Mr. Businessman, but there is a gentleman here who has been waiting twenty minutes for the "News" to become available. And if you would be so charming as to trade it with him for the *Cotta'sche Zeitung*.[29]

UNGER: With *plaisir*, my friend, with *plaisir*.—I can only wonder, Deputy Headmaster, at how the classifieds are getting out of hand. Can you believe that a week ago I found a wedding announcement in the *Journal*?

MORITZ: I don't know if you read the *Leipziger Zeitung*, but I have heard they publish entire pages filled with nothing but classified ads. But in England that was already customary in the newspa-pers fifteen years ago.

FIRST MAN OF LETTERS: I believe, my good gentlemen, that everything that ties the newspapers more closely to civic life, to the everyday, is to our advantage. In my opinion, newspapers should not be written only for men of state and members of Parliament, nor just for professors and scribblers. Newspapers belong in the hands of everyone.

PASTOR GRUNELIUS: You would not wish in the end, esteemed sir, to see the newspapers in the hands of the uneducated public. You see, I don't want to say that I am *au courant* on everything these gentlemen are discussing, but you can trust me on one thing: as a pastor, I am better placed than anyone to survey the appalling

---

26 Johann Kaspar Lavater (1741–1801), Swiss poet, mystic, and prominent Counter-Enlightenment Protestant figure known for his interest in physiognomy and the occult.

27 Johann Kaspar Lavater, *Sittenbüchlein für Kinder des Landvolks* (Frankfurt: Kessler, 1789).

28 See Moritz, *Versuch einer Kleinen praktischen Kinderlogik* (Berlin: Mylius, 1786).

29 The *Allgemeine Zeitung*, a famous newspaper established by the eminent publishing house J. G. Cotta.

epidemic of reading to which our public has fallen prey—and the less educated they are, the more hopeless it is. People read today who would not even have thought about books twenty years ago. And in my youth, if the citizen or craftsman took up a book, then it was an honest, time-honored tome, a chronicle, an old herbal, a homily. But today? The bourgeois girl who belongs in the kitchen is reading her Schiller and Goethe in the hallway, and the uncouth country girl trades her spindle for Kotzebue's plays.[30] My dear brother, the High Court preacher Reinhard, is absolutely right when he says that domestic problems—concerning which one hears so many complaints—can be directly traced to this ghastly habit of reading.[31]

SECOND MAN OF LETTERS: This much is true—as I recently read at the German Museum—musketeers in the big cities are borrowing books from the lending library to take with them to the barracks.

UNGER: The lending library. Yes, there you have said it. They are the source of all our misery.

PASTOR GRUNELIUS: Forgive me, I don't mean to interrupt, but when you speak of musketeers, I can tell you which books they are bringing to the barracks. I had the opportunity recently to cast a glance into a consignment they sent to the Grand Consistory for appraisal. I will tell you the titles, my good gentlemen, nothing but the titles: *Augustea, or the Confessions of a Bride before Her Wedding*; *The Story of Justine, or So It Must Be to Remain a Virgin*; *The Peregrinations of Henriette*. And for something of this kind one indicates Istanbul or Avignon as the place of publication, to thumb one's nose at the censors.

FIRST MAN OF LETTERS: I certainly don't wish to take up the defense of such books, but shall I tell you whom we have to thank for them? Those selfsame censors, esteemed sirs, who provided us with their miserable edict of July 9, 1788.[32] It is the censor who robs the common man of respectable and beneficial writings, and turns his curiosity and desire to read toward the

---

30 August Friedrich von Kotzebue (1761–1819), German novelist and prolific playwright. His plays were once immensely popular.
31 Franz Volkmar Reinhard (1753–1812), preacher at Dresden, influential German Protestant theologian.
32 On July 9, 1788, King Frederick William II, under the influence of the recently appointed Minister of Ecclesiastical Affairs, Johann Wöllner, enacted the "Edict Concerning Religion." It was followed on December 19, 1788 by the "Edict of Censorship," which forbid the publication of books that were deemed to question religious orthodoxy.

most cunning imposters. You know as well as I that it was only because of the censor that our *Berlin Monthly* had to move to Jena. That they suppressed the publication of Kant's *Religion within the Boundaries of Mere Reason*,[33] that they have forbidden Mr. von Humboldt to print two absolutely innocent lines on a garter in celebration of the marriage of the duchess of Lottum,[34] that they . . .

UNGER: *Herr Magister*, you see how you are upsetting our good Pastor. Let us leave these trifles aside. Let us be happy that they have not forbidden us all writings on the circumstances in France, as they have in Austria; that we, in contrast to the Viennese, may still at least read Mendelssohn, Jacobi, Bürger, and Sterne, not to mention the *Iliad*.

MORITZ: You don't mean to say that the *Iliad* is forbidden in Austria!

UNGER: The *Iliad* has been forbidden in Austria, just as the *Aeneid* is still forbidden today in Bavaria.—But I did not wish to speak of that. Only of something about which no honest, thinking human being can remain silent, that is, the answer they gave to the petition presented by the Berlin book trade last year: "We will not hear any objections contending that the book trade would suffer. For evil must be controlled, even if it means the book trade goes under."[35]

MORITZ: What do you expect? The censors have to live too. I'm telling you, it's not an easy living. For one pamphlet the poor wretch only makes two cents. I've been told, though, that it's more for poetry. Presumably because rhymed wickedness is harder to detect.

UNGER: Listen, this is not the right approach. You were just speaking, in passing, of your *Logic for Children*. That is a book that accomplishes ten times more for education and Enlightenment

---

33 Kant published the first part of what would become *Religion Within the Boundaries of Mere Reason* [*Die Religion innerhalb der Grenzen der bloßen Vernunft*] in the *Berlinische Monatsschift* in April, 1792. Forbidden by the censors to publish its continuation, the magazine shifted publication to Jena.

34 See *Alexander von Humboldt: eine wissenschaftliche Biographie*, ed. Karl Bruhns, vol. 1 (Leipzig: F. A. Brockhaus, 1872), 74; *Life of Alexander Humboldt*, trans. Jane and Caroline Lassell (London: Longmans, Green and Co., 1873), 63.

35 See King Frederick William II to Cabinet Minister Count von Finckenstein on February 4, 1792, in Friedrich Kapp, ed., *Aktenstücke zur Geschichte der preußischen Censur- und Preßverhältnisse unter dem Minister Wöllner* (Part 1: 1788–1793). In *Archiv für Geschinchte des Buchhandels*, vol. 4 (Leipzig: Börsenvereins des Deutschen Buchhändler, 1879), 153.

than a hundred censors, be they the most excellent and best inten-
tioned, which I absolutely refuse to believe of them all. And if you
could write me a second volume, it would arrive just in time.
Quite aside from the fact that it would be the best way to introduce young readers to my new typeset.

FIRST MAN OF LETTERS: Finally, Deputy Headmaster! I have
always wanted to tell you that I study your book with my small
circle—all children from respectable families. And would you like
to know what I most esteem? The incomparable passage in which
you acquaint the children with the gods. I had them learn it by
heart:

The real world exists in the ideas of human beings, but the world
of ideas differs in that, beyond the ideas of human beings, it is
simply not there. All stories of witches and ghosts are fairy tales;
all of mythology and the doctrine of the gods likewise pertain to
this world of ideas, which, since the most ancient times, has populated the world with countless new beings, none of which exist
anywhere beyond the boundaries of human imagination. Including: Apollo, Mars, Minerva, Jupiter, and all the gods and goddesses
of Olympus.[36]

PASTOR GRUNELIUS (*clearing his throat*): I believe it's time for me
to go, my good gentlemen. At seven we have a meeting in the
consistory. My respects to all.
Murmurs of leave-taking.

FIRST MAN OF LETTERS: He won't have taken that the wrong way,
will he, old Grunelius?

UNGER: Whatever are you thinking? He's the most good-natured
man in the world.

SECOND MAN OF LETTERS: Beautiful and true, what you say here
to our little ones about Olympus. Yet there is also another way to
free children from superstition and whim, and I know of someone
who steers clear of the old gods and heroes even more unabash-
edly. It is Doctor Kortum from Mülheim.[37] And if it were up to
me, and I had a Prize for Enlightenment to award, he and no
other would have to have it.

FIRST MAN OF LETTERS: But you cannot possibly be serious. You

---

36 Moritz, *Kinderlogik*, 82.
37 Karl Arnold Kortum (1745–1825), German physician and writer, author of the
satirical epic *Die Jobsiade* (1784).

would present this *Jobsiade*, which is nothing but one long run of boorishness, as a model to the Enlighteners?

SECOND MAN OF LETTERS: Because it has what all of you lack, namely, humor. And in the long run, knowledge without humor leads back to obscurantism, dogmatism, and despotism. That's what is so good about this Kortum, that he also has no respect for the Enlightenment. He groups everything together, gods, heroes and professors, pastors and courtly ladies, lords of the manor and candidates. Just like his friend Death. You know, the one who closes the first book of the *Jobsiade*:

> Inasmuch as friend Death makes not the smallest
> Distinction between the lowest and tallest,
> But cuts down all both low and high,
> With the strictest impartiality.

> And, as he ever slyly watches,
> The cavalier and the clown he catches,
> The beggar and also the great Sultán,
> The tailor and also the Tartar Khan.

> And with his scythe his rounds he goeth
> And honorables and lackeys moweth,
> The herdsmaid and the titled dame,
> Without distinction of place or name.

> He listens to no compromises;
> Both crowns and bag-wigs he despises,
> Doctor's hats and the stag's horns
> And whatever else men's heads adorns.

> A thousand things he has command of,
> By which he us can make an end of,
> And now the dagger, and now the pest,
> And now a grape-stone, gives us rest.

> Now a law-suit and now a splinter,
> Now a bad woman and now a bad winter
> Now a noose or other snare,
> Of which may Heaven help us beware.

> Misshapen Esop his fables tellin',
> And the Grecian beauty, world-famed Helen,
> Unhappy Job and King Solomon,
> Gave up the ghost and now are gone.
>
> Not one of them found time for fleein',
> Not Nostradamus nor Superintendent Ziehen:
> With doctor Faust, dreamer Swedenborg, too,
> He made a clean sweep and went through.
>
> Orpheus, the great musician,
> Molière, the comedian of the Parisian nation,
> And the famous painter Apellés,
> Friend Death has swept away all these.
>
> Summa Summarum, the long and the short is,
> That in none of the chronicles do we find notice,
> That friend Death has ever any one passed
> Without coming back for him at last.
>
> And what he has not eaten already
> He will not fail to remember when he's ready:
> Alas! dear reader, also thee,
> And what is worst of all, even me![38]

Well, what do you think of that?

MORITZ: Maybe it's a bit quirky, but I am strangely moved to see how at the end the man turns back to himself, is at home with himself. That has always been my greatest desire. I know, gentlemen, you cannot understand. But I would like to recount a little memory from my childhood that sometimes haunts me when skies are gray. I was ten years old at the time. When the skies would darken and the horizon would narrow, I felt a kind of dread, as though the whole world was also enclosed under just such a roof as that of the room in which I lived. And when I followed my thoughts out beyond this vaulted ceiling, this world itself seemed too small, and it struck me that it too must be enclosed in another, and so on.[39]

---

38 Translation from Kortum, *The Jobsiade: A Grotesco-Comico-Heroic Poem*, trans. Charles T. Brooks (Philadelphia: Frederick Leypoldt, 1863), 176–80. Benjamin has skipped several verses from the poem.

39 See Moritz, *Anton Reiser*, ed. Ludwig Geiger (Heilbronn: Henninger, 1886), 31–2.

UNGER: I believe I understand very well what you wish to say. What good is even the most beautiful Enlightenment, if it makes human beings feel uneasy and disquieted, rather than at home with themselves?

SECOND MAN OF LETTERS: Kortum has also dealt successfully with this. He wrote treatises for the farmers of Hanover on beekeeping or the virtues of the new Lutheran hymnal, or how to treat infectious diseases.[40]

MORITZ: That is the right approach, and so it should be. For in the entire compass of a kingdom one can only ever really live in just one city and in that whole city, in one house, and in that entire house, just one room. But man is as deceived by place as by time. He believes he is living years, and only lives moments. He thinks he inhabits a country, a city, but he only inhabits that one spot where he stands or lies, the room where he works, the chamber where he sleeps.[41]

The sound of a gong.

THE ANNOUNCER: "Where he sleeps."—I, the Announcer, will take up this sentence. And with it send this small society you have just been hearing to their rest. And now, I have a few things to say about Germany, where I collected these voices for you. For whatever Deputy Headmaster Moritz might say about the Gray Cloister School, these voices are not just from Berlin but also from Germany.[42] But they didn't know it, because Germany slept, and the lower the class of the inhabitant, the deeper the sleep. Germans still existed almost completely under the sign of manufacture, cottage industry, and agriculture: everything or almost everything they needed was produced locally. This gave rise to narrowness of horizon, psychological insularity, and intellectual inertia, but also to a warm intimacy and noble self-sufficiency. Three-quarters of the population lived in the country; most cities were not much more than large villages, rural cities, and big cities like Paris, London, or Rome didn't yet exist. Further, there were no machines or only machines similar to tools, and that meant no

---

40   See *Die Schriften von Karl Arnold Kortum: Bienenkalender* (Wesel, 1776); *Grundsätze der Bienenzucht, besonders für die Westphälischen Gegenden* (Wesel, 1776); *Über das alte und neue Gesangbuch und die Einführung des letzteren in die lutherischen Gemeinden der Grafschaft Mark* (Mark, 1785); *Anweisung, wie man sich vor allen ansteckenden Krankheiten verwahren könne* (Wesel, 1779).

41   See Moritz, *Kinderlogik*, 154.

42   The Gray Cloister School was the oldest gymnasium in Berlin. Moritz became its Deputy Headmaster in 1780.

exact, abundant, and inexpensive production of commodities and no light, fast, and extensive transportation. The unreliability of transport, international commerce, and political circumstances were offset by the great reliability of small proprietors and local commerce, based on the uniformity of the area of distribution, the lack of competition, and the uniformity of the means of production and consumer base. The human being of that time was asked to spend his whole life wool-gathering and fantasizing, just as today he is prevented from doing so. From these conditions arose the Classical Era of German literature. While others sweated and hustled—England panting after bags of gold and sacks of pepper, America on the verge of transforming itself into the desolate mega-trust it is today, France laying the political groundwork for the triumph of the bourgeoisie on the European continent—Germany slept an honest, healthy, refreshing sleep.

The following Voice of Romanticism should be spoken by the actor playing the Second Man of Letters.

THE VOICE OF ROMANTICISM: But what dreams it had in this sleep!

THE ANNOUNCER (*after a pause*): This voice is familiar to me.

THE VOICE OF ROMANTICISM: I should think so. While in the dense smoke of a Berlin coffeehouse the voice of Romanticism could reach you but dimly, now it should ring out more clearly.

THE ANNOUNCER: I would be glad to know your name.

THE VOICE OF ROMANTICISM: I imagine that you would be comfortable with Bernhardi, Hülsen, or Steffens, not to speak of Novalis and Ludwig Tieck.[43] But the voice of Romanticism has no name.

THE ANNOUNCER: The voice of Romanticism . . .

THE VOICE OF ROMANTICISM: . . . comes from the enchanted horn on which Clemens Brentano[44] blew, and from the imperti-

---

43 These names, some now better known than others, are all figures associated with early German Romanticism: August Ferdinand Bernhardi (1769–1820), German linguist and writer; August Ludwig Hülsen (1765–1809), philosopher and educator who, like Bernhardi, was a contributor to the *Athenaeum* (1798–1800), the literary journal founded by the Schlegel brothers; Henrik Steffens (1743–1845), a Norwegian-born Danish philosopher associated with *Naturphilosophie* and with German Romantic circles in Berlin and Jena; Novalis (pseudonym of Friedrich von Hardenberg) (1772–1801), a leading figure of German Romanticism; Ludwig Tieck (1773–1853), a prolific German novelist, translator, and critic.

44 Clemens Brentano (1778–1842), coeditor with Achim von Arnim of *Des Knaben Wunderhorn* [The Boy's Magic Horn] (1805–1808), a collection of German folk songs and poems.

nence with which Friedrich Schlegel offered his deepest discoveries, from the labyrinth of thoughts Novalis traced in his notebooks, from the laughter of Tieck's comedies that terrified the petit-bourgeois, and from the darkness in which Bonaventura[45] held his night watches. Therefore the voice of Romanticism has no name.

THE ANNOUNCER: It seems to me it just doesn't want to spit out its name, this voice. It's afraid to expose itself, and with good reason. I'd like to propose the name Jean Paul.[46] This darling of German readers around 1800, the most overblown, lachrymose, undisciplined, and rudderless writer who has ever written a novel.

THE VOICE OF ROMANTICISM: That a poet should write pedagogy need not bespeak aimlessness.

THE ANNOUNCER: You are speaking of *Levana*.[47] Listen to how Jean Paul describes a young boy. You will have to admit, he doesn't have the stuff of an educator. He's an incorrigible dreamer, nothing more.

The following text is read by the Announcer in an especially flat and uncomprehending manner up until the sound of the gong. After the gong the Second Man of Letters takes up the reading, expressively, though in a fine monotone.

He burst into a mingling flood of tears at once of joy and sorrow, and the past and the future simultaneously stirred his heart. The sun with ever-increasing swiftness dropped down the heavens, and the more swiftly did he climb the mountain, the quicker to follow its flight with his eye. And there he looked down into the village of Maienthal, that glimmered among moist shadows ... Then the earth, tuned by the Creator, rang with a thousand strings ...[48]

---

45 Bonaventura, pseudonym of Ernst August Friedrich Klingemann (1777–1831), German writer, thought to be the author of Romantic prose text *Nachtwachen* [Night Watches], anonymously published in 1804.

46 Jean Paul Friedrich Richter (1763–1825), a writer whose works are often considered unclassifiable. See Benjamin's description of Jean Paul's imagination as one of "extreme exuberance," in "Notes for a Study of the Beauty of Colored Illustrations in Children's Books: Reflections on Lyser," SW, 1, 265.

47 Jean Paul's *Levana, oder Erziehungslehre* [Levana, or Pedagogy] (Braunschweig: F. Bieweg, 1807), a classic work on education.

48 From Richter's *Hesperus, oder 45 Hundposttage: Eine Lebensbeschreibung* (1795). Translation from *Hesperus or Forty-Five Dog Post Days: A Biography, Vol. 1*, trans. Charles T. Brooks (Boston: Ticknor and Fields, 1865), 240.

The sound of a gong.

SECOND MAN OF LETTERS: "... the same harmony stirred the stream, divided into gold and gloom, the humming flower-cup, the peopled air, and the waving bush; the reddened east and reddened west stood stretched out like the two rose-taffeta wings of a harpsichord, and a tremulous sea gushed from the open heavens and the open earth . . ."[49]

HEINZMANN: This can't be the place, Mr. Unger. They are reading aloud in there.

UNGER: I know my way around Leipzig, my dear Heinzmann. That's the basement of Breitkopf's. You can see the signboard with the titles of new arrivals.

HEINZMANN: You will not run across Breitkopf so early in the morning.

UNGER: Could be that he is himself already out after commissions. Then we'll wait for him. Given the voices within, we are not the first.

SECOND MAN OF LETTERS (*reading*): "At his feet, and on this mountain . . ."[50]

UNGER: If we're disturbing you, I beg your pardon.

SECOND MAN OF LETTERS: Mr. Unger, it is no surprise to see you in Leipzig, but it is a great pleasure.

UNGER: May I introduce a business friend, Mr. Heinzmann from Bern. Distinguished Scholar.

We hear the murmured exchange of greetings, compliments, etc.

UNGER: Are we disturbing you, my most esteemed sir? What were you reading?

SECOND MAN OF LETTERS: What I prefer to read in the morning, an evensong.

HEINZMANN: That doesn't look at all like a prayer book.

SECOND MAN OF LETTERS: It is also more than a prayer book.

HEINZMANN: More?

SECOND MAN OF LETTERS: *Hesperus*, by Jean Paul. But hear for yourself:

At his feet, and on this mountain, lay, stretched like a crowned giant, like a transplanted spring-island, an English park. This mountain toward the south and the one toward the north met and formed a

---

49 Ibid.
50 Ibid.

cradle in which the peaceful village rested, and over which the morning and the evening sun spun and spread out their golden veil. In five
gleaming ponds trembled five duskier evening heavens, and every
wave that leaped up painted itself to a ruby in the hovering fire of the
sun. Two brooks waded, in shifting distances, darkened by roses and
willows, over the long meadow-land, and a watering fire-wheel, like a
pulsating heart, forced the sunset-reddened water through all the
green flower-vases. Everywhere nodded flowers, those butterflies of
the vegetable world, on every moss-grown brook stone, from every
tender stalk, round every window, a flower rocked on its fragrance,
and scarlet lupines traced their blue and red veins over a garden without a hedge. A transparent wood of gold-green birches climbed, in
the high grass over there, the sides of the northern mountain, on
whose summit five tall fir-trees, as ruins of a prostrated forest, held
their eyrie.[51]

A brief pause, following which the Second Man of Letters continues:
I am pleased to see that you have made yourselves comfortable.

UNGER: Yes, you have found a good corner. I think we can wait
for Breitkopf here in peace. If it's alright with you, Mr.
Heinzmann.

HEINZMANN: Of course. What does not sit well with me is Jean
Paul.

IFFLAND: You won't want to say anything against Jean Paul . . . Do
you know the epigraph of *Hesperus*? "The Earth is the *cul-de-sac*
in the great city of God,—the camera obscura of inverted and
contracted images from a fairer world,—the coast of God's
creation,—a vaporous halo around a better sun,—the numera-
tor to a still invisible denominator, in fact, it is almost nothing
at all."[52]

HEINZMANN: You know that by heart?

IFFLAND: I'm not ashamed of it.

HEINZMANN: "In fact, it is almost nothing at all." You see, it is
these turns of phrase that spoil Jean Paul for me. We already have
enough whimsical minds with us in Switzerland. I don't need to
tell you about Lavater.

SECOND MAN OF LETTERS: To utter the name of a poet and a
charlatan in the same breath.

---

51 Ibid., 240–1.
52 Ibid., epigraph.

HEINZMANN: I already told you, I speak as a Swiss. We are a sober people, but we are also an old democracy. We feel how the countless small courts have duped you Germans and deprived you of your independence. Precisely in the case of Jean Paul we feel that. A stunted subaltern intellect has sucked the marrow from his characters' bones. Even in contrast to the lowliest serf, they appear dishonorable.

IFFLAND: No, there I cannot agree with you. For I know better than anyone how little cause the author has to think differently than you concerning the bourgeoisie and the nobility. I have known his misery and I am proud that it was my friend Moritz in Berlin—my friend and classmate, I should have said—who found the publisher for Jean Paul's first book.

SECOND MAN OF LETTERS: Classmate, you say?

IFFLAND: Yes, and you will never have guessed that Moritz's consuming desire when we were together in school was to become a great actor. Indeed, there was a time when we were rivals.

We hear a commotion. Voices, etc.

IFFLAND: But what is all this uproar?

SECOND MAN OF LETTERS: Young people from the Museum Club, who, as I heard, are holding a rehearsal.

HEINZMANN: I am sorry to be tiresome, but if we don't use the book fair, Mr. Businessman, to speak out concerning our profession, then I don't know when we ever will. So let me tell you that we have an excess of novels, of *belles lettres*, of political hot air. What are we in need of? Natural science and history, history and geography, travel diaries. But the works of natural science should not be metaphysical. Nor should they be pedantic. Enough books on minerals and insects. What we need are popular writings. They should awaken thoughts of the Creator, the order and omnipotence of the natural world, they should show us the great, the beautiful, and the sublime, and the more closely they unite that with everyday life, with practical economics and work, with mathematics and mechanics, the better.

UNGER: Your ideal, if I understand correctly, is Defoe, who besides his *Robinson* and 200 other books created the first fire and hail insurance companies, and the first savings bank.

HEINZMANN: And we are proud to have such a Robinson-writer in Switzerland. That is Pastor Wyss with his *Swiss Family Robinson*.[53] But I didn't mean to speak of that. For I openly

---

53   Johann David Wyss published *Der Schweizerische Robinson* in 1812.

concede to you, my gentlemen, I did have an ulterior motive. I have my ideal of an author in my coat pocket and I would like very much to share it with you. It is the book of a poor and uneducated man. But just as the travel account of an itinerant journeyman is ten times more valuable than a scholarly treatise, so too something truly special emerges today when a poor, uneducated man sits down to narrate his life.

IFFLAND: You are making us exceedingly curious.

HEINZMANN: That was my intention. And now, I ask that precisely you, Mr. Iffland, read this page for us. Such prose you will have seldom have recited. With the exception of your own, I'm quite sure.

UNGER: But aren't you going to tell us who wrote it? The folder doesn't betray anything.

HEINZMANN: The author's name is Bräker. The book came out with Füßli and is entitled *Life Story and Real Adventures of the Poor Man of Toggenburg.*

IFFLAND: Not that the shepherd's life is all fun and games. Not a bit of it! There are hardships enough. The worst for me by far was leaving my warm little bed so early in the morning, and tramping poorly clad and barefoot out into the cold fields, especially if there's been a really harsh hoar-frost or a thick mist hung over the mountains. When the latter lay so high that I couldn't surmount it by climbing with my flock up the mountainside, and couldn't reach the sunshine, then I cursed the mist and told it to go to Jericho and hurried as fast as my legs could carry me out of the gloom into a dell. If, however, I did win the field and gained sunlight and the bright sky above me, with that great sea of mist under my feet and here and there a mountain jutting up like an island—why, what joy, the glory and the gladness of it! Then I wouldn't leave the mountains for the whole day, and my eye could never see its fill of the sun's rays playing on this ocean, and waves of vapor in the strangest of shapes swaying about over it, until towards evening they threatened to rise over me again. Then I wished I had Jacob's ladder, but it was no use, I had to go. I'd grow sad and everything would blend into my sadness. Lonely birds flapped around overhead, dull and sullen, and great autumn flies buzzed so dismally about my ears that I couldn't help weeping. Then I'd freeze even worse almost than early on and feel pains in my feet, even though they were as hard as shoe-leather.

Most of the time I also had injuries or bruises somewhere or other on me; and when one wound was healed then I went and got myself another, either by landing on a sharp stone and losing a nail or a piece of flesh from a toe, or else giving my hand a gash with one of my tools. There was seldom any question of getting them bound up; and yet they were usually soon better. Added to this, the goats, as I've said, caused me a great deal of trouble at the outset because I didn't know how to handle them properly.[54]

An uproar of voices drowns out the final words, until the following becomes audible again:

IFFLAND: My god, has Hell been unleashed in there? To resume: "If you want to run a decent home, be sure to leave pigeons and goats alone," writes our poor man. "So you see: the shepherd's life also has its share of troubles. But the bad times are richly compensated by the good, when I'm sure there's never a king so happy. In Kohl Wood stood a beech . . ."[55]

We hear again, this time more intense, an uproar of voices.

IFFLAND: This is completely intolerable. Just a moment, we will soon have some peace. That would be even better.

The creaking of a door is heard, followed by two unknown voices.

PASTOR: It pleases me to find you in such a good mood. Once again, I have one or two favors to ask of you.

HEAD FORESTER: Of me? How so—why—how so?

PASTOR: You should be well used the fact that I'm always begging on someone's behalf when I stop by.[56]

UNGER: But my dear Iffland, that's . . . those are . . .

IFFLAND: Yes, I can't believe my ears.

UNGER: *The Hunters.*

IFFLAND: Act Two, Scene Seven. And how hard these good people are trying.

UNGER: But still they are amateurs? A small private society, perhaps?

IFFLAND: Shhh. Listen.

PASTOR: The poor old man has a sick wife, many children. It's a horrible fate.—In his youth—a hussar, beaten almost to a cripple and no pension—discarded in his old age—he is left to wander in despair.

---

54 Ulrich Bräker, *Lebensgeschichte und Natürliche Abenteuer des Armen Mannes im Tockenburg* (Zurich: Fußli, 1789). Translation from Ulrich Bräker, *The Life and Real Adventures of the Poor Man of Toggenburg,* trans. Derek Bowman (Edinburgh: University Press of Edinburgh, 1970), 69.

55 Bräker, *The Life and Real Adventures of the Poor Man of Toggenburg,* 70.

56 See Iffland's play, "Die Jäger" [The Hunters] (1785), II, 7, in Iffland, *Dramatische Werke,* vol. 3 (Leipzig, 1798), 74–5.

HEAD FORESTER: Poor fellow.

PASTOR: If we could just get him through the winter—I have taken up a small collection.

HEAD FORESTER: May God make it worth your while. I would like to make my contribution. He who gives right away, gives twice as much.

PASTOR: But no—it's too much.

HEAD FORESTER: It's a hard winter.

PASTOR: That is really a lot. Please, less money, but a little wood.

HEAD FORESTER: The wood belongs to the Prince—the money is mine.[57]—Tonight I will sleep soundly, and, God willing, just as soundly when I must depart for good.

PASTOR: Well, God willing, we are still far from that. But yes. Why not bear it in mind. Truly, one must have lived well, and what great joy not to be disturbed by *that* thought. All the same, life has no less worth.

HEAD FORESTER: It always pains me to the soul when people try so hard to paint the world and life in black and white.

PASTOR: Human life contains much happiness. But we should be taught early on not to think it of it as glorious and uninterrupted. Within the circle of a well-maintained household there are a thousand joys, and tribulations well borne are also a happiness. The dignity of the father is the first and most noble I know. A philanthropist, a good citizen, a loving spouse and father, in the midst of . . .[58]
The voice suddenly breaks off.

HEINZMANN: You could see it didn't hold his attention. He went inside.

UNGER: The good man, now he will teach these well-behaved Leipzig children to perform *The Hunters*, and in the ceremonial performance they will be able to say: directed by Iffland.

SECOND MAN OF LETTERS: I know, Mr. Unger, that you are on good terms with Iffland. But, just between us, may I ask you, can that be endured? Can one still listen to these tirades concerning humanity and this love of man? Are you not sometimes overcome with disgust at a virtue that is nothing but instinctive goodness of heart without content? Sometimes I catch myself feeling the way I do when I read in the newspaper yet again of a murderer who was good to his dog or his horse.

---

57   Ibid., 75–6.
58   Ibid., 159.

330 TALKS, PLAYS, DIALOGUES, AND LISTENING MODELS

HEINZMANN: You are right about one thing. The ostentation of these pieces about do-gooding pains any finer sensibility.

UNGER: You could well say that of Kotzebue. But it's unkind of you to lump my friend Iffland together with that scribbler.

SECOND MAN OF LETTERS: Let's put Iffland to one side. And I'd even venture to say I am indebted to Kotzebue. Have you seen his unpalatable *The Indians in England?*[59] If one really wants to understand what Kant meant by the categorical imperative, with this iron "should" that annihilates every contingency, not just as a moral law, but as the inner stay of every poetic character, then one need only take a look at the mollusks with which our most celebrated playwright has populated the German stage.

UNGER: At any rate, we might sometimes wonder who we are actually working for in Germany, if it is still possible today to publish a rag such as the one Clas peddles in Berlin.

HEINZMANN: I don't know what you're talking about, Mr. Unger.

UNGER: Sells for twelve groschen. You haven't seen it? A literary magazine in which he brings Goethe and Schiller together with Kotzebue and Iffland.

SECOND MAN OF LETTERS: Outrageous. You are right about that. But there is another side to the story that is perhaps even sadder It shows that the likes of Kotzebue have come to think of Goethe and Schiller as competitors at best, but never as real, dangerous, enemies to the death.

UNGER: You are forgetting the *Xenien.*[60]

SECOND MAN OF LETTERS: The *Xenien?* The *Xenien?* You know as well as I how they foundered. And that's putting it mildly.

HEINZMANN: I cannot share your outrage. In the end, you must take the public as it is. You know that in the last twenty years, I haven't missed a single book fair. You speak with all kinds of people there, and you hear things they don't shout from the rooftops. Do you know how many subscriptions Göschen got for the Goethe edition he published between 1787 and 1790? I have the figure from the man himself: six hundred. As for the individual volumes, the sales were even worse. For *Iphigenie* and *Egmont*, 300—not to speak of *Clavigo* and *Götz*.

---

59 Kotzebue, *Die Indianer in England* (Leipzig, 1790).

60 *Die Xenien* (1795/1796), a collaboration between Goethe and Schiller, written in response to their critics, and motivated by the negative criticism surrounding Schiller's journal, *Die Horen*.

UNGER: My dear man, you can't blame that on the public. You know how much we suffer from pirate editions. For every legal exemplar there are ten, twenty illegal copies.

HEINZMANN: Well then, let me tell you something else. On my return journey this time, I spent an evening in Kreuznach. The previous year, my friend Kehr made a name for himself by establishing a lending library: Schiller, Goethe, Lessing, Klopstock, Wieland, Gellert, Wagner, Kleist, Hölty, Matthisson, and more.[61] Nobody wanted to read any of it. In the neat phrase of Bürger, there's a difference between an audience and a crowd.[62]

SECOND MAN OF LETTERS: We will not be able to breathe freely until we have ended the stubborn, pretentious reign of Nicolai, Garve, Biester, Gedike, and whatever else this Berlin riffraff calls itself, and put Schlegel and Novalis in their rightful place.[63]

HEINZMANN: You love a good joke.

SECOND MAN OF LETTERS: There is no victory without a fight. If Schiller and Goethe don't want to fight, then we must place our hopes on a younger generation.

HEINZMANN: I can give you a taste of the tricks of these young people. Friedrich Schlegel considered increasing the sales of the *Athenaeum* by offering free spice cakes with each issue.

UNGER: A very modern idea. But in this, Schiller is even more Machiavellian. When *Die Horen* was failing due to poor sales, he wanted Cotta to insert an article threatening the state in the final volume, so that they would go down in glory.[64]

HEINZMANN: I cannot say, my good gentlemen, that any of this

---

61   In 1797, Ludwig Christian Kehr (1775–1848) opened a commercial lending library in Kreuznach. He later started a publishing house and bookshop, and published translations and pirate editions, arguing that the reprinting and wider distribution of books was a means to greater social justice.

62   Benjamin invokes a distinction attributed to the German poet Gottfried August Bürger (1747–1794). The phrase opposes *Publikum*, German for audience, with the made-up word *Pöblikum*, a pun on crowd or rabble.

63   Friedrich Nicolai (1733–1811), editor of the *Allgemeine deutsche Bibliothek*; Christian Garve (1742–1798), German translator and writer; Johann Erich Biester (1749–1816) and Friedrich Gedike (1754–1803), co-founders of the *Berlinische Monatsschrift*. While Nicolai and Garve are sometimes associated with a popularization of Enlightenment thought, Biester and Gedike are less easily placed in an opposition between the popular and the philosophical. Benjamin invokes a once common opposition between the Enlightenment, broadly represented by these figures, and Romanticism, associated with the poets Friedrich Schlegel (1772–1829) and Novalis (1772–1801).

64   Schiller's journal, *Die Horen*, which appeared from 1795 to 1798, was published by the Cotta publishing house.

sits well with us. At any rate, I can still feel my bones from the trip in the postal coach. And we cannot assume that Breitkopf will be arriving before noon. How about a short stroll to the Café Richter?

We hear a drum, a horn (or the like) accompanied by the voice of a

CRIER: All ye honorable guests of the book fair, especially our esteemed book venders, publishers, collectors of rare books, also scholars, pastors, and all other persons of high standing—we announce that the great sale of rare books organized by Mr. Haude and Mr. Spener in Berlin, collections of the King and of the Academy of Scholarly Booksellers, has begun at the Silver Bears.

UNGER: As for me, I'll be having my breakfast at the Silver Bears.

SECOND MAN OF LETTERS: That would be the first book sale you missed, Mr. Businessman ... Don't inconvenience yourself, Mr. Heinzmann. We will meet again.

THE AUCTIONEER: *Political and moral discourses on Marci Annaei Pharsalia*, by Mr. Veit Ludwigs von Seckendorf, Privy Advisor and Chancellor to the Elector of Brandenburg and Councilor of the University of Halle in Saxony, presented in a special new edition in German with facing translations in Latin on each page and accompanying annotations of obscure and difficult figures of speech as well as an indispensable index, Leipzig 1695 ...

VOICE OF A BIDDER: Eighteen groschen.

UNGER: One would no longer dare print such a title. Here, neither publisher nor author wishes to puff himself up in the title.

The sound of the gavel.

THE AUCTIONEER: Number 211. "Mirror for the Prince, Anti-Machiavelli, or the Art of Governance," Strasbourg 1624.

VOICE OF ANOTHER BIDDER: One thaler.

UNGER: The Latin edition of 1577 would be considered rare, but the German far more and only a few are aware of it ... Two thalers.

VOICE OF THE OTHER BIDDER: Two thalers and ten groschen.

UNGER: Three thalers.

THE AUCTIONEER: Going once, going twice ... Sold.

The pounding of the gavel.

THE AUCTIONEER: Sold to?

UNGER: Johann Friedrich Unger, Bookseller, Berlin.

THE AUCTIONEER: Number 212. The Works of Johann Wolfgang von Goethe, Leipzig: Georg Joachim Göschen, 1787–1790. Unfortunately, we only have the seventh volume of this handsome edition.

UNGER: The seventh volume, distinguished scholar, but that's . . . *The sound of a gong.*

THE VOICE OF THE NINETEENTH CENTURY: *Faust!*[65] The world legend of the German bourgeoisie, beginning on the worldly stage, ending in the proscenium of Heaven, beginning with the infernal devil of black magic, rising to the earthly devil of state-craft, beginning with appearances, ending in voices. A small puppet show opens at the annual fair to address the sufferings and humiliation of the German bourgeoisie, but also its history, and at the heart of this history the image of antiquity, Helen, and the Palace at Sparta.

THE ANNOUNCER: Silence! How dare you steal my lines?

THE VOICE OF THE NINETEENTH CENTURY: I am the nine-teenth century, and have already stolen the lines of many others. I anticipated the Classical authors before they had even finished writing, and was greeted by the greatest among them before he had even glimpsed a quarter of me, with such words that I have the right to be heard here.

THE ANNOUNCER: How is it, in your opinion, that he greeted you? I believe we are speaking here of Goethe?

THE VOICE OF THE NINETEENTH CENTURY: I see that you are still in school. Goethe said of me:

> Everything nowadays is *ultra*, everything perpetually transcendent in thought as in action. No one knows himself any longer, no one under-stands the element in which he moves and works, no one the subject which he is treating. Wealth and rapidity are what the world admires, and what everyone strives to attain. Railways, quick mails, steamships, and every possible kind of facility in the way of communication are what the educated world has in view, that it may overeducate itself, and thereby continue in a state of mediocrity. Properly speaking, this is the century for men with heads on their shoulders, for practical men of quick perceptions, who, because they possess a certain adroit-ness, feel their superiority to the multitude, even though they

---

65   Goethe's *Faust: Ein Fragment* appeared in the seventh volume of the Göschen edition (Leipzig, 1790).

themselves may not be gifted to the highest degree. Let us, as far as possible, keep that in mind with which we came hither; we, and perhaps a few others, shall be the last of an epoch that will not so soon return again.[66]

THE ANNOUNCER: You have no cause to be proud of such a greeting.

THE VOICE OF THE NINETEENTH CENTURY: I lived up to it. I expanded a middling culture generally, as Goethe prophesied.

THE ANNOUNCER: A middling culture? As long as your nineteenth century lasted, the Germans didn't open their greatest volume of poetry. And only recently did Cotta sell the last copy of the *West-östlicher Divan* from the publishing house.[67]

THE VOICE OF THE NINETEENTH CENTURY: It was too expensive. I brought editions to the market that reached the people.

THE ANNOUNCER: People who didn't have time to read them.

THE VOICE OF THE NINETEENTH CENTURY: At the same time, my century gave the mind the means to expand itself more quickly than by reading.

THE ANNOUNCER: In other words, it founded the tyranny of the minute, the lash of which we still feel today.

We hear quite clearly the ticking of the second hand of a clock.

THE VOICE OF THE NINETEENTH CENTURY: Goethe himself embraced this cadence, and advised his grandson to adapt himself to it.

The following poem is read briskly to the cadence of the second hand:

> Sixty are in every hour.
> Fourteen-forty in a day.
> Each one, son, provides some power
> To achieve or flit away.[68]

"Was die Deutschen lasen, wahrend ihre Klassiker schrieben," GS, 4.2, 641–70. Translated by Diana K. Reese.

---

66   See Goethe's letter to Zelter, dated June 6, 1825, abridged by Benjamin. The translation is from Goethe and Carl Friedrich Zelter, *Goethe's Letters to Zelter: With Extracts of those of Zelter to Goethe*, trans. A.D. Coleridge (London: George Bell & Sons, 1892), Letter 183, 246–7.

67   Goethe's *West-östlicher Divan* [West-Eastern Divan], published by the Cotta publishing house in 1819.

68   Translation from *Goethe's World View Presented in his Reflections and Maxims*, ed. Frederick Ungar, trans. Heinz Norden (New York: Frederick Ungar Publishing, 1963), 69.

Broadcast on Radio Berlin, February 16, 1932, from 9:10–10:10 pm. Announced as part of the series "1789–1815" in the Funkstunde *(Schiller-Lerg,* Walter Benjamin und der Rundfunk, *233).*

In September 1932, the radio magazine Rufer und Hörer *published an excerpted version of the text, which differs from the above version in that the excerpt contains simplifications as well as the "germanization" of foreign words (see GS, 4.2, 1054–71). Along with the excerpt, the magazine also published Benjamin's programmatic statement, "Two Kinds of Popularity," which can be found in this volume (369).*

CHAPTER 39

Lichtenberg

A Cross-Section

Dramatis Personae

NARRATOR

I. Moon Beings:

LABU, *President of the Moon Committee for Earth Research*

QUIKKO, *Manager of Machinery*

SOFANTI

PEKA[1]

> *The voices of the Moon Beings reverberate, as if coming from a room in a cellar.*

II. Humans:

GEORG CHRISTOPH LICHTENBERG

THE LORD CHAMBERLAIN OF THE ENGLISH KING

THE ACTOR DAVID GARRICK

MARIA DOROTHEA STECHARDT, *Lichtenberg's girlfriend*

EBERHARD, *Justice Pütter's servant*

JUSTICE PÜTTER

A TOWN CRIER

A SELLER OF SILHOUETTES

FIRST, SECOND, AND THIRD CITIZENS OF GÖTTINGEN

A PASTOR

NARRATOR: As the Narrator, I find myself in the pleasant situation of taking a position above all the parties—I mean, planets.

---

1 Benjamin borrows the names of the Moon Beings Labu, Sofanti, and Peka from Paul Scheerbart's novel *Lesabéndio: Ein Asteroiden-Roman* (1913) [Lesabéndio: An Asteroid-Novel]. For Benjamin on Scheerbart, see Benjamin, "On Scheerbart," in SW, 4, 386 ("Sur Scheerbart," GS, 2.2, 631), and "Paul Scheerbart: Lesabéndio" (GS, 2.2, 618–20).

Because the following events take place between Earth and Moon—or rather, sometimes on one, sometimes on the other—I would violate the laws of interplanetary codes of behavior if I, as Narrator, represented the position of either the Earth or the Moon. In order to adhere to the proprieties, I will inform you that the Earth seems as mysterious to the Moon, which knows everything about the Earth, as the Moon does to the Earth, which knows nothing about the Moon. You can infer that the Moon knows everything about the Earth and the Earth knows nothing about the Moon from the single fact that there is a Committee for Earth Research on the Moon. You will have no trouble following this Committee's negotiations. But in order to enable you to easily gain an overview, please allow me to point out the following. The Lunar Committee's negotiations are very brief; the time allotted for speaking on the Moon is greatly restricted. The Moon-dwellers obtain nourishment exclusively from the silence of their fellow citizens, which they therefore only reluctantly interrupt. It is also worth mentioning that one Earth year amounts to only a few Moon minutes. Here we are dealing with the phenomenon of temporal distortion, a phenomenon with which you are doubtlessly familiar. I hardly need to mention that photographs have always been taken on the Moon.

The Society for Earth Research's machinery is limited to three apparatuses that are easier to use than a coffee grinder. First, we have the Spectrophone, through which everything happening on Earth is heard and seen; a Parlamonium, with the help of which human speech—often aggravating for the inhabitants of the Moon, who are spoiled by the music of the spheres—can be translated into music; and an Oneiroscope, with which the dreams of Earthlings can be observed. That is significant because of the interest in psychoanalysis that is prevalent on the Moon. You will now listen in on a meeting of this Moon Committee.

Gong.

LABU: I hereby open the 214th Session of the Moon Committee for Earth Research. I welcome the committee members, who are all assembled: the gentlemen Sofanti, Quikko, and Peka. We are nearing the end of our work. Now that we've sorted out all the Earth's essential parts, we have decided, in accordance with the many requests from Moon laymen, to conduct a few additional, short experiments concerning humans. It has been clear to the Commission from the start that the material is relatively unproductive. The samples taken over the last millennia have not yielded a single case in which a human has amounted to anything. Taking this established scientific fact as a basis for our investigations, our meetings from now on will deal solely with proving that this is a result of the unhappy human condition. Opinions differ on what is to blame for this unhappiness. Mr. Peka would like the floor.

PEKA: I would like permission to speak on a matter of the rules of procedure.

LABU: On the rules of procedure.

PEKA: I suggest that before we move on to other points on the agenda, we take note of this lunar map, which has just been published based on research done by Professors Tobias Mayer and Georg Christoph Lichtenberg in Göttingen.[2]

QUIKKO: In my opinion, the Moon Committee for Earth Research can expect nothing from this map. I notice that not even the huge crater C.Y. 2802, where we hold our meetings, is marked on it.

LABU: The Moon map is dispatched to the archive without further debate.

SOFANTI: Excuse me, but who is Tobias Mayer?

LABU: According to the Earth Archive, Tobias Mayer was a professor of astronomy in Göttingen who died a number of years ago. Herr Lichtenberg concluded Mayer's work.

SOFANTI: I motion that we thank Herr Lichtenberg for his interest in Moon research by making him the subject of our own investigations, for, as Mr. President has just rightly noted, our Committee's final sessions will deal with humans.

LABU: Any objections? No objections have been raised. The Committee passes the motion.

QUIKKO: I have the privilege to present a photograph of Lichtenberg.

ALL: Let us see it, please.

PEKA: But there are twenty people in it.

---

2 Tobias Mayer (1723–1762), German astronomer known for his studies of the moon, and Georg Christoph Lichtenberg (1742–1799), German writer, satirist, aphorist, and scientist. During the years 1931–1932, Benjamin had "prepared, for a commission, a complete bibliography of the writings of and about G. C. Lichtenberg" (Benjamin, "Curriculum Vitae [VI]," SW, 4, 382). The bibliography, commissioned by the Berlin lawyer and Lichtenberg collector Martin Domke, was never published and, apparently, does not survive. A card index for the bibliography is, however, extant (GS, 7.2, 837).

QUIKKO: This is Pastor Lichtenberg from Oberamstädt near Darmstadt together with his esteemed wife and his eighteen children. The smallest one is the aforementioned moon researcher.

SOFANTI: But now he is supposed to be over thirty.

LABU: Gentlemen, the time allotted for the Committee meeting is up. I request that Mr. Quikko tune the Spectrophone in to Göttingen.

QUIKKO: Spectrophone to Göttingen.

A series of purring and ringing signals can be heard.

QUIKKO: He's not in Göttingen.

LABU: Then you'll have to search for him, but without a sound. It's our silent hour now. *Pause.*

QUIKKO (*whispering*): London. He's in London. In the Drury Lane Theater. They're performing *Hamlet*. The great actor Garrick is playing Hamlet.[3]

GARRICK: Rest, rest, perturbed spirit! So, gentlemen,
        With all my love I do commend me to you:
        And what so poor a man as Hamlet is
        May do t'express his love and friending to you,
        God willing, shall not lack. Let us go in together;
        And still your fingers on your lips, I pray.
        The time is out of joint. O cursed spite!
        That ever I was born to set it right!
        Nay, come, let's go together.[4]

A burst of applause; then music.

LORD CHAMBERLAIN: It will get somewhat noisy in here during the intermission, Herr Professor. Furthermore, His Majesty has particularly asked me to give Mr. Garrick the privilege of making the acquaintance of one of Europe's greatest scholars.

LICHTENBERG: Your courteousness, my Lord Chamberlain, goes too far. His Majesty well knows that he will be fulfilling a long-cherished wish of mine by making it possible for me to become acquainted with Garrick. His acting, I can see, is beyond compare.

---

3 Lichtenberg met David Garrick (1717–1779), the influential English actor, playwright, and theater manager, in London in 1775. Lichtenberg wrote about the encounter in his "Letters from England," on which Benjamin loosely bases the scene that follows. See Lichtenberg, *Briefe*, eds. Albert Leitzmann and Carl Schüddekopf, 3 vols. (Leipzig: Dieterich, 1901–1904), vol. 1, 237. See also Lichtenberg, *Vermischte Schriften*, vol. 3 (Göttingen: Dieterich, 1844), 197ff.

4 Shakespeare, *Hamlet*, Act I, Scene V.

LORD CHAMBERLAIN: As you will see, his manners are in no way surpassed by the art of his acting. He is equally at home in the gilded court of St. James as in Hamlet's paper court.

LICHTENBERG: Will you show me to his dressing room?

LORD CHAMBERLAIN: We will be there directly.—Please announce us to Mr. Garrick.

LICHTENBERG: I was told that the acoustics are bad, but I understood every word.

LORD CHAMBERLAIN: The acoustics really are bad. But when Garrick acts, not a sound is lost. It is deathly quiet, and the audience sits as if they were painted on the wall.

DRESSING ROOM ATTENDANT: Mr. Garrick will see you now.

GARRICK: I am happy for this chance to greet you. The King already let me know you would be coming.

LICHTENBERG: I am far too caught up in the impression left by your acting to be able to greet you in the way I would wish.

GARRICK: The honor of seeing you here before me is greater than any greeting.

LICHTENBERG: Some of my friends warned me against seeing you. They were afraid that I would no longer have any appreciation of the German stage upon my return home.

GARRICK: I cannot take that seriously. Or do you think we have not heard of the reputation of an Iffland or an Eckhof here?[5]

LICHTENBERG: Unfortunately, they seldom have an opportunity to play Lear or Hamlet. Here, Shakespeare is not merely famous, but rather sacred. His name is intertwined with venerable ideas, songs by him and about him are sung, and so a large segment of English youth knows him earlier than they learn the ABCs or the one-times-one table.

GARRICK: Shakespeare is our "High School," although I can't forget what I have learned from my friends Sterne and Fielding.

LICHTENBERG: I think I could fill many pages with what your conduct in front of the ghost taught me.

LORD CHAMBERLAIN: Then you won't forget an anecdote I was recently told about Mr. Garrick. A few weeks ago, there was an audience member sitting in the balcony who believed that the ghost in Act I was real. His neighbor told him it was an actor. "But," responded the first, "if that's the case, why was the man dressed in

---

5 August Wilhelm Iffland (1759–1814) and Konrad Eckhof (1720–1778), renowned actors of the German stage.

black himself so frightened by it?" The man dressed in black—that was Garrick.

LICHTENBERG: Oh, yes, the black garment! I wanted to talk about that. I have frequently heard you being reprimanded because of it, although never between the acts or on the way home or at a meal directly afterwards, but always only after the first impression has lost its force, during a cool, sober conversation. And I never quite understood this reproach.

GARRICK: Yes, I'll admit to you that I have reasons why I dress this way. It seems to me the old costumes on the stage can easily become a masquerade. They are beautiful when they are pleasing, but the deception that then comes into play is rarely offset by the pleasure in their beauty.

LICHTENBERG: You feel the same way about actors in old costumes as I do about German books in Latin script. To me, they are always a kind of translation.

GARRICK: Allow me to speak about my combat with Laertes in the last act. My predecessors wore a helmet in that scene. I wear a hat. Why? I absolutely feel the fall of a hat during a fight; I feel the fall of a helmet far less. I don't know how firmly a helmet should fit; but I feel every slight shift of a hat. I think you understand me.

LICHTENBERG: Perfectly. It is not the business of an actor to awaken the antiquarian in the audience.

GARRICK: I once read something by an old Spaniard who said that theater is like a map. Valladolid is only a finger's breadth away from Toledo. One has barely seen a person who is sixteen years old when he appears again at sixty on the stage. That is true theater; one should not hamper the trade with pedantry. (*A gong sounds.*) Please excuse me. My scene approaches.

QUIKKO: I trust the gentlemen of the Committee will not think me high-handed for switching it off. But I think our material is complete. I am convinced that we can conclude our debate without further ado. The unhappiness of Professor Lichtenberg can no longer be a mystery to us. You have seen him in the most dazzling society and at that moment in his existence when the world seemed to open up for him. He was a marvelous guest at the English royal court; he had the privilege of speaking to the great actor Garrick about the secrets of his art; he visited England's great observatories and got to know the wealthy nobility in their castles and seaside resorts; the Queen opened up her private gallery and Lord Calmshome opened up his wine cellar for him. And now he is supposed to go back to Göttingen and his cramped rental apartment, which his publisher has allocated him as payment for his writing. He must exchange his box at the theater for his window seat. He must struggle with the students who are sent to him for room and board by distinguished Englishmen. He, who calculates lunar eclipses and planetary conjunctions, is supposed to simultaneously calculate the pocket money of the young lords and idlers boarding with him. Don't you see how the misery of this existence—with its intrigues at the university, the gossip of the professors, the resentment and the narrowness—must embitter him and turn him into a misanthrope before his time? His unhappiness? Do you really need to look for it? It is called Göttingen and lies in the kingdom of Hanover.

LABU: I think I speak in the name of all the citizens of the Moon and especially of our research committee for the study of the Earth when I most gratefully thank our colleague and technical director for his interesting remarks. We are dealing here with very illuminating comments, whose special beauty is that they are kept within the frame of our short speeches. However, I would like to oppose the proposal that we break off our research at this point. Because why, even if the Professor is trapped in the narrowness of his small university town, should he not rise high above it on the wings of his dreams?

SOFANTI: In the attempt to tune the Spectrophone in to Göttingen, it turned out that it is now nighttime there. There is absolutely nothing for us to investigate.

LABU: That seems to me a welcome opportunity to prove my conjecture correct and put the Oneiroscope into operation. Give the directive to headquarters.

A series of purring and ringing signals can be heard.

LABU: May I request you, Mr. Quikko, to proceed to the Oneiroscope and tell us what you perceive therein.

QUIKKO: I see Herr Professor Georg Christoph Lichtenberg as he sees himself in a dream.[6] He is floating far above the Earth across from a transfigured old man, whose appearance fills him with something greater than mere respect. When he opens his

---

6 See Lichtenberg, *Vermischte Schriffen* (1844), vol. 6, 50–3.

eyes and sees him, an irresistible feeling of worship and trust pervades him, and he is just at the point of prostrating himself in front of him when the old man speaks to him: "You love investigations of nature," he says. "You shall see something here that might be useful to you." And now he is passing him a blue-green sphere, here and there dotted with gray, which he holds between his index finger and his thumb. Its diameter is not more than a few centimeters. "Take this mineral," continues the old man, "examine it and tell me what you have found." Lichtenberg turns around and sees a beautiful hall with all kinds of tools. I can't describe them to you, however. Now he takes a look at the sphere and feels it; he shakes it and listens to it; he touches it to his tongue; he tests it against steel, glass, a magnet, and determines its specific weight. But all these tests show him that it is worth little. He remembers that in his child-hood he bought the same ball—or one that was not so very different—at a cost of three for a kreutzer at the Frankfurt fair. He finds some clay soil, about as much chalky soil, a lot of silica, and finally some iron and some common salt. He is very exact in his investigation because as he adds up everything that he found, it comes to exactly 100. Now the old man steps in front of him, glances at the paper, and reads it with a gentle, almost imperceptible smile.

(The following must be read so that in Quikko's voice the two speakers —God and Lichtenberg—can clearly be distinguished from one another.)

"Do you know, mortal, what it was that you were examining?"

"No, immortal, I don't know."

"Then know—it was, on a smaller scale, nothing less than the entire Earth."

"The Earth?—eternal, great God! And the oceans with all their inhabitants, where are they?"

"There they are, in your napkin. You wiped them away."

"Oh dear, and the skies and all the splendor of solid ground!"

"The skies, they should be caught there in the cup of distilled water. And your splendor of solid ground? How can you ask? That is dust; there's some on the sleeve of your jacket."

"But I didn't find a single trace of silver and gold, which make the world spin!"

"Bad enough. I see that I must help you. Know this: with your fire-steel you have smashed all of Switzerland and Savoy and the most beautiful part of Sicily, and in Africa, an entire stretch of more than a thousand square miles is totally ruined and uprooted. And there, on that glass plate—they just crashed down—the Cordilleras were lying there. And that thing that flew into your eye when you were cutting glass, that was Chimborazo."

To my regret I must announce that the image is getting blurry. The dream seems to be nearing its end. Morning must be dawning in Göttingen.

A series of purring and ringing signals are heard.

SOFANTI: Finally! The Professor's science laboratory.

DOROTHEA (*opening a door*): Oh, how stuffy it is in here. And the shutters are still closed.

Sound of shutters being pushed open.

Oh, beautiful air, a beautiful morning! But what dust. He has made himself cozy here while I've been home for eight days. And even the dust cloth is nowhere to be found.

Brief pause.

Well, now, look lively!

She sings:

> Rise up, dear little children!
> The morning star with its bright light
> Lets itself be seen freely like a hero
> And shines over the whole world.
>
> Be welcome, dear day!
> Night does not want to stay.
> Shine into our hearts
> With your heavenly glow.[7]

The tinkle of shattering glass can be heard.

For heaven's sake! (*Again, even more aghast.*) For heaven's sake!

LICHTENBERG (*can be heard opening the door*): What happened? Impossible! The electrification machine!

DOROTHEA *is heard crying.*

---

7 "Steht auf, ihr lieben Kinderlein!," a church song written by the Lutheran Erasmus Alberus in the mid-sixteenth century, was collected in a number of Lutheran hymnals as a "morning song." Clemens von Brentano and his brother-in-law Ludwig Achim von Arnim included it as "Morgenlied" in their collection of romanticized folk poems and songs *Des Knaben Wunderhorn* (1805–1808). It was later set to music by Anton von Webern, Max Reger, and Armin Knab among others. [Trans.]

LICHTENBERG: Yes, that is my just punishment for sleeping late. What was it that my esteemed teacher Tobias Mayer always said: life consists of the morning hours. And that is why I have made it a rule for myself that the rising sun shall never find me lying in bed as long as I am healthy.[8]

DOROTHEA *is heard crying.*

LICHTENBERG: Well, then we will just have to write to Braunschweig and order a new cylinder for two Louis d'or, and we'll just have to see how we can manage without artificial lightning for the next weeks.—Well, what is there to cry about? You can't be crying about the damage?—I know, you're crying about your toy box. But what more could happen to it now; I really wish you had completely different toys. You should have been with me that time in London to see Mr. Cox's museum.[9] You wouldn't have been able to keep from moving among all the magical apparatuses on your tiptoes. There you would have found snakes climbing up trees; butterflies moving their wings, studded with diamonds; tulips opening and closing; waterfalls flowing from sinuous glass tubes that quickly spun on their axes; golden elephants with golden palaces on their backs; swans swimming away across mirrors; crocodiles eating golden spheres.

DOROTHEA: Will you take me to London some time?

LICHTENBERG: London! I become quite agitated when I think about London and about how it is that those popinjays, Armstale and Smeeth and Boothwell, who sit in my lectures and waste my time with their visits to the house—how it is that they deserve to live in London! And yet England remains the nation that has produced the greatest, most active people. Not those who are the greatest at promoting themselves or at book learning, but the most steadfast, the most magnanimous and bold, the most intelligent. There is nowhere that humanity is more respected than in England, and there everything is enjoyed with both body and soul, in a way in which we who live under military governments can only dream of. Dream! That reminds me, I wanted to tell you about a dream I had today. But

8   Lichtenberg, *Vermischte Schriften*, ed. Ludwig Christian Lichtenberg and Friedrich Kries, vol. 1 (Göttingen: Dieterich, 1800), 40.

9   James Cox (1723–1800) was a London jeweller, toy maker, goldsmith, clockmaker, and inventor whose firm produced elaborate automata and mechanical figures. He opened his museum in the 1770s.

you must keep it to yourself. It wouldn't help my reputation if it was known that a natural scientist dreams. I think that sometimes dreams open the way for doubts that I don't acknowledge to myself during the day. And then in the morning, when I remember them, I am not at all unhappy to see them. To doubt is human. In short, I dreamt of open space, far away from our Earth, near the Moon—

DOROTHEA: Eberhard's coming with a letter.

LICHTENBERG: Well, it's high time he returned, because there seems to be a thunderstorm approaching.

A knock.

LICHTENBERG: Come in!

EBERHARD: Good morning, Herr Professor. The Justice has sent me. The Justice has received a letter from Gotha for the Herr Professor.

LICHTENBERG: I thank you. Please send the Justice my respects.

EBERHARD: Good morning.

LICHTENBERG: Just let it sit. I don't really want to open it.

DOROTHEA: Why don't you want to open it?

LICHTENBERG: I have an apprehension.

DOROTHEA: What do you mean?

LICHTENBERG: I have an unpleasant foreboding.

DOROTHEA: But why?

LICHTENBERG: It's my superstition again. In every object I see an omen, and I turn one hundred things a day into oracles. I don't need to describe this to you. Every creeping of an insect serves to answer questions about my fate. Is that not strange in a professor of physics?[10] (*Pause.*) Perhaps it is, and perhaps not. I know that the Earth turns, and yet I am not ashamed to believe it's standing still.[11]

DOROTHEA: But what could be written in the letter?

LICHTENBERG: I don't know, but when I heard the glass shattering just now, it seemed to herald bad news.

DOROTHEA: You must allow me to open it.

LICHTENBERG: That wouldn't help; you can't read the gentlemen's handwriting.

DOROTHEA: Gentlemen? What kind of gentlemen?

---

10 See Lichtenberg, *Vermischte Schriften*, eds. Lichtenberg and Kries, vol. 1, 26.

11 See Lichtenberg, *Aphorismen*, ed. Leitzmann, 5 vols. (Berlin: B. Behr, 1902–1908), vol. 4, 47.

LICHTENBERG: No doubt the gentlemen from the life insurance.[12]

DOROTHEA: What is that, a life insurance?

LICHTENBERG: A company. They would have paid you something after my death.

DOROTHEA: I don't like to hear you talk that way.

LICHTENBERG (*audibly tearing a letter open*): My premonitions were reliable. At least this time. The gentlemen write: "Dear, especially highly esteemed Herr Professor! In response to your letter of the 24th of this month, we regret to inform you that on the basis of the report made by our doctor, to whom we submitted the certificates and documents you provided, we are unable to offer you a life insurance policy." That should feed my morbid thoughts.

DOROTHEA: What does the letter mean?

LICHTENBERG: The thoughts that it leads me to are much worse than the letter itself. Hypochondriacal, if you know what that means.

DOROTHEA: How would I?

LICHTENBERG: Hypochondria is fear of going blind, fear of insanity, fear of dying, fear of dreams, and fear of waking up. And when one has awakened, it means observing the first crow to see if it swoops by the tower to the right or to the left.

DOROTHEA: I didn't imagine this morning to be like this.

LICHTENBERG: It is a quite beautiful morning, although humid. And when I look outside into the greenery, I can no longer make rhyme or reason of the odd ideas I had last night. Imagine: yesterday when I was half asleep it seemed to me suddenly that a man was like a one-times-one table, and later I awoke when I heard my own voice saying, "It must cool so splendidly," and thought of the Principle of Contradiction, which I had visualized as if edible before me.[13]

DOROTHEA: Don't you want to close the window? A wind is springing up.

LICHTENBERG: And a strong one it is. There will be a thunderstorm soon. At least we no longer need to mourn our cylinder, because in a few minutes we'll have the most beautiful lightning sent directly to our laboratory for our use.

DOROTHEA: Is the lightning rod finished?

---

12 The denial of a life insurance policy ("Sterbethaler Direktion") is mentioned by Lichtenberg in a letter to Friedrich Heinrich Jacobi dated February 6, 1793 (see Lichtenberg, *Briefe*, vol. 3, 69). However, Benjamin probably invents the letter from the insurance company.

13 See Lichtenberg, *Aphorismen*, vol. 2, 180.

348 TALKS, PLAYS, DIALOGUES, AND LISTENING MODELS

LICHTENBERG: Yes, since yesterday noon the first German light-
ning rod can be seen on this house, and now dear God wants to
put it into operation directly.
Thunderclaps.
QUIKKO: There's a thunderstorm in Göttingen right now.
Unfortunately, we are faced with the necessity of switching off.
SOFANTI: Perhaps I may use this intermission to announce some
observations I have made relating to the subject of our
discussion.
LABU: Mr. Sofanti has the floor.
SOFANTI: I'm afraid I cannot agree with our dear Mr. Quikko's
remarks regarding the German philosopher Lichtenberg.
Anyone who has followed this conversation with his girlfriend
must conclude that it is not the external circumstances that are
ruining his life, but his own temperament. Yes, gentlemen, I
won't hesitate to describe the poor professor as sick. Please
recall—a professor of physical science, a man who is used to
linking the phenomena of the world to their causes and effects,
and who bases his life's happiness and his peace upon insects
and crows, dreams and intimations. Whether this man was in
London or Paris, Constantinople or Lisbon, the most vivid of
lives and the most refined of courts would be lost on him, as he
would just sit there, all hunched up and mournful, like a night
owl. Such a man can certainly not amount to anything. Do we
need proof of that? Gentlemen, I submit the evidence for the
perusal of the academy. Photographs of the *Göttinger
Taschenkalender* [Göttingen Pocket Almanac],[14] courtesy of a
resourceful operator on Neptune. Take a look at the entries
written by the quill of this Herr Lichtenberg. Are these subjects
worthy of a scholar? Observations about the preparation of ice
cream in India and about English fashions, about first names
and about samples of strange appetites, about the use of flogging
by diverse peoples, about bells and about animals' aptitude to
learn, about carnival customs and about menus, about marriage—
LABU: I am reluctantly obliged to make our esteemed member Mr.
Sofanti aware that not only is he, in the understandable excitement that accompanies his remarks, on the point of exceeding his
time for speaking but also that, due to the well-known

14 The *Göttinger Taschenkalender* was a popular almanac founded by Lichtenberg's
publisher, Johann Christian Dieterich (1722–1800). Lichtenberg was a prominent contributor
and, from 1777 to his death in 1799, its editor.

phenomenon of time warp between the Earth and the Moon, we have lost a year in our contact with the subject of our observations, Herr Lichtenberg. We will try to tune the Spectrophone to Göttingen again.

A series of purring and ringing signals can be heard.

QUIKKO: The Herr Professor is not in the laboratory but in the office of his present apartment in the house of his publisher, Dieterich. Using the files in our archive, we have been able to establish that Herr Dieterich lets Professor Lichtenberg live with him for free so that the Professor will write for his *Göttinger Taschenkalender* for free. Now Herr Lichtenberg is seated at his desk. We are adjusting precisely and are thus able to follow his hand, which holds the quill. The candle is to the right of the writer; the light conditions are quite favorable.—

My very dearest friend,

I call that true German friendship, dearest man. A thousand thanks for your thoughts of me. I have not answered right away, and heaven knows how things have been for me! You are, and must be, the first to whom I confess it. Last summer, soon after your last letter, I suffered the greatest loss of my life. What I am about to tell you, no other person can ever know. I met a girl in the year 1777, a burgher's daughter from this town. At the time, she was just a bit older than thirteen years old. Such a model of beauty and gentleness I had never seen in my life, even though I had seen many. The first time I laid eyes on her, she was in the company of five or six others, who, as the children here do, were selling flowers to passersby on the ramparts. She offered me a bouquet, which I bought. I was accompanied by three Englishmen, who ate and lived with me. "What a charming creature she is," said one of them. I had noticed that, too, and because I knew what a Sodom is our refuse-heap of a town, I thought seriously that I should remove this splendid creature from such trade. I finally spoke to her alone and asked her to call on me at my house. She wouldn't go to any fellow's quarters, she said. When she heard that I was a professor, however, she came to visit one afternoon with her mother. In a word, she gave up the flower trade and spent the entire day with me. And I found that this splendid body was inhabited by a soul such as I had long searched for but never found. I instructed her in writing and arithmetic and in other branches of knowledge that, without turning her into a bluestocking, developed her intellect ever further. My scientific apparatus, which cost me over 1,500 thaler, attracted her at first because of its gleam, but finally the use of it became her only entertainment. It was then that our acquaintance was raised to its highest point. She went away late and came back with the day, and all day long her concern was keeping my things, from necktie to air pump, in order. And all with such heavenly gentleness, which I had never before thought possible. The result was, as you will have suspected by now, that as of Easter 1780 she stayed with me completely. Her inclination toward this kind of life was so great that she didn't even go downstairs except to attend church. She was not to be torn away from it. We were continuously together. When she was at church, I felt as if I had sent away my eyes and all my senses. In the meantime, I could not look at this angel, who had entered into such an association, without the greatest emotion. That she had sacrificed everything for me was unbearable to me. So I asked her to join at the table when friends ate with me and gave her the clothing that her situation demanded and loved her more with every passing day. It was my serious intention to also unite with her before the eyes of the world. Oh dear God! And this heavenly girl died on the 4th of August, 1782, in the evening as the sun went down. I had the best doctors. Everything in the world was done. Consider that, dearest man, and allow me to end here. It is impossible for me to continue.

G. C. Lichtenberg.[15]

LABU: Unfortunately, gentlemen, we are forced to recognize once again what lamentable afflictions are caused on Planet Earth by the existence of death, which is so interesting in itself, and which, as you are well aware, is unknown to us here. I believe I act in accordance with your wishes if we let music accompany the soul of the deceased little flower girl on its path into space.

A very short snatch of music follows.

LABU: To my regret, I must announce that the Spectrophone has meanwhile shifted so far that it will take us all a great deal of effort to bring Herr Lichtenberg back into focus.

A series of purring and ringing signals are heard.

QUIKKO: Indeed, there has been a shift of a millionth of a milli-degree. We are no longer in Göttingen. According to my

---

15   Letter from Lichtenberg to G. H. Amelung written at the beginning of 1783. See Lichtenberg, *Briefe*, vol. 3, 291–3. Benjamin quotes the same letter in his "German Men and Women: A Sequence of Letters," SW, 3, 169–70, first published under his pseudonym Detlef Holz from April 1931 to May 1932 in the *Frankfurter Zeitung* (GS, 4.1, 149–233).

measuring instruments, it must be Einbeck, which is not far away.—Silence!

LICHTENBERG: Herr Professor, I think—

QUIKKO: Silence! Listen to Lichtenberg's voice. It comes from Einbeck.

LICHTENBERG: Herr Professor, we should retreat to the tavern; the noise threatens to become too distracting here.

PÜTTER: Here comes the whole crowd marching behind the town crier.[16]

TOWN CRIER: The citizenry of the town of Einbeck, on the orders of the laudable municipal authorities of this town, are hereby informed that the infamous, unworthy, and learned apprentice of murder Heinrich Julius Rütgerodt will be sent from life to death today, the 30th of June, this afternoon at three o'clock, on the hill outside our town. The same Heinrich Julius Rütgerodt[17] was a respected citizen of our town of Einbeck, who enjoyed, in addition to his food, 1,500 thaler in income. But he killed his mother because she, so he said, ate too much. He invented a machine, which, according to the opinion of exceptional professors and university technologists, is of the greatest credit to the human intellect. He placed a certain number of boards together in a barn in such a way that, as soon as his mother stepped foot on one of them, she set them all into motion, causing them to collapse on her head. He achieved his goal without a single nail and without any other injury being necessary. He beat his wife to death because one morning she didn't make his coffee the right way. He could name no other motive at the trial. He struck his maid dead in the cellar, because he no longer wanted to feed her small child. All the professors and justices agree, however, that despite his inclination toward the greatest inhumanity, there must have been hours when his conscience tortured him. For he never could tolerate daylight; instead he sat the entire day with his shutters closed. And, incidentally, it has been certified that his senses were healthy and his mind whole, indeed he was among the most acute of men. This monster in human form will now publicly be sent from life to death, on which account his offenses will once

16   Johann Stephan Pütter (1725–1807), German jurist, writer, and professor of law at the University of Göttingen.

17   Heinrich Julius Rütgerodt (1731–1775), murderer executed in Einbeck in 1775. Rütgerodt appears in Johann Caspar Lavater's influential theories on physiognomy, which were satirized by Lichtenberg.

more be held up to him and his confession taken in front of the assembled people.

PÜTTER: I do reproach myself, dear Herr Lichtenberg, for encouraging you to join me on an excursion during which your ears must be assaulted by such a vulgar outcry.

LICHTENBERG: I would have asked the innkeeper to close the windows if I didn't note in myself a certain interest in criminal cases such as these, Justice.

PÜTTER: Say what you like, but I know that it's only because of your friendship with me that you consented to join me in such a dubious adventure as this execution, such as executions are.

LICHTENBERG: I trust we won't be witnesses of it. At least as far as concerns myself, I must . . .

PÜTTER: Whatever are you thinking of? For me, it's simply a matter of getting my hands on the files directly after the delinquent has been put to death.

LICHTENBERG: Don't tell me you are working on a Pitaval[18] of our kingdom of Hanover.

PÜTTER: I cannot deny it, dear Professor.

LICHTENBERG: Well, then perhaps you will allow me to tell you about a short play I saw years ago at a London marionette theater. *There are loud voices outside.*

PÜTTER: Just allow me to close the window. The noise is beginning to get too loud after all.

LICHTENBERG: Well, there was a puppeteer who had set up his tent in the open near Covent Garden. For a few pence, one could sit there for hours. There is one piece among those in his repertoire which I have never forgotten. It was, as I said, a puppet theater. But whereas usually the puppets in such a theater represent people, in this one they truly only represented what they were: marionettes. Five, six, seven of these marionettes were hanging in front of a curtain: a merchant, a soldier, a clergyman, a housewife, a judge. They swayed back and forth in the breeze and conversed. What about? You'll never guess: it was about freedom of the will. It was a peaceful conversation, because there was really only one opinion among them all: reason, nature, and religion combined their weight in favor of free will. Only one puppet,

---

18   François Gayot de Pitaval (1673–1743), a French legal writer, compiled a multi-volume collection of famous criminal cases, *Causes célèbres et intéressantes, avec les jugemens qui les ont décidées* (1734–1743). After the work was translated into German in the mid-eighteenth century, "Pitaval" became a synonym for anthologies of true crime.

which hung somewhat to the side—I think I forgot to mention it before—was not so resolute. I think this puppet was a philosopher, or maybe a professor of physics. But the others didn't set great store by his opinion. All at once, a broad cardboard hand appeared from above.—This was supposed to represent a human hand.—It took away one puppet after the other. It was very clear. The marionette player was taking his puppets off their rack. As one after the other floated up into the heights, the ones that were left asked why they went away. And each one had some sort of excuse. But the hand of the puppeteer was never mentioned. And finally the philosopher or professor of physics was left alone on the empty stage.

PÜTTER: I'm not sure what you're trying to say, dear colleague.

LICHTENBERG: I don't mean to say anything; at best I want to ask something. Whether, when we break a murderer on the wheel, we don't make the same mistake as the child who hits the stool he bumps against.[19]

A PEDDLER: Excuse me, gentlemen, for bothering you. If I could ask the gentlemen to glance at my collection. The best assortment of silhouettes you can find anywhere. One for a silver coin. The king of Hanover, the king of Prussia, the gentlemen Danton and Robespierre, of whom so much is said, and Herr von Goethe, Assistant Legal Secretary of Weimar and author of *Werther*, Herr Bürger of neighboring Göttingen, the great world traveler Herr Forster, the gentlemen Iffland and Kopf, the pride of the Berlin theater, Mademoiselle Schröder of Weimar,—I can't count them all for you. No interest! (*Pause.*) Well, then the gentlemen will certainly not spurn a little memento of the day. I present to you the finely cut silhouette of our local monster. Please take a look at the text by Herr Lavater on the back.

PÜTTER (*reading*): An inveterate murderer, full of quiet evil burrowing in on itself, an assassin of women, a mother-killer, a miser such as no moralist could ever have thought up, no actor portrayed, no poet written about. He reveled in nocturnal gloom, turned midday to midnight by closing his shutters, locked his house, averse to light, averse to people, he buried his stolen treasures in the earth, deep within cellar walls, under floors and in fields. Spattered with the blood of innocence, he danced, laughing, on the wedding day of the woman whom later he struck dead at the grave she had herself

19   See Lichtenberg, *Aphorismen*, vol. 4, 120.

unknowingly prepared at his behest and in his presence. All this can be read in his likeness: his eyes look at nothing, his smile is like the open grave, and his fearsome teeth are the gates to Hell.[20]

PÜTTER: This leaflet is worth a silver coin to me.

LICHTENBERG: And to me it's even worth two, because there's a story behind it.

PÜTTER: What do you mean?

LICHTENBERG: I don't mind letting you in on a little story. I indulged myself in a joke; but it has to remain between us.

PÜTTER: Discretion is part of my job.

LICHTENBERG: I know. Even so, I wouldn't dare to tell you if I didn't know that we hold the same opinion of Lavater's theory of physiognomy, which has become quite the rage these days.

PÜTTER: What surprises me about Herr Lavater is that he, so attentive to the signs that allow character to be intuited, should have failed to notice that people who write the way he does are absolutely not to be believed. We, however, know that the manner in which a testimony is presented can sometimes be more important than the testimony itself.[21]

LICHTENBERG: All right then, listen to my story. Circumstances, which I do not wish to touch upon here, made it possible for me to send the silhouette of this monster, whom they are finishing off out there, to Lavater. And I did it in such a way that he neither knew who was portrayed, nor that I was the one who sent it. And now, listen to his response; I carry it with me. Such a leaflet is worth more than a kingdom.

PÜTTER: Let's hear it.

LICHTENBERG: This profile undoubtedly belongs to an extraordinary man who would have been great if he had a little more mental acumen and more heartfelt love. Whether I err in thinking I have discovered in him the aptitude and inclination for the establishment or dissemination of a religious sect is an open question. I can say nothing more. That is already too much.

PÜTTER: I never heard a truer word. That's a fortunate experiment you did with the physiognomist.

LICHTENBERG: If physiognomy becomes what Lavater expects it

---

20 See Johann Caspar Lavater, *Physiognomische Fragmente*, vol. 2, Fragment XVIII, "Zerstörte menschliche Natur, Rütgerodt" (Leipzig: Weidmanns, Erben and Reich, 1776), 194–5.

21 See Lichtenberg, *Aphorismen*, vol. 3, 110.

will, then children will be hanged before they have done the deeds that deserve the gallows.[22]

PÜTTER: But perhaps we shouldn't speak of the gallows here, so near the gallows' mound.

LICHTENBERG: I am glad that the noise has moved on. I still shudder when I think back to the morning when I saw, for the first and last time, someone who was awaiting the gallows. It was in front of the court of assizes in London. The poor fellow stood in front of the jury, and as they read the death sentence, the Lord Mayor of London was sitting there reading the newspaper.[23]

PÜTTER: I think it's time to depart. The moon is already shining through the window.

LICHTENBERG: A waning moon, and murky as well. There is nothing I hate more than the sight of the moon when it ...

QUIKKO: Gentlemen, you hear the attacks that Herr Lichtenberg is just about to make against us. It is beneath our dignity to follow this any longer. I am switching it off.

LABU: Without wishing to condone the impulsive actions of our esteemed colleague Quikko, I will now give the floor to Mr. Peka for his observations.

PEKA: Esteemed sirs, you will all have noticed that the Spectraphone's images were clearer than ever this time, perhaps as a consequence of the thunderstorms that purified the Earth's atmosphere. We all had time for a close look at Herr Lichtenberg, and I think I speak for all of you when I say: We can rest assured that the solution to our problem is closer than we suspected. Herr Lichtenberg is an unhappy character. Not because of the external circumstances that keep him in Göttingen, not because of his inner constitution that has turned him into a hypochondriac, but quite simply because of his appearance. It cannot have escaped you that he is a hunchback. Yes, gentlemen, it's easy to explain why a hunchback has nothing good to say about the science of physiognomy. He has scarcely any other choice but to form his own opinion about everything, because he cannot agree with public opinion on at least one very important point, I mean as far as the hunch is concerned. We should also not be surprised to hear him speak ill of Lavater, as of enthusiasts and geniuses.

22 Ibid., 218.

23 In a letter to Dieterich written on October 31, 1775, Lichtenberg reports that he saw a number of executions in London. See Lichtenberg, *Briefe*, vol. 1, 242.

Anyone whose physique invites criticism such as his does is left with no choice but to go on the defensive as a critic himself.

LABU: We thank Mr. Peka for his clear and timely explanations. But whether he is correct to say that such a hunchback is entirely incapable of enthusiasm or surges of feeling is something we should put to the test.

SOFANTI: A report has just come in from Venus about an occurrence that I consider of great interest to us. The fifty-year-old Lichtenberg, that enemy of sentimentalists, who has been loyal to reason his entire life, is about to betray it with the Muse. He is composing verse, that is to say, he is declaiming.

LABU: A welcome opportunity to deploy our Parlamonium. We will listen to the beginning of this poem and then translate it into music.

SOFANTI: Quiet, please.

The gong sounds.

LICHTENBERG (*in a stately voice unlike his usual tone*): What if at some point the sun did not return, I often thought, if I awoke in a dark night and was glad when I finally saw day break again. The deep stillness of early morning, the friend of reflection, combined with the feeling of increased strength and renewed health awoke in me then such a powerful trust in the order of nature and the spirit that guides it, that I believed myself as secure in the tumult of life as if my fate lay in my own hands. I thought then that this sensation, which you can neither force to come about nor feign and which grants you this indescribable feeling of well-being, is certainly the work of precisely that spirit, and it loudly tells you that now, at least, you think correctly. Oh, do not disturb with guilt this heavenly peace within, I then said to myself. How would this dawning day break for you, if this pure mirror-brightness of your being no longer reflected it into your interior? What else do you expect from the music of the spheres, if not these contemplations? What else is the chiming together of the planets but the expression of this certainty, which the spirit, at first with a storm of raptures, then gradually more and more—[24]

The recitation has already been undercut with music and at this point it changes into the melody of a hymn, perhaps one by Haydn or Handel. After a while, this music changes into a funeral march.

---

24   See Lichtenberg, *Vermischte Schriften*, vol. 5 (1844), 334–5.

FIRST CITIZEN: Quite a splendid cortege.

SECOND CITIZEN: Hush, you're not allowed to talk here in the funeral procession. Wait until we're there.

FIRST CITIZEN (*more quietly*): It's quite a splendid cortege, is what I wanted to say. When I think back to the time they buried Bürger here. Three men followed the coffin: Professor Althof—

SECOND CITIZEN: Shh, you'll get us into trouble.

FIRST CITIZEN: Now the head of the procession has already arrived. The music will stop soon, and then it'll get serious. Speeches will be made.

THIRD CITIZEN: He's said to have believed in the transmigration of souls. I heard it from Poppe the mechanic himself, he's the one who built him his instruments.

SECOND CITIZEN: Do you see where I'm pointing? Do you know what it is?

FIRST CITIZEN: That's impossible. You're right. His window. So he could look down from his laboratory at his grave site. That's what I call having all your affairs in order.

THIRD CITIZEN: He's said to have stood at that window and watched Bürger's burial through a telescope. But when he saw the hearse rolling through the churchyard gate, his servant, who was in the next room, could hear sobbing. He could not bear to watch the body being taken off the wagon. He closed the shutters and shut the window.[25]

SECOND CITIZEN: His whole life he flirted with death. This happened seven years ago, but I remember it as if it were yesterday. "The angels have let me know for some time in no uncertain terms that they feel a strong inclination to haul me to the churchyard in a small, portable house as soon as possible."[26] Yes, he wrote that to me seven years ago.

THIRD CITIZEN: It's said that he was a believer in the transmigration of souls.

SECOND CITIZEN: If his soul is transmigrating, then he could land on the Moon. He always loved long journeys.

FIRST CITIZEN: I can hardly credit that he was a professor of physics. "What is matter?" he's supposed to have said. "Perhaps there's nothing of the kind in nature. One kills matter and later pronounces it dead."[27]

THIRD CITIZEN: You shouldn't believe everything they say about

25 See Lichtenberg, *Briefe*, vol. 3, 115ff.

26 Ibid., 12.

27 See Lichtenberg, *Aphorismen*, vol. 3, 189.

him; he hadn't gone out in public for a long time.—There's movement over there. They've lowered the coffin into the depths.

FIRST CITIZEN: It is an outrage that the professors didn't even find
it worth their while to cancel their seminars today.

SECOND CITIZEN: It really is quite a beautiful funeral cortege. If
you remember Bürger's funeral, where—

DIFFERENT VOICES: Shh! Shh! Shh! What insolent behavior.
Disrespectful bunch.

THE PASTOR: Highly esteemed mourners, most particularly the
honorable representatives of the university and the esteemed citizens of the town!

LABU: I open the last meeting of the Moon Committee for Earth
Research. By a lamentable turn of events, the subject of our observations, the University of Göttingen Professor Lichtenberg, died
before we could conclude our work. However, if I have switched
off the funeral service, whose initial sounds you just heard, it is by
rights, as our Committee has every reason to hold a separate
funeral ceremony for Herr Lichtenberg. For what would our
scientific honor be worth, gentlemen, if we did not concede that
we had amends to make to the deceased?
Murmuring is heard from the Committee members.
   Admittedly, gentlemen, it has been confirmed that humans are
not happy. But we have too hastily drawn conclusions from that.
We concluded that they can therefore amount to nothing. Now, it
might seem that Professor Lichtenberg confirms that; you will all
have inspected the extensive catalog of works the deceased wanted
to write but never wrote. "The Island of Cebu" and "Kunkel" and
"The Parakletor" and "The Double Prince" and whatever else they
are called. But, gentlemen, perhaps he didn't write books simply
because he knew what their fate would be. As he said, for every
one book that is read thoroughly, thousands are merely leafed
through. Thousands more lie quietly around, others are wedged
on top of mouse holes, or thrown at rats. And on top of others, so
he says, people stand, sit down, drum, bake gingerbread. Others
are used to light pipes, or to stand beneath windows.[28] Caring
little for books, Lichtenburg cared all the more for thought.
Thanks to our methods of photography we possess today the
entries he wrote in his diaries, which will likely one day gain a

---

28   Ibid., 85–6.

reputation for themselves on Earth. As I'm sure you will have ascertained for yourselves, gentlemen, these diaries are full of curious, deep, and wise insights, at which he might perhaps never have arrived had he possessed the untroubled cheerfulness that is ours on the Moon. I therefore venture, most esteemed gentlemen, to call into question the basis of our research, that is, that humans can never amount to anything because they are never happy. Perhaps it is their unhappiness that allows them to advance, some of them as far as Professor Lichtenberg, who is worthy—and not merely because of his Moon map—of all the honor we can bestow. I therefore propose that we elevate Crater No. C.Y. 2802, in which we hold our meetings, into the company of those craters here on the Moon that we have dedicated to the minds on Earth we deem worthy. The craters—those at the edge of the cloud sea, those on the heights of the lunar mountains—that bear the exalted names of Thales, of Helvetius, of Humboldt, of Condorcet, of Fourier should accept into their ranks the Lichtenberg Crater, which lies clearly, purely, and peacefully in that magical light that illumines the millennium and is comparable to the light that begins to shine from the writings of this earthly Lichtenberg. We conclude the research of our Committee and switch on the music of the spheres.
Music.

"Lichtenberg, Ein Querschnitt," GS, 4.2, 696–720. Translated by Lisa Harries Schumann.

Radio play commissioned by Radio Berlin. In April 1932, Benjamin noted in a letter to Scholem that, after the "great success" of both What the Germans Were Reading While Their Classical Authors Were Writing *and* Much Ado About Kasper, *he had been commissioned by Radio Berlin to write* Lichtenberg *(*The Correspondence of Walter Benjamin, *391). By February 1933, Benjamin's opportunities for employment on the radio had ceased. On February 28, 1933, he wrote to Scholem that he had spent the day on "the dictation of a radio play, 'Lichtenberg,' which I must now send in, in accordance with a contract, the better part of which has long been fulfilled . . . 'Lichtenberg,' though commissioned, is not sure to be produced" (Ibid., 402). The radio play was never broadcast.*

SECTION IV

Writings on Radio, Off Air

Included here are some of the texts Benjamin wrote specifically on the subject of radio, but that were not planned or delivered as radio broadcast material.

CHAPTER 40

Reflections on Radio

It is the critical error of this institution to perpetuate the fundamental separation between performer and audience, a separation that is undermined by its technological basis. Every child recognizes that it is in the interest of radio to bring anyone before the microphone at any opportunity, making the public witness to interviews and conversations in which anyone might have a say. While people in Russia are drawing these inevitable conclusions from the apparatus, here the dull term "presentation" rules, under whose auspices the practitioner confronts the audience almost unchallenged. This absurdity has led to the fact that still today, after many long years of experience, the audience, thoroughly abandoned, remains inexpert and more or less reliant on sabotage in its critical reactions (switching off). Never has there been a genuine cultural institution that was not legitimized by the expertise it inculcated in the audience through its forms and technology. This was as much the case in Greek theater as with the Meistersingers, on the French stage as with pulpit orators. Only this most recent age, with its relentless fomenting of a consumer mentality among operagoers, novel-readers, leisure travelers, and the rest, has created dull, inarticulate masses—an audience in the narrow sense of the word, one with no standards for its judgment, no language for its sentiments. Via the masses' attitude toward radio programs, this barbarism has reached its peak and now appears ready to recede. It would take just one move: for the listener to focus his reflections on his real reactions, in order to sharpen and justify them. But the task would be insuperable if this behavior were, as the programming directors and particularly the presenters like to believe, largely incalculable, or else solely dependent on the content of the programming. The slightest consideration demonstrates the contrary. Never has a reader snapped shut a book he has just begun as willfully as listeners switch off the radio after the first minute of some lectures. It is not the remoteness of the subject matter; this would often be a reason to listen for a while, uncommitted. It is the voice, the diction, the language—in short, too frequently the technological and formal aspect makes the most interesting shows unbearable, just as in a few cases it can captivate the listener with the most remote material. (There are speakers one listens to even for the weather report.) Only this technological and formal aspect can ever develop the expertise of the listener and stem the barbarism. The matter is self-evident. One need only consider what it means that the radio listener, as opposed to every other kind of audience, receives the programming in his home, where the voice is like a guest; upon arrival, it is usually assessed just as quickly and as sharply. And why is it that no one tells the voice what is expected of it, what will be appreciated, what will not be forgiven, etc.? The answer lies solely in the indolence of the masses and the narrow-mindedness of those in control. Of course, it would not be easy to adapt the behavior of the voice to the language, for both are involved. But if radio were to rely only on the arsenal of impossibilities that grow more plentiful each day, drawing, for example, only on negative attributes to create something like a humorous typology of speakers, it would not only improve the standard of its programming, it would also have the audience on its side, as experts. And nothing is more important than that.

"Reflexionen zum Rundfunk," GS, 2.3, 1506–7. Translated by Jonathan Lutes.

Written in 1930 or 1931, no later than November 1931. Unpublished during Benjamin's lifetime.

CHAPTER 41

Theater and Radio

On the Mutual Supervision of
Their Educational Roles

"Theater and Radio": an unbiased consideration of these two institutions does not necessarily evoke a sense of harmony. The
competitive relationship here is not quite as fierce as between radio
and the concert hall. Yet one knows too much of the ever-expanding
activities of radio and the ever-deepening crisis in the theater to
even begin to imagine a collaboration between the two. Such a
collaboration nevertheless exists, and has existed for quite some
time. To the extent that it has occurred, it has only been of a peda-
gogic nature. Southwest German Radio recently initiated such a
collaboration, and with considerable enthusiasm. The station's
artistic director, Ernst Schoen, was one of the first to turn his attention to the works recently put forward for discussion by Bert Brecht
and his literary and musical colleagues. It is no accident that while
these works—*Der Lindberghflug*, *Das Badener Lehrstück*, *Der Jasager*,
Der Neinsager, etc.—are unequivocally pedagogical, they also
constitute a bridge between theater and radio in a wholly original
way.[1] The basis for these programs soon proved viable. Similarly
structured serial programs, such as Elisabeth Hauptmann's "Ford,"
were soon broadcast on school radio, while issues confronted in
daily life—the upbringing and education of children, techniques
for professional success, marriage difficulties—were casuistically

---

1 Brecht's *Der Lindberghflug* [Lindbergh's Flight], with music by Kurt Weill and Paul
Hindemith, based on Brecht's radio play *Der Flug der Lindberghs* [The Flight of the
Lindberghs] (1930); *Das Badener Lehrstück vom Einverständnis* [The Baden-Baden Lesson
on Consent], cowritten by Brecht with Elisabeth Hauptmann and Slatan Dudow, with music
by Hindemith (1929); and *Der Jasager* [He Who Said Yes], by Brecht with music by Weill
(1930); and Brecht's *Der Neinsager* [He Who Said No] (1930).

addressed through examples and counterexamples.[2] The Frankfurt radio station (together with that in Berlin) provided the impetus for such "listening models," written by Walter Benjamin and Wolf Zucker.[3] The breadth of these activities allows for a closer look at the principles of this work, while simultaneously preventing it from being misunderstood.

Such a scrutiny must not cause us to overlook the obvious issue at hand: technology. It would behoove us to leave all sensitivities aside and to state the matter outright: the radio, in relation to the theater, represents not only the newer, but also the more exposed technology. It cannot yet harken back to a classical epoch, as can the theater; the masses that embrace it are much larger; and finally and above all, the material elements on which its equipment is based, and the intellectual elements on which its programs are based, are closely intertwined to the benefit of the listeners. For its part, what does the theater have to offer? The use of a living medium, nothing more. Perhaps the crisis facing the theater stems from no question more important than this: What does the use of a living person contribute to the theater? In response, two starkly contrasting notions arise—one reactionary and one progressive.

The first sees itself in no way obliged to take notice of the crisis. From its perspective, the harmony of the whole is and remains unclouded, with man as its representative. It regards him as being at the peak of his powers, as the lord of creation, as a personage (even in the case of a mere wage-earner). His realm is the culture of today, over which he reigns in the name of "humanity." This proud, self-assured theater, which takes as little heed of its own crisis as it does that of the world; this haut-bourgeois theater (whose most cele-brated magnate, however, has recently stepped down)—whether now proceeding with plebeian dramas in the new style, or with Offenbachian libretti, it always perceives itself as a "symbol," a "totality," a "total work of art."

We are characterizing the theater of education and of distrac-tion—so contradictory in appearance, yet merely complementary phenomena within the saturated stratum for which all things become stimuli. But in vain does this theater seek to compete with

---

2 Elisabeth Hauptmann (1897–1973) was a German writer who collaborated with Brecht on works including *The Threepenny Opera* (1928) and *Happy End* (1929).

3 On Benjamin's collaboration with Wolf Zucker, see, in this volume, "A Pay Raise?! Whatever Gave You That Idea!" (292), and "Listening Models" (373).

the attraction of million-mark films, replete with complicated machinery and massive crowds of extras; in vain does its repertoire encompass all epochs and all corners of the world, while broadcasting and cinema, with a much smaller apparatus, have room in their studios for ancient Chinese drama along with new forays into Surrealism. Competing with the technology available to radio and cinema is pointless.

But the ensuing controversy is hardly pointless. Above all, this is what is expected from progressive theater. Brecht, the first to theorize it, calls this theater "epic." Epic Theater is thoroughly sober, especially regarding technology. This is not the place to expound on the theory of Epic Theater, much less to demonstrate how the development and structure of *Gestus* amount to nothing but a retro-transformation of the methods of montage so critical to broadcasting and film—from a technological undertaking to a human one. Suffice it to say that the principle of Epic Theater, like that of montage, is based on interruption. Only here, interruption acts not as a stimulus, but as a pedagogical tool. It brings the action to a temporary halt, forcing the audience to take a critical position toward the proceedings and the actor to take a critical position toward his role.

Epic Theater pits drama's laboratory against drama's total work of art. It draws in a new way upon theater's reliable old prospect—the exposure of those present. Its experiments revolve around man in the present crisis, man eliminated by radio and cinema, man, to put it somewhat drastically, as the fifth wheel of technology. This diminished, neutralized humanity is subjected to certain ordeals and evaluative tests. Consequently, events are alterable not at their climaxes, not through virtue and resolve, but only in their strictly habitual processes, through reason and practice. To construct from the smallest elements of behavior what Aristotelian dramatic theory refers to as "action": that is the meaning of Epic Theater.

Epic Theater confronts conventional theater by replacing culture with training, and distraction with groupings. Concerning the latter, anyone who follows the changes in radio will be familiar with the recent efforts to more narrowly define listener blocs in terms of social class, interests, and milieu. Similarly, Epic Theater is attempting to cultivate a group of interested parties, who, independent of criticism and advertising, are keen to see their own concerns, including political ones, realized in a series of actions (in the above sense) by a consummately trained ensemble. Notably, this development has led to older dramas undergoing major transformations (*Eduard II*; *Dreigroschenoper*) while newer ones have been subjected to a kind of controversial treatment (*Jasager*, *Neinsager*);[4] this may shed light on what is meant by replacing culture (of knowledge) with training (of judgment). Radio is particularly bound to take advantage of established cultural goods, which it does best through adaptations that not only correspond with technology, but also comply with the demands of an audience that is a contemporary of its technology. Only thus will the apparatus remain free from the halo of a "gigantic educational enterprise" (as Schoen puts it),[5] scaled back to a format fit for humans.

"Theater und Rundfunk, Zur gegenseitigen Kontrolle ihrer Erziehungsarbeit," GS, 2.2, 773–6. Translated by Jonathan Lutes.

Published in Blätter des hessischen Landestheaters *in May, 1932.*

---

4 Brecht's *Eduard II* [Edward II] (1924); *Dreigroschenoper* (Threepenny Opera) (1928); *Der Jasager* [He Who Said Yes], and *Der Neinsager* [He Who Said No].

5 See Benjamin, "Gespräch mit Ernst Schoen" (GS, 4.1, 548); "Conversation with Ernst Schoen" (trans. Thomas Y. Levin in *The Work of Art in the Age of Its Technological Reproducibility and Other Writings on Media*, ed. Michael Jennings et al. [Cambridge, MA: Harvard University Press, 2008], 397).

CHAPTER 42

Two Kinds of Popularity
Fundamental Principles for a Radio Play

The radio play *What the Germans Were Reading While Their Classical Authors Were Writing*, a few samples of which have been excerpted for readers of this issue, attempts to take into account some fundamental considerations on the popularity to which radio ought to aspire in its literary dimension.[1] For all of radio's revolutionary aspects, it is in relation to our understanding of popularity that it is, or should be, most innovative. According to the old conception, popular representation—no matter how valuable it may be—is derivative. And that is easy enough to explain, given that before radio there were hardly any forms of publication that actually correlated to popular or educational aims. There was the book, the lecture, the newspaper, but these forms of communication in no way differed from those through which the progress of scholarly research was disseminated among circles of experts. Consequently, popular representation was undertaken in scholarly forms and had to forgo its own original methods. It found itself constrained to clothe the content of certain domains of knowledge in more or less appealing forms, in some cases relating it to shared experience and common sense; but what it produced was always secondhand. Popularization was a subordinate technique, and public estimation of it testified to this fact.

Radio—and this is one of its most notable consequences—has profoundly transformed this state of affairs. On the strength of its unprecedented technological potential to address unlimited

---

1 Benjamin refers to his own play, *What the Germans Were Reading While Their Classical Authors Were Writing*, an excerpted version of which was published with "Two Kinds of Popularity" in the radio journal *Rufer und Hörer* in September, 1932.

masses simultaneously, popularization has outgrown its well-meaning, humanistic intentions and become an endeavor with its own formal laws, one that has elevated itself just as markedly from its former practice as did modern advertising technology in the previous century. In terms of experience, this implies the following: popularization in the old style took its point of departure from a sound basis of scholarship, imparted in the same way that scholarship itself had developed it, but with the omission of more difficult lines of thought. The essence of this form of popularization was omission; by and large its layout remained that of the textbook, with its main parts in large print and its excursus in small. However, the much broader, yet also much more intensive popularity sought by the radio cannot content itself with this approach. It demands a total transformation and rearrangement of the material from the standpoint of popular relevance. It does not, therefore, suffice to attract interest with some timely inducement, only to once again offer the curious listener what he can hear in any old lecture hall. To the contrary, everything depends on convincing him that his own interests possess objective value for the material itself; that his questions, even when not spoken into the microphone, call for new scholarly findings. In this way, the external relationship between scholarship and popularity that prevailed before is supplanted by an approach that scholarship itself cannot possibly forgo. For here is a case of a popularity that not only mobilizes knowledge in the direction of the public, but mobilizes the public in the direction of knowledge. In a word: true popular interest is always active; it transforms the substance of knowledge and has an impact on the pursuit of knowledge itself.

The livelier the form in which such an educational endeavor claims to proceed, the more indispensable the demand that a truly lively *knowledge* unfold, and not just an abstract, unverifiable, and general liveliness. This applies especially to the radio play, insofar as it has an instructive character. The literary radio play in particular is as little served by the arts-and-crafts cobbling together of so-called conversations, plucked from anthologies and from excerpts of works and letters, as by the dubious audacity of having Goethe or Kleist at the microphone, reciting the words of the script writer. And because the one is as questionable as the other, there is only one way out: to address the scholarly questions directly. And that is what I am aiming for in my experiment.[2] It is not the heroes of German intellectual history themselves who make an appearance, nor did it seem appropriate to make heard the greatest possible number of excerpted works. In order to gain depth, the superficial was taken as a point of departure. The aim was to present the listeners with what is in fact so prevalent and so gratuitous that it invites this typification: not the literature, but rather the literary *conversation* of the day. Yet this conversation, unfolding in coffeehouses and at fairs, at auctions and on strolls, was preoccupied with poetry schools and newspapers, censorship and the book trade, secondary education and lending libraries, Enlightenment and obscurantism in unforeseeably diverse ways; this conversation simultaneously maintains an intimate relationship to the questions posed by an advanced literary scholarship ever more concerned with researching the historical factors that determined literary production. To reconstruct the debates over book prices, newspaper articles, lampoons, and new publications—in themselves the most superficial debates imaginable—is anything but superficial as a scholarly undertaking, for such retroactive invention also makes considerable demands on the investigation of facts with respect to their sources. In short, the radio play in question strives for the closest possible contact with the research recently undertaken in so-called audience sociology. It would see its highest confirmation in being able to captivate the specialist no less than the layman, even if for different reasons. And with that, the concept of a new popularity appears to have found its simplest definition.

"Zweierlei Volkstümlichkeit: Grundsätzliches zu einem Hörspiel," GS, 4.2, 671–3. Translated by Jonathan Lutes and Diana K. Reese.

Published in the radio magazine Rufer und Hörer, *September 1932.*

---

2 See Benjamin, *What the Germans Were Reading While Their Classical Authors Were Writing.*

CHAPTER 43

The Situation in Broadcasting

The chaos of programs is inefficient and confusing. To address this problem, each station's programming will now be broadcast on several other stations. So far so good, in terms of a simplification of the work involved; however, the following is now occurring: the many large stations abroad are interfering with the reception of the smaller German stations, to such a degree that their radius is limited to only forty or fifty kilometers. Conferences have been arranged to eliminate these disturbances through a sensible allocation of wavelengths. Without waiting for the results of these conferences, it has now been decided to build nine or ten large broadcasting stations, allegedly to ensure that reception will be free of disturbances. (Of course, there will again be separate programming for these stations. What is simplified at one extreme is lost at the other. A victory for double-programming across the board.) But the real reason for building these stations lies elsewhere: in politics. Long-range propaganda instruments are desired in case of war.

"Situation im Rundfunk," GS, 2.3, 1505. Translated by Jonathan Lutes.

Unpublished during Benjamin's lifetime. Likely written between 1930 and 1932. For further context, see the exchange of letters between Benjamin and Schoen from April 1930, where they discuss Benjamin's plan to publish, in the Frankfurter Zeitung, *an essay on the current political issues in broadcasting (GS, 2.3, 1497–505). This essay was, apparently, never realized. Benjamin's comments also register an acknowledgment or anticipation of the reorganization of radio under the Papen government, introduced in the summer of 1932, which transferred control over broadcasting to the state and prepared the way for the takeover of the airwaves by the Nazis at the end of January, 1933.*

CHAPTER 44

Listening Models

The underlying purpose of these models is a didactic one. The subject matter of the instruction consists of typical situations taken from everyday life. The method of the instruction is to juxtapose example with counterexample.

The speaker appears three times in each listening model: at the beginning he announces to the listeners the topic that will be covered; he then introduces to the audience the two partners who appear in the first part of the listening model. This first part contains the counterexample: how *not* to do it. After the first part, the speaker returns. He indicates the mistakes that were made. He then introduces the listeners to a new figure, who will appear in the second part and show how the same situation can be handled successfully. At the end the speaker compares the wrong methods with the right ones, and frames the moral.

Thus, no listening model has more than four principal voices: 1) that of the speaker; 2) that of the model figure, who is identical in the first and second parts; 3) that of the inept partner in the first part; 4) that of the adept partner in the second part.

Radio Frankfurt presented three listening models from 1931 to 1932:

1. "A Pay Raise?! Whatever Gave You That Idea!"
2. "The Boy Tells Nothing But Lies."
3. "Can You Help Me Out Until Thursday?"

The first listening model showed one inept and one clever employee, negotiating with their boss. The second showed a ten-year-old boy who tells a fib. In the first part his father questions him, driving him deeper and deeper into his untruth. In the second part his mother demonstrates how to make the boy aware of his naughtiness without provoking defiance. The third listening model showed the clumsy behavior of a man who asks his friend for money and gets turned down, followed by the skillful actions of someone else in the same situation.

"Hörmodelle," GS, 4.2, 628. Translated by Jonathan Lutes.

Unpublished during Benjamin's lifetime. "Listening Models" was possibly written in early 1931, in conjunction with the broadcast of "A Pay Raise?!" Benjamin did produce at least one additional listening model, perhaps in collaboration with Wolf Zucker: a piece entitled "Frech wird der Junge auch noch!" [The Boy Is Getting Fresh, Too!], likely a version of the above-mentioned "The Boy Tells Nothing But Lies," was broadcast from Frankfurt on July 1, 1931, and perhaps from Berlin as well (see editors' notes in GS, 2.3, 1442; see also Schiller-Lerg, Walter Benjamin und der Rundfunk, *196–7, 213–16).*

Appendix:
Walter Benjamin's Radio Broadcasts

The Appendix, a chronological presentation of Benjamin's known broadcasts and, where possible, their titles, is intended to provide the reader with an overall sense of the scale and timing of Benjamin's broadcast output. It is indebted to Sabine Schiller-Lerg's seminal study, *Walter Benjamin und der Rundfunk* (see in particular her chronological listing of the broadcasts, pp. 530–2; for programming categories, see especially pp. 540–1), as well as to the editors' notes to Benjamin's *Gesammelte Schriften*. Both of these sources provide detailed information concerning the archival status, dating, and location of Benjamin's broadcasts. Where indicated, the information comes from another source.

Below the individual translations in this volume, we have provided further information, where available, concerning the archival sources from which the dates of broadcast have been determined. There, where possible, we also indicate the length and time of the broadcasts.

For broadcasts that are translated and included in *Radio Benjamin*, the reader is referred to this volume. For broadcasts that do not appear in this volume but that have been translated elsewhere, the reader is referred to the relevant translation. For broadcasts that do not appear in this volume and, as far as we know, have not been translated elsewhere, the reader is referred to the relevant pages in the *Gesammelte Schriften*. In the last instance, the titles appear first in German, with a translation provided in brackets.

A word on the "lost or missing" broadcasts: these are known to have taken place in the sense that other archival traces, including announcements in radio journals such as the Berlin station's *Funkstunde* or the Frankfurt station's *Südwestdeutsche Rundfunk-Zeitung*, testify to the fact. These broadcast-events, for which there is no remaining typescript of the material in its broadcast form, fall into at least two categories: broadcasts for which there is no related, surviving "textual witness" to the broadcast material, in other words no existing material other than the mention of the broadcast in a radio journal or in Benjamin's other broadcasts, letters, or other work; and broadcasts for which there exist other, related versions of the material, such as print versions published elsewhere by Benjamin. For the latter category, we refer the reader to the relevant pages of the related material in the *Gesammelte Schriften*, and, where possible, relevant translations of the related texts.

For dates on which a broadcast is known to have taken place but for which the precise title or content is not known, the relevant, if incomplete, information is given in brackets under the title column. These dates should be read in tandem with Table 2, which gives broadcast texts for which the precise date of broadcast is not known.

Table 3 provides information about radio texts that were planned or completed by Benjamin but were never aired, as well as about broadcasts that might have taken place but for which there is no further information.

Table 1: Chronological list of broadcast dates

	Date	Station	Title	Programming Category / Broadcast Type	Reference
1.	3/23/1927	Frankfurt	"Junge russische Dichter" [Young Russian Writers]	Talk	Lost or missing. See related text, "Neue Dichtung in Russland," GS, 2.2, 755–62.
2.	8/14/1929	Frankfurt	"Die Romane von Julien Green" [The Novels of Julien Green]	Talk on the book-hour	Lost or missing. See related text, "Julien Green," GS, 2.1, 328–34. Translated in SW, 2, 331–6.
3.	8/15/1929	Frankfurt	"Children's Literature"	Talk	In this volume.
4.	8/20/1929	Frankfurt	"Reading of Works by Robert Walser"	Reading	Lost or missing.[1]
5.	9/4/1929	Frankfurt	"Vorlesung aus eigenen Werken" [Readings from My Own Work]	Reading	Lost or missing.
6.	10/29/1929	Frankfurt	"Johann Peter Hebel"	Talk on the book-hour	GS, 2.2, 636–40.
7.	10/31/1929	Frankfurt	"Gides Berufung" [Gide's Vocation]	Talk	GS, 2.1, 257–69.
8.	11/9/1929	Berlin	[On a Berlin-related theme; title unknown]	Youth radio	Lost or missing.
9.	11/23/1929	Berlin	[On a Berlin-related theme; title unknown]	Youth radio	Lost or missing.
10.	11/30/1929	Berlin	[In a series entitled "Tales and Adventures"; title unknown]	Youth radio	Lost or missing.

1 Information on this broadcast was provided by Thomas Küpper, coeditor (with Anja Nowak) of Benjamin's radio writings in the new critical edition, *Werke und Nachlaß* (Berlin: Suhrkamp, forthcoming). The announcement of the broadcast was discovered by Mr. Gregor Ackermann, who found in the newspaper *Frankfurter Nachrichten*, vol. 208, no. 230 (August 20, 1929), a listing indicating that "Walter Benjamin would read the works of Robert Walser on Frankfurt radio the same day" (email from Thomas Küpper, February 8, 2013). Unfortunately, no surviving text for this broadcast has been found.

11.	12/7/1929	Berlin	"Berlin Puppet Theater"	Youth radio	In this volume.
12.	12/14/1929	Berlin	[On a Berlin-related theme; title unknown]	Youth radio	Lost or missing.
13.	12/15/1929	Frankfurt	"Bücher von Thornton Wilder und Ernest Hemingway" [Books by Thornton Wilder and Ernest Hemingway]	Talk on the book-hour	GS, 7.1, 270–1.
14.	12/16/1929	Frankfurt	"Sketched in Mobile Dust"	Reading	In this volume.
15.	1/4/1930	Berlin	[On a Berlin-related theme; title unknown]	Youth radio	Lost or missing.
16.	1/23/1930	Frankfurt	"Pariser Köpfe" [Parisian Minds]	Talk	GS, 7.1, 279–86.
17.	1/24/1930	Frankfurt	"Friedrich Sieburgs Versuch 'Gott in Frankreich?'" [Friedrich Sieburg's Essay "God in France?"]	Talk on the book-hour	GS, 7.1, 286–94.
18.	2/1/1930	Berlin	[On a Berlin-related theme; title unknown]	Youth radio	Lost or missing.
19.	2/8/1930	Berlin	[On a Berlin-related theme; title unknown]	Youth radio	Lost or missing.
20.	2/15/1930	Berlin	[On a Berlin-related theme; title unknown]	Youth radio	Lost or missing.
21.	2/25/1930	Berlin	"Demonic Berlin"	Youth radio	In this volume.
22.	3/7/1930	Berlin	"Berlin Guttersnipe"	Youth radio	In this volume.
23.	3/15/1930	Berlin	"Berlin Toy Tour I"	Youth radio	In this volume.
24.	3/22/1930	Berlin	"Berlin Toy Tour II"	Youth radio	In this volume.
25.	3/26/1930	Frankfurt	"E. T. A. Hoffmann and Oskar Panizza"	Talk	In this volume.

26.	3/28/1930	Frankfurt	"Reuters *Schelmuffsky* und Kortums *Jobsiade*" [Reuter's *Schelmuffsky* and Kortum's *Jobsiade*]	Talk on the book-hour	GS, 2.2, 648–60.
27.	3/29/1930	Berlin	[On a Berlin-related theme; title unknown][2]	Youth radio	Lost or missing.
28.	4/5/1930	Berlin	"Borsig"	Youth radio	In this volume.
29.	4/12/1930	Berlin	[On a Berlin-related theme; title unknown][3]	Youth radio	Lost or missing.
30.	4/14/1930	Berlin	"Theodor Hosemann"	Youth radio	In this volume.
31.	5/9/1930	Frankfurt	"Prescriptions for Comedy Writers: A Conversation between Wilhelm Speyer and Walter Benjamin"	Dialogue	In this volume.
32.	5/11/1930	Frankfurt	"'Die Angestellten – Aus dem neuesten Deutschland' von S. Kracauer" ["White-Collar Workers: The Latest from Germany," by S. Kracauer]	Talk on the book-hour	Lost or missing. See related text, "Ein Aussent-seiter Macht sich Bemerkbar, Zu S. Kracauer. 'Die Angestellten,'" GS, 3, 219–25. Translated as "An Outsider Makes His Mark," SW, 2, 305–11.
33.	5/24/1930	Berlin	"Besuch im Kupferwerk" [Visit to the Copper Works]	Youth radio	Lost or missing.
34.	6/22/1930	Berlin	Erzählung der Woche [Story of the Week]	Reading	Lost or missing.

2 Based on comments made by Benjamin in both "Borsig" and "The Rental Barracks," Schiller-Lerg speculates that Benjamin's broadcast for March 29, 1930 was on the subject of "Baugeschichte Berlins unter Friedrich Wilhelm I" [The Building History of Berlin under Frederick William I] (*Walter Benjamin und der Rundfunk*, 141–3, 530).

3 Schiller-Lerg suggests that "The Rental Barracks" was most likely broadcast on this date (*Walter Benjamin und der Rundfunk*, 112, 142, 532).

35.	6/23/1930	Frankfurt	"Neues um Stefan George" [Something New About Stefan George]	Talk	Lost or missing. See related text, "Wider ein Meisterwerk: Zu Max Kommerell, 'Der Dichter als Führer in der deutschen Klassik,'" GS, 3, 252–9. Translated as "Against a Masterpiece," SW, 2, 378–85.
36.	6/24/1930	Frankfurt	"Bert Brecht"	Talk	GS, 2.2, 660–7. Translated in SW, 2, 365–71.
37.	7/1/1930	Berlin	["A Visit to the Brass Works"]	Youth radio	In this volume.
38.	7/12/1930	Berlin	"A Visit to the Brass Works"	Youth radio	In this volume.
39.	7/16/1930	Berlin	"Witch Trials"	Youth radio	In this volume.
40.	9/20/1930	Berlin	"Das Leben des Autos"[4]	Youth radio	Lost or missing.
41.	9/22/1930	Frankfurt	"Myslowitz–Braunschweig–Marseille: Die Geschichte eines Haschisch-Rausches" [Myslovice–Braunschweig–Marseilles: The Story of a Hashish Trance]	Reading	Lost or missing. See related text in GS, 4.2, 729–37. Translated in SW, 2, 386–93.
42.	9/23/1930	Frankfurt	"Robber Bands in Old Germany"	Youth radio	In this volume.
43.	9/27/1930	Berlin	"True Dog Stories"	Youth radio	In this volume.
44.	10/2/1930	Berlin	"Robber Bands in Old Germany"	Youth radio	In this volume.

4 There is some debate on the title and subject-matter of this broadcast, as well as that of the subsequent broadcast on January 17, 1931. Schiller-Lerg lists "Vom Leben der Autos" as the title for the broadcast on September 20, 1930, and "Das Leben des Antos" for the broadcast on January 17, 1931. Her discussion of the broadcast makes a compelling case for a focus on "Autos," or cars (*Walter Benjamin und der Rundfunk*, 169). The editors of the GS, however, dispute the spelling of "Autos" and insist that the title ought to be "Das Leben des Antos" (GS, 2.3, 1442).

45.	10/23/1930	Berlin	"The Gypsies"	Youth radio	In this volume.
46.	11/8/1930	Berlin	"The Bootleggers"	Youth radio	In this volume.
47.	11/22/1930	Berlin	"Kaspar Hauser"	Youth radio	In this volume.
48.	11/23/1930	Frankfurt	"Alte und neue Graphologie" [Graphology Old and New]	Talk	Lost or missing. See related text in GS, 4.1, 596–8. Translated in SW, 2, 398–400.
49.	12/17/1930	Frankfurt	"Kaspar Hauser"	Youth radio	In this volume.
50.	12/29/1930	Frankfurt	"Carousel of Jobs"	Talk	In this volume.
51.	12/31/1930	Frankfurt	"The Bootleggers"	Youth radio	In this volume.
52.	1/16/1931	Berlin	[theme and title unknown]⁴	Youth radio	Lost or missing.
53.	1/17/1931	Frankfurt	"Das Leben des Autos"	Youth radio	Lost or missing.
54.	1/30/1931	Berlin	"Dr. Faust"	Youth radio	In this volume.
55.	2/8/1931	Berlin	"Wie nehme ich meinen Chef?" [How Do I Deal with My Boss?] (with Wolf Zucker)	Listening model	See "A Pay Raise?! Whatever Gave You That Idea!" in this volume.
56.	2/11/1931	Frankfurt	"Theodor Neuhof, der König von Korsika" [Theodor Neuhof, the King of Corsica]	Youth radio	Lost or missing.
57.	2/14/1931	Frankfurt	"Cagliostro"	Youth radio	In this volume.
58.	3/22/1931	Frankfurt	"Tag des Buches: Vom Manuskript zum 100. Tausend: Gespräch zwischen Ernst Rowohlt und Walter Benjamin" [Day of the Book: From Manuscript to One Hundred Thousand: A Conversation between Ernst Rowohlt and Walter Benjamin]	Dialogue	Lost or missing.

5 Schiller-Lerg suggests "Postage Stamp Swindles" as a possible candidate for this broadcast (*Walter Benjamin und der Rundfunk*, 165).

59.	3/26/1931	Frankfurt	Listening Model I: "A Pay Raise?! Whatever Gave You That Idea!" (with Wolf Zucker)	Listening model	In this volume.
60.	3/28/1931	Frankfurt	"Dr. Faust"	Youth radio	In this volume.
61.	3/28/1931	Frankfurt	"Das öffentliche Lokal, ein unerforschtes Milieu" [The Local Bar, an Unexplored Milieu]	Talk	Lost or missing.
62.	4/27/1931	Frankfurt	"Unpacking My Library: A Talk about Collecting"	Talk	Lost or missing. See related text translated in SW, 2, 486–93.
63.	4/29/1931	Frankfurt	"The Bastille, the Old French State Prison"	Youth radio	In this volume.
64.	5/9/1931	Frankfurt	"Naples"	Youth/School radio	In this volume.
65.	7/1/1931	Frankfurt	"Wie die Zauberer es machen" [How the Magicians Do It]	Youth radio	Lost or missing.
66, 67.	7/1/1931	Frankfurt and Berlin	Hörmodell II: "Frech wird der Junge auch noch!" [Listening Model II: The Boy Is Getting Fresh, Too!] (with Wolf Zucker)	Listening model	Lost or missing.
68.	7/3/1931	Frankfurt	"Franz Kafka: *Beim Bau der Chinesischen Mauer*"	Talk on the book-hour	GS, 2.2, 676–83. Translated in SW, 2, 494–500.
69.	9/16/1931	Frankfurt	"Wie die Tierbändiger es machen" [How the Animal Tamers Do It]	Youth radio	Lost or missing.
70.	9/18/1931	Berlin	"The Fall of Herculaneum and Pompeii"	Youth radio	In this volume.
71.	10/31/1931	Berlin	"The Lisbon Earthquake"	Youth radio	In this volume.

72.	11/5/1931	Berlin	"Canton Theater Fire"	Youth radio	In this volume.
73.	1/3/1932	Frankfurt	"Funkspiele: Dichter nach Stichworten" [Radio plays: Poets by Category]	Radio play	Lost or missing.
74.	1/6/1932	Frankfurt	"The Lisbon Earthquake"	Youth radio	In this volume.
75.	1/19/1932	Frankfurt	"Auf der Spur alter Briefe" [On the Trail of Old Letters]	Talk	See the related material in GS, 4.2, 942–4. Translated in SW, 2, 555–8.
76.	1/21/1932	Frankfurt	Länder-Querschnitt III: "Frankreich in seiner Kunst" [Countries in Profile III: France in Its Art]	Talk	Lost or missing.
77.	2/3/1932	Frankfurt	"Canton Theater Fire"	Youth radio	In this volume.
78.	2/4/1932	Berlin	"The Railway Disaster at the Firth of Tay"	Youth radio	In this volume.
79.	2/16/1932	Berlin	*What the Germans Were Reading While Their Classical Authors Were Writing*	Radio play	In this volume.
80.	3/10/1932	Frankfurt	*Much Ado About Kasper*	Radio play for children	In this volume.
81.	3/23/1932	Berlin	"The Mississippi Flood of 1927"	Youth radio	In this volume.
82.	3/30/1932	Frankfurt	"The Railway Disaster at the Firth of Tay"	Youth radio	In this volume.
83.	5/16/1932	Frankfurt	*The Cold Heart* (with Ernst Schoen)	Radio play for children	In this volume.
84.	7/6/1932	Frankfurt	"Denksport" [Mental Exercise]	Youth radio	See "A Crazy Mixed-Up Day: Thirty Brainteasers" in this volume.

85.	9/9/1932	Cologne	*Much Ado About Kasper*	Radio play for children	In this volume.
86.	1/19/1933	Frankfurt	"Von Seeräubern und Piraten" [On Pirates and Privateers]	Youth radio	Lost or missing.
87.	1/29/1933	Frankfurt	"Aus einer unveröffenlichten Skizzensammlung *Berliner Kindheit um 1900*" [From an unpublished collection of sketches, *Berlin Childhood around 1900*]	Reading	Lost or missing. See the related material, translated as *Berlin Childhood Around 1900*, in SW, 3, 345–413.

Table 2: Broadcasts whose precise dates are not known

These titles should be read in conjunction with the dates listed in Table 1, where the exact title or content, as indicated in brackets, has not been determined.

	Date	Station	Title	Category	Reference
1.	[probably Nov. or Dec. 1929]	Berlin	"Berlin Dialect"	Youth radio	In this volume.
2.	[probably end of 1929 or beginning of 1930]	Berlin	"Street Trade and Markets in Old and New Berlin"	Youth radio	In this volume.
3.	[probably 1929/1930]	Berlin	"Fontane's *Wanderings Through the Mark Brandenburg*"	Youth radio	In this volume.
4.	[probably spring or summer, 1930]	Berlin	"The Rental Barracks"	Youth radio	In this volume.
5.	[probably the second half of 1930]	Berlin	"Postage Stamp Swindles"	Youth radio	In this volume.
6.	[probably 7/6/1932]	Frankfurt	"A Crazy Mixed-Up Day: Thirty Brainteasers"	Youth radio	In this volume.

Table 3: Broadcasts that were planned, started, or completed, but never delivered on air, or broadcasts for which there is no further information

	Status	Title	Category	Reference
1.	Completed, but never broadcast	*Lichtenberg: A Cross-Section*	Radio play	In this volume.
2.	Started	"*Leben, Meinung und Taten des Hieronymus Jobs* von Kortum" [Kortum's *Life, Opinions, and Deeds of Hieronymus Jobs*]	Youth radio	Lost or missing.
3.	Planned	[Radio play on Spiritism]	Radio play	No known text was ever produced.
4.	Planned	Hörmodell III: "Kannst Du mir bis Donnerstag aushelfen?" [Listening model III: Can You Help Me Out Until Thursday?]	Listening model	Lost or missing.
5, 6, 7.	Possibly broadcast with Wolf Zucker	[Listening models IV–VI]	Listening models	Lost or missing.

Notes on Contributors

Jonathan Lutes is a translator living in Berlin.

Lisa Harries Schumann lives outside Boston, Massachusetts, and is, among other things, a translator of texts whose subjects range from penguins to Heidegger and Brecht.

Diana K. Reese is the author of *Reproducing Enlightenment: Paradoxes in the Life of the Body Politic* (Walter de Gruyter, 2009). She has taught German Literature at Cornell and Harvard Universities. She currently lives in New York City and translates for *Artforum.*

Lecia Rosenthal is the author of *Mourning Modernism: Literature, Catastrophe, and the Politics of Consolation* (Fordham University Press, 2011). She has taught at Columbia and Tufts Universities. She lives in Los Angeles.

Index